A HISTORY OF THE ROYAL ARMY
VETERINARY CORPS

WILLIAM PERCIVALL, 1ST LIFE GUARDS, 1792–1854
(From a miniature in the possession of his grandson, Mr. C. W. Percivall, M.A.)

Frontispiece.

A HISTORY OF THE ROYAL ARMY VETERINARY CORPS
1796-1919

BY

MAJOR-GENERAL SIR FREDERICK SMITH
K.C.M.G., C.B.
FORMERLY DIRECTOR-GENERAL ARMY VETERINARY SERVICE
FELLOW AND HON. ASSOCIATE OF THE ROYAL COLLEGE OF VETERINARY SURGEONS

The Naval & Military Press Ltd

Published by

The Naval & Military Press Ltd
Unit 5 Riverside, Brambleside
Bellbrook Industrial Estate
Uckfield, East Sussex
TN22 1QQ England

Tel: +44 (0)1825 749494

www.naval-military-press.com
www.nmarchive.com

In reprinting in facsimile from the original, any imperfections are inevitably reproduced and the quality may fall short of modern type and cartographic standards.

DEDICATED

TO THE MEMORY OF

WILLIAM PERCIVALL
1792–1854

MEMBER OF THE ROYAL COLLEGE OF SURGEONS AND
VETERINARY SURGEON 1ST LIFE GUARDS

WHOSE RESEARCHES CONTRIBUTED SO MATERIALLY TO

THE ADVANCEMENT OF VETERINARY KNOWLEDGE,

BOTH IN CIVIL LIFE AND IN

THE ARMY VETERINARY SERVICE.

PREFACE

THIS book is the outcome of a practice begun when I entered the Army, of reading military history and making notes of all matters pertaining directly or indirectly to our Service. It was not, however, until retirement placed me in a favourable position to take up the subject as a serious study, that it was possible to make any real use of the data collected. History cannot be written in a hurry; as Kaye[1] says, it is not the outcome of inspiration but of evidence; this evidence has to be dug up and then slowly and laboriously examined.

Colonel Duncan, in his *History of the Royal Artillery*, says that it is impossible to overrate the influence of history as a power to awaken *esprit de corps*, and so create a sympathy with the past and cohesion with the present. Lord Kitchener was not satisfied that *esprit de corps* was sufficient; he urged *esprit d'Armée*.[2] Unquestionably he was right; it is the broader spirit which is so frequently absent. It is *esprit d'Armée* which should be sedulously cultivated by our Service.

The first veterinary school in this country, and our Army Veterinary Service, were the outcome of the French Revolution. The Revolution drove Sainbel to England and antagonism to the Revolution involved Europe in war. In 1794, when Coleman took Sainbel's place in London, steps had been taken to increase the size and efficiency of our Army; many of its services were in a deplorable condition, for example transport, supply and medical, while a Veterinary Service did not even exist.

Until the year 1793 there was no artillery in our Army to cooperate with cavalry. The existing artillery worked entirely with the infantry and the horses and drivers were hired! So backward were we in the art of war that cavalry was sent to do the work of infantry; at the time we are writing of there were eight cavalry regiments serving in the West Indies, in Pitt's senseless campaigns against the French in those islands!

It is evident that reorganization was required; attempts were made to improve defective services, fresh infantry regiments were created, and veterinary officers were appointed to cavalry

---

[1] *History of the Sepoy War* 1857-58, J. W. Kaye, F.R.S.
[2] *Under Ten Viceroys*, Major-General N. Woodyatt, C.B., C.I.E.

and artillery. The Royal Horse Artillery, and the Seaforth, Cameron and Gordon Highlanders are only three years our seniors in point of creation, while many fine regiments, including the Rifle Brigade and Argyll and Sutherland Highlanders, are our juniors. Such observations enable a mental picture to be formed of the Army as it was at that date. Other landmarks may be added; Napoleon had recently been promoted a Captain of Artillery, Wellesley (subsequently Wellington) had not been heard of, and Nelson was a Captain in the Mediterranean.

Our Service was created two years after Coleman assumed the Professorship of the London School. The actual date of its birth is 24th May 1796, precisely 131 years ago. The circumstances attending its birth form an essential part of the text. In its subsequent growth it will be observed how each generation has stood on the shoulders of its predecessor. This is as it should be and is evidence of progress. After eighty years of preparatory spade work, a further period of twenty-seven years was required to bring into existence and mould our Corps. At this distance of time we are apt to forget those who laid the foundation of our future expansion.

The designation "Veterinary Surgeon" was not found in the English language before April, 1796. Sainbel spoke of the "Veterinary Physician"; John Hunter of the "Veterinarian."[1] The Board of General Officers which sat in the above year (see p. 39) must have been puzzled how to distinguish in the cavalry between the surgeon of men and the surgeon of horses; accordingly they solved the difficulty by coining a compound designation. This subsequently became applied to the entire civil profession. It is, of course, a misnomer; we have ever been more physician than surgeon.

All sources of reference have been quoted in the text, though special acknowledgment must be made to the Hon. Sir John Fortescue's *History of the British Army*. His references to the creation of our Service enabled me to consult the originals in the Public Record Office; this suggested the possibility of other documents existing which would throw light on our history, and the text will show that such was the case. Unfortunately there are many documents in the Public Record Office relating to events as far distant even as the Crimea, which are not yet accessible to the public. Since the year 1906, each Director-General of the Army Veterinary Service has left on record a history of his period of office, so that the future historian will be saved much trouble.

[1] The word "Veterinarian" first occurred in the English language in 1646 in Sir Thomas Browne's *Pseudodoxia Epidemica*.

The account of my administration as originally drafted was brief; but an event which occurred shortly after it was written suggested that its brevity failed to give a true conception of a period of remarkable difficulty. It was accordingly rewritten, and an outline given of the attempt made to render our Service fit for war. Hitherto we had never been prepared, for the reason that we had to depend on others to furnish our requirements as an act of grace; but with the introduction of a Corps in 1903, it was possible to render our Service efficient as a war unit. The position secured in 1903 was but the first step; it had to be built up, consolidated, and rendered a sound working organization. The officers of the Corps provided ability, energy and zeal; as the text states they took their duties seriously, were determined to master the difficulties of their new position, and to train their men to be a credit to this new branch of the Army. But without organization and modern equipment they could effect little, and both of these had to come from above. It was the struggle to obtain them which occupied my period of office. How the effort was received by the Authorities of that period is dealt with in the text; it is clear that the terrible waste of animal life in the War in South Africa, 1899-1902, had made little or no impression. The period occupied by this struggle is now rapidly sinking into the past, the chief actors have disappeared from the stage, and those who follow will wonder why in the interests of efficiency any difficulty ever existed.

I have to acknowledge my obligations to officers who have furnished me with information. The late Inspecting Veterinary Surgeon J. J. Meyrick, C.B., was an invaluable source; his memory at 90 years of age might well have been the envy of a young man. Colonel W. B. Walters, C.B., another veteran, has never spared time or energy to reply to my many questions. It is a singular coincidence that our three oldest officers, Dr. Evans, the father of the profession, the late I.V.S. J. J. Meyrick, and Colonel Walters, all belonged at the same time to the old 4th Brigade of Artillery, then stationed in Canada.[1]

Major-General H. T. Sawyer, C.B., D.S.O., Director-General Army Veterinary Service, has been good enough to give me access to the Records of Service of Officers, and to Lieut.-Colonel J. W. Rainey, C.B.E., I am very greatly indebted for the laborious work

---

[1] The 4th Brigade was noted for the number of distinguished Artillery officers it produced. In addition to the Veterinary Officers already named, there was another, Adam Elijah Clarke, an inventor. While in Canada he brought out the "Acme" skate, which, I believe, has never been improved upon, and towards the end of his life he devised a time-fuse which was adopted by the Artillery, and for all I know may still be in use.

of making a copy. He also copied out the names of all officers serving in the Great War, but it was found impossible to publish this formidable list. It has now been deposited in the Royal College of Veterinary Surgeons for permanent record.

Colonel A. G. Todd, C.B.E., D.S.O., and Major H. E. Gibbs, D.S.O., have both been good enough to undertake enquiries for me, and in other ways have been most helpful.

The portrait of William Percivall, kindly furnished by his grandson, is acknowledged in the text.

The subject of the uniform worn at different periods was found to be more suitably presented as an Appendix. The question was not a simple one, as explained elsewhere, but Mr. Percival Reynolds, an authority on the subject, has been good enough to help me out of my difficulties. The Rev. P. Sumner, another authority, has afforded me information on the matter of the Farriers' distinctive uniform.

Captain A. E. Haswell-Miller, M.C., R.S.W., undertook the coloured drawings; every detail had to be gone into, and in this respect he tells me of the great help he received from Mr. Percival W. Reynolds and Mr. L. E. Buckell, while to Captain P. Durand, late H.L.I., he was indebted for the loan of material. Captain Haswell-Miller's skilful work has rendered this subject attractive.

The Corps badge on the cover is from the pen of Mr. R. O'Reilly, a late member of the Corps.

The manuscript and proofs have all been critically read by Mrs. F. Bullock, M.A., LL.B., to whose conscientious care and accuracy I am, as in the past, very deeply indebted. My labours have been considerably lightened by her earnest work, which includes the preparation of the index.

The production of this book is due to the Committee of the Royal Army Veterinary Corps Officers' Fund, which has undertaken the cost of publication. Without this relief from the financial burden the text could never have seen the light in its present form. The work has been a labour of love, and it has afforded me great pleasure to make over to the Fund the copyright of the book, with my sincere thanks to the Committee for its liberality and co-operation.

F. S.

LONDON,
May, 1927.

CONTENTS

CHAPTER	PAGE
I. INTRODUCTION	1
II. THE ARMY FARRIER, 1600-1796	5
III. THE GENESIS OF THE ARMY VETERINARY SERVICE AND THE COLEMAN ADMINISTRATION, 1796-1839	27
IV. ADMINISTRATION UNDER CHERRY AND WILKINSON, 1839-1876	112
V. THE EVOLUTION OF THE ARMY VETERINARY SERVICE, 1876-1919	161

APPENDICES

APPENDIX	
I. THE UNIFORM OF THE ARMY VETERINARY SERVICE, 1796-1911	243
II. NAMES OF VETERINARY OFFICERS SERVING IN THE PENINSULAR WAR	253
III. NAMES OF VETERINARY OFFICERS PRESENT IN THE WATERLOO CAMPAIGN	255
IV. VETERINARY OFFICERS OF THE KING'S GERMAN LEGION	256
V. NAMES OF VETERINARY OFFICERS PRESENT IN VARIOUS CAMPAIGNS, 1799-1908	256

CORRIGENDA

Page 74, par. 3, line 7, *for* 1802 *read* 1801.

Page 76, par 4, line 8, *for* J. Price *read* G. Price.

Page 131, par 3, line 4, *for* that *read* those.

Page 208, par. 3, line 8, *for* p. 102 *read* p. 162.

A HISTORY OF THE ROYAL ARMY VETERINARY CORPS

CHAPTER I

INTRODUCTION

A HISTORY of the Royal Army Veterinary Corps is now due, for our hopes for the creation of an effective branch of the Army have been fully realized. The gracious spontaneous recognition accorded by His Majesty to our Service is the crown of our success.

These pages are intended to show step by step how this success has been won. There are big gaps which cannot be filled in the early part of our history, especially during the long period of office of the first Principal Veterinary Surgeon, who published nothing relative to his office, and so far as we know left no records. From the year 1828 onwards, when the *Veterinarian* first appeared, we have good knowledge of our history, superior in completeness to many regimental histories. For this we are indebted to our periodical professional literature, conducted, curiously enough, from 1828-54 and 1876-94, by two officers of our Service, who, though mainly catering for the civil profession, never lost sight of the necessity of placing on record Army facts and news. This information has been invaluable in the construction of this work. Percivall compared the pages of the *Veterinarian* to a safe, where records could be placed in custody for future generations. Our pages will show how largely we are indebted to the ability and foresight of Percivall, Youatt and Fleming.

Editors of periodicals have very largely to depend upon their correspondents for the matter that fills their pages, and the members of the profession in the Army are as backward in recording their experiences as their brothers in civil life. Of all the officers of our Service who went through the long war in the Peninsula and the brief Waterloo Campaign only one has left behind any material useful for our purpose, while the Service in India has been a notable example of such neglect. The Veterinary Service of the East India Company was established in 1826 and abolished in 1858. Thus it took part in every epoch-making campaign, but the officers carried the information they acquired to their graves: not a syllable was written by any one of them. The Crimea is another example of lost opportunities; with two exceptions the only officers who recorded their experiences were those temporarily employed outside the sphere of active hostilities. In recent times we have done rather better, but not well enough. It is precisely the personal experiences which are so valuable and on which reliable history is based.

The unravelling of history is a slow process. Imagination cannot be substituted for facts, and facts have to be unearthed. This task is frequently laborious; a week may be spent in obtaining information capable of being expressed in less than a line of print. The Public Record Office is a mine of information for the English historian, but successful work there is largely a matter of chance, as there is no subject index to the millions of papers housed in that stately building in Chancery Lane. No doubt there is much there I have not had the good fortune to find, but what I have found throws a flood of light both on our genesis and development, and on the aims and character of the first Principal Veterinary Surgeon to the Cavalry, Edward Coleman.

To Coleman was given the task of constructing our Service; whether he did it well or ill each will judge for himself on the facts narrated, which whenever important have been documented so that future writers may know what has already been consulted.[1] Our great reformer, James Collins, came into office in 1876; evidently he did not value the records of his predecessors, for he sent them to the Royal Arsenal to be destroyed. A waggon-load was burned! Only four bound books escaped destruction, one of them being John Percivall's Register of Sick and Lame Horses of the Artillery from 1802-06. These four books in due course came into my possession, and are now lodged for safety and reference in the Library of the Royal College of Veterinary Surgeons. But for Collins' act of vandalism our Service would probably have possessed a record of unique completeness.

This history divides itself naturally into four periods. The earliest, from 1600 to 1796, is the period of our predecessor the Farrier. There is very little written about him excepting that he was very ignorant and very inefficient. This was the fault of the times in which he lived, a period of ignorance and in-

---

[1] All Public Record Office papers quoted by me are indicated as P.R.O.

difference. It was not until the end of the 18th Century that public opinion was sufficiently enlightened to demand something better.

The main feature of the second period, 1796-1839, which covers the long reign of Coleman, is the entrance of the professional man into the Army. It has not always been possible to separate Coleman's civil from his military duties, nor indeed could this have been done without sacrificing important features in our history; for example, it has been necessary to notice the attitude of Professor Dick to the London School, and the subsequent effect of his intervention in securing a military instead of a civil head for our Department.

The opening of the third period, 1839-1876, brings into power a confirmed enemy of Coleman. F. C. Cherry was a soldier with a fine record of active service. The story of his succession as Principal Veterinary Surgeon, and the ousting of " St. Pancras " from control of the Army Veterinary Department, has never previously been made public. Cherry was a man of rigid integrity, stern, unforgiving, and a disciplinarian of the Peninsula period. He was the first to give our Service a military character, and it is to be deplored that he did not succeed to office at an earlier age. His successor, John Wilkinson, was Chief throughout the Crimean period and long after. He will reveal himself as the record is unfolded.

We who live in days when changes in administration are frequent, and all for the public good, almost gasp in realizing that these three men alone occupied office for no less than eighty years!

The fourth and last period, 1876-1919, is the era of sweeping reform or more accurately of regeneration. Every forward step was slow, fettered by the unwillingness of conservative military authorities to realize that under their eyes a body had come into existence as different from the parent structure as anything could well be. This body when fully developed proved itself a power for good if given opportunities; all its lessons were learned in the hard school of professional experience both in peace and war. It was struggling to be free of the bonds which restricted its full usefulness, and was prepared to accept responsibilities which would have caused the earlier administrators to quake. Young, buoyant, optimistic, above all trained to know what to do and how to do it, all the Department desired was the freedom of action necessary, as much in the interests of the public purse as in those of the Service to which it was proud to belong. This freedom was slowly won; it was yielded grudgingly, but by the greatest good fortune sufficient time elapsed between the emancipation and the Great War to enable us to consolidate the position gained.

The initial step in this great forward movement was taken by James Collins (Plate 1) in 1876. It is doubtful whether even he then realized what would be the ultimate extent of the structure the foundation of which he so well and truly laid. A new generation had to be born, trained and proved, in order to develop the advantages of, and effectively control, the new position.

Having reached that stage this History must close. The end of the Great War is a suitable halting-place. To the future historian will fall the duty of chronicling our further progress on more advanced lines, or else of closing the record for ever. There are indications that the use made of mechanical science has rendered possible the passing of the horse in war, in which case we have now reached our zenith, and, as the horse gradually disappears from the Army, our sun will "draw towards its setting."

PLATE I

JAMES COLLINS, 1830-95
Principal Veterinary Surgeon, Army Veterinary Department.

To face p. 4.

CHAPTER II

THE ARMY FARRIER, 1600-1796

THOUGH the subject of this chapter is the Army Farrier during the period 1600-1796, yet it will be convenient to include an outline of his subsequent career.

He was the progenitor of the Veterinary Surgeon, and for the purpose of this history there is no necessity to go further back than the 17th Century, in order to learn what were the first provisions made for the care of sick and lame animals in War.

A very early reference is by Sir John Smythe in 1591. In his *Certen Instructions and Orders Militarie* he urges that the Muster-Master should be accompanied by "a skilful Ferrar" who can judge of lameness and soundness. This remark suggests that skilful men existed and that their services were appreciated. Our army at this time was practically conscripted, and the duties of the Muster-Masters were to ascertain by personal inspection that men, horses and arms were efficient.

Gervase Markham, a cavalry soldier who wrote numerous treatises on subjects he did not understand, including worthless and retrograde works on the diseases of the horse, published in 1625-27 a purely military work entitled *The Souldier's Exercise*. In this he could have told us much about the troop farrier; he neither mentions him nor the troop horse, though on both subjects he was specially qualified to write. His brother, Francis Markham, published *The Epistles of Warre in* 1622, and remarks on the need for "an excellent smith or Farryer, who shall ever be furnished with horse shooes, nayles and drugges both for inward and outward application."

We are more indebted to Captain H. Hexam, who in the *Principles of the Art Militarie* 1637, tells us with some precision what the duties of a Farrier then were:—" His dutie is as occasion serves to drench and lett bloude the horse of the troupe, and allwaies either upon a march, or in quarter, to have in readinesse his buggett (wallet) of tooles, horse shoes and nailes, whensoever he shall be called upon by his officers, or when any gentleman or souldier of the Troupe shall have use of him, and for this reason that he must duely attend upon the troupe, he is freed from other duties and hath a greater paye than an ordinary horseman." Hexam does not state the rate of pay, but we know that in 1639 the farrier received 2s. 6d. a day and his two " servants " each a shilling.[1] In 1661 the farrier of Cuirassiers received 3s. 6d. a day, of Harquebusiers 2s. 6d. and of Dragoons 1s. a day, together with one shilling a day for his horse.[2] In 1678 the farriers of the Royal Dragoons at Tangiers received 2s. a day and rations.[3] In the Train of Artillery the pay was higher; the Master Farrier from 1681-1740 received 4s. a day with from 2s. to 2s. 6d. a day for his " servants,"[4] but these artificers had technical work to perform in connection with carriages. I do not know what deductions, if any, were made from these rates of pay, but in the eighteenth century they were heavy. Fortescue[5] shows that a Dragoon in receipt of 1s. 9d. a day pay never saw a penny of it; he paid for his clothing and necessaries, food for himself and horse, paid the doctor for medicines, the farrier for shoeing, the armourer for repairs, the riding master for instruction, and after all these stoppages 5 per cent. of his pay was taken by the Paymaster General! The Farrier of both branches of Artillery prior to 1797 received 2s. $9\frac{1}{2}$d. a day with deductions; in 1797 his pay was raised to 3s. $2\frac{3}{4}$d., with deductions amounting to $5\frac{3}{4}$d. a day.[6]

During the Civil War one farrier per troop was the recognized establishment in the Parliamentary Cavalry; he, however, seldom appears in the tables, being included in the total of Privates; this held good in the Cavalry until well into the nineteenth century. In *Pallas Armata*, written by Sir James Turner in 1670 (though not published until 1683), the social status of the military farrier abroad is shown us. In the German Cavalry the gentlemen of the troop would not permit the saddler or farrier to ride in the ranks with them, but Turner adds that all who now ride in the ranks are not gentlemen, so that the difficulty regarding these " profitable members " is removed. It is quite certain that no

---

[1] *Military Antiquities*, F. Grose.

[2] *Brief Instructions for Exercising the Cavalry* 1661, by J. B.

[3] *Dartmouth MSS.*, Historical Manuscripts Commission.

[4] *Notes on the Early History of the Royal Regiment of Artillery*, Colonel Cleveland R.A., also P.R.O. W.O. 55/352.

[5] *The British Army* 1783-1802. Staff College Lectures 1905, by the Hon. J. W. Fortescue.

[6] P.R.O. W.O. 47/2391.

snobbery of this kind existed in the Cromwellian Cavalry, where men were appointed to positions of trust and responsibility without respect to their social status.

In the British Museum there is a manuscript, Harleian 7018, which gives considerable details concerning the army from 1687 to 1693. Among the Head Quarter Staff is a "Martiall to ye Horse." Colonel Walton in his *History of the British Standing Army 1660-1700* refers to this manuscript; he was evidently puzzled regarding this official and suggested he was a Master of the Horse, but this is unlikely as the daily stipend is given at 7s. and the Master of the Horse is a high functionary of the State. I have been disposed to regard him as a Superintending Farrier of the Cavalry, but nowhere have I seen any reference to such an appointment, and he was probably a Provost-Marshal.

The term "Marshal" as indicating the Farrier is many centuries old and still exists in the French Army. It was a word not in general use in this country, though it occurs with sufficient frequency to show that its meaning was well known.

The author of the article entitled "Marshal" in *Chambers' Encyclopedia* 1908, appears to me to have fallen into an error in ascribing a very dignified position to the "Royal Farrier" in feudal times. He represents him as being a great officer of State, conjointly with the Constable a judge in the Courts of Chivalry, and an inspecting officer of troops, camps, arms, colours, etc. The Marshal to whom these duties were assigned was not the Royal Farrier, much as we may regret it. Further there were several Marshals. In this country the Royal Farrier was almost invariably referred to as the Serjeant Farrier; "Serjeant" indicating employment as the head of a department of the Court. The title Serjeant Surgeon long survived.

From 1693 to 1778 there is no information on the farrier, but during that period a standing army had become firmly established and definite regulations governing the army farriers no doubt existed. Thus we find a contract between the farrier and the State for the shoeing and medical treatment of the horses. It is from the 18th Century, so barren in records, that we begin to trace the development of our branch of the service. Towards the end of this period a work entitled *The Discipline of the Light Horse* by Captain Hinde, published in 1778, gives much information on the interior economy of the cavalry. We learn that the contract rate for shoeing and medicine was one halfpenny a horse per diem. No wonder that the farrier purchased his drugs in the cheapest market! The farrier on parade took post on the right of his troop; in a squadron both farriers were on the right. In the march past they were at the head of the squadron. In the field the position was that of serrefile in their respective troops.

It is interesting also to know that as far back as 1778 a regimental pattern of horse-shoe existed, and a farrier found guilty of making a shoe of any other than the established pattern, besides receiving corporal punishment for the offence, lost the iron of such shoes and had to replace those destroyed. If a horse was rendered lame by careless shoeing, such as lowering the foot too much, the Farrier received corporal punishment and was confined, "in order that he may be prevented drinking any liquor but water," until the horse was sound. "Under pain of the severest punishment Farriers are to keep strictly to the methods and medicines inserted in regimental orders; when any complaint happens to horses not mentioned therein, they are not to perform any operation nor administer any drugs without the approbation of the Commanding Officer of the Troop." This last order supports the view that the lines of treatment were laid down regimentally; unfortunately they are not given. Among the duties of an officer, it is stated that he should "acquire a knowledge of the diseases to which horses are liable and the medicines proper to be employed."

Captain Hinde gives us an account of a Farrier's funeral. A Sergeant's party attended (presumably for a Farrier Major); the usual "mourning" horse followed and three volleys were fired. On his coffin were laid the axe, pair of pincers, hammer and horse-shoes. In passing it may be noted that at this time a surgeon had a drawn sword, pair of pistols, amputating knife and saw placed on his coffin. I do not know when this custom became obsolete.

Another account is given of the Army Farrier by the 10th Earl of Pembroke 1734-94, in his work on *Military Equitation* 1778, an account which is as severe as it is doubtless just. He knew Bourgelat and James Clark of Edinburgh, and was therefore in a position to estimate the standard capable of being attained by skilled men. He urged the formation of an institution for the training of Farriers; he pressed for their better education and encouragement, and for skilled supervision of their work. He says that as matters stood in his day he would rather be without them. But how were these men to be trained? There was no Veterinary School in this country until 1791; Pembroke helped it into existence, and lived long enough to see it at work.

Throughout the whole of the eighteenth century the superintending care of the horses of a troop was committed to a Warrant Officer known as a Quartermaster. He was responsible for the feeding and management; it was he who ordered the shoeing of horses, and together with the farrier inspected the backs when the regiment was on the march. He would appear in part to have corresponded to a Farrier Major but was without his technical knowledge. As to how the troop farrier was trained in veterinary duties we have no information; doubtless he used regimental prescriptions unless he had had some experience in civil life. He was very ignorant, and it was for this reason that a senior farrier, a Farrier Major, was appointed to supervise the troop Farriers. The earliest definite date I can give for the Farrier Major is 1795, but his office existed long before that though there was no such rank on the establishment; the appointment, if made, rested with the Commanding Officer. In some regiments no Farrier Major was appointed, perhaps because no man was qualified for the post, or else that the Commanding Officer did not consider it necessary. In those days, and for long after, regiments were practically the private property of the commanding officer.

In the 18th and early part of the 19th Century there was a Standing Board of General Officers which recommended improvements in arms, equipment, personnel, and organization The proceedings of this Board are extant and may be consulted at the Public Record Office. Generals of Cavalry appear to have predominated on it, and questions relative to the welfare of the troop-horse were constantly under discussion. It is anticipating matters to say that it was the recommendations of this Board which ultimately created the Army Veterinary Service.

The Board attached great importance to the presence of a Farrier Major in a regiment, and whether such an appointment had been made was one of the questions which had to be answered in the report of the General who inspected the regiment. In one of the letter books of the Board (P.R.O. W.O. 3/27), under date 31 May 1788, it is remarked that distinctions for non-commissioned officers and farriers have been generally adopted in all regiments, which "appears very proper," and it is proposed these shall be continued; unfortunately we are not told their nature. In W.O. 7/36, p. 126, under date

13 July 1811, fifteen years after the Veterinary Service was created, the Board recommends a Farrier Major to be appointed to each regiment. In the same year they recognized that one farrier per troop was insufficient and recommended a second, together with a Squadron Farrier with the rank of Corporal to supervise the farriers of the squadron. In this connection it must be remembered that in those days regiments were frequently broken up into detachments scattered over the country, particularly for the prevention of smuggling or breaches of the peace, and that supervision by the regimental staff was difficult. In December 1811, the Board once more represents the necessity of a regimental Farrier Major with the pay and allowances of a Sergeant. He was to rank as a Staff Sergeant on the same footing as the Saddler and Armourer Sergeants. They define his duty as being the superintendence of all the Farriers under the direction of the Veterinary Surgeon. An earlier Board had used the expression "Command of the Farriers," but evidently it was felt this was going too fast, so that the word "superintendence" was substituted.

At a meeting of the Board held in March 1812 "in answer to a further question," evidently addressed to it by the Financial Authorities, they record that the appointment of a Farrier Major, or as styled in these proceedings Farrier Sergeant, is "indispensable and necessary." In spite of these representations no Farrier Major was officially sanctioned for the Cavalry until 1852. Nevertheless long before this date one was to be found in every regiment, and his conditions of service were peculiar. He was a private soldier receiving 1s. 3d. a day pay, with the protection stripes of a sergeant. He received from the full Colonel of the regiment an allowance of six guineas a year; from the Officer Commanding five pounds a year, together with the allowance for the shoeing of a troop, for which he had an assistant, to whom he paid 5s. a week. He had also the shoeing of the horses of the Regimental Staff. These allowances, no doubt, varied slightly in different regiments; those quoted are on the authority of Veterinary Surgeon Gloag of the 10th Hussars.[1]

[1] *Veterinarian*, vol. xii., 1839.

In a book entitled *Jottings from my Sabretasche* 1847, by "A Chelsea Pensioner" who served in the ranks of the 15th Light Dragoons in the Peninsular, we have a picture of the Farrier Major of that regiment. This man was constantly in trouble, and though always by title the Farrier-Major, his actual rank varied from sergeant to corporal and private according to his conduct. He is described as a big, jovial, rollicking, devil-may-care tippler, who soon killed himself; he was a fellow of infinite jest; when

It was on 16 June 1852 that a Farrier Major at last was officially appointed to every Cavalry regiment with the rank and pay of a Sergeant. He replaced the Saddler Sergeant (who was subsequently restored), but at the outset no appointment was authorized until a vacancy occurred among the Sergeants on the establishment.

On 4 February 1860 a Royal Warrant was published revising the rates of pay of Farrier-Majors and Farriers. The Farrier Major was given the rank and clothing of a Quarter Master Sergeant, together with pay at 3s. 8d. a day, and the pension of that rank on discharge. His chevrons were now worn on the cuff. A memorandum by the C.-in-C., dated June 1860, was attached to the warrant, providing that the Farrier-Major may be reduced for misconduct to the rank and pay of a farrier at the discretion of his Commanding Officer. It adds that he and the Farriers may, if approved by the C.O., be members of the Sergeants' Mess.

In July 1881 the rank of Farrier Major was abolished and that of Farrier Quarter Master Sergeant substituted. In 1904 the rank of Warrant Officer was conferred on a limited number of Farrier Quarter Master Sergeants, and they became Farriers Sergeant Major.

We digress for a moment to observe that no rank was attached to the trade designation of a Farrier other than the Farrier Major. In July 1881 this was remedied, and compound rank was granted; it was only relative, and conferred all the obligations attached to rank but not all its advantages. We have seen above the change in rank effected for the Farrier Major in 1881. At the same time the " Farrier " became a Sergeant Farrier (not Farrier Sergeant). This application of compound rank affected all branches of the Service, excepting that in the Household Cavalry the ranks were otherwise designated, the Farrier Major becoming Farrier Quarter Master Corporal, and the " Farrier " a Corporal Farrier. Curiously enough, though the year 1881 saw this important and beneficent change in the various Farriery ranks of the Cavalry and Artillery, compound rank had for some time

---

he acted as auctioneer in the sale of cast horses the Spaniards broke into peals of laughter at his eloquent descriptions, in a mixture of Spanish and English, of the favourable points of the horses, for which he succeeded in obtaining good prices. This man had a great reputation for the treatment of sore backs, and his services were often requisitioned by other regiments. He had had a good early training, for he served under the celebrated Veterinary Surgeon Castley, 15th Light Dragoons.

previously existed in the Royal Engineers and the Army Service Corps. In the R.E. the Farrier Major was originally known as "Farrier and Carriage Smith Major"; in 1881 he became Farrier Quarter Master Sergeant. Prior to 1881 the Engineers had "Sergeant Farrier and Shoeing Smith" a combined rank, and this remained unaltered in 1881. The A.S.C. had the following ranks prior to 1881: Farrier Major, Farrier Sergeants, Corporals acting as Farriers and Carriage Smiths, and in addition the appointment of Shoeing and Carriage Smiths. In 1881 these ranks became Farrier Quarter Master Sergeant, Sergeant Farrier, Corporal acting as Farrier and Carriage Smith. It will be observed that in the highest ranks the trade designation came first and in the remainder the military rank came first. In 1896 in all branches of the Service the trade designation was placed before the rank.

To resume—June 1852, as stated above, was the date of the official appointment of the Farrier Major of Cavalry, but there existed in the Artillery, certainly in 1850, the equivalent of a Farrier Major; he was called a "Staff Farrier" and was on the Brigade and not Battery Staff. He disappeared before 1876, but two Farriers Major of Artillery then existed, one with the Riding Establishment, the other with the Artillery Remount Depôt. The Farrier Major of Artillery wore a crown; the shoe was placed over the chevrons, and of course the latter were on the cuff. In the Cavalry the shoe was worn above the chevrons and there was no crown. The pay of an Artillery Farrier Major in 1850 was 3s. $10\frac{3}{4}$d. a day in Horse Artillery and 3s. $8\frac{3}{4}$d. a day in "Marching Battalions"; it is necessary to remember that he was also a skilled Carriage Smith.

The position of the 18th Century farrier himself presents, however, no such difficulty as we have had in determining that of the Farrier Major of Cavalry. In the Cavalry and Artillery he was merely "the farrier" without rank. In the Cavalry he was a private soldier with the pay of 1s. 3d. a day together with an allowance for shoeing, and for the provision of medicine. There was also a small regimental allowance for the repair of collar chains. In 1860 he was given a Sergeant's stripes as a protection and authority, also better pay, but he was not a Sergeant and certainly in the Cavalry could be reverted to the ranks or to Shoeing Smith without a Court Martial. In spite of this statement the memorandum quoted above by the C.-in-C., dated June 1860, distinctly states that the Farrier could only be reduced and the Shoeing Smith "displaced" by sentence of Court Martial, excepting in instances of inefficiency, when the case could be disposed of by the Colonel of the Regiment. The Sergeant Farrier was given no authority on parade, and if occasion arose he could be commanded by a Corporal!

In the Farrier's warrant of 1860, it is stated that the Farrier shall have the *relative rank* and clothing of a Sergeant, with pay at 2s. 6d. a day, and on discharge a special rate of pension equal to that of a Sergeant. It was not until January 1893 that he obtained the substantive rank of Sergeant Farrier, and a further rank of Staff Sergeant Farrier was created. In 1896 the rank was amended to read Farrier Sergeant, Farrier Staff Sergeant, etc. This took place first in the Cavalry and later in the Artillery. Even now Farriers of any rank are not entitled to command on parade unless specially detailed. On the other hand, in matters of discipline they exercise the full authority attached to their rank.

In the Artillery the Farrier was a trained gunner and a carriage smith. He drew an allowance for shoeing, one halfpenny per day per effective horse, but not even in the old days did he draw an allowance for medicine; the Board of Ordnance supplied their own. In 1850 his pay in Horse Artillery was 3s. $4\frac{3}{4}$d. per day, and in "Marching Battalions" 3s. $2\frac{3}{4}$d. He received no rank until 1881, when he became a Sergeant Farrier. Though the Artillery is the most punctiliously exact branch of the Service, I never heard the Sergeant Farrier called by his rank. He was never anything but "the Farrier" to anyone from the Commanding Officer downwards, but there was no hesitation in giving him command, and under stress I have seen him Sergeant of the Guard and that at a time when he was a Farrier with only relative rank.

In an Artillery return of 1810, Farriers and Carriage Smiths are shown together, but in 1815 Farriers are in one column and Shoeing Smiths in another. The earliest date, as far as I am aware, at which the designation "Shoeing Smith" appears is 1805, and it then refers only to the Artillery.

Shoeing Smiths for Cavalry date from 1860; up to that time they were called "Assistant Farriers." The Royal Warrant of 1860 defines the Shoeing Smith as "Assistant to the Farrier," and fixes the number at one per troop with the rank of Private and rate of pay at 1s. 11d. a day. In January 1893 the rank of Corporal Shoeing Smith was created. Shoeing Smiths of

Artillery were originally known as Carriage Smiths. In 1797 the pay was the same as the Farrier's, 3s. 2¾d. p.d. with deductions. It remained the same in 1801, but in 1850 a Shoeing Smith of Horse Artillery received 2s. 3¼d. p.d. and in "Marching Battalions" 2s. 1¼d.

Reference has been made to the Farriery Allowance, and on this question we must touch. The earliest information we have is in 1778 when it amounted to one halfpenny per horse per diem. In December 1795 it was raised to one penny a day per effective horse. The allowance was a contract between the State and the farrier to cover the cost of iron, nails, fuel, tools and medicines for the horses. When Professor Coleman became the Principa Veterinary Surgeon of the Cavalry in 1796, he was appointed contractor for drugs, instruments and dressings, for which he received the sum of three shillings per horse per annum; this amount was deducted regimentally from the farriers' allowance, and paid over to the P.V.S. In the proper place we shall have much to say on this question; it was made by his detractors the basis of a campaign against Coleman which was carried on for years. There were repeated attempts by the Financial Authorities to reduce the allowance to Farriers, or to extract greater service for it. For example, it was proposed to draw upon it in payment of the bills of private practitioners, but the Board of General Officers stuck to the Farrier, and resisted every attempt to reduce his only source of remuneration. The Finance Department, however, succeeded in reducing it to a halfpenny a day when on service, probably for the reason that ready-made shoes were largely supplied in the Field. With this exception, and for a short period in 1802 when it was three farthings, it remained at one penny per day from 1795 to 1852, perhaps a little longer. In 1860 the farriery allowance was one halfpenny per day with no deductions, and it remained at that until the contract system of shoeing was abolished in the Cavalry in April 1888. For over a century and a half the Farrier received a private's pay and nothing for his work excepting what he could save out of his allowance; it was this that recompensed him for being the hardest worked man in the army, serving in the double capacity of soldier and artificer. What he actually cleared is not definitely known. In 1811 the Board of General Officers calculated that his income from the allowance amounted to from £11 to £13 a year, little enough for the rough work he undertook.

Before closing this subject attention may be drawn to the

Regulations of 1881 for the *Supply of Stores in the Field*, in which it is laid down that on taking the Field every horse was to be newly shod, and 4 spare shoes were to be carried on the saddle for each animal; in addition sets of shoes up to 15% of the strength of the unit were to be carried regimentally; all of these were provided by the Sergeant Farrier. In addition he had to pay for all shoes, nails, coal and tools drawn by his C.O. from Government stock, at the rate of one shilling per set of shoes and nails. Coal was charged him at cost price; it is laid down that shoes and coal are to be " carriage free "! It is evident that on service there was little made out of the contract system. Perhaps this was recognized, as there was an order in March 1878, stating that on " Foreign Service " if the halfpenny a day was insufficient a farthing a day might be added to it.

The ethics of the question of Government having a contract with its servants will be fully considered later, when the abolition of the farriery contract is dealt with.

During the 18th and part of the 19th Century there were two men in a Cavalry Regiment dressed differently from all others, one was the Trumpeter, the other the Farrier, but whereas the Trumpeter's dress was elaborate and handsome, that of the Farrier was plain and sombre. Most Cavalry regiments in the 18th Century, excepting the " Blues," were dressed in scarlet, and distinguished by their facings and pattern of tunic. All the Farriers were dressed in blue, blue tunic waistcoat and pants, with a collar and cuffs of the same facings as the regiment, excepting in Royal Regiments where the facings were red. The head-dress was a bearskin cap resembling that worn by fusiliers, but lower; on the front was a black metal plate bearing a silver-plated horse-shoe, and sometimes a hammer and pincers. They wore boots or black leggings. The saddle-cloth and housings were blue with a cross hammer and pincers in the corner opposite the flank. In other ranks this corner bore the regimental device. The housings covering the wallets were blue, and bore a horse-shoe; the wallet cover was black bearskin. This is the uniform as laid down in 1768, but there were frequently small regimental departures, for example, a white waistcoat, white breeches and regimental saddle-cloth. (See Plate 2.) The wallets were large circular contrivances technically known as " churns." They carried shoes, nails, tools and such veterinary appliances as were taken to the field. The leather of the saddlery was frequently black. The man was generally mounted on a black horse, though in some regiments greys were used. On parade the farrier wore a white apron hanging down on the right thigh, the left side being tucked up. He carried an axe in a case suspended from a belt which passed over the right shoulder. When the men drew swords the farriers drew axes, the tool being carried by the haft resting on the right thigh, edge forwards. He had no other arms. The Farrier Major carried an axe but also wore a sword.

The dress shown in Plate 2 belongs to a somewhat earlier period, about 1750-55, to that described above. At the back of this cap is a piece of scarlet cloth; the plate on the front is red edged with silver; the apron is tucked up so as to hang down the *left* thigh; the cloak is of the same colour as that worn by the regiment; the fur covering the "churns" is white, that worn by the men was brown.

There is a painting of a Farrier of 21st Dragoons in the possession of W. E. Manners, who wrote the life of Lord John Manners, Marquis of Granby. This regiment, raised by the Marquis, existed from 1760-63. The Farrier is clothed much as in Morier's picture, but wears white epaulettes; the cap is like a busby, and the shoe on it appears to be upside down.

Nothing is known of when the Farrier's distinctive dress was introduced; it is fully described in a Royal Warrant, 19th December 1768.[1] Its purpose perhaps was the quick identification of the man should his services be required. The headdress appears to have been the first part to go; in 1828 the Farrier of the Life Guards wore a chako-shaped fur cap with a peak and brass chain chin-strap; he also wore a sword. The distinctive dress of the Farrier has now disappeared, excepting in the Life Guards, where the black plume to the helmet and blue tunic remain, and all farriers in the Household regiments carry the axe. It was in 1878 that the distinctive blue dress of Farriers of Dragoons and Dragoon Guards was replaced by scarlet. In the Artillery no axe was carried, and the farrier wore a sword; it is also believed that he wore the headdress of the regiment; the same dress existed in the Royal Waggon Train.

Among the other duties of the Farriers was that of inflicting corporal punishment; in some regiments this was carried out by the Trumpeters, in others alternately by Trumpeters and Farriers. The Farriers were trained in the art of flogging by the Trumpet Major. The victim had to pay the Trumpet Major for the "cat,"

[1] P.R.O. W.O. 30/13.

PLATE II

FARRIER, 11TH DRAGOONS, ABOUT 1750-55

The outline is from a photograph of a copy of the original which is at Windsor Castle, and was painted by David Morier. The copy was made by the Rev. P. Sumner, and is now in the War Office Library.

To face p. 10.

but the Farrier's services appear to have been unrewarded. In the Artillery the duty was originally carried out by Trumpeters, later by Shoeing Smiths. Flogging for certain offences was still in existence during the early part of my service. It was carried out by Farriers, who were informed beforehand that if they failed in their duty they would be themselves punished.

On parade the troop farrier carried in the "churns" a case of phlemes, a bleeding stick, drenching horn, clyster pipe, and two bandages. As late as 1852 these formed part of the man's kit and had to be produced at inspection. For years after the introduction of the Veterinary Service the farrier did all the bleeding. When we remember that in those days blood-letting in health and disease was a regular practice (even before the horses were turned out to grass),[1] it must be acknowledged that he was kept very busy and doubtless became extremely expert. He was also responsible under the Veterinary Officer for "docking" and for "nicking" when the latter was practised. He has probably always been responsible for the correct numbering of the horses. The numbers in 1804 were cut in the hair. I do not know when branding of the hoof was introduced.

The first issue of *Rules and Regulations for the Cavalry* was published on 1st October 1795; they are especially interesting to us as very full information is given regarding the farriery department, and further they show us the exact situation existing immediately before the Veterinary Service was established.

In these Regulations the duties of the Quartermaster are laid down; he is defined as the principal non-commissioned officer of the troop responsible, *inter alia*, for "everything relative to the horses." Care, management, watering, feeding, stables, shoeing, etc. He was, in fact, the Regimental Horse-Master and visited the stables with the Farrier three times a day, a night visit included.

The following extracts from these Regulations are of interest:—

Farrier Major

He is to rank in the Regiment as a Sergeant, and he receives an extra allowance of six Guineas per Year in consequence of his appointment.

He is to make himself intimately acquainted with the Standing

---

[1] The horses were "turned out" every year as an economical measure. The money thus saved, technically known as "Grass Money," went to the purchase of necessaries for the Dragoon.

Orders of the Regiment, as far as relates to the Stable duty, Farriers, etc., and attend punctually to their execution.

He must, by his proper, soldier-like, manly, obedient conduct, and decent appearance, set an example to the Farriers, over whom he has perfect authority; and, if ever he finds a Farrier acting in disobedience to his directions, he is to confine him immediately, reporting him to the Quarter-Master of the Troop, and to the Officer Commanding it, as also to the Officer Commanding in the Quarter.

He is to stand at the head of the Farriers on all foot parades, and act towards them as a sergeant.

On no account whatever is he to drink with a Farrier.

He is to direct the Farriers in the treatment of every horse who is ill with grease or any other complaint. He is to watch carefully over the treatment of every such horse, and constantly to inspect the shoeing. He has free access to the stables of every troop at all times; he must frequently visit them, and inspect the shoeing and sick horses, and he must report to the Officer commanding in the quarter, whether he sees anything amiss, either in the management of sick horses, or in any part of the stable duty.

Farriers

The greatest attention is to be paid to the shoeing exactly according to the regimental order; and if a Farrier is found to deviate from it in the least, he must be instantly reported, and he will be brought to a Court Martial. If any horse is ill or lame, the Farrier Major, if in the Quarter, must be applied to immediately by the Farrier of the Troop, and he is to make his report on the subject to the Officer commanding the Troop, being attended by the Farrier of the Troop, by which means every sick or lame horse will be under the care of the Farrier Major; and if any Farrier presumes to do anything without his direction, he will be brought to a Court Martial for disobedience of orders.

The Farrier Major is to have free access to every stable of the Regiment whenever he chooses, and he is ordered to go frequently into the cantonments of the different Troops, and examine the horses' feet; and if he finds a shoe contrary to the regimental pattern, or anything amiss, he is to report it immediately to the Officer commanding the Regiment. In all his duty, he is to receive the utmost support from every Officer and Quarter Master; and any Farrier that dares to disobey him will be punished.

Whenever anything is the matter with a horse, or a nail out of his shoe, or the shoe displaced, the man is immediately to mention it to the Farrier; who is not on any account to give the horse physic, or bleed him, without directions received from the Officer commanding the Troop through the Quarter Master.

When the Farrier goes round, after riding out, or exercise on horseback, he must carry his hammer, pincers, and some nails, to fasten any shoe that may be loose; and, in general, all shoeing must be done after dinner, unless a horse should have cast a shoe by accident, which of course must be put on again before riding out.

When a horse is particularly unwell at an Out-Quarter, or has any obstinate lameness, it must be reported to the Head Quarter of the Regiment for the information of the Farrier Major, who, if he cannot prescribe for him at a distance, must be sent to see him if practicable.

No Farrier must presume to make up any medicine, or any external application, contrary to the receipt given him by the Farrier Major, on pain of being severely punished.

Whenever a horse has been shod, he must be pointed out by the Farrier to the Officer Commanding the Troop on the next horse parade, who will immediately examine his foot; and if he finds the shoeing contrary to order, he will confine the Farrier.

If any Farrier, through carelessness or inattention, lames a horse belonging to a Detachment of another Troop, that Farrier shall be at all the expense in curing the horse so lamed, and not the Farrier of the Troop to which he belongs.

It has been the custom of the Farriers of the Regiment, when they have had horses of a Detachment of another Troop under their care, and any horse of that Detachment required medicine, to charge the Farrier of the Troop to which such horse belonged in a very extravagant unreasonable manner.

To prevent this in future, the Farrier Major shall order at a Druggist's, whose articles are as cheap and reasonable as can be obtained, such things as at any time are necessary for such Detachment horses, and place them to the account of the Farrier of the Troop to which the horse so required belongs; and the Non-commissioned Officer who has the charge of that Detachment must see such medicines given, according to the order received with them. The amount to be paid the 24th of every settling month, by the Clerks of troops to which such Detachments belong.

Any Non-commissioned Officer having a Detachment or Party from the Regiment under his care, and no Farrier belonging to the Regiment with him, shall see that the horses are shod according to the pattern of the Regiment; and he is to give an extra account of the day of the month on which each man's horse is shod to the Farrier, or to the Clerk of the Troop to which the horse belongs, for the Farrier's information.

If any dispute arises between the Farriers respecting charges made from one to another, the Farrier Major must settle it.

The Farriers must be decent in their appearance and orderly in their Quarters, and in every respect well behaved Soldiers. They must understand, that being a Farrier is no privilege for dirty appearance and drunkenness.

The Farriers, excepting the Farrier Major, are to inflict punishments when ordered.

Dress of the Farrier Major

His dress is the same as another Farrier, excepting when under arms on foot or on horseback, or on Sunday he must have a Sergeant's feather in his hat or cap,[1] and his coat is laced like that of a Sergeant; he has also a Sergeant's cane; he must always wear his gloves when under arms, or on Sunday, and have a Sergeant's sword and belt, worn exactly as they wear theirs.

At field days he wears his hat and feather, and hatchet; at a review of course his full-dressed cap, and on this occasion he must have a clean white apron hanging down on the right thigh, and tucked up on the left side.

Whenever he turns out on horseback, his hat or cap, whichever he wears, must be tied on quite fast.[2]

When he turns out in watering order, he wears his stable dress.

Dress of the Farriers

When out in watering order the Farriers are in the regimental blue stable dress, trowsers, and foraging caps,[3] hair clubbed in the regimental manner, but not powdered. In this dress they may be allowed to appear, excepting at any parade, when they must be dressed in their exact uniform, and black leather caps, unless it is a parade under arms, with the men in hats; or on Sunday, when they must also be in hats. In short when the men are in hats they must be so, if ordered to parade with them; and they must be powdered or not as the men are. They must also wear black leggings. Each Farrier must have always a clean white leather apron to wear at a review; it must be tucked up on the left side, and hang down the right side.

At a field day the Farriers must wear their hats.[4] At riding-house or horse-drill, caps.[5] When at a review the full uniform cap.[6] At all times when under arms on horseback, they are to have their axes, which must be kept in perfect order, and the belts and plates clean.

Whenever a Farrier is ordered on parade of any kind, he must be exactly as neat and clean in his dress in every particular, and as exact as any other Dragoon. His hair as well clubbed[7] and powdered when so ordered, and his belt as clean.

When they are out on horseback of course they are booted and spurred, and every part of their accoutrements, etc., must be put on exactly as well, and be in as good order, as those of any of the Dragoons. Their coats must be hooked as before mentioned.

Whenever they turn out on horseback, their hats or caps, whichever they have on, must be tied quite fast.

[1] The hat referred to is the three cornered hat of the period. The Cap is the full dress bearskin.

[2] The three cornered hat was a most difficult headdress to keep in its place. After a rapid movement the ground was littered with hats.

[3] This was a flat cap of black leather.

[4] This is the three cornered hat.

[5] This is the above mentioned black leather forage cap.

[6] This is the headdress seen in Plate 2.

[7] A "club" was formed by turning up the queue or pig-tail, and tying it according to regimental pattern.

Shoeing

A pattern shoe, and a set of nails, are to be in the possession of each Quarter Master.

A set of shoes for one horse is not to weigh more than four pounds four ounces, excepting for some particularly large feet, when an extra allowance of two or three ounces will be made, and these must be in exact conformity to the pattern shoe in length, breadth, and thickness of the web; and this weight never to be exceeded on any account or pretence. In Shoeing, the old shoes are to be taken off in so careful a manner as not to injure the feet, the toes to be cut sufficiently low; the seat of the shoe is the only part of the foot ever to be touched with the buttress; the bars, sole, and frog, never to be pared on any account nor anything taken off them but the loose ragged pieces. No hot shoes are to be tried on the foot, nor any bar shoes ever to be used, except a horse has got a wound in his foot that absolutely requires one, and then it is to be discontinued as soon as the wound is well. The shoes to be perfectly flat on both sides, no longer than the foot; the nails not too large but well tempered, and so ingrooved that their heads may be level with the shoe; the clinches made level with the hoof, and the foot well finished, and taken as short as it can bear.

When the horses are turned to grass, the toes of the fore feet to be taken short, and cut as low as they will bear, and the edges of the hoof to be rasped quite round, the bars, sole, and frog, being left as above.

When the half of the time is expired for the horses remaining at grass, the feet must again be pared as above described, but not quite so much.

The Quarter Masters to see that the horses are always so well shod as to be fit to march on any unforeseen expedition.

The Dragoon is always to take his horse to the shop, and stop till he is shod.

In frosty weather the shoes may be turned a little up if necessary, but in general it is better to make use of frost nails only.

No apology is offered for this long extract; the book is rare, the occasion important. Coleman never ceased to eulogize his work in the Cavalry. The system of shoeing he found has been described as ruinous. No one reading the instructions for Shoeing in the Cavalry Regulation of 1795 will admit this. How far, indeed, do they differ from the present day regulations? The fact is that the regulations for shoeing there given were drawn up by the tenth Earl of Pembroke in 1778, and were based on his study of the subject under the tuition of that great veterinarian, James Clark of Edinburgh. It by no means follows that the system of shoeing laid down by regulation in 1795 was that followed throughout the Cavalry, but it shows that at this date, before Coleman had ever seen a Troop horse, there existed in the army a very clear conception of the cardinal principles of shoeing.

Further, it is interesting to note that even in the 20th Century we have nothing more practical than frost nails for troops moving in the winter.

The following Standing Orders dealing with Farriers of other branches of the Service may conveniently be given here:—

STANDING ORDERS OF H.M. ROYAL WAGGON TRAIN, 1804

Farriers and Shoeing

The pattern shoe weighs 17 oz.; no farrier is to presume to use one heavier or different in shape, excepting under the orders of the Veterinary Surgeon.

No Farrier is to administer any medicine to a horse, apply external dressings or perform an operation, without the sanction and authority of the Veterinary Surgeon, or the Officer Commanding the Troop.

The buttress is never to be used to the frog; ragged parts are to be pared off with a knife. Hot shoes are never to be applied. The Shoe should be made to fit the foot, not the foot the shoe.

The Farrier is to execute all punishments inflicted by sentence of Regimental Court Martial.

STANDING ORDERS FOR THE ROYAL ARTILLERY, 1847

The Farrier is to report every evening to the Commanding Officer the state of the sick animals; the number of horses shod to be stated on a return, also the quantity of medicines expended.

STANDING ORDERS FOR THE ROYAL ARTILLERY, 1864

The Farrier is to set an example to the Shoeing Smiths by his steady soldier-like conduct. Over the Shoeing Smiths he has perfect authority as far as regards general conduct, sobriety, and attention to work. Any disobedience of orders by them will be met by confining the man and reporting the circumstances.

He is to order all medicines, unless serving under a Veterinary Surgeon, subject to the approval of the officer on duty, or the Commanding Officer, without whose knowledge no medicines are to be administered excepting in case of necessity.

He is to attend foot and riding drill once a week and all stable hours. On the march he will examine the horses' backs and shoulders at the first stable hour.

No private shoeing is permitted without the permission of the C.O.

The Shoeing Smith is to observe implicitly the instructions given him by the Veterinary Surgeon and the Farrier.

He is to examine the feet of his horses every morning and report any horse sick, to keep the feet properly marked; never to lose his temper or strike a horse he may be shoeing.

He is to inflict corporal punishment when required to do so by the C.O.

The rational treatment of disease was practically unknown in the Service before Coleman's day. He began his duties as Principal Veterinary Surgeon to the Cavalry with the most trifling experience but unlimited confidence. He depended for results on his experimental observations grafted on his knowledge as a surgeon. His early efforts in the treatment of disease gave no indication of being any improvement on the past, if indeed they were not inferior to it. Look, for example, at his *Instructions for Farriers* issued in 1796; of this pamphlet in later years he must have been grievously ashamed. The second edition published in 1803 was a decided improvement. The two editions of this work will be carefully considered later, attention is drawn to it here in consequence of an attack made upon it by an ex-Farrier Major.

John Lane, late Farrier Major 2nd Life Guards, who placed the letters A.V.P. after his name, published in 1800 *The Principles of English Farriery Vindicated*, containing strictures on the erroneous and long exploded system lately revived at the Veterinary College, etc., etc. In the Preface we read that "the writer against whom my attack is principally directed, has with unmerited obloquy and invective, vilified the character of one of the most useful bodies of men in the Kingdom, charging them with ignorance and brutality of which they are perfectly innocent, and all this with no other view but to promote his own interests." There are ninety-seven pages of destructive criticism of this kind. Lane especially attacks the *Instructions for Farriers*. He speaks of his 45 years' experience, and referring to a particular type of nail mentioned by Coleman as something new, he says he has known it for fifty years. He tells us he served with the Inniskilling Dragoons in Scotland in 1771 and that later he was "Superintending Farrier" to the Yorkshire Light Dragoons. (Can this have been the title before that of Farrier Major was introduced?) Incidentally he gives us a short treatise on diseases, which enables us to see army practice as it was immediately prior to the advent of the Veterinary Service. Lane concludes by declaring Coleman to be contemptibly ignorant of the art he was practising. The whole booklet is directed against the change in the old order of things, but it is written with ability and the criticism is just. It is well to know that such as he were to be found where ignorance and stupidity commonly prevailed.

The farrier was uneducated, as were most people of the 18th Century. When education became available in the Army, about the middle of the 19th Century, the senior men were too old to learn, and the lowest educational standard was selected by the Authorities for the younger men. This was a grave error, and defective education has always held this class back.

The Principal Veterinary Surgeon in India in 1870, Mr. R. J. G. Hurford, an officer of then nearly forty years' experience, wrote of the farriers' education as follows:—[1]

"The result of my experience of the farriers of the army is that they are generally men entirely without any education, save of a mechanical description, and are in consequence incapable of understanding and appreciating even the most rudimentary instruction in the veterinary profession; the simplest language in which such instruction could be conveyed would be a mystery to the majority.

I believe I am within the truth when I assert that not one half of the Shoeing Smiths of the British Army can read their own language distinctly or write it legibly, and without a good primary education it is impossible to convey sound technical knowledge to a man."

We had to be satisfied with this type, whose educational defects are not exaggerated by Mr. Hurford, as may be seen from Plate 3, which corresponds to the period at which he wrote.

Their defective education was not without its humorous side as the following letter received by a Veterinary officer from a Battery Sergeant Farrier reveals:—

"Sir, I have given the medicine you ordered, and the horse is now dead."

I had an admirable Artillery Sergeant Farrier who always referred to the clinical thermometer as the "clinometer," thereby betraying his artillery bias, while the vagina became the "virginia." "Antimony" for "anatomy" was a universal error in the Farriers' classes, and "carbonic acid" was always spoken of as "carbolic acid"!

No doubt the worst result of their defective education was the extraordinary confidence and conceit they displayed after having acquired a little insight into hospital work. This was more apparent in Artillery than Cavalry. The Farrier Major of Cavalry obtained more clinical experience in three months than the Battery Sergeant Farrier did in twelve, and the wider his experience the more cautious he became.

Looking back through a long life I can say that the Farrier Majors I met, or who came under me, were a credit to their regiments and the officers who trained them. The Farrier Sergeants of Artillery had generally less polish and perhaps less education

[1] *Veterinarian*, vol. xl., 1870, p. 921.

PLATE III

DISEASE.
Paralysis, Fever and tendency to Lock-jaw.

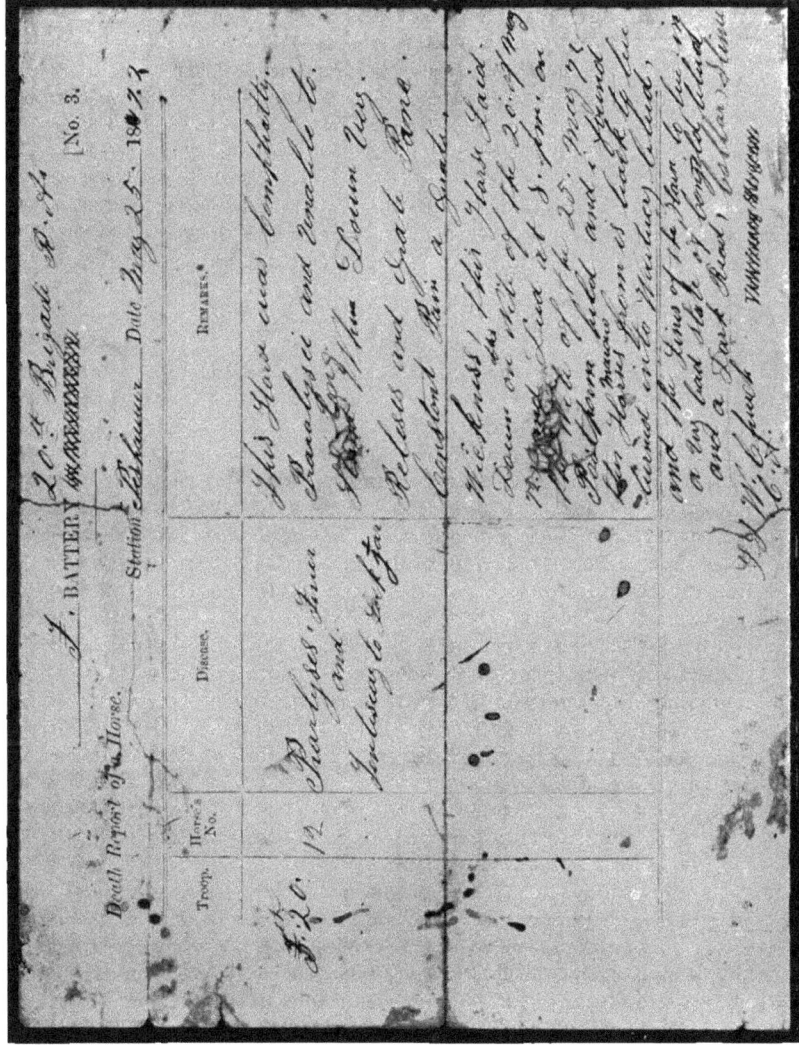

REMARKS.
This horse was completely paralysed and unable to stand long. When down very restless and great pain. Constant pain a great weakness. This horse laid down on the night of 20th of May, '72, and died at 3 p.m. on the night of the 25th May, '72. Post-mortem held, and I found this horse's marrow from his back to be turned into watery blood, and the loins of the horse to be in a very bad state of congested blood and a dark red colour slime.

DEATH REPORT OF A HORSE

than the Farrier Majors of Cavalry. Many hundreds of farriers of all ranks and of every branch of the army have passed through my hands; during my soldiering days I met no better men. None could work or did work as hard; as a soldier and artificer he had the duties of two men to perform. On return from the Field or after a march his second duties began while his comrades were resting; he was never spared, and in consequence on Service the wastage of Farriers is out of all proportion to that of other ranks.

The general opinion I formed of the Army Farrier was certainly not held by all. There is an article in the *Veterinarian*, Vol. 43, 1870, on "Army Farriers and Shoeing Smiths" which presents the other side of the shield. At that time this officer's experience had been wholly in the Artillery. Among other recommendations he urges that the Farriers should have nothing to do with the sick and that a subordinate veterinary service should be formed and represented in every battery and squadron. It is interesting to know that as far back as 1870 the need for such a branch as the Royal Army Veterinary Corps was recognized by our officers.

The greatest defect of the Farrier in days gone by was his inability to exercise discipline. This was owing partly to a deficiency in self-respect and partly to having to work with the men he had to command. The gulf which exists between the ranks is easily bridged when they are thrown closely together. If a squadron sergeant major had to take off his jacket and groom a horse during stable hour his authority would end.

The intemperance of Farriers was a bye-word. I am sure that in my day they were not more intemperate than other ranks, but the chances of detection were infinitely greater as in theory they were never off duty.

So far as the Royal Army Veterinary Corps is concerned the Farrier has passed away; his place is taken by a man of good education whose training is in the hospital and not in the forge. Nevertheless, those of us old enough to speak of the system of the past will surely remember with gratitude the rough, attentive nurse who did his best, and after a hard day's work would willingly sit up at night with a serious case; enthusiasm and interest were seldom wanting. In his heart he frequently claimed credit for the recovery, and I should have been sorry to deny him this small return for his devotion.

There has never been a shortage of army farriers in time of

peace; there have always been difficulties in war. The earliest I have met with is given by Rymer in his *Fœdera*, p. 586. It occurred in the reign of Henry V.; the entry reads " 6th June 1415. Orders were given to arrest forty smiths for the King's Expedition to France." A month or two later these men were present at Agincourt.

In June 1813 an order was published permitting boys to join regiments of dragoons with the object of learning a trade, among others that of farrier. They were enlisted for an unlimited period and bound for four years. I do not know whether the scheme was successful. This order may have stimulated the East India Company to initiate in the Cavalry and Artillery of the Madras Army a system of pupilage for farriers. The sons of old soldiers of good character received preferential treatment. The system still exists in the Madras Cavalry, the pupils being Eurasians.

CHAPTER III

THE GENESIS OF THE ARMY VETERINARY SERVICE AND THE COLEMAN ADMINISTRATION, 1796–1839

FOR a clear understanding of this chapter, it is necessary to give a biographical sketch of the man who by the accident of his position was called upon to bring our Service into existence.

Edward Coleman, F.R.S., 1765–1839, was born in Kent; at the age of sixteen he was apprenticed to a Surgeon at Gravesend. Proceeding to London in 1789 to " walk the hospitals," he entered as a pupil the house of Mr. Cline the celebrated Surgeon of St. Thomas's, to whom Coleman afterwards said he was indebted for his surgical and physiological knowledge. Cline had three other house pupils, of whom the most famous was Astley Cooper; between Coleman and Cooper a friendship sprang up which lasted throughout their long lives. Their hospital was the "Borough Hospitals," consisting of Guy's and St. Thomas's; in addition both took out John Hunter's course of lectures. While a student Coleman showed aptitude for physiological work, and made many experiments connected with Asphyxia, which were subsequently published in 1791. In the same year he qualified in medicine, left Cline's house and started practice in Fenchurch Street. In 1792 he made some observations on the comparative anatomy of the eye, but these were not published. In 1793 his opportunity came. Sainbel of the Veterinary College died and a successor was required. Through the influence of John Hunter and Cline, Moorcroft and Coleman were appointed as joint professors. Moorcroft only occupied the position a few weeks, and on his retirement Coleman was instituted sole professor at the age of twenty-eight, with no knowledge of the subjects he was appointed to teach. Forty years later he stated that he brought with him some knowledge of comparative anatomy and physiology, and the grand principles of medical science; this was his equipment for training the thirteen veterinary students he found in the school, and, at the end of his life, he rightly admits that he " had everything to learn."

Two years after his appointment to the London School Coleman was charged by the Commander-in-Chief with the creation of the Army Veterinary Service. He was made Principal Veterinary Surgeon to the Cavalry, his Commission being dated 21st September 1796, and also appointed Veterinary Surgeon to the Board of Ordnance (Artillery) in a civil capacity, with, at first, the designation of " Medical Superintendent." One of the earliest duties imposed on him was the production of a handbook for the guidance of Army Farriers, and in 1796 an official publication appeared entitled, *Instructions for the use of Farriers attached to the British Cavalry and to the Honourable Board of Ordnance*. To this virgin veterinary publication we have already referred on page 23, and of it we shall later have something more to say. There was a second edition in 1803. In order to justify his appointment to the Veterinary College, he published in 1798 the first volume of his work on the *Structure and Diseases of the Foot*. The impression Coleman intended to convey by this book was that the true principles and practice of shoeing had been discovered by him. Judging from the text one would think that no such men as La Fosse, Osmer and James Clark had ever lived! Their views on the structure of the foot and shoeing are adopted but not acknowledged; in fact he mentions no previous worker, but he thanks Cline for directing his attention to the subject and giving him much information! Incidentally it may be said that Cline knew nothing of the foot or shoeing. In 1800 he published a work on the *Formation and Uses of the Natural Frog*, and recommended a patent article of his own invention for use in the stable to give frog pressure. This latter hasty, ill-informed work was an advertisement, and it is extraordinary, considering his position, and that his school was in possession of a Parliamentary grant, that he should have protected any remedy he regarded as valuable to the public. In 1801 appeared the *First number of Veterinary Transactions*. It was intended to be an annual publication issued by the College, indicating the progress made in improved methods of practice during the year. The first number was the last. In 1802 followed the second volume of the *Structure and Diseases of the Foot*, with beautiful anatomical plates, the injections for which were made by John Percivall, though his name is not mentioned. The volume consists mainly of a tedious account of his differences with Moorcroft over the principles of shoeing.

It is remarkable that though Coleman wrote on subjects which he either did not understand or understood imperfectly, nowhere did he record the outstanding observation of his life, and his only claim to be remembered as a scientist: namely, the transmission of glanders to the ass by transfusing blood from a glandered horse. If one wishes to read an account of it, one has to turn to the 3rd vol. of Percivall's *Hippopathology* 1858, pp. 208, 261, 297. Percivall never saw Coleman perform the experiment, and was dependent on what he had been told by eye-witnesses, and his notes of Coleman's Lectures.

There is a distinct object, which will appear in due course, in thus presenting a list of Coleman's publications.

We must now turn to a consideration of the man himself. Sir Astley Cooper tells us that Coleman's reading was not extensive, and that his knowledge was in great measure empirical. He adds that he was a cheerful and delightful companion, on terms of intimacy with the choicest spirits and many intellectual persons. Sir Benjamin Brodie, President of the Royal Society, referring to Coleman's death, said his intellect was of a high order and gave indications of genius,

PLATE IV

EDWARD COLEMAN, F.R.S., 1765-1839
Principal Veterinary Surgeon to the Cavalry.

but admits that in many subjects he was behind the knowledge of the day. James Turner, by no means a friend, speaks of his " transcendent abilities."[1] William Percivall says that those who only knew Coleman from his works could form but an imperfect estimate of him. He describes him as possessing talent combined with a happy gift of imparting knowledge in its plainest and most pleasing forms. His reforms in Army Hygiene, he considers, place him on an eminence of distinction.[2] He, however, condemns Coleman's wild theorizing. We must remember that Percivall knew him intimately and had known him all his life. The above was written years after Coleman's death and after there had been a rift in the lute, so the testimony is the more valuable.

Coleman was undoubtedly a man of great personal charm, as his enemies readily admit, with all the cleverness of a woman in turning this advantage to account. Simonds describes him as facetious, humorous, suave in manner, with great kindness of disposition. Another pupil, J. Mayer Senr., says he possessed genius, a tact peculiar to himself and a generous and warm heart towards his pupils. The present writer admits that many years ago his hero-worship of Coleman was pronounced, but with the study of his history a revulsion of feeling has occurred. He is not singular in having misplaced his worship. John Gamgee as a pupil came under his magnetic spell, but renounced his allegiance later in life.[3]

In appearance Coleman was rather below the middle height; a very close observer tells us that his walk, attitude and gesture were those of a man confident of himself, a little prone to be indifferent to others, and far more disposed to lead than to follow. He describes his features as irregular, yet in the aggregate peculiarly expressive of intellectual energy, mingled at times with a deal of the severity of thought.[4] There was a consensus of opinion that his bust by Sievier, made when he was seventy years of age, was a remarkable likeness. Youatt says " the very man!" Its most marked characteristic is great flattening of the cheek bones. I am indebted to the Governors of the Royal Veterinary College for a photograph of an autographed engraving, made when Coleman was probably under forty years of age (Plate 4).

Coleman's official and private character will be revealed in the text as occasion affords.

Sir Astley Cooper and Coleman held identical views on the social position and future of the infant profession of which they assumed the charge. Let this truth be fully realized, Sir Astley Cooper ruled our profession for forty years, and his determination was to keep us bottom dog. Coleman was the instrument ready and fit to achieve this object. The attitude of the Medical to the Veterinary profession in the 18th century has been fully reviewed in my *History of Veterinary Literature*, vol. ii., dealing with that period. Coleman as a struggling

---

[1] *Veterinarian*, 1853. [2] *Ibid.*, 1851.
[3] *Edinburgh Veterinary Review*, vol. vi., 1864, p. 75.
[4] *Veterinarian*, vol. vii., 1834, p. 103.

surgeon condescended to come to our only Veterinary School and teach that of which he had absolutely no knowledge or experience. Throughout his long life he held that the practice of the veterinary art was a simple matter, that the diseases were few and easily learned, that consequently veterinary materia medica was equally simple, and the required remedies few. But in this nonsense there was an underlying object; it explained his sudden grasp of an alien subject, and also why as medicine contractor to the British Cavalry he permitted the use of only a few simple drugs. Nor is this all; the simplicity of the subject admitted of its being understood by men without education and of mediocre intelligence. Accordingly Coleman swept away the high standard of training introduced by Sainbel, who with all his faults had been intent on producing a well-educated and respectable profession. Though Coleman advertised for medical men to join the College with a view to obtaining Commissions in the Cavalry, he maintained all his life that they made the worst veterinary surgeons and that the sons of farriers, grooms and stable keepers made the best. Naturally the latter class were more submissive and unlikely to question his authority, whereas the trained surgeon was a thorn in his side during the early years. Thus he favoured the sons of the forge and stable, and as far as possible excluded the surgeons from the Army, and by such means stamped our profession with the brand of social inferiority. His love of power, his passionate clinging to office when a physical wreck, his jealousy, even of those who had been his pupils, his malignity towards those whom he disliked and envied—failings not, however, peculiar to Coleman—were the striking characteristics of his latter days. He had an intense love of money which influenced his acts throughout life. He came to us as a poor man, he died extremely wealthy. We shall see later how he sold his self-respect for a few shillings a day. To his greed the social ruin of our profession was largely due; he willingly took large numbers from the lower strata of life as students; the question of their educational fitness did not arise; the whole of the fees passed into Coleman's pocket and not into the exchequer of the College. With such principles, his long life was an unmitigated evil, for the moulding of the future profession had lain solely in his hands. With a full consciousness of the value of words, and after reading everything he wrote and everything written for and against him, I concur with the opinion of F. C. Cherry, expressed ninety-six years ago, that Coleman was the greatest enemy the profession has ever had in its highest ranks.

Yet he had an immense reputation. This cannot have been based on his published works, of which I have given a complete list. These works were immature, and all written within *nine years* of his joining a profession of which he previously knew nothing. Though he lived for thirty-seven years after the last work was printed, during that time *he never published a line* containing his ripe experience and judgement. His students obtained his mature views through his admirably delivered lectures, which were rigidly guarded from publication, pressmen being excluded from his theatre. His opinions were final; there was no appeal; they never underwent revision; he made no mistakes. These characteristics he shared with the Duke of Wellington. The same lectures were repeated year by year, and the same errors and prejudices disseminated. He never quoted any veterinary writer as an authority, not even one of his own pupils; there was only one man in the profession and his name was Coleman.

It must not be supposed that his faults were unrecognized in his lifetime; we shall show how his Army functions were attacked. No man in our profession was ever more vigorously assailed and insulted, for even a statement of facts may be so expressed as to be insulting. Yet Coleman never openly resented an attack, but continued imperturbably on his way. To what then was his success due? In the first place unquestionably to the influential support of the Governors of the College, of whom the most powerful was his bosom friend Sir Astley Cooper, and secondly to the attractive personality, natural ability and consummate audacity, which had made him master of the situation and secured him a firm position in the College within ten years of his appointment.

We are now about to study Coleman's introduction to the Artillery branch of the Army, first prefacing an outline of the constitution of the body which controlled the Artillery.

The Board of Ordnance was a very ancient body, originally created to furnish the Navy with warlike stores. In due course it took on functions naval, military and civil, and became the most powerful public body in the kingdom. Its affairs were conducted by a Board over which presided the most important person in the kingdom after the Prime Minister, the Master-General of Ordnance. In discharge of its military functions, the Board controlled the Artillery, Engineers, and the Civil Staffs of both services. It was a law unto itself, made its own regulations, issued its own warrants for pay and promotion, and took no notice of Army warrants unless so disposed. The Master-General was appointed usually from among the distinguished servants of the State; he might be either a soldier or civilian, and was responsible only to the King.

The Artillery of the Army at the period on which our interests are centred, 1793, was merely a tactical unit of the Infantry, each infantry battalion having two guns, hence the term then and for long after in use, "Battalion Artillery." The horses employed in the Battalion Artillery were hired from contractors, who also provided the drivers, non-enlisted men, who wore a white smock, walked by the side of their team, carried a long carter's whip, and were officially known as "waggoners." The care of the hired horses was confided to a Commissary of Horse, who had subordinates known as conductors; neither the Commissary nor conductors were Artillerymen. In action the drivers frequently disappeared, and in the year of which we are speaking, 1794, it was decided to form a Corps of Captain Commissaries and enlist the drivers. The Commissary was responsible for training the men, and for feeding and looking after the horses, but from the moment these were hooked into the guns, the whole came under the officer commanding the guns, who then, no matter how junior in point of service, became senior to the Commissary.

It is difficult to realize that the Battalion Artillery (Field Artillery of the present day) required a special corps for the care of its horses; nevertheless, such existed under various designations until 1822, when it was swept away. During all these years friction and bitter hostility existed between the Corps of Artillery Drivers and the Royal Artillery.

In the year 1793 also another Artillery came into existence, still under the Board of Ordnance, the Horse Artillery. Unlike the Battalion Artillery each troop possessed its own horses, the drivers were enlisted men, and the whole were under the control and management of Artillery officers.[1]

Having said so much of the constitution of the mounted Artillery of the period, we may now turn to Coleman. On the 19th February 1796 the D.A.G. of Artillery, who commanded the Corps of Captain Commissaries, reported to the Board of Ordnance on the diseased state of the Artillery horses located in Kent. At this time there were practically no military stables, and the horses were scattered over the country, both for military reasons and facility of accommodation. Under instructions from the Board of Ordnance, Mr. Coleman, Professor of the Veterinary College, was directed to investigate the disease and report thereon.[2] Coleman reported that the disease was glanders, and on his recommendation many horses were destroyed. These animals were the property of the contractor and had, of course, to be paid for. In his report Coleman suggests that the " prodigious loss " was due to skilled advice not being sought at the beginning. The authorities at Woolwich thereupon strongly represented to the Board that an appointment which would secure Mr. Coleman's attendance, would pay for itself in a very few months. They

[1] It has been stated by a distinguished officer of Artillery that the pre-eminence of the Horse Artillery as horsemasters "was acquired by them in the Peninsula from their intercourse with the Cavalry of the King's German Legion."—*History of the Royal Artillery*, Captain (afterwards Colonel) F. Duncan.

[2] P.R.O. W.O. 55/1350.

pointed out that as matters stood there was nothing to prevent the extension of the disease if it were left to the management of ignorant farriers.

Further, in the previous year, 1795, the horses of the Ordnance were known to have been affected with glanders. Animals had also arrived from overseas from the Expedition to Quiberon, only a fraction of which survived owing to a disease "which appeared to be infectious," and the Officer Commanding the Corps said he could not hear of any Farrier under the Ordnance, whose judgement could be depended upon to deal with this serious situation.

Coleman, having made his inspection at the request of the Board of Ordnance, followed it up with a letter, dated 27 February 1796, in which he suggested that a portion of the stables at Woolwich should be set apart as an Infirmary, that he should attend once or twice a week, and that there should be in residence his representative, a pupil from the Veterinary College, who should remain there until the Farriers were sufficiently instructed in the treatment of disease.[1]

There is no allusion in this letter to the fact that Coleman prior to his appointment to the Ordnance had been lecturing to the officers of the Army Medical Staff at Woolwich, chief of whom at this time was Dr. Rollo, the Surgeon-General to the Ordnance. Twenty years later Coleman refers to some lectures, saying that so greatly were they appreciated that a memorial was signed by Dr. Rollo and his officers, suggesting Coleman's appointment as Veterinary Surgeon to the Ordnance.

This reference to Rollo and the officers of the Medical Staff of the Ordnance would be inexplicable, but for a few lines which occur in the autobiographical account of Delabere Blaine, contained in the first section—the History of Veterinary Medicine—of his *Outlines of the Veterinary Art*. Blaine was a rolling stone; from 1794-95 he was surgeon to one of the troops of Horse Artillery at Woolwich, "with which I remained more than two years,[2] extending my knowledge of human medicine by witnessing the judicious management of the Woolwich Artillery Hospital under the direction of the late ingenious Dr. Rollo. Nor had I less opportunity also for improvement in the veterinary art, *from the circumstance of all the sick horses belonging to the establishment being placed under my inspection.*"[3] In studying the biography

[1] P.R.O. W.O. 44/687, Bundle No. 88.
[2] Blaine gives his year of joining the Artillery as 1793, but the R.A. List shows his appointment as 1st April 1794 and resigned 15th August 1795.
[3] The italics are mine.—F. S.

of Blaine, I have often been puzzled to explain the italicized sentence. I finally put it down to bombast and self-advertisement, of which Blaine, in spite of his ability, had more than his share; but in the light of War Office paper 44/687, which I only unearthed at the P.R.O. in 1925, it is possible to reconstruct matters, and to explain Coleman's appearance at Woolwich. Never in any of the official correspondence of the period is there a hint of the medical branch of the Ordnance interesting itself in veterinary practice, but we have seen the difficulties the authorities had in obtaining skilled advice, and as Blaine had served a year in Sainbel's dissecting room in 1791-2, we can readily imagine his chief, Dr. Rollo, mentioning to the Artillery authorities at Woolwich his previous connection with the Veterinary College, and can understand that Blaine's advice may have been requested, as he has above stated. At this time Blaine knew very little of veterinary practice and Coleman but little more. It is evident that when Coleman learned Blaine had left the Service in August 1795, he visited Woolwich and saw Dr. Rollo, and by lecturing before him and his officers, demonstrated his capacity for taking up the work Blaine had recently been doing gratuitously. Certainly there can be no doubt that it was Dr. Rollo who suggested to the Artillery authorities at Woolwich to call in the services of Professor Coleman when disease broke out, though Blaine in his historical notice never mentions the name of Coleman as his successor at Woolwich.

Coleman's proposals for his weekly attendance at Woolwich, and the residence there of one of his pupils, were accepted. His pay was fixed at 10s. a day, that of his assistant at 6s. a day, and the appointments of both took effect from 25 March 1796. Coleman's designation on appointment was "Medical Superintendent"; there is nothing to show when this was changed. The Assistant appointed was John Percivall, father of William Percivall; he had qualified in 1795. Coleman, in his letter of 29 February, already quoted, suggested to the authorities at Woolwich what his remuneration and that of his assistant should be. He was also careful to provide for inspection duty, the horses, as we have seen, being very scattered. A rate of double pay on inspection days and travelling allowance of 1s. 3d. a mile were sanctioned. Nor did the supply of medicines escape his attention. The medicines in use he regarded as "improper"; he desired to supply his own, a capitation grant being suggested by one of the officers of the Artillery of 4d. a week per horse ! Coleman made no demur, but as this worked out at over £1,000 a year for the 1,200 horses then on charge, the Board very properly regarded it as excessive, and decided that medicines should be supplied by their own Druggist, both for general purposes and for chests. This must have been a disappointment, for the contract for medicines was well worth securing.

Coleman's duties with the Ordnance were to examine for soundness all " recruit " horses, advise on the treatment of disease, inspect at outstations, bringing in such cases as he thought necessary for treatment at Woolwich, to lecture occasionally to the Officers, Artillery Cadets and Farriers, and to direct the Shoeing. He found the horses of the Ordnance saturated with disease, "violent" grease, canker, quittor, contracted feet, mange, blindness, farcy and glanders; when he left many years later, he claimed that all such conditions belonged only to the past. This is not accurate; no branch of the Service was free from glanders until long after Coleman's death; but there was an immense and beneficial change, a complete revolution for which Coleman claimed the credit. As the responsible official, it must be granted him; in fact, the clearance of disease among the horses of the Ordnance was not entirely Coleman's work, but largely that of his assistant. Coleman attended once a week at Woolwich, every Tuesday, and did so for twenty years. The assistant was in residence; with more than double the amount of practical experience of the master, he rivalled him even in clinical knowledge and judgement.[1] Before the assistant had been there many years he became, in 1805, an officer in the veterinary branch of His Majesty's Ordnance, highly respected, trusted, and in due course acquired wide experience. He examined and passed into the Service all horses for the Artillery, and he also lectured to the officers and farriers. His judgement in the selection of horses was universally recognized. The master, on the other hand, was never an officer of the Ordnance, his appointment was purely civilian, terminable at a day's notice, as indeed it subsequently was terminated.

It has not been possible in giving a consecutive history of Coleman's connection with the Board of Ordnance to avoid anticipating, and it is now necessary to return to the year 1796 to learn how the Cavalry fared in the matter of a veterinary service.

[1] We must not forget that in February 1796 Coleman had only two years' experience of veterinary work, and later we shall give evidence of his knowledge at this time.

There have been few more gravely unsatisfactory campaigns carried out by the British Army than that which terminated in Holland in 1795. Large bodies of mounted troops were engaged, and the losses from disease, neglect and ignorance were startling. In the field were Generals of sound common sense, who recognized that improvement in the care of horses (and men) was possible with proper organization and training, and the Commander-in-Chief, the Duke of York, though a very unsuccessful soldier, was by no means blind to the chief causes of inefficiency. If sick men and animals cannot be cared for on a campaign there is something wrong. It would be really difficult to say whether the men or the horses were the more neglected in Holland, but so deep an impression was created on the military authorities, that a determined effort was made on the termination of hostilities to prevent any such recurrence. Fortunately for the project, the Duke of York had witnessed the chaos and neglect, and was all in favour of rational reform. He has been given credit, by the most careful, precise and widely read historian of the British Army, the Hon. Sir John Fortescue, for initiating veterinary reform in the Cavalry. I am inclined to think that the real inspiration lay elsewhere.

In 1793 it is known that William Moorcroft had a large practice in London, further that on the death of Sainbel in that year he was invited to take his place at the Veterinary College. This his private practice did not permit, so that the College authorities appointed Edward Coleman as co-professor; Moorcroft's engagement was therefore a part-time one. The Moorcroft-Coleman arrangement lasted only from February to April 1794; the men evidently did not agree; they were as wide apart as the poles, and Coleman was left in possession. Moorcroft was a man of great breadth of view who knew the possibilities of his profession, and was indeed at this time the only man in the kingdom who was properly qualified to practise, having graduated at Lyons in March 1791. His practice brought him into contact with many distinguished people in London, among whom was Lord Heathfield, a governor of the Veterinary College, to whom his work on Shoeing, subsequently published in 1800, is dedicated, and with whom he was on terms of friendship. There can be no doubt that Moorcroft and Coleman impressed on Heathfield, who at that time commanded the 29th Dragoons, that nothing effective could be done to control loss in the Army until the management of the horses and treatment of disease were given into skilled hands.

Heathfield was in a position to secure not only the co-operation of his brother Generals, but also the important interest and help of the Commander-in-Chief (Duke of York), who in 1795 returned to this country from Holland. Among Sainbel's pupils, all able men, was one William Stockley, still little more than a boy, but who must at that time have given evidence of the strength of character and great ability which subsequently characterized his long career. Stockley was known to Moorcroft. When Coleman assumed the sole control of the Veterinary College he appointed Stockley as Demonstrator of Anatomy. In 1795, probably September, Lord Heathfield desired to prove experimentally the utility of introducing Veterinary Surgeons into the Army generally, and at his suggestion, as an experimental measure, Stockley was sent to the 1st Fencible Cavalry for six months. At the end of six months Colonel Villiers, who commanded the regiment, certified to the ability and diligence of Stockley, and the great advantage the Service had derived from his appointment.[1] The experiment was at an end, and active measures were taken to push forward a scheme for introducing a Veterinary Service into the Army. The facts just narrated would necessarily be unknown to the learned author of the *History of the British Army*, whose study of the official correspondence in the P.R.O. would reveal to him the remarkable interest taken by the Duke of York in horses, farriers and forge carts, but there can be little doubt that Moorcroft, Coleman and Heathfield were the instigators of the movement, and that William Stockley, at nineteen years of age, had by his personality, zeal and ability, won over the authorities. His name must never be forgotten.

William Stockley, 1776–1860, entered the Veterinary College in 1792 at the age of sixteen, and obtained his diploma in 1794. When posted to the 1st Fencible Cavalry he was placed under the surgeon of the regiment, whom Stockley describes as a man of great eminence and who knew a good deal about horses; he bent the boy's service life in the right direction. On the conclusion of the experiment above mentioned, Stockley declined Coleman's invitation to return to a post in the College. He had taken a great liking to soldiering, and remained with the 1st Fencibles until the regiment was disbanded in 1800.

He was then transferred to the Artillery in Ireland, where he served until 1822, when he was placed on half pay on reduction of establishment. He was restored to full pay in 1838 and went to Canada; returning in 1844 he served in Ireland and England until 1858, when he was

---

[1] *Veterinarian*, vol. xxx., 1857, p. 353, and vol. xxxiii., 1860, p. 426.

retired as Senior Veterinary Surgeon of the Ordnance at the age of eighty-two!

He was a man of great physical and mental energy, ability and diligence, of warm temperament, outspoken, good-natured and an entertaining companion. His fund of Service anecdotes, it is said, would have filled a volume. He was extraordinarily popular with all ranks. During his service he did everything to maintain the status of the profession, and was ever zealous of its advancement and of its rights. He did not hesitate to bring officers of high standing before higher authorities for interfering with his practice. He was the first to move for an improvement in the pay of the Army Veterinary Surgeon. Stockley's success in the experimental trial was a valuable asset to his future service; a failure at this critical time would have altered the course of our history. Stockley always regarded himself as "the most fortunate man in the profession." Whatever good fortune came to him he deserved. He was elected President of the Royal College of Veterinary Surgeons in 1857 and died in 1860.[1]

At the time we are writing of, and for many years subsequently, a standing "Committee of General Officers" sat in London and periodically dealt with all questions of Army organization. We have already referred to it at p. 9. The committee appears to have consisted entirely of Cavalry officers, and two of its members were Lords Heathfield and Pembroke.[2] On 3rd March 1796[3] the Adjutant-General of the Army addressed the President of this committee, directing it, under instructions from H.R.H. the Duke of York, to report on several subjects connected with Cavalry, and the letter concludes: "The Veterinary College and whether its instruction is such, according to the opinion of the Board, as to enable it to furnish the means of improving the present practice of farriery, and whatever may appertain to that very important branch of the Cavalry Service, reporting such particular mode or system as may appear to them most advisable to adopt for so essential and so salutary a service."[4]

---

[1] The authority for this outline of Stockley's life is the *Veterinarian*, vol. xxx., p. 353; vol. xxxiii., p. 426.

[2] This was the 11th Earl, not the author of *Military Equitation*, who died in 1794.

[3] It will be observed that the date is twelve days after the Board of Ordnance had been addressed on practically the same question by the D.A.G. of Artillery at Woolwich. There could not have been any collusion between the Cavalry and Artillery authorities, for the Ordnance lived a life of extreme official isolation. We conclude therefore that Coleman had worked up interest in the Ordnance through the Medical Department of that service, and in the Cavalry through Lord Heathfield. The Adjutant-General of the Army was a Cavalry officer and a friend of Heathfield; he was also well disposed towards the proposed veterinary service.

[4] P.R.O. W.O. 3/15.

The Report of the Board was made in April 1796,[1] and is as follows:

The Board having taken into consideration the heavy loss of horses continually accruing to the Cavalry from the total ignorance of those who have at present the medical care of them, as well as from the very inadequate allowance made for that Department, which precludes all possibility of procuring persons better skilled in the knowledge of Farriery, are of opinion that the Veterinary (in the original " Vertinary ") College may afford the means of great improvement in this essential part of the service, and that a proper pecuniary compensation given to persons taken from that seminary to be attached to each Regiment of Cavalry, will be a most advisable measure to adopt and would ultimately beyond all doubt prove a considerable saving to the public. The Board, therefore, begs leave to suggest that the Veterinary Surgeon to be attached to each Regiment of Cavalry should receive the Pay and Warrant of a Quarter Master, and that he be furnished with a necessary set of instruments, as also with a chest of medicines at such stated periods as shall be deemed expedient.

That until the Regiments of Cavalry shall be supplied with Veterinary Surgeons, each of them not so supplied should be allowed to charge half of the above pay for the subsistence of a student whom they shall send to the College to be educated for that purpose, the name of which student should appear at the foot of the Monthly Return of each regiment, and the allowances be charged with contingent half-yearly accompt, accompanied by a certificate from the Commanding Officer and the Professor of the Veterinary College.

It may be here necessary to add that it has been proposed by the Governors of the Veterinary College that they will defray the charge of Board, Lodging and Instructions for six pupils at a time, who may be willing to enter into the Service and who upon such conditions shall be considered as engaged in it, if suitable emoluments are held out to them as soon as they have passed their examination.

But as the pupils to be educated in the College will probably occupy near three years in their studies, the Regiments of Cavalry cannot be supplied for many years with a sufficient number of Veterinary Surgeons from the Fund, for which reason it is that in the interim the Board have thought it proper to propose that a certain additional number of students, to be provided either by the Regiments or the College, should receive half pay from Government during the time of their studies, which expense, whenever the regiments are once supplied, will no longer be necessary if the College will continue, as they have offered, to instruct six pupils at their own expense for the use of the Army.

It may be proper also to mention that the Governors of the College state that there are at least four pupils who have nearly completed their education, and who are willing to engage in the Service upon

[1] P.R.O. W.O. 4/164, p. 286.

terms which may be deemed an adequate compensation for their time and the expense they have incurred.

This epoch-making report is signed by W. A. Pitt, General; W. Harcourt, Lieut. General; D. Dundas, Harrington, Heathfield and Pembroke, Majors-General; all Cavalry Officers of experience and anxious to remedy an obvious blot on military organization.

It will be observed from these proceedings that Veterinary Surgeons were to be appointed to Cavalry Regiments under the warrant of the Colonel and not under the King's Commission. Regiments were also invited to send a man to qualify, towards whose maintenance at the College half the proposed daily pay of a Veterinary Surgeon was approved. This amount is stated to be 2s. 6d. per diem. It is remarkable that the College authorities in their anxiety to secure the Service as an outlet for their pupils, undertook to train and *maintain* at their own expense six men every year, who were ultimately destined for the Army! What most impressed the Military Board was the delay which must occur before the trained students could be available. Three years was the period fixed by Sainbel and accepted by the Governing Body. It was also the period now accepted by Coleman. This period is of vital importance from a historical point of view, as Coleman, very shortly afterwards, reduced it from three years to *three months!*

On the 24th May 1796 Colonels of Regiments were informed by letter of the above arrangements (which by now had obtained Treasury sanction and the approval of the Duke of York), for "improving the practice of Farriery in the Corps of Cavalry," and that a person properly educated and having received a certificate from the medical committee of the Veterinary College, would be attached to each regiment under the name of Veterinary Surgeon;[1] that the appointment is by Warrant for not less than seven years, and that the Veterinary Surgeon shall have exactly the same pay as a Quarter-Master of Cavalry, viz. 5s. 6d. per diem. They are further directed that Regiments may send a student to the College for whom 2s. 6d. will be allowed by the State, but prior to admission he must be attested to serve for at least seven years, reckoned from the date of joining the regiment as Veterinary Surgeon, and that from the date of his attestation he is, either as student or surgeon, liable to be tried and punished by G.C.M. for disobedience of orders, or any offence against military discipline.

[1] P.R.O. W.O. 4/165, p. 29.

PLATE A

What part Coleman played in these transactions is not evident. There is no evidence of any protest by him against the position offered, or the rate of pay, or the prospective " flogging " for breaches of military discipline, to which at that time all under commissioned rank were liable. Was Coleman satisfied with these offers ? This will ever be a question of opinion; he gives me personally the impression of possessing such contempt for the calling of which by accident he became the head, that I do not for one moment think he regarded the terms as unsuitable or derogatory. That he did not protest is shown by his acceptance in 1801 of Warrant rank for the Veterinary Surgeon of the Ordnance, John Percivall, for no Commissions were given in that branch until 1805.

Apparently there was no response by the students to the terms offered by the State in the letter of 24 May 1796. Further, Coleman saw that unless he could turn out men in less time than three years, the chance of supplying the Cavalry might be lost; he therefore introduced a distinctly astute scheme. His proposal was addressed to medical men recently qualified, asking them to join the veterinary ranks, and by passing " a very moderate space of time " at St. Pancras,[1] qualify themselves for the practice of veterinary medicine in the Army.

This circular or announcement gave great offence to the army medical authorities, as we shall see later. Its importance for us is that Coleman lowered the standard of professional education to meet an emergency; he might have been justified in doing so as a temporary measure, and solely for candidates possessing a medical qualification, but this standard became applicable to all, and before long anyone could obtain the diploma of his school by a few months' study. This condition of affairs lasted throughout Coleman's life. The evidence in proof of this is found in the *Veterinarian* thirty-four years later. In the issue for September 1830 an anonymous writer says that in the selection of army candidates men of character and education had met with no preference; private considerations had trodden down all meritorious right, and the army been disgraced by the appointment of grooms, farriers, and men of low character and education. He draws attention to the dedication to King George III. of Coleman's work on the Foot, in which he thanks His Majesty for conferring commissions, and so inducing medical men of liberal

[1] I employ here the designation current at the time and for many years later.

education to devote their services to the Army, and asks, if this was true in 1805, how is it that he "stuffed the army with canaille," and for years set his face against medical men? In the following number another correspondent says that he has often heard senior cavalry officers deplore the difficulty in getting a good veterinary officer, while still another writes in the same issue, and openly charges Coleman with introducing grooms and farriers as veterinary surgeons into regiments.[1] He also asserts that the list of candidates is unfairly kept, and that Coleman forwards the names of favourites and rejects those of others. The writer takes no exception to his " enlisting his friends and relatives into the service," but deplores the introduction of the low ignorant characters he places in such a station. " What might not have resulted had the army always been supplied with professional gentlemen?" The Editor of the *Veterinarian*, knowing the truth of these charges, suggests that they might well form the subject of an enquiry, especially "considering his (Coleman's) well-known objection to medical men." It is significant that though these and many similar statements were made during Coleman's lifetime, there was no attempt at refutation.

Such then we must believe were the students sent to the Army, and though surgeons had been specially invited to join the College in 1796, with a view to entering the Service, Coleman always said in after life that they made the worst veterinary surgeons, while the sons of farriers made the best! It was rather a two-edged argument to employ. Thirty-four years later, at the opening lecture of the College in November 1830—*i.e.*, in the month following the issue of the last *Veterinarian* from which we have quoted—he denied having made such a statement, but admitted that medical men, owing to their previous ignorance of the horse, laboured under a disadvantage. " I have had 130 medical pupils, but if asked where they are I could not tell. I cannot find them, at least in the Metropolis." He then narrated the case of a medically educated veterinary surgeon who had to be withdrawn

[1] This charge against Coleman is so serious that it is impossible to avoid quoting the most trustworthy evidence on the point. R. Darvill, Veterinary Surgeon 7th Hussars, in his *Treatment and Training of the Race Horse*, published in 1828, gives his personal history. A groom in a racing stable, he one day took a horse to the College for treatment; he was bitten with the idea of qualifying as a Veterinary Surgeon, and saw Professor Sewell, the mouthpiece of Coleman, who informed him " *that men of a similar description to myself were the most fit persons to become Veterinary Surgeons.*" (The italics are mine.—F. S.)

from a regiment because he mistook the lame leg. To be charitable to Coleman we must believe that his memory was failing him in 1830: the evidence against him is overwhelming. We have not quoted all, though that contained in the *Veterinarian*, vol. vii., 1834, p. 103, should perhaps not be omitted. The Editor of the *Veterinarian* in publishing the November 1830 address asks Coleman how many non-medically educated veterinary surgeons had been compelled to leave their regiments or to be excluded from mess. No reply was given.

The absurdly short period of study adopted by Coleman was due in the first place to his own ignorance, but all his life he proclaimed the simplicity of veterinary as compared with human medicine, and that the number of diseases from which the horse suffered was small! He even boasted that he could carry in his waistcoat pocket all the drugs necessary in veterinary practice. The significance of this statement will be apparent when we consider him as army contractor for the supply of drugs.

To return, however, to the appeal made to young medical men in 1796 to join the Army Veterinary Service. While Coleman was pledged to do his best to obtain men the State had also a part to play. The 2s. 6d. a day bribe to induce regimental farriers to be educated, was now to be converted to another purpose and added to the 5s. 6d. daily pay already promised, making a total of 8s. a day pay. The War Office announced these terms, also the scheme for obtaining men from the medical profession, in a letter addressed to Colonels of Regiments on 21st September 1796, adding that the *College having now been placed on a more respectable footing than had been originally proposed*,[1] candidates approved by the medical committee of the school shall receive their appointment by Commission under His Majesty's Royal Sign Manual.[2] It is quite clear that some such concession was necessary if medical men were to be obtained for the Veterinary Service. As regards the terms the letter above quoted gives the rate of pay at 7s. per diem, 6s. being "subsistence" and 1s. "arrears." Evidently 7s. was a mistake, but the 1s. arrears was not. Later on, the 1s. a day was stated to be for his horse. This, however, was a mean financial move, for

---

[1] The italics are mine. This was a gratuitous insult, for which Coleman was doubtless responsible. As a matter of fact the pupils of Sainbel were of outstanding ability and gentility. If Coleman had admitted only the same type of man, our profession would to-day occupy a very different position in public opinion.

[2] P.R.O. W.O. 4/166, p. 72.

when the officer was placed on half pay it was calculated on seven shillings and not on eight as originally promised.

In the Medical Service of the Cavalry the senior officers, at any rate, had long been commissioned and by 1796 the commission had been extended to the junior or "mate." What chance was there then of recruiting medical men for the Veterinary Service on a non-commissioned basis? It has been necessary to deal with this question, as Coleman has been credited with obtaining Commissions for our Service; not only is there nothing to support that contention but there is evidence to the contrary. Commissions were the outcome of the attempt to supply a large number of cavalry regiments with veterinary assistance by enlisting human surgeons and giving them a veterinary certificate and commission.

Coleman in his work on the *Structure and Diseases of the Foot* 1798, thanks H.M. the King for conferring commissions on Army Veterinary Surgeons, and says that by so doing he has done more to promote the veterinary art than could otherwise have been effected in centuries. "This single act has raised the art from contempt to respectability, and induced many medical students to devote their services to its improvement." But in his statement to the public he makes no claim to having secured this concession. Compare this silence with the claims made in the last years of his life, to be precise on 10 March 1835 (*Veterinarian*, vol. viii.) that he bethought how he could give respectability to a profession containing many men who had nothing estimable in their conduct and still less in their practice. The mode of effecting this was soon afforded; veterinary surgeons began to be appointed to the Cavalry regiments; and "I prayed and demanded that they should be appointed in the same way as human surgeons, that they should be commissioned officers, that they should rank as gentlemen. With some difficulty I obtained my object and thus gave to the veterinary profession a new character and importance." This statement, made thirty-nine years after the event, is the first in which he claimed that the act was his. His memory must have been at fault, for his assertion does not square with the known facts, nor was the class of man he welcomed at his school calculated to give the profession "character and importance" or provide "gentlemen" for the Army!

If, as he said, it was he who obtained commissions for his officers in the Cavalry he signally failed in the Artillery. Surgeons and Hospital Mates of the Ordnance in 1796 served on warrant issued by the Master-General of the Ordnance, and the veterinary surgeon appointed by Coleman had also to serve on warrant. A curious anomaly in consequence existed, both in the medical and veterinary services of Cavalry and Artillery, the Cavalrymen being commissioned, the latter not! It was not until 1804 that the Medical Service and (1805) the Veterinary Service of the Ordnance received commissions, though not without a struggle, in which Coleman gave no assistance. It was the prospective candidates for the Ordnance Veterinary Service who indignantly refused to serve without commissions. Applications made to Coleman on this subject were not forwarded to the Authorities. The candidates accordingly addressed the Commander-in-Chief direct, and when commissions were approved, Coleman did not inform the petitioners until several appointments had been made.[1]

Meanwhile Coleman was not neglecting his own interests. The letter of the 21st September 1796 previously mentioned (p. 43) informed Colonels of Regiments that Mr. E. Coleman, Professor of the Veterinary College, had been appointed by His Majesty to be Principal Veterinary Surgeon to the Cavalry, with an allowance of 10s. per diem. This appointment, it will be observed, carried with it the King's Commission, and was granted to a man already tied down to civil life by his school duties, and simultaneously mixed up with another branch of the Army (the Ordnance) from which he also obtained a daily stipend but no commission. Impossible as these conditions are in the 20th century there was precedent in the 18th and early part of the 19th century. John Hunter was Surgeon-General in the Army Medical Service while conducting his school and immense practice, but he had already served in the Army, while Coleman had not.

Nor did Coleman's extraordinary good fortune end here. We have seen that in March or thereabouts he was anxious to provide the Ordnance Service not only with veterinary advice but with drugs. The figure mentioned for drugs (p. 34) was so startling that it was at once rejected, and never throughout the years that he attended that branch of the Service did the question of supplying his own drugs ever again crop up. It was otherwise in the Cavalry. I suggest that Coleman had learned his lesson in March, and when the Cavalry drug question arose in August

[1] *Veterinarian*, vol. iii., September 1830 and vol. xxxii., 1859, p. 639. This contains a statement by one of the candidates.

[We may here note that the cost of preparing a Commission for a Veterinary Surgeon in 1796 was £5 0s. 6d.; by 1830 the charge had fallen to 30s.]

or September, we find the four shillings a horse per month, proposed for the Ordnance, though not by Coleman personally, reduced to three shillings per annum per head for the Cavalry!

The State no longer has contracts with its servants; they were common in Coleman's day, and they were not rare when the writer entered the Service. At that time the farriers held a contract for shoeing the horses; the commanding officer (in India) held a contract for supplying blankets, nose-bags, picketing gear and horse slings, and the Veterinary Officer held a contract (India) for the supply of certain "bazaar medicines." All this has rightly been swept away, but in Coleman's time Colonels of Regiments held immense contracts, the largest being the supply of uniform to the men, while medical officers contracted for drugs and dressings, so that Coleman's contract was nothing unusual. The contract for drugs for the men had always been regarded with particular favour. Some Apothecaries - General became immensely wealthy, and the money could not have been saved out of their pay.[1] An Apothecary-General under a Royal Warrant of 1747 secured the reversion of his appointment for his son;[2] evidently it was a position worth having. Coleman, who combined in a peculiar degree science with business aptitude—a very unusual alliance—secured the right to supply the Cavalry not only with drugs but also with the necessary surgical appliances at the above-mentioned rate of three shillings per annum for all troop horses and chargers at duty. The method of paying him is laid down in the historic letter of 21 September 1796, and we need not enter into it excepting to say that the money was found by taking it from the Farrier's contract for shoeing and medicines. In 1796 this amounted to one penny per diem per effective troop horse, and in his evidence before a Royal Commission in 1808, to which we shall presently refer, Coleman said this sum consisted of shoeing one halfpenny and medicines one halfpenny. This statement was incorrect; Coleman knew perfectly well that it did not cost 15s. a year to provide each individual horse with medicine; he was merely anxious to show by comparison how small his charge of 3s. a year really was. This sum he received not only for the regular Cavalry but also for the Fencibles.[3]

Great importance was attached by the State to the quality

---

[1] See Farrington's Diary under date 20 January 1807.

[2] Fortescue: *History of the British Army*, vol. iv.

[3] Fencible Cavalry were regular troops enlisted for the duration of the war and for Home Service only.

of the medicines to be supplied; the Farriers in their day no doubt bought in the cheapest market, and the adulteration of drugs at that time is beyond belief, especially of those intended for veterinary practice. This was to be changed. Coleman was bound by the terms of his contract to obtain his drugs from the Apothecaries' Society, while their undue expenditure by regiments was specially provided against by excluding private practice of every kind by regimental veterinary surgeons, Commanding Officers being informed by the King's order that not only was this to be prevented, but not " the smallest deviation from this order" permitted. Nevertheless there were exceptions even to this positive order. J. Field, Veterinary Surgeon 2nd Life Guards, was partner with Moorcroft and permitted to practise privately. On Moorcroft proceeding to India in 1808 the whole of this immense practice passed into the hands of Field. John Percivall practised privately, also the Veterinary Officer of the 1st Life Guards.

The same letter informed Colonels that those regiments not yet supplied with veterinary aid would be furnished by Mr. Coleman with a chest of medicines, with ample directions for use, describing the symptoms and treatment of common diseases, and the preparations adapted to each complaint. The letter concludes that with the chests will be forwarded pattern hoofs shod according to the new principle, so " that the Farrier may be able immediately to adopt the mode of shoeing recommended by the Principal Veterinary Surgeon."

On the same day that this letter was sent to Colonels commanding Cavalry regiments, Coleman was informed that the King had been pleased to appoint him P.V.S. to the Cavalry, and that his commission would bear the date of that letter, 21 September 1796.[1] The letter also informed him of his rate of daily pay, of the amount of the instrument and medicine contract, and urged him to use every exertion to obtain and provide the necessary men. In the same month 28 regiments of Fencible Cavalry were included in Coleman's contract for medical and surgical supplies, in addition to those of the regular service, so that the number of horses for which he drew was something considerable. By the year 1799 there were 40,000 Cavalry in England !

At p. 23 reference has already been made to the book of

---

[1] P.R.O. W.O. 4/166, p. 92. Nevertheless his gazette in the *Gentleman's Magazine* is dated 10 August 1796. I cannot trace his appearance in the Army List before the year 1817.

Instructions for Farriers, which Mr. Coleman undertook to supply with each chest of medicines he issued to the Cavalry, and we have noted there the resentment shown by an ex-Farrier-Major of the Life Guards. We must now examine the work itself.

This booklet of 41 pages of large type is entitled *Instructions for the use of Farriers attached to the British Cavalry and to the Honourable Board of Ordnance*, London 1796.[1] He deals with his subject in the following order and without any attempt at system: Inflammation of the Eyes, Inflammation of the Chest, Inflammation of the Intestines, Spasm of the Intestines called Gripes, Inflammation of the Feet, Inflammation of the Kidneys, Recent Strains and Bruises, Gunshot and other Recent Wounds, Staggers, Coughs and Colds, Grease, Thrushes, Glanders, Farcy, Hidebound, Worms and Bots, The Treatment of Horses in Camp, The Treatment of Horses in Quarters returned from Camp or Grass, The Actual Cautery, The Principles and Practice of Shoeing.

Each disease is considered under Symptoms and Treatment. The symptoms are few, excepting those of glanders, which he mixes up with ozœna, and continued so to do throughout his life. He regarded the head as the seat of disease and directed it to be buried "several feet underground." The value of this booklet in the history of Coleman is beyond measure. He here lays bare to us the actual knowledge he possessed in 1796 after two years' experience. He is self-convicted; his ignorance is as great as that of the men he sets out to teach, while the ferocity of the treatment advised by him could not be credited to-day if it were not that a copy of the pamphlet is in existence. In Pneumonia he instructs the Army Farrier to apply the "actual cautery to the sides," if the disease is violent, with rowels in the brisket and under the chest. In Enteritis rowels and cautery are to be applied to the belly, which is then to " be covered with five or six sheep skins "!—presumably just removed. He does not say how he proposes to place that number on one belly. In Nephritis the actual cautery was to be applied to the loins. In Grease the limb was to be superficially fired. In Farcy " the part to be fired in straight lines." His treatment of " Staggers " was appalling; besides the liberal bleeding (always four quarts at a time), the poll was to be blistered, two rowels placed in the belly, the hair clipped off the pasterns (presumably all four) as high as

[1] A copy of this rare publication exists in the Library of the Royal Veterinary College, London. From the notes it contains it was evidently Coleman's personal copy.

the fetlock, and *boiling water poured on the part twice a day!* Nothing is said of the treatment of ordinary wounds, injuries, and lameness, though these formed three-fourths of the cases the Farrier would have to deal with.

This disgraceful booklet is the first army veterinary publication! No wonder that John Lane, the ex-Farrier-Major of the 2nd Life Guards, attacked him in 1800 (see p. 23) and stated that his " medical instructions to the Farriers of the Army were cruel and destructive . . . and a disgrace to the age and nation for which they are written." We agree.

A second edition appeared in 1803. This time Coleman's name is on the title page. The same groups of diseases are dealt with, but the actual cautery and boiling water are no longer directed to be employed. He does, however, instruct for " Inflammation of the Eye " the one-sixth part of a teaspoonful of common salt to be inserted daily under the lids! The bleedings are also smaller. In this edition there are instructions for the management of young horses. In both editions Coleman is extremely brief and appears to take for granted the diagnostic skill of the farriers. It is convenient to note here that these were not the last instructions published for Farriers. In 1824 John Percivall, Senior Veterinary Surgeon to the Ordnance, published *Directions for the Farriers of the Royal Artillery*, approved by the Board of Ordnance, and issued as an official publication.

Of the first thirty-four years of Mr. Coleman's administration we have but meagre information; there was no professional periodical published until 1823, and it was not until 1830 that the Coleman administration was attacked by that journal. From these attacks we are able to reconstruct much of what had occurred. Meanwhile Coleman ruled with an iron hand both in military and civil life. He was a Dictator and long outlived most of his contemporaries. He provided officers of the calibre and training above described. But his work was not without merit, for he improved the health of army horses beyond recognition. By a better understanding of glanders he brought this disease under control, and by great improvements in the hygiene of stables, ventilation, drainage, the principles and practice of dietetics, he effected throughout the Cavalry service vast and permanent reforms, which many times over covered the cost of his department. Beginning, as we have seen, in 1796 with no knowledge of his subject, he was as a man of observation bound to learn, and in due course he acquired considerable aptitude and knowledge, which he imparted to his pupils. But apart entirely from any consideration of improved methods of treatment, what we have to thank him for more particularly is the lessons he taught in the prevention of disease. He was apt in his lectures to exaggerate his successes in this direction, great as they were; he adopted a dogmatic attitude, posing as the man who stood alone in the field, as the one person possessing superior knowledge, but we can forgive him these foibles in consideration of the great work he carried out. It is remarkable that he should have done so well with so many other irons in the fire—the Ordnance, the School, his consultations in various parts of the country, and his supervision and inspection of the Cavalry. On retrospect two features stand out: one is that when he came into power veterinary conditions among the horses of the army were so bad that improved methods were bound to show good results; the other is that in spite of his reduction of the period of school training from three years to a few months, he sent to the Service, in his early days, several able men many of whom in time rivalled the master in ability. Like Coleman they improved their originally meagre stock of knowledge by self-education, and they were not content to accept the finality of Coleman's views. For example there was James White of the Royal Dragoons and Thomas Peall of the Royal Artillery, whose careful study of glanders and the methods of infection may be read to-day with the greatest interest. Both worked on the system of experimental enquiry. Coleman never acknowledged their work nor that of others in his adopted profession. Then there was James Turner of the Royal Waggon Train, the discoverer of navicular disease and an accomplished practitioner. Similarly there was at Woolwich a quiet, plodding, observant man whose knowledge and experience had grown to considerable proportions, who had struck out for himself, and by ability and persistence acquired a deservedly high reputation, to which even Coleman might aspire. John Percivall, the assistant who had been placed temporarily at Woolwich in 1796, and whose services the Board of Ordnance had hoped soon to dispense with when the Farriers were taught, never left Woolwich for the remainder of his life, but on the other hand, as previously stated, was given a commission and became an Artillery Veterinary Officer and the father of his service. Can it be believed that Coleman's weekly visit to Woolwich brought about the wondrous change in the health of the horses of the Artillery Service? It was John Percivall and other good men, such as Stockley,

William Percivall, Peall, J. Turner and J. Goodwin, to whom the Artillery of that day were indebted. Then there was James Castley of the 12th Lancers, an ideal type of cavalry veterinary officer, whose communications to the early numbers of the *Veterinarian* can be read with profit to this day, and whose style of presenting his case has a charm of its own.

It appears invidious to select these few names among some dozens of officers employed, especially as no reference has been made to the work of many who wrote on the subject of their profession,[1] but our object is, while giving every credit to Coleman for launching the craft, to remind the reader that there were other forces at work with which Coleman was not in touch, inasmuch as he never did a day's soldiering in his life. It was in the regiments that all the work was done; if a good man found his way there the results were good; if an indifferent man, Coleman was asked to provide someone better. He did not always do so, inasmuch as we find Commanding Officers threatening to find their own.[2] The results of the work could be gauged by the returns of disease, all of which were transmitted to the P.V.S. by Commanding Officers. Where Coleman failed was that he gave no credit to the men who did the work; he was jealous; the merit was alone his. He had long outlived his utility to the Service and to the profession before he died, yet there was no falling off in the results; on the other hand they steadily improved.

During his days another Veterinary School arose; he struggled desperately to keep all Service patronage in his own hands, and exclude candidates from elsewhere. But he met his equal in a man who was immensely his superior professionally, who was more acid in character, of equal if not greater persistence in having his own way, and whose private interest would cause even a Government to hesitate. William Dick's pupils were excluded by Coleman from the Army. It is difficult to find sufficiently restrained language to express the wickedness of this attitude, which did so much to keep the veterinary surgeons of the north

---

[1] I wish it were possible to deal with their work, but that is outside the scope of this History. The following is probably a complete list of Army Veterinary Surgeons who published books up to the end of Coleman's life. It is a good record in point of numbers, while the quality in many cases left little to be desired: Boardman, Causer, Cherry, Denny, Darvill, Feron, Grellier, Gauly, Goodwin, Gloag, Hodgson, Peall, Percivall, Ryding, Shipp, Smith, Turner and White. This does not include men, such as Castley, Purves, and others, who contributed to periodical literature.

[2] *Veterinarian*, October 1830.

and south of Britain in a state of antagonism. Finally it turned, as we shall see, to the advantage of the Army Veterinary Service. Dick in due course beat Coleman and subsequently sent his best men to the Army, the State reaping the advantage of their sound training. A large number passed into both the Home and Indian Armies, though none succeeded in passing the examination during Coleman's lifetime! It is well to remind ourselves that Edinburgh under Professor Dick furnished, among many others, J. Anderson, J. and F. F. Collins, G. Fleming, J. H. B. Hallen, W. Lamb, J. Lambert and J. Owles.

Returning to the historic year 1796, we may enquire how far Coleman was able to carry out his promise of supplying veterinary surgeons to regiments by reducing the period of instruction? Only one Veterinary Surgeon was appointed to the Army in 1796 (exclusive of John Percivall, who until the year 1801 was purely a civilian); his name is worthy of record. John Shipp joined the 11th Light Dragoons on 25 June 1796; he must therefore have entered as a Warrant Officer, but was commissioned the following year. He saw service in Holland in 1799, Spain in 1809, being present at Talavera with the unfortunate 23rd Light Dragoons, and with the same regiment was in the retreat from Quatre Bras and at the Battle of Waterloo in 1815. He died November 1834. Excluding Stockley, appointed as an experiment (see p. 37), Shipp was the first qualified man to enter the Army.

In the year 1797, commissions meanwhile having been granted, sixteen officers entered, including the classical scholar Bloxham, appointed to 1st Life Guards; James White to the Royal Dragoons, a man of singular ability; Thomas Boardman to the 3rd Dragoons, author of the first Veterinary Dictionary by a qualified man in this country; and James Siddall, for many years father of the " Blues." In 1798 eight entered; in 1799 ten, of whom five went to India. We shall have more to say about these five presently. In 1800 nine more graduates joined the Cavalry. In five years Coleman had furnished 44 veterinary surgeons to the Army, so that it must certainly be held that he had acted up to his undertaking. How many of these were medical men we do not know; Coleman never stated the number of these which passed into the Army.

A very curious case came to light in 1797; one James Harrison had been appointed Veterinary Surgeon to the 16th Light Dragoons in 1789, evidently a regimental appointment probably from Farrier Major. This man held no qualification, and Coleman succeeded in obtaining his removal in 1797.[1] In the Army List of 1808 he is shown on half pay as "Chief Veterinary Surgeon," under "Officers of Hospitals on the Continent, late under the Command of the Duke of York." In 1822 his name is still in the Army List as "Chief Veterinary Surgeon" on half pay September 1799, this time under the head of "Miscellaneous," and in the year 1829 his death is announced, still as "Chief Veterinary Surgeon." How this man succeeded in obtaining the title of "Chief" will probably never be known.

An appointment which was probably unique was that of John Denny. He was a Surgeon's Mate in the 10th Light Dragoons from June 1795 to May 1797. On the latter date he became Veterinary Surgeon to the same regiment and served as such until 1803. He then returned to medicine and became Asst. Surgeon of the 10th Light Dragoons until 1808, being present in the Retreat on Corunna. He was transferred as Surgeon to the 62nd Regiment in September 1809, and owing to ill health, the result of his service in Spain, he retired on half pay a few months later.[2] We may add that Denny was the author of a worthless *Treatise on the Diseases of Horses*.

Another medical man, R. S. Cumming, M.D., who had previously served in the Army as a Surgeon, was commissioned as Veterinary Surgeon 7th Light Dragoons in 1797 and in April 1805 to the Artillery. With the latter he was present at the siege and capture of Copenhagen in 1807.

From the year 1814 to 1819 two Veterinary Surgeons are shown as belonging to the "Blues" both bearing the name of Siddall. James, the elder, joined the regiment in 1797, John in 1812; no doubt they were father and son. The two appointments to one regiment can in part be explained by the fact that the "Blues" had two squadrons serving in Spain, Belgium and France, from 1814 to 1819. James died in 1821, John in 1856, so that the regiment was served by them for seventy years. In Old Windsor Church there is a memorial to John Siddall bearing the following inscription:

"A just tribute to private worth and great professional merit, this tablet in memory of John Siddall is inscribed by the Officers Royal Horse Guards (Blue), in which regiment during a period of 53 years he discharged with zeal and diligence the duties of Veterinary Surgeon, and was the last surviving member of all ranks in the Household Brigade of Cavalry present at Waterloo. Died 2 Oct. 1856 in the 69th year of his age, and is interred at the Church of Old Windsor in this country."

It will be observed according to the dates I have given, which are extracted from the Army Lists of the period, that John served in the "Blues" for 44 years. The tablet states that he served 53 years, in which case he must have joined the regiment at 16 years of age! The Siddall case is easily a record in length of regimental service. We shall later meet with a John Siddall, Veterinary Surgeon in the Bengal Army, a very gallant soldier, who I have assumed belonged to the same family, for the name is uncommon.

[1] P.R.O. W.O. 40/8.   [2] P.R.O. W.O. 44/688.

We have seen earlier that the authorities hoped to obtain Veterinary Surgeons by sending regimental farriers to Coleman for education. Only one, so far as can be traced, succeeded. Thomas Smith served with the 2nd Dragoon Guards certainly in 1784. In 1793 and again in 1795 he was on active service in Holland. In 1799 he was commissioned as Veterinary Surgeon in his old regiment and was placed on half pay in 1813. In this year he published a *Treatise on Glanders*, in many respects an interesting work. It is mainly devoted to proving the spontaneous origin of the disease as the result of unhygienic surroundings, which theory he had imbibed from Coleman. Of far more interest are his attacks on the interior economy of his old regiment, especially on watering and feeding of the horses, which were neglected in favour of leather work, brass buckles and foot parades. He understood all the causes of regimental horse-neglect, such as have been known to our Service for the past 130 years.

We have already referred to five of the ten officers who entered in 1799 proceeding to India: Joseph Erratt, 19th Light Dragoons, was the first officer of our profession to enter that country. He was shortly followed by Thomas Burrowes, 8th Light Dragoons; James Grellier, 22nd Light Dragoons, Richard Davies 27th Light Dragoons, and Samuel Newman, or Newnan, 29th Light Dragoons. We can dismiss Grellier and Davies as they were invalided to England; Erratt, Burrowes and Newman were the stout men of the party, and stout men were required in the days when regiments campaigned during all seasons, wore English clothing, including the leather stock strapped around the neck, English head dress which afforded no possible protection from the sun, and lived the careless and intemperate life usual then and long after. Erratt's chief distinction is that he was with his regiment at the Battle of Assaye, the first serious enterprise of the future Duke of Wellington; but the great interest of the Mahratta War of 1803 centres around Samuel Newman. He and Burrowes were both present in General (subsequently Lord) Lake's Campaign, which for rapidity of movement and violent fighting has no equal in India, not even during the Mutiny. Newman greatly distinguished himself at the Battle of "Laswaree," which is regarded by historians as the most decisive in India, as it laid the foundation for the destruction of the Mahrattas, then the greatest warlike power in India. Precisely what Newman did I have failed to ascertain. One record, referring to him as "Surgeon," says that it was through his exertions that many wounded were rescued from the field, where no quarter was given. That, however, would not be sufficient justification to a Commander-in-Chief for conferring a combatant commission on him in the Field, and that is what occurred. Samuel Newman was created a Cornet in his regiment, dated the day of the battle, 1st November 1803, and in his monthly return for January 1804, Lord Lake asks not only for a Veterinary Surgeon in his place, but also for a Cornet, as he had already promoted Newman to a Lieutenancy. No Veterinary Surgeon was, however, received for some years and meanwhile Newman carried on in a dual capacity. He subsequently became Captain and was among the seniors of that rank when the regiment was broken up many years later. This rare case, the first but not the last in our Service, is referred to in the *Veterinary Record* for April 1850, but the distinction is attributed, curiously enough, to Veterinary Surgeon Burrowes of the 8th Light Dragoons who was present at the same battle. In the Regimental History of the 8th Hussars the battle of " Laswaree " receives a long notice, and Burrowes is referred to as " Cornet " Burrowes: it is stated that he had a hand-to-hand encounter with a French officer in the service of the Mahrattas, and as a result was badly wounded in the face; in spite of this he later led his men when an appeal for a charge was made. There was no Cornet Burrowes in the regiment at that time, nor for several years later, and there is no officer bearing this name among the list of wounded. The story is evidently incorrect in detail, but that Burrowes, as well as Newman, did something on that day to attract attention appears almost certain. Though we cannot give an account of Newman's distinguished service we hope to have rescued his name from oblivion.

During the Peninsular War two German officers were appointed to British regiments, and after the Waterloo Campaign Coleman obtained some officers from the King's German Legion. This magnificent force, consisting of all arms, was broken up at the end of the Napoleonic Wars and at least three of their officers were posted to our Cavalry. All had taken Coleman's diploma before appointment to the Legion. These were not the only foreigners in our ranks. There was a Frenchman, perhaps two, in our Service. The regiment known as the York Hussars were all foreigners, including at one time the Veterinary Surgeon.

An unusual appointment was that of one Ensign Browne, who entered the Service as a combatant officer in 1813 and was appointed Veterinary Surgeon 6th Dragoon Guards in July 1834.[1] This officer must have been about forty years of age on appointment, but in those days there was no age limit and several of our officers on joining were already advanced in life. James Siddall, already referred to, was thirty-seven years of age. Feron, a Frenchman, was forty-five when appointed to 13th Light Dragoons; C. Blinman of the Carabineers was forty, and there were others.

It is convenient to quote here another unusual case, though it did not occur in Coleman's day. In the year 1856 Opie Smith, Veterinary Surgeon 2nd Dragoon Guards, then in the Crimea, is shown in the Army List as acting in two capacities in his regiment, viz. as Assistant Surgeon and Veterinary Surgeon. This case is probably unique; he doubtless drew the pay of both appointments, as this must have had official approval to appear in the Army List.

As we have already stated, the great difficulty under which Coleman's officers worked was that their chief had no experience as a soldier; he was not in touch with military questions, and he

[1] P.R.O. W.O. 43/107730.

does not always appear to have realized some of the disadvantages under which his officers laboured. For instance, a rate of pay was fixed but no provision made for increase of pay for length of service; nor was the relative rank of his officers fixed. Similarly, nothing was done on the important questions of half and retired pay, ill health, or wounds received in action, yet no doubt his officers brought these points to his notice. Many years later it is over and over again stated in the *Veterinarian* that representations made to him on various subjects met with no sympathetic consideration, nor were they always transmitted to the Authorities. Nevertheless there is some evidence to the contrary. In December 1798 a general order was issued concerning the rates of pension for widows. The widow of the Veterinary Surgeon was awarded £20 per annum, the same as the Chaplain's widow, but £10 a year less than the widow of the Surgeon and £6 less than that of the Assistant Surgeon. It is not to be supposed that Coleman had any voice as to the amount of the pension, but on the question of principle he may have been consulted. In connection with this order it may be noted that it was not until it came to be applied that the widow found she received no pension unless her husband had ten years' full-pay service. The Finance branch of the Army has never been distinguished for the liberal interpretation of its own orders. In an article in the *Veterinarian* for 1839, vol. xii., p. 276, Mr. Gloag, V.S. 10th Hussars, states that he wrote a letter on the question of Widows' Pensions to his Chief, who transmitted it to the Secretary at War. On 26th May 1803 the War Office issued a circular to the Colonels of Cavalry Regiments stating that on Mr. Coleman's representations, Veterinary Surgeons were in future to be allowed sixpence a mile travelling expenses both ways, when ordered to attend horses at a distant "outpost," whenever that distance exceeds 25 miles from the Head Quarters of the Regiment. Up to that time they had to find their own expenses. In the article already referred to Mr. Gloag, dealing with the question of travelling expenses, says: "I have heard Professor Coleman say that he has repeatedly applied to the Secretary at War on this subject without avail."

It is evident from the above that complaints were not always withheld, but it is impossible to believe that the *Veterinarian* would have permitted its pages to be employed in the dissemination of untruthful statements regarding Coleman's administration.

While defending Coleman against the charge of wholly neglecting the interests of his officers, it is only right for us to note that he did not neglect his own. In 1804 he asked the Board of Ordnance for an increase in pay,[1] which, we may add, was refused.

We have already referred to the peculiar organization of the mounted portion of the Royal Artillery. Up to the year 1801 two civilians were in veterinary attendance, Coleman and his assistant John Percivall. In 1801 Percivall was appointed Veterinary Surgeon to the Brigade of Gunners and Drivers under warrant from the Master-General of the Ordnance. In the year 1804 two veterinary surgeons were approved for the Brigade of Gunners and Drivers, Stockley being the second. In the year 1805 both J. Percivall and Stockley received His Majesty's Commission and six other officers were appointed in a veterinary capacity to the newly designated Corps of Royal Artillery Drivers. These officers were posted to districts throughout the country, evidence that John Percivall had done first-class work and that the Board of Ordnance was anxious to extend it. The establishment remained at eight until September 1807, when it was raised to ten, which number it never exceeded, not even in 1815, and in some years was only nine. The story of commissions being granted in 1805 has already been told.

It should be clearly understood that these officers were appointed to the Royal Artillery Drivers and not to the Royal Artillery. They appeared on the monthly returns of the Artillery, but in the column devoted to the Drivers, whereas Medical Officers are shown with the Royal Artillery. The Drivers were looked down upon as being outside the regiment though an essential part of it. The Horse Artillery had no body of Drivers distinct from the regiment. On the establishment of each troop there was a surgeon, but there was no veterinary surgeon of Horse Artillery until 1861. In the Army Lists of the first quarter of the nineteenth century the Veterinary Surgeons of the Ordnance are shown under the Corps of Drivers and also under the "Ordnance Medical Service"! The Ordnance possessed a Medical Service of its own quite distinct from and independent of the Army Medical Service, but I cannot explain why our officers figured in it. After the great reduction of the Army in 1816 and subsequent years only two veterinary surgeons were retained with the Ordnance, but in 1828 a third was sanctioned. The three were J. Percivall, H. Coward and C. O'Connor. In this year all three for the first time appeared in the Royal Artillery list, though not assigned to any special Horse Brigade or Battalion. With the expansion of

[1] P.R.O. W.O. 45/67.

the Royal Artillery in 1854 the veterinary establishment was greatly increased—viz., from three to eleven; in 1856 there were twenty-two, and in 1861 twenty-eight veterinary officers. In November 1861 six veterinary surgeons were at last appointed to the Royal Horse Artillery, and in both Horse and Field Artillery they were for the first time appointed to Brigades. This organization lasted until 1878, when on the introduction of the Departmental System veterinary officers automatically disappeared from the Royal Artillery list.

The Royal Horse Infirmary at Woolwich (Plate 5) was built about 1804. It was not only a Hospital, but contained veterinary stores for the Artillery; it was also a seat of research and the adjacent quarters were the home of the Percivalls, father and son. At the Infirmary Coleman visited every week for years. Here both Percivalls did their pioneer work in anatomy, physiology and clinical medicine. One of Percivall senior's three museums was here; it was located in a specially constructed place over the Guard Room and was still in evidence in my early days. John Percivall died in his quarters at the Royal Horse Infirmary, and it is believed that Stockley, who then became Senior Veterinary Surgeon to the Ordnance, resided there until his retirement. After Stockley the quarters were occupied by John Wilkinson, who resided there during his long tenure as Principal Veterinary Surgeon. For many reasons therefore this building possesses for our Service great sentimental interest.

As our Service expanded Woolwich became its Head Quarters, where recently commissioned officers joined. The Royal Horse Infirmary saw them all until the School at Aldershot was opened in 1882. It was James Collins who broke the tradition that Woolwich was the home of the Department and office of the Principal Veterinary Surgeon, by getting himself moved to the War Office, and sending probationary veterinary officers to Aldershot.

I have been puzzled over the accepted designation "Royal Horse Infirmary." Was it a Royal establishment? I spent much time going through documents but found nothing on the subject. In 1823 W. Percivall addressed his *Veterinary Lectures* from the " Royal Horse Infirmary," so that the designation goes back a long way. Recent enquiries for me on the spot by Major H. E. Gibbs, R.A.V.C., to whom I am much indebted, suggest that the title in full would have read " Royal Horse Artillery Infirmary." As " Royal Horse " was a recognized abbreviation,

PLATE V

OFFICERS' QUARTERS
House occupied successively by J. Percivall, W. Stockley, and J. Wilkinson.

GUARD-ROOM
Over this was J. Percivall's Museum, the windows of which can be seen.

STAFF QUARTERS
On the ground floor to the right was the Pharmacy, and on the left a room used as an office by the Veterinary Officers of the garrison in the time of J. Wilkinson.

ROYAL HORSE INFIRMARY, WOOLWICH
(Now an Artillery Remount Depôt.)

it seems to me that this explanation is the correct one. About 1903 the building was given up in exchange for a modern structure at Woolwich, but it still retains its old name and will no doubt do so to the end. It is unchanging in appearance; it looks to me to-day as it did fifty years ago. If the Percivalls came back they would probably say the same. Even the guns which flank the entrance have been there for untold years, probably since the place was built.

Among the Veterinary Surgeons gazetted to the Ordnance Service between 1805-06 were Joseph Goodwin and Thomas Peall. Both were cultured men of outstanding ability. A biographical notice of Goodwin appears later. We are here concerned only with Peall. He was at the Veterinary College in 1795, for he refers to his experiments on glanders carried out at that institution, stating he conveyed the disease to an ass by placing material from a horse affected with farcy within the nostrils, without damaging the mucous membrane; the animal was affected with glanders in eight days. He qualified in the year 1796. In 1802 he was in Dublin, Veterinary Professor to the Dublin Society, at whose Institution he delivered an annual course of lectures of which the syllabus is extant. In November 1806 he joined the Veterinary Service of the Board of Ordnance. He was the ringleader in refusing to join until commissions were granted. In 1814 he was in Cork, and in this year published a work on the *Diseases of the Horse*. He held his Professorship at the Dublin Society, though at the time he was still in the Service. His work on the Diseases of the Horse is written with great grace and charm: it is a wonderful book also in respect of the profound knowledge exhibited. He distinguishes between glanders and strangles, diseases confused long after his day; he stresses the identity of glanders and farcy, and actually recommends State legislation: in so doing he hopes he is not quitting his " proper department "! He is convinced that the most common mode of infection in glanders is by ingestion. We see in this important respect how completely the pupil has broken away from the master, for Coleman all his life maintained that it was the miasma of the stable which produced the disease. In 1817 Peall was placed on half pay on reduction of establishment. In 1822 he produced a work on *Foot Rot*: he was still with the Dublin Society, but after that date, unfortunately, all trace of him is lost; he was certainly dead in 1830. Peall was undoubtedly a great man. He was also a modest man and disclaimed the merit of any positive discovery.

It is obvious that the Board of Ordnance in 1805 could not engage officers without drawing up terms of service. What these terms were I found in a paper in the P.R.O.[1] which, though dealing with another matter, quotes a portion of the Ordnance Veterinary Warrant of 1805 of which we have not previously heard. In

[1] W.O. 44/687.

this communication it is stated that for the first three years of service the pay was 8s. p.d.; for the next seven years 10s. p.d.; for the next ten 12s. p.d., and on completing twenty years' service 15s. p.d. It is stated that the half pay was half the full pay of which the officer was in receipt. Finally it is said that the widow receives £30 a year and additional for her children. I have not found the original of this Ordnance Warrant of 1805, and feel sure that the above data are not complete.

When this warrant was brought out for the Ordnance Service, the Cavalry Veterinary Service was in the identical position it had occupied in 1796. During the nine years which had elapsed since its creation nothing had been done to obtain an increase in pay for length of service; no provision had been made for half or retired pay and the relative rank of the officer was not fixed. For these reasons I feel quite certain that Coleman had no say in the Ordnance Veterinary Warrant of 1805, and that the whole thing had been carried through without his being consulted. He now realized that the Cavalry officers could no longer continue to serve without terms of service being arranged. Accordingly he wrote to the War Office, and after pointing out the necessity of holding out greater encouragement to the Cavalry Veterinary Surgeons he submitted proposals on all the points hitherto left unprovided for. We shall presently deal rather fully with this correspondence, but it is convenient at this point to state that his recommendations were approved and in May 1807 a warrant was issued for the Cavalry, practically identical with that of the Ordnance Service of 1805 excepting as regards the widow. She still remained at £20 p.a. The 1807 warrant is careful to say that the daily rate of pay for the officer includes one shilling for his horse; and this fiction (which was also a breach of faith; see p. 43) enabled the half pay to be reduced by sixpence a day. It is convenient to note here that in 1815 an order was issued directing that the period of service necessary for the Veterinary Surgeon to qualify for increase of pay could include any actual service he had rendered as Assistant Surgeon, Surgeon's Mate or Hospital Mate. Two points in the Cavalry Warrant of 1807 do not appear in the extract of the Ordnance Warrant of 1805 given above; these were the right to retire at twenty years' service on 7s. a day, and a retiring rate after thirty years' service of not less than 12s. p.d., the actual amount to be fixed by the Treasury. By the above Warrant of May 1807 the Cavalry Veterinary Surgeon obtained the same rate of pay and retiring allowance as his brother of the Ordnance, but he had had to wait two years in order to obtain it. As some compensation for this injustice the warrant was made to take effect from March 1806.

Another point dealt with in the Cavalry Warrant of 1807 was the vexed question of travelling allowance; the warrant states that this has been improved on Mr. Coleman's recommendation, 6d. a mile being allowed for any distance over forty miles travelled in one day. Previously 6d. a mile was allowed for the whole distance, when the " outpost " to be visited was over twenty-five miles from Head Quarters. Under the new rate, when the outpost necessitated above forty miles of travelling a conveyance was approved, but no allowance was given if the distance was under forty miles. Gloag, writing in 1839, when the rate had been in operation thirty-two years, tells us how hard this was, especially on poor officers. In the P.R.O. there is a claim by John Percivall for travelling allowance on inspection duty in November 1805 from Woolwich to Chatham. He is informed that as he drew forage allowance for two horses he should have ridden there and back the same day!

It has been convenient to deal with the Cavalry Warrant of 1807 in the above position, but we must now retrace our steps and study the correspondence with the authorities, which led to its production: the subject is historically of supreme importance, for it brings us once more in contact with the medical authorities of the Army, and we now learn the view they took of any attempt to improve the position of the Cavalry Veterinary Surgeon.

Coleman's representations to the Secretary at War on behalf of the Cavalry officers were started in September and October 1805. The War Office referred his letter to the Army Medical Board, who were asked to report on the several details of the proposed amelioration of the Veterinary Service. The reply of the Medical Board[1] was not received for six months; it is dated March 1806 and begins by attacking Coleman's proposals of 1805. The Board had never forgiven him for his attempt in 1796 " to seduce Medical Students to the Veterinary Department," and in their letter of the above date they " earnestly deprecate anything like equalization with the Medical Department of the Army," and ask that before any further encouragement is given to the Veterinary Service by increasing the pay or allowances, an enquiry should be made into what benefit may have accrued to this service

[1] Given in full in *5th Report of the Commissioners of Military Enquiry* 1808, Appendix 12(B), p. 127.

by "their late approximation to the Medical Department." The Board concludes its letter by begging that it may be excused from reporting on the several proposals of Mr. Coleman. In spite of this opposition the warrant of 7th May 1807 was issued. This caused the Army Medical Board, in the person of Mr. Knight,[1] Inspector-General of Army Hospitals, to return to the attack. His letter addressed to the Deputy Secretary at War is dated 27th May. It is remarkable for its length and tone of extreme irritation. He expresses his "mortification" at the improved rates of pay granted to the Veterinary Service, to the betterment of which the Government appears to set no limitations. What can "Medical men of science feel at such seeming association of merit and value?" He is persuaded that the Government cannot be "more anxious for the safety of the sick horse than of the wounded soldier." Yet "such an unfavourable inference may be drawn," for the student of medicine in 1796 was "expressly invited to quit the surgical for the veterinary pursuit. If Surgeons are tempted to become Farriers (*sic*) it might be expedient to substitute Farrier-Surgeons for the Barber Surgeons of old!" But Mr. Knight's feelings will not allow him to pursue the subject further than to express the hope that if the two departments are to be assimilated, the long and expensive education of the medical candidate may be reduced to that of the three years' slender study of the veterinary department.[2] He asks permission to quit the unsavoury subject, and to submit a scheme for the improvement of the Medical Department of the Army, bearing in mind that the supply of medical recruits is very unequal to the demand. He then asks for relative rank with its corresponding advantages in choice of quarters, and rate of prize money, for improved pensions, submitting a table of his proposals. Even now he cannot dismiss the subject without stating that "the Medical Staff of the Army is sunk and depressed by the approximation and better encouragement to the veterinary department"; to support this statement he presents a table comparing the pay and advantages of the Medical and Veterinary Departments.[3]

[1] Francis Knight, to whom reference has been made, was originally Surgeon to the Coldstream Guards; he became a member of the Medical Board in 1801.

[2] Mr. Knight little knew how sadly even that brief period had been reduced by Coleman.

[3] We trust that the charge of the sunken and depressed state of the Medical Service being due to its approximation to the Veterinary Department had no real foundation. At any rate this was not the excuse adopted by the authorities, who in 1810 swept away the Medical Board

This correspondence is not pleasant reading and but for the "Commissioners of Military Enquiry" would never have seen the light of day. Before this Commission Mr. Coleman was examined on oath in the year 1808. His evidence appears in the *8th Report* of the Commissioners, printed in 1809, Appendix No. 20, p. 221. His principal examination centred around his contract to supply the Cavalry with drugs, dressings and instruments, and gradually drifted into the expenditure connected with the provision of veterinary surgeons to the Army. It is convenient to take both questions here. From his examination we learn a good deal which was not generally known. I published it in full in the *Veterinary Record* of 5th August 1893, to which reference may be made for details.

It transpired from Mr. Coleman's evidence that though the Apothecaries' Society was designated in his contract as the invariable source of supply, the Secretary at War had permitted this stipulation to be departed from very soon afterwards, in consequence of a report from the Army Medical Board—before which Coleman had laid a list of the medicines used in veterinary practice—that it was unnecessary to purchase such medicines at the Society, and they were accordingly obtained from Messrs. Howard, Druggists to the Board of Ordnance. The Commissioners then point out that Coleman found by experiment that several of the medicines, of powerful efficacy when given to man, had no effect on the horse. These were in consequence omitted from the authorized list of drugs supplied to the Veterinary Service, the Commission dryly remarking *that they appear to have been the most expensive of the drugs originally employed!*[1] The check on the quality supplied was furnished by the officers who used the drugs and who received instructions never to use a single article of doubtful quality, but to return it to the druggist, sending at the same time a sample to Mr. Coleman. Asked as to the frequency of complaints he believed there had not been twenty since 1796, and some of these were unfounded. "It would be contrary to my interest, as well as that of the public, to use weak and ineffective medicines." It also came out in evidence that besides the Artillery, which provided their own medicines, four regiments were excluded from Coleman's contract, the Life Guards, Royal

---

owing to its ineptitude. It had existed since 1756 and for years had been a reproach; its members also quarrelled among themselves for patronage and their fights became known to the public.

[1] The italics are mine.—F. S.

Horse Guards, and 10th Hussars. The veterinary surgeon of each of these regiments himself received the three shillings per annum per horse and provided his own drugs, etc. Coleman took the opportunity to add in evidence that he understood the officer of the 2nd Life Guards was out of pocket by the contract. Nevertheless twenty years later, when the Life Guards became vacant, he pressed the newly appointed officer to renounce the contract and permit him (Coleman) to add it to the others he was holding!

Asked by the Commissioners as to the saving effected by his contract as compared with the old system of the Farriers purchasing the drugs, he calculated that on an average of 15,000 Cavalry horses the saving had been £9,000 a year, or £108,000 since 1796, on the assumed basis that the farrier as contractor for medicines as well as shoeing, received one halfpenny of the penny a day allowed him per horse for shoeing, and one halfpenny for medicine (see p. 46). But, he added, if only one farthing of the penny be regarded as having been spent by the farrier on medicines, the saving by the new contracts was £3,453 per annum, or £41,457 since 1796. Coleman was naturally anxious to present his contract in the most favourable light, but the Commissioners point out that the saving effected does not go to the public but to the Farriers, and they recommended an enquiry into the allowance paid to Farriers of Cavalry.

When the *Veterinarian* in 1830 opened fire on Coleman's administration, his contract was frequently referred to in terms which leave no doubt in the mind of the reader of the value of this source of revenue, while the terrific attacks launched by his implacable enemy Bracy Clark in the *Hippiatrist* of the same year, forcibly directed attention to the question. We may close the subject at present by saying that in 1832 he lost his contract for medicines, no doubt in consequence of the articles which appeared in the above Journals. As compensation his pay was raised from 10s. to 20s. a day as P.V.S. Cavalry.[1]

The other subject ventilated in Coleman's examination before the Commissioners was the syllabus of professional training at the Veterinary College. A system prevailed by which students obtained external teaching at the various London hospitals, in human anatomy, physiology, surgery, materia medica, chemistry, and the practice of physic. Coleman stated that whatever the qualifications possessed by candidates in these subjects a mini-

[1] P.R.O. W.O. 43/90055.

mum of three months' attendance on his lectures and practice at the College was essential before an examination could be claimed. He insisted on the value of the examinations conducted by the Medical Committee of the College,[1] assisted by himself, before a candidate could present himself for a commission in the Army.

The Commissioners accepted the independent testimony of Brigadier-General Bolton, who had long served with the Cavalry, as to the appointment of Veterinary Surgeons having been productive of much benefit to the Army; this witness stated that those he had met were properly qualified for their position, and that great improvement had been made in the shoeing of army horses since the introduction of the veterinary system. The Commissioners then examined the views held by the Army Medical Board, with which we have already dealt, and concluded by saying that there was no evidence before them of any actual injury being sustained by the Medical Department of the Army, from the superior encouragement supposed to be given to the Veterinary Surgeons. It is strange that Coleman was not asked by the Commissioners the precise number of medical men he had induced to enter the Army, for only he knew.

The facts noted above show the nervousness of the Army Medical authorities on what they describe as "the close approximation of the Veterinary to the Medical Service." It is an old feeling, even now far from dead. Assuming, for the sake of argument, that the approximation had the effect of debasing the Medical Service, it must be admitted that there were reasons for the apprehension felt; for instance, before the date under review, and for many years afterwards, the Veterinary Surgeons of the Ordnance Service, as already mentioned, were shown *in the same list* as the Ordnance Medical Service; in 1807 a book of *Financial Regulations* was published by the War Office, one section of which is entitled *Medical Department of the Army including the Veterinary Branch*. Subsequent to the period under notice—viz., in 1815 and even in 1837—the War Office in a Veterinary Warrant refers to the Veterinary Officer as serving "in any capacity as a medical officer on full pay," and as late as July 1860, all probationary

---

[1] He gives their names and appointments: Drs. Baillie, Babington, Cooke, Pearson, and Messrs. Cline, Horne, Abernethy, Wilson and Astley Cooper, truly a wonderful collection of the leading medical and surgical talent of the day. Nevertheless not one of the number knew anything about the diseases and injuries of animals, and, owing to Coleman's opposition, it took years of fighting to displace them and instal veterinary examiners.

veterinary officers were gazetted under the heading "Veterinary Medical Department." There were, no doubt, other disquieting facts of which we have no record to-day, but it is significant that thirty-one years later than the period we are dealing with—*i.e.*, on the death of Coleman—it is stated, as we shall see in due course, that it was the intention of the Secretary at War, on the death of Coleman, to place the Veterinary Department under the Army Medical Board. Secretaries at War come and go; they bring no knowledge of details nor even of principles with them, for they may never have seen a soldier in their lives excepting in the streets, so that the "intention" was not a personal idea, but a scheme absorbed from the permanent civilian staff of the War Office, who have always regulated the financial aspects of the Army in accordance with their judgement, experience and prejudices.

We have defended Coleman against the charge that he did nothing for the interests of his officers. In 1812, as already noted, pensions for wounds received in action, or rather for the loss of a limb or an eye in action, were made applicable to the Veterinary Service, £50 a year being given, the amount awarded to a Cornet or Assistant Surgeon. It will be observed that there was no provision made for the dependants of a veterinary surgeon killed in action. This was not granted until June 1826, when £40 was allowed, the lowest rate in the scale, the same as that allotted for a Hospital Mate and Deputy Purveyor. These questions must have been represented by Coleman. Presumably representations made in 1811 brought to the front the question of relative rank, the basis of departmental position, for in that year all veterinary surgeons, no matter how long they had served, were, "as an indulgence," classified as Cornets "for choice of quarters only."

In 1811 Confidential Reports on all officers were introduced, and a printed set of questions applied to each rank or appointment. In the case of the Veterinary Surgeon "of Cavalry"—for apparently no army regulation affected the Ordnance branch unless initiated or approved by the Board of Ordnance—the Inspecting General Officer had to say whether the Veterinary Surgeon was "intelligent and competent," whether the horses were shod in conformity with Regulations; whether the Farriers were expert at their work and well instructed; what number of men were trained to put on shoes in an emergency; whether glanders or other contagious diseases had affected the regiment since the last report, and if so whether the veterinary measures of repression had been attended by success. In this report the Commanding Officer had to describe the system of ventilation adopted in the stables and state whether orders had been issued to prevent the supply of fresh air being interfered with. I cannot claim to have done more than peruse these voluminous reports, which are all in the P.R.O. So far as the officers are concerned they are generally described as good and sometimes as highly satisfactory. I noted one bad report, and several complaints of the officers being too old for work. It is obvious that the purely veterinary questions in this report should have been dealt with by the P.V.S.; this also was urged in the *Veterinarian* Vol. 3, September 1830.

In 1812 War Office Instructions were issued regarding the casting " of men and horses," and commanding officers reminded that the Commander-in-Chief was the casting authority. The form of casting return for horses is almost identical with that used at the present time.

Regulations dealing with the *Transport of Horses by Sea* appeared in 1813. They were the first military instructions issued on the subject, though in 1797 a London corn merchant, S. Lawson, had published a book in which most advanced views were laid down for the carriage of horses and mules by sea! Coleman must have been consulted in the matter of these Regulations, though he had no practical experience of the subject. His views on the cause of glanders, and his belief in his knowledge of what occurred during the Walcheren Expedition as the result of the hatches being battened down, were matters which throughout his long life remained ever fresh in his memory. The Regulations were issued on 6th December; they are interesting as introducing the sponging of the face and nostrils with vinegar and water in bad weather, and the giving of nitre with the food, fetishes which remained in the Regulations for the next seventy or eighty years. The provision of a vacant stall on either side of the sick, ventilation of the hold by windsails, and the employment of slings in cases of illness or accident, were sound measures probably suggested by veterinary officers, several of whom had by that time considerable experience with horses at sea. That this is more than conjecture may be judged from the direction that the arrival overnight of the horses for embarkation is essential so that they may be got on board when cool; care in feeding, and care and exercise on disembarkation, were other important features which would occur only to those with practical experience of the subject.

It is hardly necessary to state that Coleman was as proud of his schemes for the improvement of army shoeing as he was of his success in controlling contagious diseases, but though in his early days his views of disease were accepted almost without question, such was at no time the case with his theory and practice of shoeing. It will not be necessary here to enter upon his qualifications for dealing with this very technical question, excepting to say that he constituted himself an authority very shortly after taking up his appointment, and the erroneous views he then formed as the result of inexperience and want of practical knowledge, he endeavoured, in spite of intense opposition, to maintain throughout his life, for he belonged to the class of men unable to admit mistakes. As a matter of fact he had to abandon some of his worst theories and practices, but he never admitted this. By the year 1811 he had, of course, acquired considerable experience as compared with the years 1798 to 1802, when he published the two parts of his work on the Foot and Shoeing. As we have already stated, after the year 1802 Coleman published nothing further on any subject throughout his long life, and but for a controversy about to be dealt with, it would be difficult to know with precision what his more mature views on the shoeing question actually were. There were other people with " views " both within and without the profession; no one of standing in the profession supported Coleman's theories and practice, and those outside were equally bitter in their attacks. These matters will be fully considered in the third volume of my *History of Veterinary Literature*, so that any reference to them here is unnecessary. On the other hand, we are well within the subject of this history in examining his views on Army Shoeing, and fortunately through a lamentable controversy we are able to state them.

Among the Veterinary Surgeons appointed to the Royal Artillery Drivers in 1805 was Joseph Goodwin (1786–1845). He had an interesting history; studying medicine at Guy's Hospital with Astley Cooper and Coleman, he qualified, entered practice as a medical man and so remained until 1798, when he entered the Veterinary College and obtained the diploma of that institution in six months. He then proceeded to Oxford, matriculated, and began veterinary practice in that city. He appears to have aspired to a chair of anatomy, presumably comparative, and started demonstrations on the anatomy of the horse for the University, but these lectures were shortly prohibited by the Chancellor. Leaving Oxford he entered the Ordnance Veterinary Service, 24 April 1805, and was appointed to the Sussex district, but in April 1809 had to retire on account of ill health. The Jockey Club now begged of him to settle in Newmarket, but he only remained there a year, when he went into practice in London with a Captain Blagrave, late of the Royal Artillery Drivers, a layman. There he conducted a large practice, when in 1812 he was officially appointed to the stables, Carlton House, the residence of the Prince Regent (subsequently George IV.). In 1815 he was appointed Veterinary Surgeon to the Prince, with whom he remained after his accession and until his death in 1830 as George IV., though in 1821 he was studying veterinary medicine in St. Petersburg. During these years Goodwin's friend and patron was Lord Bloomfield, an Artillery officer, an intimate friend of the Prince Regent and member of his staff. Goodwin was a man of very strong and decided opinions, with a mind not cast in the ordinary mould. An enthusiastic follower of Coleman's doctrines in his early days, he soon discovered mistakes in regard to shoeing and spent the remainder of his life in studying and writing upon that subject, basing his observations on his vast experience. He not only exposed the fallacy of Coleman's views, but endeavoured for twenty-five years to bring about a reorganization of the College. He was also an inventor and received from the Society of Arts a medal for his *operating table for horses* designed to prevent the risk and inconvenience of casting; the "dumb jockey" was also his invention, as well as a balling gun and hobbles.[1]

We have given this outline of an active and useful life in consequence of what follows: Captain Blagrave of the Royal Artillery Drivers was interested in horses; he was especially interested in shoeing and invented a shoe. It is likely that he and Goodwin had served together. After Blagrave left the Service, from which he and his friend appear to have retired about the same time, he published an account of this shoe, and started an establishment in Oxford Street which he described as an "Institution for the Practical Improvement of Veterinary Science." Here, as we have seen, he was joined by Goodwin, and it is quite likely that the whole affair was prearranged.

In advertising his shoe, reflections were cast by Blagrave on Coleman's system; moreover, it was stated that the Blagrave shoe was under the patronage of the Prince Regent. Thereupon a George Price, Veterinary Surgeon to the Ordnance of the Medway District, wrote a letter to the Prince Regent,[2] on paper eighteen inches in length, of which three sides are covered with writing, in which, after approaching the "presence" with due humility, he points to "the bold and unqualified untruths asserted by Captain Blagrave in his address to the public." Goodwin by his

[1] *Veterinarian*, vol. xviii., January 1845.
[2] P.R.O. W.O. 44/532.

association with Blagrave is accused of prostituting his profession, and putting back the clock of progress. Price says that as Mr. Coleman has taken no notice of Blagrave's advertisement, he (Price) is impelled to address H.R.H. on the fallacy of the Blagrave method. He gives an account of his own service and experience, and states that he has never known Coleman's system of shoeing productive of anything but benefit. The tone of the letter, as well as its length (subsequently printed it occupies eleven pages of type), is far from pleasing; he refers, for instance, to the " ci-devant Captain and his renegade Vet "! How a letter addressed to the Prince Regent got into the hands of Captain Blagrave does not appear, but, as Lord Bloomfield was an equerry to the Prince and a friend of Blagrave's, is easily surmised. The next stage is the publication of a pamphlet by Captain Blagrave entitled: " An Epistle to Mr. Professor Coleman on the effects his Practice has had on the Cavalry of the United Kingdom, with remarks on a letter . . . addressed to H.R.H. Prince Regent." London. No date appended. The public is informed that a copy of the pamphlet can be obtained from the " Institution for the Practical Improvement of Veterinary Science, Oxford Street."

Blagrave's pamphlet consists of 16 pages, and though addressed to Coleman it opens with a vulgar attack on Price, in which it is stated that he was originally intended for a dealer in bonnets, sarcenets and shoe ties, but forsook this calling when his cousin, Edward Coleman, attained to eminence and professional preferment, and by taking out a twelve months' course at the College was dubbed a doctor. Then follow reflections on Price's judgement and practical skill. Coleman is invited to say whether Price's production was not concocted between the cousins. This is followed by an attack on Coleman, vulgar and personal. The correspondence found its way to the Board of Ordnance, which, on 29th October 1811, calls upon Coleman to say what method of shoeing is now practised on the horses of the R.H.A. and R.A. Drivers; whether the practice originally instituted by him corresponds with the present practice and what deviations, if any, have been made therefrom. He is also requested to report his opinion on the system of shoeing as practised under Captain Blagrave.

Coleman's reply, dated 8th November 1811, covers nine pages of foolscap and is holographic. He informs the Board that his systems of 1796 and 1811 differ in no material points; he follows this up with a dissertation on the use of the frog and then says:

" But the leading principle of shoeing beyond all others, and which from fifteen years' experience we have found highly beneficial to H.M. Service, is to make the horny *sole concave* with a drawing knife, and the crust to project below the sole, which effectually prevents corns or bruises or any pressure from the shoe. This practice, Sir, is, and in my opinion ever will be, of much greater importance than the form of the shoe inasmuch as it is a *principle* in the shoeing of horses, meaning by a principle, an invariable rule with any kind of shoe, for all horses, of all ages, of every description, used for all sorts of work, on all kinds of roads, and in every country."

Then he goes on to say that as regards the shoe itself no one pattern can be applicable to various and opposite kinds of feet, " but that as a general shoe for the army I have recommended, *under certain circumstances* and *certain restrictions*, a shoe with heels thinner than the toe." This is followed by a long account of the care necessary in fitting this pattern in order to avoid damage to the leg. At this period of history no reference to shoeing would have been complete without some mention of " contraction," so the Honourable Board of Ordnance is informed: " I made a few years since, as I humbly conceive, an important improvement in the practice of shoeing, by employing a clip at the inner part of each heel of the shoe, so as to embrace the inner heel of each bar, and thereby prevent (during the necessity of using thick heeled shoes) those diseases which are the general result of raising the frog above the ground, viz., contracted heels, thrushes and canker. . . . These, Sir, are and always have been my principles of shoeing. They may be founded in error, but after much labour and many years' experience I have seen no cause to alter my opinion." He goes on to say that he does not know whether the practice of any of the Veterinary Surgeons in H.M. Service has been at variance with these principles, but he warns the Board that officers like Captain Blagrave, from being acquainted with the exterior of the horse, believe themselves capable of understanding the mechanism and economy of the foot, the principles and practice of shoeing, and even the treatment of disease, and " the Veterinary Surgeons, rather than be at variance with their Commanding Officers, and doubting their own authority to resist, have quietly permitted the Farrier to apply any sort of shoe most agreeable to their officers' wishes. Such instances have come to my knowledge. . . . It is not for me to expatiate on the good effect of my own system," so he refers the Board to certain General Officers who for fifteen years have watched his practice, and paid the most marked attention to the subject.

Coleman continues that he has read Captain Blagrave's prospectus over and over again, but cannot form a conjecture as to what the system is; the great object, he says, appears to be to inform the world that he has a new Institution for the care and cure of the diseases of horses. In this prospectus objection is taken to thin-heeled shoes. Coleman says that he understands Blagrave's shoe has thick heels and that both project backwards beyond the hoof. This type of shoe he condemns as the cause of thrush, canker, etc., and adds that before the appointment of " District Veterinary Surgeons in the Ordnance, more horses of the R.A. Drivers at outstations were diseased with thrush, canker, corns and grease, than have been seen at Head Quarters from the year 1796 to the present period. In fact, corns, thrushes and canker among the horses of the R.H.A. and R.A. Drivers at Woolwich are rarely ever seen." He concludes by offering a demonstration of his system.

The Board transmitted a copy of the above to the Prince Regent, and notified H.R.H. that the Master-General and the Board entirely concurred in the opinion given by Mr. Coleman. Evidently Coleman was asked whether he had any objection to Mr. Price seeing his report, for on 20th November 1811 he replies that he has already sent him a copy through Mr. Percivall, but as he (Coleman) may hereafter find it necessary to vindicate his professional character and as his report would form part of his reply to the libel, he objects to an official copy being sent to Mr. Price.

The next correspondence is from Price to the Board of Ordnance, dated 28th January 1812, in which he delicately imparts to the honourable body, that he has only just been informed that the Grub Street publication of his antagonists has been handed to the Board, and that the *Thing* (sic) of an author has thought fit to be his biographer. He then gives an account of his life: articled to an attorney, next in the Norfolk Militia, later holding a commission in a Light Infantry Regiment, finally in the Service as a Veterinary Surgeon. He states that he and Coleman are related by marriage, but for years he has experienced his deep and deadly hatred, and the interests of a numerous offspring have constantly met from Coleman decided and rancorous enmity. He promises to reply to his cowardly biographer and

PLATE B

To face p 72

raise the blush of shame to his cheeks, as soon as his health, damaged during the Expedition to the Scheldt, permits.[1]

Next a letter from Coleman to the Board on 31st March 1812, asks that an official report may be called for from Woolwich as to his system of shoeing, as he understands Blagrave threatens to eject the Coleman system and establish his own. He then draws up certain questions for the reporters and Mr. Percivall to answer, saying that the latter is entitled to a large proportion of the merits of the system, the practice of it having been carried out under his eye, and that he (Coleman) is ready to acknowledge his "great attention and ability." He is informed in reply that the Board took the question up under instructions from the Prince Regent, and does not think it necessary to revive the subject.

This was a skilfully conceived plot to discredit the Coleman system of shoeing, in which the Prince Regent was utilized.[2] It failed, as the Board of Ordnance supported Coleman, but for the historian it has useful results. Nowhere, not even in his lectures, do we obtain so clear a conception of Coleman's views on shoeing. Price's account of the character of his relation by marriage confirms all that has been written by Coleman's detractors, and as a side and unexpected issue, is valuable as well as dramatic.

In the year 1815 the Veterinary Department of the Army was nineteen years old and all the officers were yet Cornets. On 14th April 1815, two months before the Battle of Waterloo, an order was published in which it is stated that for the first ten years of his service the Veterinary Surgeon is to *class* as a Cornet, after ten years as Lieutenant, and after twenty years' service as Captain. The Veterinary Surgeon is further reminded that this order gives no claim whatever to military command. The Medical Service was "classed" a few months earlier, in December 1814, and the same warning issued, Assistant Surgeons obtaining the relative rank of Lieutenant and Hospital Assistants that of Ensign. Thus the Veterinary Officer waited ten years for the rank that the Assistant Surgeon received on appointment. According to the Order just quoted the highest rank the Veterinary Surgeon could attain was that of Captain, and there was no change for the next forty-four years!

[1] Price died at Cadiz a few months later, November 1812, during the Peninsula War. As he was present in the Campaign in Holland in 1799 he was among the first of our Department to proceed on active service.

[2] The Prince Regent had a peculiar sense of humour. I doubt whether he entered into the plot with any other object than to extract amusement.

It is said that the constant disputes and dissatisfaction respecting choice of quarters led to the regimental staff officers being "classified," see *Veterinarian* Vol. 3, September 1830; the article adds that "the tag, rag and bob-tail set" which Coleman from time to time "pushed" into the Service were unworthy of rank.

The reticence of Coleman during his long period of office, and the destruction of the records mentioned at p. 2, left us in absolute ignorance of the veterinary arrangements for the campaigns occurring between 1799-1815, and even of the names of the officers who took part. Considerable time has been spent in endeavouring to collect a little information; the monthly "States" in the Public Record Office for this period have been examined, and we now know at least the names of the officers who served. It is very desirable to place on record the services of our officers during these long years of war, especially as the information is entirely new.

The first Expedition for which Coleman had to provide was that sent to Holland in 1799. With the Artillery Drivers was G. Price. The Cavalry Force consisted of the 7th, 11th, 15th and 18th Light Dragoons, with which were R. S. Cumming, J. Shipp, J. Trigg and F. Marsh. These five officers were the first of our newly created branch to proceed on active service. The next campaign was in Egypt under Abercrombie in 1802, in which C. O'Connor was present with the 12th Light Dragoons and S. Coxon with the 23rd Light Dragoons. In 1803 occurred the second Mahratta War. Coleman's responsibility only extended to the provision of veterinary officers for the British Cavalry regiments; to this sufficient reference has been made at p. 54. In 1807 an Expedition was sent to Copenhagen. R. S. Cumming was present with the Artillery at the Bombardment, together with the following veterinary surgeons of the King's German Legion: Hilmer, Eicke, Erdmann and Precht. In the same year an Expedition proceeded to South America, and in the attack on Buenos Ayres Veterinary Surgeon G. Lander, 9th Light Dragoons, was killed. In 1808, among the troops in Portugal were the 18th and 20th Light Dragoons, with which were J. Nesbitt and J. Darley. Both of these officers were present at the battles of *Roleia* and *Vimeira*.

In the same year an Expedition was sent to Sweden under Sir John Moore, but it never disembarked, and after being four months at sea was landed in Portugal in August 1808. With it were H. Coward, Artillery Drivers; F. C. Cherry, Waggon Corps; and F. Erdmann, 3rd Hussars K.G.L. These troops, together with the 18th Hussars, formed part of a force with which Sir John Moore marched into Spain. The Cavalry Brigade for this force, 7th, 10th and 15th Light Dragoons, came from England in November and was landed at Corunna. With the 7th was J. Parker, but Lord Vivian, who commanded, says in his *Memoirs* that Parker was arrested at Portsmouth, so presumably he did not accompany the regiment. [It is only fair to the memory of Parker to add that his offence could not have been serious, as his name remained in the Army List for the next two or three years.] With the 10th there was no veterinary surgeon, but as J. Denny had just exchanged his veterinary for a medical commission in the same regiment (p. 53), it may be assumed the horses did not suffer by the exchange. With the 15th was J. Castley, an able man. There was no time to "condition" the horses on arrival at Corunna; the brigade was urgently required by Moore, and, while still quite unfit, set off by forced marches to join him. A few weeks later they returned by the same route, together with Sir John Moore's Army, seeking their ships at Corunna with Napoleon at their heels. In this disastrous winter retreat were Coward, Cherry, Denny, Castley, Nesbitt and Erdmann. Curiously enough Coward had with him a veterinary pupil, J. H. Hodgson, who subsequently joined the Bengal Veterinary Service. We shall meet with him again. Why a civilian was permitted to accompany an army does not here concern us; we have only to remember that in those days women and children accompanied armies going out to fight.

The next campaign was in Holland in 1809, generally referred to as the Walcheren Expedition. It also was a disaster. With this force were the 3rd Dragoon Guards, 9th and 12th Light Dragoons, the Waggon Train, and 2nd Hussars K.G.L. J. Blanchard, J. Gain, J. Feron, F. C. Cherry and F. Eicke were present. I cannot trace the name of the officer with the Artillery.

In 1809 another Expedition was sent to the Peninsula which kept the field until 1814. With it in 1809 were five British and one German regiment—viz., 3rd Dragoon Guards, T. Rose; 4th Dragoons, T. Bird; 14th Light Dragoons, R. Thompson; 16th Light Dragoons, J. Peers; 23rd Light Dragoons, J. Shipp; 1st Hussars K.G.L., F. Precht; and Artillery Drivers, C. O'Connor. The battle of *Talavera* was fought in July, Bird, Thompson, Peers, Shipp and Precht being present. Rose was absent through sickness, and O'Connor was on duty at Lisbon, where he remained throughout the whole campaign. The 23rd Light Dragoons were practically destroyed at Talavera, and the regiment returned to England to refit, its place being taken by the Royal Dragoons: veterinary officer, W. Ryding.

In 1810, with the arrival of the 13th Light Dragoons (S. Chard), the number of British Cavalry regiments was six, and of German one. The battle of *Busaco* was fought in September, Chard and Peers being present. Thompson was absent, being on duty at Lisbon. Precht was sick, and died a few months later. During the whole of this year the Artillery at the front had no veterinary officer.

In 1811 seven additional cavalry regiments arrived, six British and one German—viz., 4th Dragoon Guards, A. Kirwan; 5th Dragoon Guards, J. Stanley; 3rd Dragoons, J. Barrington; 9th Light Dragoons, J. Gain; 11th Light Dragoons, R. Gouldthorpe; 12th Light Dragoons, J. Castley; 2nd Hussars K.G.L., F. Eicke. The twelve British regiments had seldom more than nine veterinary surgeons available owing to sickness; the two German regiments were also incomplete for some months. During this year the Artillery at the front had the services of J. Lythe. The Cavalry shared in the battles of *Fuentes d'Onor* and *Albuera*, both in May. At Fuentes d'Onor Ryding and Thompson were present, Peers absent through sickness; at Albuera were Rose and Bird, Chard being sick. No German veterinary surgeon was present at either battle.

Practically throughout 1812 the number of British Cavalry regiments remained at twelve, but the German were increased to four by the arrival of the 1st and 2nd Dragoons K.G.L.: Veterinary Surgeons Heuer and Hogrefe. Owing to sickness there were seldom more than seven officers available for the twelve British regiments. This year the Waggon Train received an officer, F. C. Cherry, and the Artillery at Cadiz was joined by J. Price, who, however, died shortly afterwards. S. Chard, 13th Light Dragoons, also died late in the year. In December three Household Cavalry regiments arrived; they brought only one Veterinary Surgeon, J. Siddall, and it was some months before officers for the 1st and 2nd Life Guards arrived: F. Dalton and J. Field. Veterinary Surgeon J. Lythe of the Artillery Drivers was present at the storming of *Ciudad Rodrigo* and *Badajoz*. The following officers were present at the battle of *Salamanca*: Barrington, Bird, Lythe, Cherry, Hueur,

Hogrefe and Power. Four officers were absent from Salamanca, either on duty elsewhere or from sickness.

In 1813 the following Cavalry regiments arrived in the Peninsula: 7th Hussars, R. Darvill; 10th Hussars, H. Sannermann; 15th Hussars, C. Dalwig; 18th Hussars, J. Pilcher. The following regiments, however, left the command: 4th Dragoon Guards, A. Kirwan; 9th Light Dragoons, J. Gain; 11th Light Dragoons, R. Gouldthorpe; and the 2nd Hussars K.G.L., F. Eicke. There were therefore sixteen British and three German Cavalry regiments in the Peninsula in 1813, and the Cavalry remained at this strength until the conclusion of the war. The number of officers available varied between ten and thirteen. The German regiments remained complete. A third officer for the Artillery arrived during 1813, William Percivall; he was posted to the Field Army, where he and J. Lythe remained until the end of the war. At no time throughout the war were there ever more than two veterinary surgeons in the field with the Artillery, while the Horse Artillery was entirely unprovided. There was much fighting in 1813. At the battle of *Vittoria* the following officers were present: Rose, Barrington, Bird, Jons (5th D.G.), Lythe, Cherry, Heuer, Hogrefe and Power; Dalwig of the 15th Hussars joined too late. The only regiment officially credited with being at the *Pyrenees* is the 14th Light Dragoons, the Veterinary Surgeon of which was absent on duty, but every regiment was employed on this difficult front. In the battle of *Nive* the Cavalry was represented by the 16th Light Dragoons, but the new veterinary officer had not joined at the date of the action. We do not know at which engagements the German officers were present.

In 1814 the Cavalry were better provided with veterinary surgeons than at any previous period in the history of the war. A vacancy in the 3rd Dragoons was filled by one Lowes,[1] and the death vacancy in the 13th Light Dragoons by J Constant, who, however, did not arrive in time for the campaign in the South of France. The closing battles of the war at which the Cavalry are credited with being present are *Orthez*—where the veterinary

---

[1] I give the name occurring in the Peninsula "States." At this date J. Blanchard was the Veterinary Surgeon of the regiment, but his name does not appear in any Peninsula return. On the other hand, the name of Lowes does not appear in the Army List. Nevertheless, J. Lowes qualified in November 1813, and no doubt this is the officer referred to in the returns. Lowes was Veterinary Surgeon to 3rd Dragoons as late as the year 1836.

officers were R. Darvill, 7th Hussars; J. Lythe and W. Percivall, Royal Artillery Drivers—and *Toulouse*, the final battle, at which were Lowes, Bird, W. Percivall, Lythe, and some German officers, names unknown.

At the close of the war there were twenty-four veterinary officers in the South of France or Spain—*i.e.*, Cavalry 16, Cavalry Staff Corps 1, Artillery 3, Waggon Train 1, German Cavalry 3.

Appendix II. presents in a tabular form the particulars of service of veterinary officers in the Peninsula. The active service of two of these stands out as a record: Thomas Bird, 4th Dragoons, and Joseph Lythe, Royal Artillery Drivers. Bird was present at Talavera, Albuera, Salamanca, Vittoria and Toulouse; Lythe at Ciudad Rodrigo, Badajos, Salamanca, Vittoria, Orthez and Toulouse. Bird's regiment was not at Waterloo, but Lythe was in that campaign. A medal for the Peninsula was not issued until 1847, and Bird, like many others, did not live to receive it. The most determined opponent to the issue of a Peninsula medal was the Duke of Wellington! He and his senior officers had been given Gold Crosses for their share in the campaign, but the services of those who had won the war were unrecognized until 1847.

The veterinary history of the Peninsula War has yet to be written. Wellington, writing to Lord Liverpool on 23 May 1811, described Spain as the grave of horses.

The Waterloo Campaign saw a considerable addition to the veterinary service of the Artillery, which had been so much neglected in the Peninsula. There were six officers present with it in June 1815, and seven in July. The names are shown in Appendix III. The Royal Horse Artillery neither in the Peninsula nor at Waterloo had any veterinary service for their 1,570 horses. It is most doubtful whether the veterinary officers of the Artillery Drivers were consulted by the R.H.A., as the bitterest enmity existed between these branches. The total number of veterinary officers in the Waterloo Campaign was twenty-one British and six German. Their names and regiments are given in Appendix III.

The two last survivors of the Peninsula and Waterloo were Henry Hogreve, 15th Hussars (formerly an officer of the King's German Legion), who died in 1865, and John Constant, 13th Light Dragoons, who lived until 1870.

After the downfall of Napoleon an Army of Occupation remained in France, but at home demobilization and retrenchment were shortly undertaken. In the year after Waterloo Coleman received a letter from the Board of Ordnance dated 23 July 1816, informing him that his services with the Corps of Royal Artillery Drivers " ceased on 20th inst."! As will be seen from the correspondence now to be recorded, this dismissal was not only unexpected but created consternation. Accordingly Coleman prepared a memorial to the Master-General of the Ordnance, which is preserved in the Public Record Office,[1] and covers nine sheets of demi paper. It is without date. Of the paragraphs of this memorial which throw light on the history of our Service and the character of Coleman we shall now give a précis.

He first states that he was appointed to the Brigade of Horse Artillery and Corps of Captain Commissaries (now termed Royal Artillery Drivers) by the late Marquis Cornwallis, that his appointment was obtained through Dr. Rollo, Surgeon-General in the Ordnance Service, who expressly assured him that the appointment was permanent, that consent was given to a weekly personal visit, and that during his absence one of his pupils was to remain in attendance. As the Board had expressly stated " that the residence of the pupil was not to be protracted longer than absolutely necessary," he concluded that his own appointment was permanent. The pupil selected (Mr. John Percivall) repeatedly refused to accept the appointment, but so great was his ability and good conduct that " your memorialist " urged him to accept, and in 1805 the Board, instead of removing the pupil from Woolwich, " as at first intended," was pleased to direct that he and eleven others trained by the memorialist should be appointed to the Ordnance Service as Commissioned Officers. This he trusts may be regarded as evidence of the success of his system. Since that time the pay of the assistant has been progressively augmented, and he is now in the position of retiring, if he please, on half pay at 20 years' service. "Your memorialist" mentions these facts not from any motive of jealousy, nor from the belief that his assistant has been too highly paid; on the contrary, he is satisfied with " the great and eminent services of his assistant," but hopes to be permitted to claim some portion of merit for having educated, selected and recommended Mr. Percivall. The next argument is an extraordinary one, for Coleman actually states that he could have selected as an assistant *an inferior type of man*, and in this way have rendered a continuation of his own services " absolutely necessary," but the good of the Service was a para-

[1] W.O. 44/687.

mount consideration! Coleman is evidently not ashamed to record the temptation he takes credit for resisting.

He then brings forward the improvements he has effected in the Service; for instance, his new system of ventilation, invented at a "considerable expense" to himself, but adopted "without any remuneration" being awarded him, though it has saved several thousand pounds to the State, and will continue to save so long as horses are kept by the Government. Further, the principles and practice of shoeing, ventilation, stable management and veterinary practice introduced by him have been adopted throughout the whole Ordnance Service.

Leaving his professional services, he turns to the terms of his appointment; he was not specifically appointed to the Royal Artillery Drivers; his assistant dealt with that branch, while his (Coleman's) services have been principally with the Horse Artillery. [It may be observed that it was the R.A. Drivers branch which was at this time under reduction.]

Dealing next with the financial aspect, he reminds the Board that he is the only Veterinary Surgeon whose pay has not been increased, nor is he allowed forage or coal, and though the senior, he is discharged without any remuneration for past services. In 1805, when Commissions were conferred upon his pupils, he had refrained "from motives of delicacy" from memorializing for a Commission, which he feels sure would not have been refused! He trusts that this act of abnegation may now operate in his favour, for a Commission in 1805 would, in 1816, have given him 15s. a day pay, with forage, a pension to his widow and children in case of death, and a claim to retire at the present time on 7s. a day.

He attaches to his appeal two testimonials from the Officers Commanding the Horse Artillery and Royal Artillery Drivers, Woolwich, in which they bear testimony to his professional skill and the benefit derived therefrom by the Ordnance Establishment. He adds that his conduct during these long years has merited their "entire approbation"; in proof of which he informs the Master-General that he has never during his service received the most trifling reprimand, or incurred in the smallest degree the displeasure of his commanding officers!

This piteously undignified appeal concludes with the request that "in kind consideration of his past services" he may be dealt with "on the same footing as every other Ordnance Veterinary Surgeon," and if this is sanctioned he would show his gratitude by lecturing to the Officers, Cadets and Farriers of the Ordnance Service, and by taking professional charge of St. John's Wood in addition to Woolwich, and by continuing to exercise great circumspection in the selection of candidates for appointment in the veterinary department of the Ordnance Service. With feelings " of highest respect and greatest humility " he begs his memorial will be taken into favourable consideration.

There is no reply to this memorial in the correspondence, but there is a letter from Coleman dated 1st May 1817, and it is easy from its contents to understand what has occurred between August 1816 and May 1817. Among other events there has been a personal interview with the Master-General, which Coleman refers to as an act of " most gracious condescension " which he will ever remember " with the most lively feelings of gratitude "! He then comes to business. The Master-General had evidently given a negative reply to the question of a commission, and would appear to have stated that Coleman's claim to remain in his position must be based solely on the benefit the public have derived from his services. Coleman therefore "implores" the Master-General to ascertain from his commanding officers their opinion of events before and during his period of service. " It is painful, my Lord, to my feelings to become an Egotist," but he hopes to be excused, and quotes extracts from testimonials received from his late commanding officers.

There follows a further sacrifice of self-respect. He begs to inform the Master-General that he has a wife, and though he does not plead poverty, he explains that he has two brothers with families who through agricultural misfortunes are much distressed and look to him for assistance ! [At this time Coleman's income was computed to be about £3,000 a year !]

On 17th June 1817, the Board of Ordnance recommended that Mr. Coleman be placed upon the same footing as every other Ordnance Veterinary Surgeon who had been reduced since the Peace, and that he be allowed 5s. per diem, in return for which he will engage to deliver lectures to the officers, cadets and farriers. This decision led to further correspondence; Coleman had not got what he wanted. He had asked to be placed " on the same footing as every other Ordnance Veterinary Surgeon," a demand by no means clear. The Board took his request at what seemed to be its face value, and added after the word Surgeon, " who had been reduced since the Peace."

On 9th July 1817, he addressed the Master-General on this

decision, saying that in his petition he made no such request, but asked to receive the same pay as every other Veterinary Surgeon of the Ordnance on the active list. He no doubt meant this, but certainly did not express it. Though he had been P.V.S. for twenty years, he had not learned the niceties and pitfalls of official correspondence, which suggests that his experience of it was very limited. He adds in this letter that a post chaise would be required to carry his preparations for the promised lectures to and from Woolwich, which would considerably diminish his allowance for lecturing!

More correspondence follows, until finally it is agreed on 15th December 1817, that his services should be retained at 10s. a day, in consideration of the benefit which " it appears " will be derived from the lectures he has " bound himself " to deliver to the officers of the Ordnance Corps at Woolwich. One would have thought that Coleman, even though thus ousted from the veterinary charge of the garrison at Woolwich, would have been glad after this shameful correspondence to allow the matter to close, but on 18th December 1817 he actually wrote to the Board to ask whether the 10s. per diem was in addition to the 5s. per diem previously offered him! On 22nd December he received a reply in the negative.

The intimate friendship between Coleman and John Percivall which endured for thirty years was not disturbed by the events just narrated, for, of course, the correspondence never leaked out of the office of the Board. Percivall never learnt of the attempt made by his friend to push him out of the Service; indeed, until the publication of these pages no one has known, for this particular bundle of papers at the Public Record Office had never previously been examined. The Coleman-Percivall friendship, however, was arrested later, as we shall presently see.

In 1818 a Register of Sick and Lame Horses was introduced; we do not know how the records in the Cavalry were kept up to that time, but certainly in the Artillery a register had been kept as far back as 1802. The order introducing this book into the Cavalry provides that it is to be frequently inspected by the commanding officer, and produced at all inspections of the regiment. A half-yearly return of sick was also ordered, and the form in which this was rendered has been very little altered, for the present annual return is almost identical with it. There was as yet no monthly return, and one is tempted to enquire by what means Coleman kept himself informed of Cavalry horse efficiency, when he had to wait half a year before knowing the amount of sickness which had occurred in a regiment. The half-yearly return was directed to be sent to the War Office, of which Coleman was not an official; presumably he received the rèturns from the War Office; in 1822, however, an order was published directing that in addition to the copy sent to the War Office, a copy should be sent direct to the " Veterinary Surgeon General."

This is not the first time Coleman had been so designated in a War Office order. In a Glanders Order of 1807 he is given the same title, to which, of course, he had no right. In 1802, on the title-page of the second edition of his work on *Natural and Suspended Respiration*, he describes himself as Veterinary Surgeon General to His Majesty's Cavalry, and again in 1803, on the title-page of the pamphlet *Instructions for the Use of Farriers of the British Cavalry and Most Hon. Board of Ordnance;* it would therefore appear that the title originated with himself; how it found its way into official orders is inexplicable. In the *Veterinarian* for September 1830, in a most interesting communication by an anonymous Army Veterinary Surgeon on the conditions then existing in our Service, occurs the following reference to the Veterinary Surgeon General: " I have heard of his existence, but have never set eyes on His Excellency; the Army List contains the name of Edward Coleman as Principal Veterinary Surgeon, but this is not synonymous with General, and indeed is no rank at all." He goes on to deplore the absence of a real head in our Service.

The regulations on glanders were first drawn up in 1796 in the *Instructions to Farriers attached to the British Cavalry*, etc. The symptoms given are those accepted at that time. Isolation was ordered, also disinfection by scrubbing and the application of size and lime wash. The head of the affected animal was directed to be buried several feet underground. No reference is made to the lungs. Treatment of Farcy was permitted. In the 1803 issue of the above " Instructions " more detailed information is given; there is still, however, the usual confusion with ozœna, although there is also evidence that by this time Coleman knew more about the affection. There is a change in the disinfection routine. After being well washed with soap and water, the manger walls, etc., are to be painted with oil colour, as " lead has no pernicious effect upon horses "! Though he states in the " Instructions " that farcy frequently terminates in glanders, he still permits it to be treated. It is evident that in 1803 he had not made the classical discovery, with which he has been credited, of the identity of the two diseases. In both editions of the "Instructions" the medicines suitable for the treatment of the case were ordered to be obtained from the chest of preparations supplied by Coleman, the nature of the various compounds not being given. In a copy of the 1803 "Instructions," to be found in the library of the Royal Veterinary College, the components of each preparation are inserted in ink. This was evidently Coleman's private copy, and it shows us that at this time he was treating farcy with sulphate of copper. In May 1807 an order was circulated to all regiments of Cavalry by the Commander-in-Chief, at the suggestion of the "Veterinary Surgeon General," designed to prevent infection by Glanders and Farcy. In the same year a second order, again suggested by the Veterinary Surgeon General, dealt with the prevention of infection; the disinfection by the washing and painting processes is again enjoined, but between these an application of quicklime is ordered. Pails, head collars, clothing, surcingles, nose bags, body brushes, mane combs and sponges are to be burned, and iron work of saddlery exposed to the fire for ten minutes! In 1822 another order by the "Veterinary Surgeon General" directed that a suspected case was to be kept tied up to the manger to prevent the infectious discharge being distributed. The disinfection was as before, except that three coats of paint were to be given. The destruction of appointments is now directed at discretion, but if the disease suddenly occurs it is advised to burn them.

Percivall (*Hippopathology*, vol. iii., 1858, p. 242) reproduces an extract from an official communication he received from Coleman as late as October 1837, urging that hot water, soft soap and soda should be employed on the stalls and fittings prior to the process of painting, though he concludes by saying that defective ventilation is much more frequently a cause of glanders than the presence of glanderous discharge!

These orders show that glanders was by no means so completely under control as Coleman had publicly stated; no returns of disease were published in those days, but the Inspection Returns of regiments are still in existence in the Public Record Office, and a perusal of them shows that cases occurred in most regiments every year down to the time of the Crimean War.

The above quotation from Coleman's official correspondence of 1837 brings to notice a theory he held throughout life, "that not one horse in a thousand or even in ten thousand" contracted the disease by infection! He blamed, as we have seen, the miasma of the foul stable, yet, as Percivall says, non-contagionist as

Coleman was, the regulations issued by him for the control of glanders "were as effectually calculated to prevent the spread of the disease by contagion as anyone of an opposite way of thinking could desire."

Thomas Peall, Veterinary Surgeon to the Ordnance, in the year 1795, while still a student at the London School under Coleman, produced glanders in the ass by smearing the discharge from a farcy ulcer inside the nostrils; the animal was affected on the eighth day. James White, Veterinary Surgeon Royal Dragoons, planned carefully conducted experiments which proved that the respired air from a glandered horse could not produce the disease, nor could the miasma of the stable, but that the disease was readily conveyed by inoculation or through the digestive canal. He also found that the virus of the disease was killed by chlorine. These were big advances, but they were never mentioned by Coleman, and Percivall, strangely enough, in his work failed to give them the position they merited. It is evident from some remarks he makes that he disliked White, who was a bold advertiser, but he could have had no such feeling towards Peall, who was a modest retiring gentleman.[1] Unquestionably to Peall belongs the credit of proving one hundred and thirty years ago the identity of glanders and farcy, while White demonstrated the all-important source of infection by actual experiment and destroyed the miasma theory by the same method. Coleman nevertheless held the field purely by virtue of his position as a dogmatic teacher of youth, knowing that not one man in a thousand of those who passed through his hands would venture to differ from him or subject his views to the crucial test of experimental enquiry. So long as the profession lasts Coleman will be credited with the discovery of the identity of the glanders-farcy poison. The mistake is of long standing. Coleman, prudently it may be, never published one syllable on this momentous discovery, though he mentioned it in his lectures (1822). Percivall is the authority, but he obtained from others an account of the actual experiment, which he did not himself witness, and, of course, he heard Coleman in his lectures claim the discovery as

---

[1] At the end of his life Percivall admitted that he had read nothing written by White between the 7th and 16th Editions, and in making a tardy apology for his neglect he admits the correctness of White's views. How he came to overlook Peall's experiment of 1795 is inexplicable. In 1823 he described him as having "no competitor as a veterinary pathologist."

his (p. 28). It was two able officers of the Army Veterinary Service who laid the first solid foundation for our knowledge of glanders.

James White entered the Royal Dragoons in 1797 and left the regiment in 1804. During his service he published his work on *Veterinary Medicine*, which ran into many editions. It is dedicated to the Duke of York. White very early broke away from his teacher, Coleman, and boldly pushed ahead. In 1802 he distinguished between glanders and strangles; he also stated that glanders and farcy were produced by one and the same poison and that the chief source of spread was contact with the diseased. In 1812 he reported experiments to show that glanders could not be conveyed by the air nor created by the miasma of a foul stable. He showed that ingestion was a frequent source of infection and credits Sainbel with this discovery. He proved that chlorine was capable of destroying the virus, and finally differentiated between ozœna and glanders. In 1812 he urged Coleman, though without effect, to publish his observations on glanders. But in spite of his silence Coleman, by the various orders he issued on disinfection, shows that he was familiar with White's work.

On leaving the Service White settled for a time in Exeter, where he had a large practice and built up a great reputation. Towards the end of his life his mind would appear to have become affected, as he published some astounding nonsense, which no doubt caused the reliability of his early work to be questioned. He lived long enough to correct his errors. He was a well-educated man, well connected, and, it is said, his own worst enemy. His most objectionable characteristics were his unblushing self-advertising and his perpetual discoveries which came to nothing. Curiously enough this very advanced thinker never throughout his life recognized a case of acute laminitis; he always attributed it to an affection of the back! White's strong point was the prevention of disease. On the title-page of the later editions of his works occurs the motto *Venienti occurrite morbo*, which Simonds adopted for the Royal Veterinary College at its Incorporation in 1879. Clearly, from its connection with White and its applicability, it should be the motto of our Service. White died in 1825.

We have now reached a period in this history when the administration and grievances of the Veterinary Service were no longer unknown to the public. The *Veterinarian* and the *Hippiatrist*, two magazines established with very different objects, appeared in 1828. The editor of the *Veterinarian* was at first W. Percivall, then Percivall and Youatt were joint editors, then for years Youatt was alone, and finally Percivall. The editor of the *Hippiatrist* was anonymous, but his identity was generally known, for his writings were peculiar and unmistakable. He was Bracy Clark, and with him was associated F. C. Cherry, an Army Veterinary Surgeon on half pay, who subsequently succeeded

Coleman as Principal Veterinary Surgeon. Both periodicals served as mouthpiece for the Army. The *Hippiatrist* was published solely with the object of exposing Coleman, and if possible of getting rid of him; the *Veterinarian* was published to advance knowledge, to advocate reform in all branches, and serve as a medium for professional communication.

The *Veterinarian* was outspoken but gentle in tone and bearing, the *Hippiatrist* was virulent, abusive and libellous. For reasons known only to Bracy Clark he changed the name of his periodical three times during the three years of its existence. The name we have selected is the most appropriate of the three. The *Veterinarian* had for one of its objects the reform of the St. Pancras School; the *Hippiatrist* was solely devoted to the destruction of Coleman by any and every means; the violent language in which it indulged was more calculated to defeat than assist its object, but it was deliberately chosen in the hope of ensnaring Coleman into legal proceedings. In this it never succeeded. It cannot be too clearly stated that there was no united action by these journals against the London School; they were, in fact, antipathetic. After Coleman there was no man Bracy Clark disliked so much as Youatt. Curiously enough, both periodicals appeared for the first time on 1st January, 1828. W. Percivall was warned by his father at the birth of the *Veterinarian* "never to show malignity or revenge, or I will disown you and the *Veterinarian*; attack and expose the measures, but spare the man."[1] Percivall senior and Coleman were, as we have already remarked, " constant companions and bosom friends," but when the son published the *Lectures on the Veterinary Art* in 1823, and the *Veterinarian* in 1828, all intercourse ceased, though Percivall senior little knew the attempt his bosom friend had made twelve years previously to get rid of him from the Service.

No time was lost by the *Hippiatrist* in coming into action. In its second issue in February 1828 appeared an article by F. C. Cherry, on half pay, and now practising at Clapham. He was a man of commanding ability, fearless, unforgiving, adamant. His son, a medical man and veterinary practitioner, was his equal in brilliancy and of identical temperament. Later in life they quarrelled over matters connected with the Royal College of Veterinary Surgeons; a bitter and unedifying warfare resulted as a consequence of the son's championship of the Royal College against the attitude of Professor Dick, whom the father supported.

[1] *Veterinarian*, vol. iv., 1831.

This quarrel has no other bearing on this history than as showing how doughty the antagonist was who had now taken the field. His attack on Coleman[1] is confined in this article to his income derived from the College fees, amounting, he says, to £1,322 last year, in addition to his salary as Professor. He makes no reference at this stage to Coleman's Army salaries and emoluments. But the article was earnest of what was to follow. In the third number appears an unsigned contribution, unmistakably from the pen of Bracy Clark, in which he compares the Veterinary College as originally constituted with its present mismanaged and corrupt state. This article is addressed to His Majesty, as Patron of the College, and the subscribers to the Institute. In it the writer points out that Coleman loses no opportunity of stating that medical pupils seldom succeed as veterinary practitioners. He, however, admits as students linen drapers, paper hangers, shoemakers and tailors, and in a few months turns them out to practise. The money which was intended for the support of the College—*i.e.*, the students' fees—goes into Coleman's pocket, which explains the readiness with which the lowest characters find admission. He goes on to state that Coleman holds nearly all the veterinary offices of emolument and patronage: Professor to the Veterinary College, Veterinary Surgeon General to the British Cavalry, Veterinary Surgeon to the Ordnance Department, Druggist General and Contractor for the Government Horses, Principal Examiner for the diploma, and Chief Receiver of fees! His salary is given at £500 a year (this is exclusive of the fees given by Cherry in the previous number), and the emoluments from his other appointments amount, it is understood, to upwards of £3,000 a year. Possessing as he does the whole patronage of army appointments, he can forward or blight the prospects of pupils at pleasure. As veterinary examiner for the diploma he can make the ordeal easy or difficult. "We do not hesitate to assert that the Veterinary College is one of the most rotten establishments in England. . . ." In the seventh issue, published in July 1828, there is an article addressed to the Duke of Clarence, afterwards William IV., who had lately become President of the College, in which he is informed of the present state of the Institute, and begged to put it in order. In the same number is a further attack by Cherry; in the twelfth issue another article by the same writer. In the twenty-first issue for May 1829 there is an unsigned letter on Coleman's army contract, in which it is pointed out that experiments with new

[1] *Hippiatrist*, vol. i., No. 2, 1828.

PLATE C

To face p 88

drugs are not encouraged, as it is not to Coleman's interest (" and those who know him will not accuse him of negligence in this respect ") to waste drugs in experiments on disease. " A pistol bullet is no expense to the contractor." In the thirty-first issue of October 1829, a surgeon, who gives his name and address, writes to say that he entered the College with the object of entering the army, and when the 11th Dragoons became vacant, asked for the regiment. It was given to one greatly his junior. He again tried for a vacant regiment through the colonel, who was informed (by Coleman) that his candidate being a medical man was deficient in practical knowledge. Nevertheless Coleman had certified his competence to practise!

In the forty-first issue, March 1830, there is a further attack on Coleman's army contract, the previous arguments are repeated, and it is added that the smaller the consumption of drugs the larger his profits, and that he discountenances the use of expensive drugs, the employment of new remedies, and the use of improved instruments and surgical appliances. In the same article is the further statement that Coleman regards the groom or farrier as making the best veterinary surgeon, and that he knew of no instance of a surgeon succeeding as a veterinary surgeon. The writer adds sarcastically that Coleman is a brilliant exception to his own law. In the forty-seventh number, for June 1830, is an article evidently by an experienced officer of the Veterinary Service. He says that Coleman as P.V.S. inspects a great number of military horses, but what does he know of the speed and stoutness of horses in the field, the ease with which they perform long marches, their maintenance of condition in a campaign, and the casualties to which they are most liable?

In the fifty-first issue, in August 1830, a serious charge is made by Cherry to the effect that a veterinary officer being about to be appointed to a regiment of Cavalry, Coleman required a promise from him that he would not take the money allowance for medicine as his predecessor had done.[1] We know from the *Report of the Commission of Military Enquiry* of 1808 (p. 63) that there were only four regiments for which he did not draw the allowance. It is impossible to reject this story, as the article is signed. Cherry continues that every Veterinary Surgeon of Cavalry has the private property of Mr. Coleman, contractor, in

[1] In this connection see p. 64, in which Coleman stated that the Veterinary Surgeon of the 2nd Life Guards was out of pocket by the contract!

his care, and that for more than the third of a century Coleman has received a premium for suppressing improvements, protecting ignorance and indolence, and that *he is the greatest enemy the veterinary profession ever had!* In estimating the gravity of these statements, it is necessary to remember that they were made by a senior officer; in fact, by the very man who became Principal Veterinary Surgeon after Coleman.

The fifty-ninth issue of this periodical was published in December 1830; its editorial is perhaps the most violent ever issued. The College is described as the seat of pelf and not of science, and the statement that grooms and farriers make the best Veterinary Surgeons is again quoted, the writer adding that he has frequently heard Coleman say so.

The *Hippiatrist* had done its work, and no further issue appeared after December 1830. Coleman, as we have seen, lost his contract for medicines, etc., shortly afterwards, in 1832.

The first two years of the *Veterinarian* (1828-29) contain only one or two matters of importance to the Army, but the College system, and Coleman as an opponent of progress, are incessantly attacked, and Youatt promises his readers that the *Veterinarian* will effect the desired reform. In the November issue of 1828, Percivall, who had not yet been joined by Youatt, deals with inadequate instruction, alleging it to be the main cause of our degradation, and says that the type of man sent as Veterinary Surgeon to some Cavalry regiments was such that he was not permitted to mess with the officers! He calls down shame on the heads of those who placed these men in such a position. A little light is thrown on the times by the next sentence. "Even when the Veterinary Surgeon is a gentleman by extraction, education and bearing, he mingles with the officers of the regiment only under painful restrictions." At the time Percivall wrote these bitter words he had been with the 1st Life Guards for eighteen months. In the June 1829 number of the *Veterinarian* is the report of a speech by Coleman at a dinner. In this he stated he was a great advocate for rank,[1] but that we ought not to place a higher stamp on our profession than the public are willing to give. We are only the younger sons of the medical profession. In the Army there is a shade of difference between the Surgeon and the Veterinary Surgeon in point of rank. "I cannot help but think it is well founded . . . we should not say that we are on a par with the medical profession." Coleman conveniently forgot

[1] By rank he here means status.

that in 1794 he was in a position to have placed the veterinary profession on a level with other learned professions by maintaining the sound educational standard on admission which he found with Sainbel's pupils, and by upholding the three years' course established by the Frenchman. In the issue for October 1829 Youatt hits at the real reason for Coleman's attitude, the innate contempt felt by him for the profession of which he was the titular head, and says we must hear no more of those favourite dicta of the Professor respecting the few diseases of the horse, which are so easily treated and comprehended, and the pharmacopœia the contents of which are so limited that it can be carried in the pocket.

Apart from Percivall's contributions, the first military literature appearing in the *Veterinarian* is from James Castley of the 12th Lancers, who writes on " Soundness," and gives other evidence of his acute professional judgement and skill. In the number for April 1830 he gives us an account of laminitis in the Cavalry Brigade in the Corunna Campaign, and corrects Napier's History of the Peninsula War. Castley made his mark in the Peninsula, and was requested by the authorities to draw up instructions for the care and management of horses on landing. There were no administrative veterinary officers in those days, nor, in fact, until the Crimean Campaign. Castley's information on everything relating to the army horse was always sound, and in addition he knew how to present his matter in a most attractive form. He was the first to liken us to the Cinderella of the Sciences in referring to the humiliation offered our profession by the University of Edinburgh when she turned her back on Dick's school at its inception. Dick was then a young man, and Castley praises his zeal, sincerity and fairness, and compares his methods with those practised in London. In this article Castley refers to his " old friend Cherry," the editor of the *Hippiatrist* (he should have said co-editor), and so either accidentally, or with approval, disclosed to the profession the name of at least one of the men who were working to unmask Coleman.

In the December number of the *Veterinarian* for 1830, and in that for June 1831, Castley writes on the troop horse and his management; the latter article would appear to have been a lecture to N.C.O.'s. In speaking of the regimental hospital, he says it is always the most useless man in the troop who is detailed to look after the sick horse; or else the duty is made a fatigue, and a fresh man sent at every stable hour. How little the Service changes! In July 1831 he deals with hereditary diseases, and recalls that when as a student he told Coleman that the breeders in Yorkshire regarded specific ophthalmia as hereditary, the Professor replied: "I know of no such thing as hereditary diseases; strictly speaking no disease can be hereditary." A large number of cases of specific ophthalmia then existed in Ireland (where he was serving), and he also saw many cases in France during the three years he served there with the Army of Occupation after Waterloo. In October 1832 he writes wisely and well on shoeing; he urges that there should not be an obstinate adherence to any one pattern, though the common seated shoe is excellent for most purposes. His last contribution was in December 1832, when he begged the Profession to cease fighting and to combine for improvement: "let us recollect that union is strength."[1] A day or two later he was dead, and the *Veterinarian* in an obituary notice emphasized to the profession the serious loss it had sustained.

James Castley was born in Westmorland in 1781 and educated under a relative who kept a school at Richmond, Yorks. From his father he acquired a knowledge of horses invaluable to him in his writings and practice. Obtaining his diploma with marked credit in May 1807, he entered the Service the following month, being gazetted to the 15th Light Dragoons, with which regiment he went through the Corunna Campaign; in 1809 he transferred to the 12th Light Dragoons and served with this regiment in the Peninsular War and at Waterloo. He is described as a firm and excellent friend. He was certainly a practitioner of outstanding ability and a man of sufficient personality to attract the attention of the military authorities of his day, no easy matter in the early years of the nineteenth century. Castley died 31st December, 1832.

In the *Veterinarian* for September 1830 occurs the article already referred to at p. 41, pointing out the disgrace incurred by sending men socially unfit to the Service. It also touches on the question of relative rank, and draws attention to the fact that the Veterinary Surgeon has to serve ten years for the relative rank a Surgeon obtains on entry. Finally, the writer deplores the absence of a real military head to the department, and asks for someone who will take a paternal interest in its welfare, and have the interests of the Service at heart. He concludes that "no department has so long been left in the background for want of a 'head.'" In October 1830 appears an equally strong article from

---

[1] Our College motto was proposed many years later by Professor Morton; he may have been influenced by Castley's observation.

the pen of "Another Army Veterinarian" expressing the gravest dissatisfaction at the existing state of affairs. He also refers to a Royal Warrant, published in July, in which the half and retired pay of Veterinary Surgeons is dealt with. He says that this warrant is not only of no use, but leaves matters worse than they were before. "Were my time to come over again I should not sacrifice twenty-five of the best years of my life to a pittance of 8s. a day." Coleman is again blamed for taking no interest in the welfare of his officers.

The Royal Warrant of July 1830 dealt with the questions of Half and Retired Pay only, and stipulated that an officer placed on retired pay or half pay on reduction of establishment or ill-health would receive:

After 3 years' service, 3/6 per diem (temporarily)
Above 3 ,, ,, and under 10 years 4/6 per diem
Above 10 ,, ,, ,, ,, 20 ,, 5/6 ,, ,,
After 20 ,, ,, 8/- per diem, if 5 years have been spent abroad; otherwise—
,, ,, ,, ,, 7/- ,, ,,
,, 30 ,, ,, 12/- ,, ,,

The right of retirement at twenty years' service on the higher rate was now dependent on the officer having served five years abroad. This warrant was no advance on that of 1807. No better insight into the great dissatisfaction existing in our department in 1830 could be obtained than in the communications referred to.

On the 13th December 1830, John Percivall died suddenly at the Royal Horse Infirmary, Woolwich. Three days before he had been hunting, returned fatigued, and had a fainting fit. The symptoms of his illness given in the *Veterinarian*, vol. iv., 1831, make it clear that he died from angina pectoris while the Orderly Corporal was reading to him the daily report of the sick in hospital. The date of his birth was February 1768, so that he was nearly sixty-three years of age. He graduated in 1795, and in 1796 was appointed by Coleman as his assistant at Woolwich. He received neither warrant nor commission at that date. We have already recorded the history of his appointment (pp. 34, 57) and the determination of the Ordnance not to lose his services. In 1801 he was appointed a Warrant Officer, and in 1805 commissioned. He had entire charge of the horses of the Ordnance, amounting during war to many thousands. He had an intuitive knowledge of conformation, understood service requirements, and all horses for the Artillery were examined by him. In 1805 additional veterinary surgeons were appointed, no doubt owing to the excellent results obtained by John

Percivall. He took an active share in lecturing to the officers and men, and carried out investigations on many subjects, especially on the action of drugs; it is said that there was not a medicine he did not test, in the hope of one day publishing his results. He was most regular and diligent, and, being especially fond of making anatomical injections and preparing museum specimens, he collected material for no less than three museums. One he sent to the Dublin Society, no doubt for the use of Peall; one was formed at the Artillery Riding Establishment, and another at the Royal Horse Infirmary, where, as has been said, it existed in my day. Being essentially a practical man he did much to control the " wildly theorizing disposition " of Coleman. He was an open, straightforward man with a somewhat blunt exterior; no officer was more respected by his seniors, and none more idolized by those who served under him. His whole soul was wrapped up in his only child, his hope and his pride, William Percivall. It is this obituary notice which is the authority for the statement at p. 82 that when W. Percivall's *Veterinary Lectures* and *Veterinarian* were produced, all intercourse between Coleman and John Percivall ceased. Percivall senior did not contribute much to periodical literature, but the *Veterinary Lectures* of his son are full of the father's observations, and indeed, from his ripe experience and sound judgement he supplied much of the material to be found there.

In the *Veterinarian* for February 1831 an anonymous contributor explains the various channels through which a commission in the Veterinary Service of the Army is obtainable, and states that interest with the Commander-in-Chief or his Military Secretary secures appointment without Veterinary interference. He also says that examinations for the Army are a farce, as the man who examines the candidates (Coleman) has only recently certified them as fit to hold a diploma! He concludes his article by saying that " the veterinary surgeon is the worst remunerated officer in H.M. Service." In the following number another correspondent suggests that Coleman should discriminate in the selection of men for the service, precisely as is done by the Director General of the Medical Service. In the same issue an anonymous contributor of very advanced views deals with the duties of the Army Veterinary Surgeon; among these he includes the care and management of the horses of the regiments. He complains that the Veterinary Surgeon is interfered with in the treatment of the sick, but does not specifically state in what ways. There were restrictions right up to the end of the regimental system in 1878, one being that no operation could be performed without the permission of the commanding officer. Judging from a statement in this paper no regulations at that time existed for the performance of veterinary duties other than those in the Standing Orders of regiments, but Veterinary Regulations certainly existed in 1847, and were not new then, so this article may have been the cause of their issue. The writer urges that the Veterinary Surgeon should be prompt in decision, firm in opinion, precise and peremptory in giving orders. Indecision, he says, is fatal, neglect of personal appearance equally so, "let him be smart and soldier-like in dress as well as active and determined in his conduct." He tells us that in the Register of Sick and Lame Horses introduced in 1818 there is no place where a record of the case can be inserted, and it thus loses much of its educational value. He critically examines the very primitive official nomenclature of diseases drawn up for the preparation of the half-yearly return, and sarcastically describes it as "a glorious achievement"! "First come grease, mange and other cutaneous diseases; then acute and chronic glanders; diseases of the lungs and chest (mind the book does not say the lungs are *not* in the chest!); and now follows a sweeper, *Diseases of the Contents of the Abdomen.*" Fractures are not even mentioned. This admirable criticism shows how completely Coleman was out of touch with the Army; incidentally it illustrates the best type of man the Service contained.

In the issue of July 1831 the *Veterinarian* publishes a further contribution on the Royal Warrant of 1830, restating the arguments against this warrant which have already been given at p. 93. The writer then deals with the supply of medicine by contract, and tells us that the regiments in Ireland furnished their own medicine, as also in India, and that the Household Cavalry and 10th Hussars have the same privilege. It is curious that there is no mention of the Irish system of supply in Coleman's evidence before the *Commissioners of Military Enquiry* in 1808 (p. 63).[1] Whoever the writer was he took a very advanced view, and urged that purveyorship of medicine was irreconcilable with Coleman's Commission as P.V.S. to the Cavalry, and that it was discreditable and impolitic that he should appear in the character of a contractor.

[1] This may be due to the fact that in the early part of the nineteenth century the Army in Ireland was quite distinct from the Army in England. Ireland possessed its own Ordnance Service; the Irish Artillery issued its own orders, and the regiments forming the garrison were permanent unless required for active service. Some cavalry regiments served continuously for over eighty years in Ireland! When our Service came into existence a commanding officer in Ireland asked Coleman for a Veterinary Surgeon for his regiment; Coleman could not send one until authority had been obtained.

As we know, Coleman lost his contract in 1832, but this loss was evidently kept secret, for his enemies never refer to it.

In the March issue of 1832 is an account of the Veterinary Service in the French Army, with their rates of pay. The Veterinary Surgeons held no commissions and were on a level with regimental artificers! More than a year later, Youatt, who had strongly espoused the cause of our French colleagues in their struggle to obtain commissions, urges them to "Agitate, still agitate, again and again . . . ere long the voice of truth and justice will be heard."

In April 1833, John Field, Veterinary Surgeon 2nd Life Guards, died at the age of sixty-five. He had joined the regiment in January 1805, and served continuously with it until his death, but he saw no active service. The J. Field who served with the 2nd Life Guards in the Peninsula and at Waterloo was a relative, a son perhaps. His influence on the profession was immense. He had a private practice in addition to his army appointment. For several years he was assistant, and then partner, with the celebrated William Moorcroft. When Moorcroft went to India in 1808, Field succeeded to the practice, the largest and most exclusive and lucrative in London. Moorcroft in a very few years had made a fortune. Field continued the practice up to the time of his death. He was naturally retiring in disposition, and was not well known in the profession in which he exerted so much power for good. So great was the public confidence in his professional judgement and rigid integrity, that his word was law, and but rarely disputed. These were the days when questions of soundness or unsoundness frequently arose, and to no man, it is said, were the public so much indebted for the exposure of many infamous frauds. The esteem in which he was held by his regiment and by his clients, all people of position, and the fortune he left behind him, were, says the *Veterinarian*, the best proofs of his professional worth.

The first public mention in this country of a Veterinary Service for India was made by Sir Astley Cooper at the annual dinner of the St. Pancras School in February 1833, from which it would appear that the College had secured the right to nominate candidates to the India House. Sir Astley's statement is not clear, but it is evident that the College had obtained recognition from the East India Company which it had not previously possessed. Some account of the Army Veterinary Service in India must now be given.

The earliest official reference I have found in connection with the Veterinary Service in India is contained in a General Order of the Bengal Army, dated 8th April 1793, in which it is stated that upon the appearance of a supposed infectious disease among the horses, the affected will be removed from the cantonment, and the matter reported to the Officer Commanding the Station, who will order the animals to be inspected "by persons who may be judged capable of distinguishing the disorders of horses." We are left in doubt as to whether these were Europeans or natives. At this time there was not a single qualified man in India and only two in England, Sainbel and Moorcroft.

Moorcroft, as we have just said, went to India, arriving on 14th November 1808; he gave up a lucrative practice to become Superintendent of Studs, and his duties were to reorganize the Breeding Studs of Bengal. Since the year 1793 India had been endeavouring to raise a type of horse suitable for Cavalry and Artillery purposes, and to this end all three Presidencies kept their own Studs. From the first their experiments were doomed to failure, as they were conducted by military officers ignorant of the subject. In Madras and Bombay they failed early and signally; in Bengal a similar total failure was averted only by Moorcroft's arrival with very large powers. He succeeded in producing a class of animal very superior to the original product, but felt convinced that no permanent improvement could be effected until he had secured the right breed of sire. He had rejected the Arab and the English horse as not producing the type at which he was aiming. He believed that the animal he required could be found in Central Asia, and thither he went in 1819. He had then been eleven years in India. He had trained a doctor as an assistant (Surgeon Gibb), and had made great progress in the suppression of contagious diseases, demonstrating what veterinary science could accomplish in this direction. At this time the veterinary care of the horses of the Indian Army was in the hands of native practitioners.[1] We cannot enter into the dramatic history of Moorcroft's life, excepting to say that from the journey to Central Asia in 1819 he never returned, and in time it was learnt that he had been murdered near Bokhara in 1825. For seven years from the time of his departure the Government of Bengal kept his appointment open, with Dr. Gibb in charge, but as soon as definite tidings of his death were obtained, Moorcroft's breeding establishments were, in 1826, returned to the control of their original incompetent superintendents, inexperi-

[1] Not so the veterinary care of British Cavalry regiments serving in India. These were furnished with duly qualified officers from home. See p. 54.

enced infantry and cavalry officers, and Dr. Gibb disappeared. This is not the place to give an account of the fortunes of the Studs during the succeeding half-century. The product was the laughing-stock of the Army and the despair of the East India Company. Not once or twice after a clean sweep of the various establishments was a fresh start made, but always under the same incompetent management. From first to last the Studs cost millions; the mismanagement was staggering and unbelievable, and the story of the repeated costly failures reads like a page of extravagant fiction.[1]

We take up the subject of their veterinary administration again at the year 1832, when even the East India Company had got tired of the terrible losses from disease, and insisted upon Veterinary Surgeons forming part of the staff of the various depots. None had been inside the Studs for six years!

But we have first to learn how the Indian Veterinary Service was formed, and much of its early history may be gleaned from an article written by J. T. Hodgson in Vol. X. of the *Veterinarian* (1837).[2] Hodgson was the first Veterinary Officer to enter the Indian Army (Moorcroft was a civilian); he joined the Company's service on 29th May 1826, but he tells us that he was in the Stud at Hissar in 1821, and refers to Moorcroft as if he had met him. In his work on the Foot he says he was at Hissar in 1815 or 1816, in which case he probably met Moorcroft. He does not tell us how he found his way to India, perhaps in charge of horses for the Government Studs, as fresh animals were sent out every season. However that may be, Hodgson was engaged in India by the Bengal Government, and prior to his regular appointment to the Bengal Army, was appointed to the Governor-General's Bodyguard at Calcutta in March 1821. Here he was directed to train eight Assistant Apothecaries, half-caste Indians, as Veterinary Surgeons for the troops of the Bengal Army. When these men were qualified, they were to be promoted Sub-Assistant Veterinary Surgeons, with the pay and allowances of an Apothecary.

Hodgson says that in May 1822 he warned the Bengal authorities their scheme would not work, and that something similar

---

[1] The India Office has been good enough to grant me every facility for examining the records and correspondence connected with the Indian Studs from 1793–1873.

[2] The title of the communication is: *Observations on the Veterinary Establishment at present in India, with a plan of amendment, presented to the Honble. Court of East India Directors and to Edward Coleman Esq., Professor, in 1824.*

had been tried at home in 1796 in endeavouring to convert the army farrier into a Veterinarian. Nevertheless he was directed to carry out the arrangement and zealously co-operate with the wishes of the authorities. The scheme came to nothing, though in the Bengal Army List for 1st August 1823 three Sub-Assistant Veterinary Surgeons are shown on the Establishment of the Army. On 5th August 1823 Hodgson submitted to the Government of India a scheme for an organized veterinary service for India. This the Government sent to the *Medical Board* of Bengal, which expressed the opinion that a few regularly educated Veterinary Surgeons might be usefully employed in the manner indicated by Hodgson; with this view the Government entirely coincided. It would appear that Hodgson was not satisfied, for he says that on 20th November 1823 he again submitted his scheme, of which he now gives a synopsis.

The East India Company was to have a professor at the London School, who should deliver a course of lectures to candidates for the Indian Service on the Breeding, Rearing, Management, and Diseases of Horses, Cattle and Camels, and Shoeing, so that prior to proceeding to India they should have some knowledge of their duties. To these lectures the Company's civil, military and medical servants were to be admitted should they desire to attend. Hodgson considered this system preferable to that adopted by Coleman of lecturing to the cadets at Woolwich. As regards the organization of the Veterinary Service in India, he proposed an officer on the General Staff of the Army in India as Principal Veterinary Surgeon; similarly an officer to the forces in the Presidencies of Bengal, Madras and Bombay, and an administrative officer to each Division; in addition, executive officers to Brigades of Horse Artillery, Regiments of Cavalry, the Studs and other departments of the Army possessing animals. He provided for sickness and death by having supernumerary officers on the spot. He drew up tables of Pay and Allowances, Promotion, Leave, Pensions, also Veterinary Regulations, and dealt with the Supply of Veterinary Stores, Portable Forges and Horse Shoes. The statement which follows is a little confusing, but reading between the lines it would appear that Hodgson's astonishingly advanced and complete scheme was not entirely the work of a civilian, as he then was, but that he was in possession of a plan for reorganizing the "Veterinary Department" of the Home Army, which was drawn up by "Veterinary Surgeon Percivall of the Royal Artillery." William Percivall must have supplied Hodgson with a copy of his projected work on the reorganization of the profession, both civil and military. This book, though advertised in 1823, was never published, for what reason we do not know, but conjecture that it offended Coleman.[1] The Government of India informed Hodgson that it did not feel competent to decide on the merits of his scheme, " which with the projected work of Veterinary Surgeon Percivall would more properly come under the consideration of the Authorities at Home, to whom it was to be submitted on that gentleman's (Hodgson's) arrival in Europe." We have had to construct the above from Hodgson's obscure account; it is quite certain, as will appear later, that he was in London in 1824 and handed over the scheme to Coleman. There is nothing I can find in the Records of the India Office to show that Coleman forwarded the proposals to the East India Company.

The Bengal Government having failed to provide a half-caste veterinary service for India, there was no help but to draw on England. In 1827 twelve Veterinary Surgeons went out for the Indian Army, in 1828 thirteen; subsequently they were supplied as casualties occurred. The establishment for the three Presidencies in 1832 was thirty-one officers. All of these men were doubtless selected by Mr. John Field of the 2nd Life Guards (see p. 96); this officer purchased all the horses for India, also the stores, and it was only when he was on his death-bed in 1833 that the Veterinary College, in the person of Professor Sewell, was appointed to inspect supplies and select candidates. This appointment explains the announcement made by Sir Astley Cooper alluded to at p. 96.

The Regulations subsequently drawn up for the working of the Indian Veterinary Service were undoubtedly compiled in India; they were satisfactory excepting in respect of administrative officers. None were appointed, not even a Principal Veterinary Surgeon. As a consequence the officers had no channel of their own through which they could ventilate a grievance professional or military; all such representations had to be made through the Superintending Surgeon of the Division! Hodgson, writing in the *Veterinarian* for January 1854, p. 11, says: " A Principal Veterinary Surgeon was in the draft of the Veterinary Department given by me to the late Principal Veterinary Surgeon Coleman in 1825 [he

[1] The title of the work was: *Observations on the Constitution, Economy and Defects of the Veterinary Department of Great Britain, accompanied with plans of amendment*, addressed with all due submission and respect to the President, Vice-Presidents, Subscribers and Members of the Veterinary College.

probably means 1824]. Why the nomination did not happen I am unable to explain." We do not think it difficult of explanation; there was only room for one Principal Veterinary Surgeon in the British Empire. The Veterinary Department of India remained without an official head or a single administrative officer for forty years!

From vol. 31 of the *Veterinarian* (1858) we learn something of the professional life of the young Veterinary Officer of the East India Company. He began by taking the oath of allegiance before the Chairman and Court at the India House. He received a sum of money for his passage, and drew pay from the date of arrival in India. He was first posted as an Assistant Veterinary Surgeon under a senior officer to learn his military and professional duties, and when reported fit he was examined by a Board for his final acceptance by the Company. The Board consisted of the *Senior Medical Officer* of the Station, together with a second medical officer, *assisted* by a Veterinary Surgeon![1] In this arrangement the influence of Astley Cooper and Coleman may be traced; this was the St. Pancras system. In the *Veterinarian* for 1863, vol. 36, p. 346, is given an amusing account of one of the examinations, and of the despair of the President at having to examine on subjects of which he was utterly ignorant.

We have now sketched in outline the organization of the Indian Veterinary Service from its beginning in 1826, and must glance at its work at the various depots of the Stud, after the East India Company had insisted, in 1832, that Veterinary Surgeons should be appointed.

The Superintendents of the various depots were opposed to veterinary aid; for six years they had repelled every attempt to bring in professional advice, and when finally they were compelled to accept it, a set of ingenious regulations were drawn up by the Stud Authorities to neutralize this assistance. These regulations muzzled the Veterinary Officers; they were forbidden to interfere with the Stud management, and ordered to confine their attention to disease and injuries. Nevertheless, so gross were the abuses, that the bolder spirits did raise objections, but were always instructed to mind their own business, and that if advice in management were required it would be asked. There was much to conceal and much to be ashamed of, but the Veterinary

[1] I have not seen the Bengal Regulations on this subject, but those of Madras, dated 1849, state that the Examining Committee is to consist of one Medical Officer and one, or if possible, two Veterinary Surgeons.

officers having no administrative head, had no means of suggesting reforms; the only person to whom representations could be made was the man who had issued instructions that none were to be offered! Peculation and irregularities were rife, especially among the natives; even the officers of the Stud came under suspicion.

How was it possible for any self-respecting man to work on without protest, while he saw young stock, never exercised, tied up to bamboo poles from yearlings until four years old? At that age those which had failed to withstand this system, as indicated by their fetlocks nearly touching the ground, were sold as useless to the Service. Further, a herd of dairy cows was at one time kept to supply milk for the yearlings. These are only two instances from a catalogue of appalling mismanagement.

It was to one of these Depots (Hauper) that J. T. Hodgson was appointed. Later trouble arose. Charges and recriminations preferred by the officers of that establishment against each other resulted in an official investigation; the Superintendent of the Depot was removed to another Depot, one of his assistants was returned to his regiment and another transferred; one Veterinary Surgeon was transferred, while Hodgson was brought to a Court Martial and dismissed the Service on 20th July 1834. The Court recommended that provision be made for Mr. Hodgson, "as that individual is labouring under symptoms of insanity." I have seen the charges on which he was tried. He alleged against various officers of the Stud neglect of duty, misappropriation of public money, and rewards for false testimony. There is little doubt from the subsequent history of the Studs that these charges were largely justified; in fact, the Superintendent who was chiefly concerned was subsequently removed from his second appointment for "incapacity." However, by this method of dealing with Hodgson the military authorities effectually sealed the lips of the Veterinary Officers with the Studs; there were no more complaints, though everything went on as before. Some years later a combatant officer of the Studs endeavoured to represent to the Bengal authorities its evil organization. He was severely punished, his promotion being stopped.

J. T. Hodgson has already been alluded to at p. 75 when as a pupil of Mr. H. C. Coward, Veterinary Surgeon to the Ordnance, he accompanied the latter, in a civil capacity, as assistant when Coward went to the Peninsula, where he served in the Corunna Campaign. Hodgson returned to England in 1809 and continued his studies with Coward. He qualified in 1814 and in 1815 went to India. He here held a civil appointment for five years in the cattle and camel breeding establishment at Hissar, and in March 1821, according to his own account, was appointed Veterinary Surgeon to the Governor-General's Bodyguard. His appointment to the Indian Army is dated 29th May 1826, and he was the senior officer on that list. He published in 1824 a work on *The Foot of the Horse, deduced Mathematically from the Structure and Function of the Hoof.* It is a remarkable book, though one never seems to fathom what lessons Hodgson wishes to convey. As this work was published in London, and as he advertises in it a proposed course of lectures on the art of preserving and defending the foot of the horse, it is evident he was at home in 1824. This would account for the statement on p. 100 that he gave Coleman a draft of the Regulations for India. He, however, returned to India and took up the army appointment of 1826. On his return home, after the events above narrated, he became a contributor to the *Veterinarian* for some years. Some of his articles are impossible to understand; the editors could scarcely have known of his previous history in India or they would have been more careful in scrutinizing his manuscript. Nevertheless, Hodgson was unquestionably an able man.

We learn nothing of the pay of the Indian Veterinary Service until we come to the *Veterinarian* for May 1834, in which J. Skeavington, who served as Veterinary Surgeon Bengal Horse Artillery, published a paper on the subject. The first scale of pay was laid down on 6th September 1826. The writer gives every detail of pay and allowances, and shows that an officer received for the first three years of his service the equivalent of nearly 24s. a day. The pay was identical with the pay at home, it was the allowances which made the difference. Several papers on the subject appeared subsequently, which showed that when all his necessary expenses were set against his income the officer had very little left to support his position.

Skeavington does not deal with contract and extra duty pay. In 1826 the medicines, etc., were supplied by the East India Company's Medical Stores at Calcutta on repayment by the Commanding Officer out of his contract allowance; but later, the date I do not know, the Veterinary Officer drew the contract money and repaid the Stores. The amount of the contract was two annas a month for each horse and one rupee for every charger. The medicines, etc., were purchased from the Medical Stores at wholesale English prices, and a liberal margin of profit resulted. Extra duty pay was drawn when an officer had in addition to his own charge the veterinary care of other units. The rate was

Rs. 12.7 for every hundred horses belonging to the extra charge in addition to the usual allowance for medicine.

In June 1834 a discussion began in the *Veterinarian* on the much-vaunted system of Ventilation introduced into military stables by Coleman. Two points have to be remembered, namely, that the earlier stables were never ventilated, ventilation being regarded as pernicious, and that until about the time Coleman took office there were no barracks or stables for the troops in the United Kingdom. Regiments were split up into detachments, stationed at considerable distances apart, the men and horses being billeted. The year 1792 saw a change, and barracks for the men with stabling for the horses were begun in many places such as Woolwich, Dover and other military centres.[1] These buildings were all erected by a certain Barrack Master General, ambitious and unscrupulous, who finally came to grief. But before this occurred a large number of barracks had been erected, and it would appear from statements made by Coleman in his lectures that the stables were built unventilated. As a consequence diseases were common and frequently fatal.[2] The high mortality had the effect of causing attention to be directed to ventilation, and Coleman, as may be remembered (p. 80), referred to his experiments on the subject, and the amount he was out of pocket in making observations. Nowhere, however, does he describe his system, but in 1834 an account of it is given by Mr. Karkeek of Truro, a practitioner of great learning and professional ability. He tells us that he took down Coleman's lectures in shorthand, and these he reproduces. Above the manger and opposite the nostrils was a hole in the wall $2'' \times 3''$ or $3'' \times 4''$ which, of course, communicated with the outside air. At the bottom of the wall close to the flooring were holes, the number and size of which are not stated. Coleman designed the lower holes as inlets, and those opposite the nostrils as *outlets*. Karkeek states that notwithstanding Coleman's views, the holes opposite to the nostrils are inlets. He, therefore, recommends another system free from direct draught, placing the inlets close to the floor and the outlets near the ceiling, as far as possible from

---

[1] See an admirable paper on "Early Cavalry Barracks," by C. R. B. Barrett, *Cavalry Journal*, vol. vii., p. 161, 1912.

[2] Nowhere does Coleman refer to the fact that several years before he appeared at the Veterinary College, James Clark, of Edinburgh, the leading veterinary practitioner of the day, had forcibly drawn attention to the subject of unventilated stables and the evils arising from them. See *History of Veterinary Literature*, vol. ii.

PLATE D

the nostrils, the inlets and outlets to be made oblique. When owing to the arrangement of the buildings it was not possible to obtain fresh air close to the ground, Karkeek admitted it above and carried it down to floor level by means of tubes. This is the system of ventilation generally attributed to Coleman, whereas we now know it was that of Karkeek of Truro.

In the September *Veterinarian* of 1834, Brett, Veterinary Surgeon 12th Lancers, has another system for the ventilation of stables. His method, where ground inlets were impossible, was to run a wooden shaft 2 feet square the whole length of the stable under the manger at the floor level. The shaft was open at both ends and communicated with each stall by means of an upright shaft 7 or 8 feet high. Additional air inlets could be constructed by carrying a shaft at right angles to the original one beneath the floor, and letting it open into the pillar or heel post supporting the stall partitions. Obviously this could only be intended for officers' stables, as all troop stables from the earliest times have, as a measure of economy, been constructed with bails. Where no difficulty existed in obtaining fresh air directly from outside, Brett employed as inlets a 2-foot tube (for each horse ?) opening outwards near the ground level, and an opening in the stall some distance above the horse's head. All outlets were through tubes in the ceiling, one for each horse, running through the men's rooms above. Brett states that the R.E. officer who is building the stables at Manchester proposes if possible to introduce this system of ventilation. We draw attention to it as a notable improvement on Coleman's somewhat crude arrangement, which would have been all right had the holes opposite the nostrils always been outlets. On the contrary, they must have always been inlets, and hence the great outcry against his system of draughty stables. It will be observed that both Karkeek's and Brett's systems of supplying fresh air and getting rid of foul have been employed under other names in the ventilation of dwelling rooms.

At the end of the year 1834 there occurred in India a case of two Lieutenants of a Native Cavalry Regiment striking a Veterinary Officer and attempting to throw him out of a window. Both officers were tried by G.C.M. and dismissed the Service.

In February 1838 the first paper on battle wounds was published. It is true these had rarely been omitted from works dealing with the injuries of horses since the days of the immortal Blundeville, but the writers were without any practical knowledge and generally made extracts from observations on human surgery. Now, however, we have an account by a member of our own body who had made the most of his opportunities in the field. J. S. Beech was Veterinary Surgeon to the Anglo-Spanish Legion which was despatched to Portugal in 1835. He writes on *Gunshot, Sabre, Lance and Other Wounds* in the eleventh volume of the *Veterinarian*, and an admirable communication it is. His style of writing and method of drawing conclusions from his material reminds us of the " Commentaries " of Guthrie, the great surgeon of the Peninsula War. Beech examined his cases post mortem. He noted in the case of a bullet wound of the intestines and diaphragm that though only a few hours had elapsed between injury and death, the four holes in the intestine were partly closed by lymph. I am not aware of any such precise records before or since his day on the subject of war wounds, and it is regrettable that we never meet with him again. There is an editorial by Youatt in the same number, referring to Beech's communication with great satisfaction, and stating that though numerically the Army Veterinary Service represents only a small portion of the profession, "it is a class deservedly respected, and on whose character and bearing our general acceptance and repute greatly depends."

The only other notice of wounds at this period, which I have come across, occurs nine years later. J. Purves of the Indian Service refers in 1847[1] to the gunshot wounds, "fearful" sabre cuts, round and grape-shot wounds, he saw in "the various hospitals of the Army" during the Punjab Campaign, and he trusts that those who had these cases under treatment will record them—a pious but unfulfilled hope. Excepting a few isolated though notable records we had to wait until 1896 for a large group of cases from the pen of the late Veterinary Lieutenant-Colonel Rayment.[2]

In the June issue of the *Veterinarian*, 1838, appears an article on *Cavalry Statistics*, copied from No. 335 of the *Edinburgh Medical and Surgical Journal*. The regiment is described as one of Heavy Cavalry, and the period over which the observations extended was eight years (1830-37). The mortality was 2·8 per cent., the castings 8·3 per cent. The chief cause of death was pulmonary trouble. There were three cases of farcy and six of glanders. Of the 168 animals cast no less than twenty-two were got rid of for blindness.

---

[1] *Veterinary Record*, vol. iii., January, 1847.
[2] *Veterinary Journal*, vol. 42, p. 32.

This was the first time that any precise statistics of the health of army horses had been published, and it is unfortunate that the name of the author is unknown. I suggest it was H. Hallen of the Inniskilling Dragoons.

In the same number, June 1838, is an editorial announcing that the graduates of the Veterinary College, Edinburgh, were in future to be admitted to the Services, both British and Indian, " subject, as all candidates for that honour have hitherto been, to the Veterinary Surgeons General of the British and Indian Cavalry being satisfied as to their competence." As there had never been a Veterinary Surgeon General of the British, not to mention the Indian Cavalry, it is a matter of speculation whether Youatt was merely being facetious at the expense of Sewell, who, as we saw at p. 100, had been appointed to represent the India House in the matter of Studs. Youatt adds that now the barrier is broken down he " cannot suppose that any unfair preference will be shown " as between the London and Edinburgh candidates. Dick, writing to Youatt the following year, February 1839 (see p. 169, *Veterinarian*), tells him this salutary change was arranged with the War Office by the President of the Highland and Agricultural Society. He does not feel too confident that his men will be fairly treated, and says that it always requires some degree of interest to obtain an appointment.

From the Memoir attached to the *Veterinary Papers of Professor Dick* we learn that the opposition to the admission into the Army of graduates of the Edinburgh School was overcome in April 1838, but it must have been a long fight, as Dick's memorial on the question is dated January 1836. Up to the time of Coleman's death, July 1839, no candidate from the northern school succeeded in obtaining admission. Dick had judged correctly; there was little probability that Coleman would pass over his own pupils and allow those from Edinburgh to be appointed.

Within a month of Coleman's death Dick addressed a letter to the Commander-in-Chief urging that an impartial judge of candidates for commissions in the Veterinary Service be appointed, and suggesting that some neutral person, unconnected with either school, be made Principal Veterinary Surgeon to the Army. The correspondence is given in full in the Memoir quoted, also the reply of the Military Secretary a month later, in which the Commander-in-Chief personally nominated a student of the Edinburgh School for a commission provided he was reported qualified by the Principal Veterinary Surgeon. By this time Cherry had been appointed P.V.S., and he and William Percivall examined and passed the first candidate from the Edinburgh School—James Robertson.

In the *Veterinarian* for 1839, vol. xii., p. 276, evidence of the awakening of the Army Veterinary Service is afforded by a paper which we have already mentioned in another connection, entitled *Hints to Veterinary Surgeons entering the Army regarding their conduct, duties, etc.*, by J. W. Gloag, 10th Hussars. This officer belonged to the new school of thought. He was ambitious that his Service should take up its true position, but felt that, scattered as they were over the face of the globe, it was impossible to bring officers together for a discussion of their status. He also recognized that it was easier to get an improved standard adopted by the young than by the old, and therefore addressed himself to those about to enter. No instructions existed for the young officer on entering, and his total lack of knowledge of military matters placed him from the first at a grave disadvantage. Gloag's advice on conduct is admirable, and might still be issued to new entrants, for wisdom never grows old. When men are placed under definite and rigid restrictions and are performing the same class of duties over and over again, even on lines widely separated by time and space, the same circumstances and difficulties arise. Throughout life Gloag acted up to the standard he set when still a young man, and the writer, who never met him, well remembers that his name and reputation as a great gentleman long survived him, and were common subjects of discussion forty years ago. Having advised the young officer of the line he should adopt in dealing with others and in moulding his own life, he reviews his position in the Army, and gives advice respecting military command, arrest, punishment, and other details, a knowledge of which were and are of the greatest importance on joining. He explains that relative rank confers status in the choice of quarters, distribution of prize money, or allowances of any kind, but confers no military authority, though a veterinary officer may order a man to be confined. Then follows an account of the rates of pay and retired or half pay, which have previously appeared at pp. 60, 93. Forage for two horses was allowed on payment of $8\frac{1}{2}$d. a day for each horse.[1] Field allowance (but not in India) was granted at the following rates: Subalterns 9d. a day,

---

[1] The Veterinary Officer of Horse Artillery and Cavalry had to pay for the forage for his chargers as long as the regimental system lasted. In all other arms forage was a free issue.

Captains 3s. 6d. In the field there was a free issue of Forage, and Rations were supplied at a charge of 2½d. per ration.

Gloag next deals with the Farriers' Department (see p. 10).

Every farrier when mounted was to be in possession of a phleme, blood stick, two linen bandages, some tow, and a clyster apparatus carried in a holster. Each troop had a chest of prepared veterinary medicines, with the use of which every farrier was expected to be well acquainted. Every soldier carried four shoes and a set of nails, which were regularly used up and replaced. Every Troop Sergeant-Major was in possession of three sets of shoeing tools. All regiments were expected to have six men per troop able to put on a shoe. Every Farrier and Assistant Farrier had to be expert in nail making (note the designation Assistant Farrier; there were no Shoeing Smiths in Cavalry in those days: see p. 13). When a farrier was ordered punishment the shoeing of his troop was taken from him and given to the senior assistant.

Full instructions are given in stable duties, watering and feeding. The horses received in barracks, hay 12 pounds, corn 10 pounds, straw 8 pounds, but on the line of march, hay 18 pounds and corn 8 pounds! Ventilation, exercise, stable vices, are all dealt with, and instructions given in the preparation of returns and record of cases. What to do in the event of an outbreak of disease is discussed, and the young officer is told *inter alia* to consult if necessary with a civil practitioner, whose fee will be paid by the War Office.

Then follow the parade and health inspection of horses, duties on the line of march, care and management of remounts; selection of remounts, though he observes that the Veterinary Officer's duties are confined to examining for soundness. He notes in passing that in Ireland the number of horses suffering from cataract is immense. Lastly comes the hospital, and the diseases most commonly found. He is most impressive in urging on the young practitioner not to bleed unless absolutely necessary, this at a time when the belief in bleeding as a necessary part of all treatment was universally held, and every farrier carried a phleme with him to the field! He feels so strongly on this matter that he repeats his advice. Coming to glanders, he advises how to act when a case occurs, and says the disease is very common in Ireland. His disinfectant was chlorinated lime, a great improvement on Coleman's instructions. Finally he directs the young officer how a horse should be destroyed by shooting, and advises him always to have a second pistol at hand, loaded, in case of an accident.

Apart from the intrinsic value of Gloag's paper (and the advice given is golden), we have here a unique opportunity of seeing our Service precisely as it was in 1838. What immediately strikes us is that in spite of Coleman's neglect of the Service for which he was responsible, a neglect intensified for years by increasing age and physical infirmity, the Department had from within evolved its own high ideals of its duties and responsibilities, and was countering the indifference of its Chief by disseminating these for the benefit of all. We must not forget that at this time, and for forty years after, our Department was on a regimental basis, and our officers seldom saw each other unless their regiments met on the line of march when changing stations;[1] each lived and worked in his own narrow regimental cell, and each had to map out for himself his official as well as his private life. There was no administrative officer other than Coleman, and in latter years he was frequently so unfit as to be unable to deliver his course of lectures at the College, so that his regimental inspections, *which were only made at request*, must have been few and far between.[2] There was no stimulus save regimental, and whether that was present or absent depended entirely on the commanding officer, who it must be remembered did not come and go as in the present day, but purchased his regiment and remained practically for life. If he happened to be a man who took no interest, his officers could not escape the deadening influence of such an administration. No praise is too great for those officers of our Service who, alive to its possibilities, sought to raise the standard of efficiency, and advance the highest ideals of social and pro-

---

[1] For forty years after Waterloo only the bare skeleton of a standing army was maintained in this country. The regiments were widely scattered performing police duties; they were untrained to operate with other arms, in fact, rarely or never saw them. There were no large military centres excepting the Artillery centre at Woolwich, which under the oppressive hand of the Duke of Wellington was finally reduced to impotence. The non-militarists of this country, as active then as now, had settled among themselves there would be no more wars; international unity, peace and concord had been secured. No improvements were desired in armament, training, or equipment by the fossils who formed the Staff of the Army; the whole machine was moribund, the only things which showed no loss of vitality were pipeclay and bath-brick.

[2] In the *Veterinarian* for September 1830 it is urged that the Principal Veterinary Surgeon, and not the Inspecting General Officer, was the proper person to furnish replies to the veterinary questions contained in the Inspection Reports of regiments.

fessional conduct. Even had Coleman been young and blessed with enthusiasm and energy, it must never be forgotten that he was a civilian pure and simple, who had never done a day's soldiering in his life, and for that reason alone was incapable of leading and directing. At the point we have reached in this history his days were numbered, and the Department was about to enter on a new and improved phase.

On the 14th July 1839, Edward Coleman died at the age of seventy-three, having been Principal Veterinary Surgeon to the Cavalry for forty-three years! No further notice of his career is necessary here; his life work so far as the Army is concerned is contained in the foregoing pages. We have referred to his inordinate love of money and the large sums gained by him from his position. He died worth £47,000.[1]

[1] *Veterinarian*, vol. xvi., November 1843.

CHAPTER IV

Administration under Cherry and Wilkinson, 1839–1876

The question of a successor to Coleman as P.V.S. Cavalry was at once taken up. Fortunately the correspondence on this question has been preserved and is in the Public Record Office, W. O. 43/90055, so that we know with absolute exactitude all that occurred.

The opening minute of this correspondence begins:

"Mr. Coleman the P.V.S. is dead, and as it was Sir John Hobhouse's intention, when this event should happen, to place the veterinary department under the Army Medical Board, it is proper to state the origin of the duties of this office."

There follows an account of Coleman's appointment, his pay, emoluments (contract), and duties from 1796. "It has always been considered that the Cavalry have derived great advantage from his skill and attentive superintendence. In 1832 his pay was raised from 9s. 6d. to 20s., but he was deprived of any profits from the supply of medicines.

"When this change was made in his pay it was the intention of the then Secretary at War that when he died or retired, the duty he performed should devolve upon the Army Medical Board; that the medicines should be supplied in the same manner as the medicines for the Army, and that the vacancies of Veterinary Surgeons should be filled up by the nomination of the Director General, upon certificate that the candidate had studied at the Veterinary College and had passed his examinations there satisfactorily. This would throw the whole duty and responsibility upon the Army Medical Board. The question now to be decided is whether Mr. Coleman's vacancy is to be filled up or not? It appears to me that there is a considerable advantage in having the judgement of the Professor of the Veterinary College both in the selection of the most competent persons to fill the situations of Veterinary Surgeons and in controlling the supply and the expenditure of medicines. There is also a security in employing a professor of the Veterinary College that the most approved mode of erecting and ventilating stables will be adopted, and there is further a considerable advantage, in the constant intercourse and occasional supervision of the Professor of the College, which would I fear be almost if not entirely lost by entrusting these duties to the Army Medical Board, who have considerations so much more important to attend to. If upon these grounds it should be deemed advisable to maintain the appointment of P.V.S., the person who may succeed Mr. Coleman as Professor of the Veterinary College would appear to be the person more properly marked out for the duties required, than any other, even to the exclusion of the Veterinary Surgeons of the Army. In time of peace these duties are not very laborious although important, and it might be sufficient to allow at first 10s. a day or £200 a year, instead of the £365 which Mr. Coleman, who had served the public for 43 years, received."

There is no signature or initial to this opening minute; it is written by one of the leading Civil officials in order to bias future suggestions. One thing is very clear: he was working for Professor Sewell to become Principal Veterinary Surgeon. He was also well aware that another civil official intended, if possible, to hand the Veterinary Department over to the Army Medical Board.

On the above minute are two marginal notes; in one the writer states that he knows nothing of the intention to place the Veterinary Department under the Army Medical Board, and fails to see why the Director General of that Service should be a proper person to select. This note is initialled, but the initials cannot be deciphered. The second note, initialled " H " (Lord Howick), says that he has spoken to Lord Fitzroy Somerset on the subject, "who will bring the question officially before me. I am adverse to the abolition of the appointment."

Then comes a letter from Lord Fitzroy Somerset, Military Secretary to the Commander-in-Chief, Lord Hill;[1] it is dated Horse Guards, August 12th, 1839. " The appointment of Veterinary Surgeon General (*sic*) having become vacant by the decease of Mr. Coleman, and the General Commanding in Chief being of opinion that it would be desirable that it should be filled by a Veterinary Surgeon who has had considerable experience in the Service, I am directed by Lord Hill to request to be informed of the rate of pay which the officer who might be selected for the situation would be entitled to receive. His Lordship is induced to make this enquiry, having understood that the pay granted to Mr. Coleman some few years ago was special and not to be given as a matter of course to his successor."

Next comes a second unsigned minute:

" Lord Fitzroy Somerset on the part of Lord Hill desires to know what pay will be allowed to the P.V.S. if that appointment be maintained. It is necessary for the consideration of this question that the Secretary at War should be informed that the General Commanding in

[1] Lord Hill was the soldier's friend; a gentle, humane man very different in disposition from the Duke of Wellington.

Chief has in contemplation to recommend an old Army Veterinary Surgeon for the appointment. It has been anticipated that a professor of the Veterinary College would succeed Mr. Coleman, in which case pay at 10s. a day would be very proper; if on the other hand the appointment is to be made a reward for the Veterinary Surgeons of the Army, it must be paid at least at the present rate of 20s. a day. Mr. Dick, whose letter has been sent to the Under Secretary at War, is a professor in Edinburgh. He strongly contends for the propriety of appointing a neutral person having no connection with the Veterinary Colleges, to ensure a fair distribution of the patronage, his belief being that Mr. Coleman had it all. This, however, Lord Fitzroy Somerset informs me was not the case, but that Lord Hill continually selected persons for the commissions from the recommendations of the Colonels of Cavalry Regiments. It was usual to send these persons before the Veterinary College for examination, but Mr. Coleman had nothing further to do with their appointment than to certify to their qualifications. The professor of the Veterinary College might still continue the supply of the medicines."

Written as a marginal note against the last paragraph of this minute, in handwriting which has not previously appeared, is this unsigned opinion:

" The Service would, it is conceived, be benefited both in respect of encouragement to the soldier and of the care of horses of detachments, by throwing these appointments open to the Regiment. It may be premature to look to any considerable increase of the Cavalry Force, but whenever it does take place there will be a large demand for veterinary proficients. If the time were more favourable for augmenting the number of non-commissioned officers, a Farrier Sergeant in each regiment might not be an ineligible appointment. He would be a sort of Assistant Veterinary Surgeon, and I am not aware that there is at present any regular provision for the case of the Veterinary Surgeon in sickness."

It would be interesting to know who this reactionary individual was; no doubt one of the permanent civil staff of the War Office. His suggestion appears to be to train men regimentally as Farrier Sergeants, and appoint them to veterinary duties as vacancies occur !

A minute by Lord Howick ends the question on lines which quite evidently had been prearranged between him and Lord Hill. He entirely approves " that the appointment should be given to a Veterinary Surgeon of the Army, if one properly qualified can be found. Whether a real injustice results or not, there is a very just objection to placing the head of one particular Veterinary College in a situation which, in appearance at least, must give him considerable influence upon the choice of candidates for employment. . . . The pay should be continued as at present, 20s. a day."

This decision is conveyed to the Commander-in-Chief, who is informed that the appointment is to be considered as a reward for service, to be granted to an Army Veterinary Surgeon, the pay to be 20s. a day.

We have therefore to thank Lords Hill and Howick and Professor Dick for securing the appointment of Principal Veterinary Surgeon for an Army Veterinary Officer, and the entire exclusion of the London or any other Veterinary School. In the September number of the *Veterinarian* for 1839, Youatt is enthusiastic over a soldier being appointed P.V.S., Mr. F. C. Cherry, a man of wide military experience. The College, he says, can know nothing of Army requirements. He further suggests a Board to examine candidates for the Army, of which the P.V.S. should be President; this was subsequently adopted.

It is perfectly evident from the foregoing that the appointment of a successor to Coleman was the occasion of a great deal of wire-pulling. Personally we suspect the civil heads of the War Office for pressing the Medical and Farrier Sergeant schemes, but we must not lose sight of Sir Astley Cooper. He was determined to keep the veterinary profession in a subordinate position, and as a Governor of the London School had opposed every step towards advancement. His professional position was of the highest, and brought him into contact with the most influential men of the day; it would be in accordance with his policy to hold the opinion that now Coleman was gone the Army Veterinary Service would be best regulated by the Army Medical Board, with Coleman's successor at St. Pancras, Sewell, as its veterinary adviser! The necessary evidence is wanting, but when we consider his attitude towards our profession for over forty years the assumption is fair.

Frederick Clifford Cherry (1779–1854), the new Principal Veterinary Surgeon, joined the Service on 28th June 1803 and was gazetted to the 11th Dragoons. With the Waggon Train he served under Sir John Moore in the Corunna Campaign, and later was present at Salamanca and Vittoria; he took part in the disastrous Walcheren Expedition, and was at the Battle of Waterloo. On the reduction of the Army after Waterloo he was placed on half pay 25th September 1819. He went into private practice at Clapham and as a practitioner had few equals. Two of his sons entered the profession, both received a medical as well as a veterinary education, and like the father both were very able men. One son, "A. H.," joined the Royal Dragoons and died in the Crimea;

the other, "W. A.," went into practice in London. He wrote some able papers, took up the cause of the College Charter very warmly, and was as warmly opposed by his father, who was on the side of Professor Dick and against the Charter (see p. 124 *infra*).

F. C. Cherry published in 1820 a six-page pamphlet entitled *On the Treatment of Horses' Feet*. In 1825 a two-page pamphlet bearing the title *On the Treatment of Horses' Feet in the Stable*. In this he introduced to the public his patent felt footpads, which took the place of clay stopping. In 1829 he published an article on *Broken Knees and their Treatment by Operation*. This describes the "Cherry operation," which was practised successfully during the late War. In 1830 appeared his translation of Solleysel on *The Art of Shoeing*, subsequently issued in book form in 1842 after he became Principal Veterinary Surgeon.[1] Finally there was a paper on *The Effects of Temperature on the Skin of Horses and Ventilation of Stables*. All Cherry's communications were written while on half-pay. After being on half-pay for fourteen years he returned to the Army on appointment to the 2nd Life Guards in 1833. The date of his promotion to P.V.S. is 17th September 1839. No tenure was mentioned; these were the days of life appointments, and it was not until thirty-seven years later that a time limit was assigned; Mr. Cherry held the appointment for fifteen years, dying in harness.

Cherry seldom spoke in public, but when he did he spoke his mind. On one occasion at the Annual Dinner of the profession, replying for the Army,[2] he said that for many years he had lived apart from the profession as things had occurred of which he disapproved. On succeeding to the appointment of P.V.S. to the Cavalry he had found affairs as *little organized* as they were when the Service was first created! He took credit for being instrumental in annulling contracts between the public and the late P.V.S. to the Cavalry, which he says were of a most injurious nature to the profession.[3] After a reference to some men striving for popularity, he concluded his short speech by saying, "Do your duty, it will be sure to bring you through in the long run." We are glad to have this glimpse into the character of Cherry. His writings we have noticed, and we have drawn attention elsewhere to his attacks on Coleman in conjunction with Bracy Clark. He gives us the impression of being a hard, stern, unrelenting, able man, possessing and acting up to high ideals; jealous of the reputation of his profession, both in and out of the Service, and prepared to safeguard its material interests. That he was right in his attitude towards the Edinburgh graduates is undoubted; his unpopularity in this country appears in

---

[1] The title page of the book shows him as having served with 2nd Life Guards, Royal Dragoons, 10th Hussars, 11th Dragoons, 12th Lancers and Royal Waggon Train. It also shows him as "Veterinary Surgeon to His late Majesty George IV. in Ireland." We think most of the above Cavalry appointments must have been of a temporary nature. The regiments to which he was gazetted were the 11th Dragoons, Royal Waggon Train, and 2nd Life Guards.

[2] *Veterinarian*, vol. xvii., April 1844.

[3] This refers to his articles in the *Hippiatrist* (see p. 88).

the first place to have been due to his advocacy of the Northern School, and later to his strange opposition to a Charter being granted the profession. Percivall (*Veterinarian*, vol. xvi., November 1843) says that under Cherry's administration a better type of man passed into the Army, that the door was closed against the incapable and characterless, and that Cherry would keep the military department of the profession sound. F. C. Cherry died at the age of seventy-five on 11th July 1854.

In the year 1845 the country was blessed in possessing a Secretary at War of a new type. Sidney Herbert (1810–1861),[1] younger son of the eleventh Earl of Pembroke,[2] then began the first of three distinct periods of office as War Minister. He was the wisest, ablest and most humane of all who had hitherto occupied that position, and the British soldier of all ranks owes him much. The country recognized his gifts, and his memory is perpetuated by his statue in Pall Mall. His first act on taking over office was to prepare a Warrant for improvement of the serving and retired pay of officers; in particular he recognized that the "Regimental Staff" (Adjutant, Paymaster, Surgeons, Veterinary Surgeon and Qr. Master)[3] had hitherto received very little attention. The entire correspondence on the Warrant is in the Public Record Office,[4] and many pages of it are in his handwriting. Having drawn up his scheme he sent it to an official in the War Office, in whom he had great confidence, for criticism and suggestions. His covering letter to him is dated 2nd October 1845; referring to the Regimental Staff he says: "I quite approve of the proposed scales of retirement. Will you draw up a draft of a letter to the Treasury, with which Board there may be perhaps some difficulty." Then follow detailed instructions on the framing of this letter as applicable to each class of officer; when he reaches the Veterinary Service he says:

"Of the Veterinary Surgeons, whose case rests on the value of their services, their increased skill and responsibility of late years, there being in their profession no upper grades or prospective advantages at all, and lastly (a great argument to a Financial Board) the small number."

It is the letter of a fair-minded man, anxious to do his best for the whole regimental staff; he consigns it to one who is "a master of the case that no one would do it better." The official

[1] Afterwards Lord Herbert of Lea.
[2] Consequently grandson to the "Patron Saint of the Troop Horse."
[3] There were no commissioned Riding Masters until 1855.
[4] W.O. 43/107730.

in question returns it with his remarks, and there follows a very long statement in Sidney Herbert's handwriting. One paragraph referring to the Staff Officers reads:

" The ranks may be divided into two classes, those that are, as it were, a separate profession, withdrawing the holder from the career and prospect of military promotion, and those that are of a temporary nature, a step in the course of military advancement, and leading therefore to further advantages. In the first class are the Paymasters, Qr. Masters and Veterinary Surgeons, in the second the Surgeon and the Adjutant. The claims of the first class are obviously the strongest. . . . The Veterinary Surgeon is a most valuable class of man, greatly improved in attainments of late years, but having had no increased advantage whatever. The number however is small, being limited to the small number of cavalry regiments. It is important that medical officers whether having the care of men or horses should not remain in their appointments after age shall have deprived their hand and eye of their quickness and certainty. I propose therefore a limited number of retirements, say five, on retired full pay, and I also propose to adopt Mr. Hanby's proposed scale of full and half pay with the exception of the last item."

The Mr. Hanby referred to gives a long statement of the conditions veterinary candidates have to comply with on entry, and the various warrants which had from time to time appeared. He refers to the warrants we have already quoted, and mentions one of the 1st October 1840, of which we had not previously heard, but which certainly does not differ from that of 1830. Reviewing the various warrants, he puts the case in a nutshell, pointing out that there has been no improvement in full pay for thirty-seven years, but that the half pay has twice been modified, and that, considering the important duties which the Veterinary Surgeon has to perform, the skill necessary, the influence his knowledge has from the point of view of finance, and the improved class of man who has entered in recent years, he considers there are abundant grounds for an increase of both full and retired pay. He gives the scale he suggests, and adds a list of serving officers of cavalry showing that only two or three would derive an immediate benefit; while for the majority the advantage would be prospective. Having some experience of War Office officials I regard this minute as the best example within my knowledge of an attitude as generous as it is rare. The Treasury, however, declined to agree to Sidney Herbert's proposals, but issued a Warrant applicable to the whole Army on 1st May 1846. The Veterinary Service was dealt with in para. 46; no increase in serving pay was given, but a small increase in retired pay. Officers above five and ten years' service obtained an increase of 6d. a day, above 20 years' service 1s. a day, and at 25 years' service 2s. The following are the rates:

If above 5 years' service, 5s. per diem.
,, ,, 10 ,, ,, 6s. ,, ,,
,, ,, 15 ,, ,, 7s. ,, ,,
,, ,, 20 ,, ,, 8s. ,, ,,
,, ,, 25 ,, ,, 10s. ,, ,,
,, ,, 30 ,, ,, 12s. ,, ,,

The Paymasters and Regimental Surgeons did much better, both being able to retire at 30 years' service on 15s. a day.

Behind the War Secretary in his fight for the regimental staff was an officer on the active list, Paymaster L. M. Prior, 12th Lancers, who had been constituted the " mouth-piece of his brother staff officers." He had interviews both with Sidney Herbert and the Treasury: his letters are in the file, and it is evident he did an immense amount of spade work; his strong advocacy of the Veterinary Service is notable.

In the correspondence we have just examined there is no evidence that Cherry had been consulted, but a month or two after the issue of the 1846 warrant we find him addressing the Secretary at War[1] in these terms: " Since I have been placed in the office which I have the honour to hold, numerous representations have been made to me respecting the disadvantages under which the Veterinary Surgeons in the Army are labouring, and my personal experience in a regimental capacity, with my subsequent opportunities for more extended observation, lead me to believe that these officers really stand in a very unfavourable position, and that it will be for the benefit of H.M. Service to make some changes." He then reviews the position and makes recommendations. He states the case of a widow, whose husband died with the relative rank of Captain after more than thirty years' meritorious service and who is in receipt of £30 a year, or six pounds less than is awarded the widow of a Cornet or Qr. Master.[2]

Mr. Cherry's proposals for an improved warrant for his officers are best considered in connection with the financial report on his scheme. This is written in the true War Office style.

[1] P.R.O. 43/108480.
[2] The widow of Mr. Bird, 4th Dragoons; this officer's Peninsula service is given in Appendix II.

The memorandum says that Mr. Cherry solicits a review of the whole position of regimental Veterinary Surgeons, their full and half pay, widows' pensions and compassionate allowance for children, with a view to some improvement in order to induce men of higher character and qualifications to enter the Service, and to secure the attachment to the Service of the officers already in it; that the present rates of full pay were established in 1807, the avowed object of the legislation being precisely that now urged by Mr. Cherry, " to induce well-qualified persons to enter," etc., and that if the intended object has not been gained by the liberal terms of 1807, " it does not seem likely that a further increase would do so." In respect of the 1807 warrant Cherry's proposal was to add a rate of pay, 17s. 6d. after 25 years' service, there being no provision in that warrant for any period of service over twenty years. The financial mind seizes hold of this point, and agrees that the 17s. 6d. rate might " be advantageously bestowed to induce the Veterinary Surgeon to continue in the Service," especially as at present it only affects two officers. On Cherry's proposals for an increase in half pay at 25 and 30 years' service, the official says that the present rates have only recently been published, and in his opinion the fresh proposals " are wholly uncalled for," and would place the Veterinary Surgeon at 30 years' service on an equality with the Surgeon, "whose claims must be considered superior." "As regards widows' pensions, an increase was recommended in 1827 by the late P.V.S. Coleman, in 1840 by Mr. Cherry, and in 1843 by Veterinary Surgeon Gloag, 10th Hussars; to the first and last a reply was sent that the Secretary at War did not see sufficient reasons for any increase. The 1840 proposal was postponed until the question of widows' pensions generally had been revised, and that has not yet been put in hand.

" The Veterinary Surgeon having no superior rank to rise to, whatever may be the length of service, is allowed (Queen's Regulations 1844) choice of quarters according to his service as follows: Under 10 years as Cornet; under 20 years as Lieutenant; above 20 years as Captain. He attains to no rank by this arrangement, as seems to be considered by Mr. Cherry, but he is put on a par with these ranks for the purpose of allotting quarters and for no other purpose. This arrangement affords no ground, therefore, for a fluctuating rate of widow's pension."

This is the first time that the subject of rank for veterinary officers arises in official correspondence, and we see the spirit of

PLATE E

hostility in which it is met. It must be remembered that the writer of this minute was a civilian.

The memorandum continues that it is worthy of consideration, as the officer must necessarily serve ten years on full pay to entitle his widow to any pension, whether the rate should not be made equal to that of a Lieutenant in agreement with the preceding scale as to quarters. At present the rate is £30, being the lowest in the scale, and only applicable to Deputy Purveyors. It is suggested that it should be raised to £40, the rate given to a *Lieutenant's* widow, but it is not proposed to alter the rate of compassionate allowance for the Veterinary Surgeon's children.

The next official who had to report on the question was more humane; he agrees with the 17s. 6d. rate after twenty-five years' service "to induce the Veterinary Surgeon to continue without grumbling," and he supports Mr. Cherry's proposal for a graduated increase of pensions for widows, but he does not suggest more than £40, even for the widow of a Captain. The Secretary at War (no longer Herbert) puts it up to the Treasury. He was entirely favourable, for there is a minute in his handwriting which reads: "This is a very useful body of men to have *good* in the Army and not always easy to be got."

The Warrant was issued on 7th October 1846: the wording is peculiar; after the usual preamble, it says, "the pay of a Veterinary Surgeon who shall have served in the army in any capacity as a medical officer (*sic*) on full pay for a period exceeding twenty-five years, shall be seventeen shillings and six pence a day." It is difficult to understand why the term "medical officer" is used, but the expression "Veterinary Officer" was very rarely employed, even by the Veterinary Service.

Cherry must be congratulated on securing a rate of pay for length of service not previously granted, and better terms for widows. He possessed what Coleman lacked, a knowledge of requirements and a determination to push his Service ahead. It will be observed that he refers to his officers by their relative rank. He recognized the importance of rank as defining an officer's position and status. It was the germ of that which took so long to come to maturity.

In February 1840 he dealt with travelling allowance for Veterinary Surgeons visiting outstations, and remedied a long-standing grievance. Regiments were still very much split up, and the amount of travelling to be done was considerable, in respect not only of the number of journeys to be made, but more especially of the distances to be covered. We have already seen (pp. 56, 61) the efforts previously made to remedy a grievance which left the officer considerably out of pocket at the end of the year. He was now allowed 5s. when visiting any outstation over ten miles from head-quarters and not exceeding sixteen. Beyond sixteen and not exceeding thirty-two miles 6d. a mile was allowed for the whole distance, after deducting the first sixteen; beyond thirty-two miles 6d. a mile for the whole distance travelled, without any deduction.

Up to the time of Cherry's assumption of office, the bare " Register of Sick and Lame Horses " was the only record kept by the Veterinary Officer; in December 1839 instructions were issued that a " Record of Treatment " of cases was to be kept in a separate book. Instructions for the correct keeping of both books were issued; it is laid down that post-mortem appearances cannot be recorded too minutely.

The introduction of railways facilitated the transfer of sick and lame horses to a new station; they had no longer to march with the regiment, or be left on the road in the care of civilians. In January 1844 Cherry issued detailed instructions on this point.

In 1847 a very painful case occurred which at the time gave rise to considerable public feeling. The Veterinary Surgeon of the 6th Dragoon Guards, G. Johnston, and his Commanding Officer, Colonel Jackson, failed to agree on points connected with veterinary duties. Johnston had only been two years with the regiment, having been gazetted from half pay, but during this time there had been constant friction with his Commanding Officer. The purchase of a batch of remounts brought matters to a head. Nineteen arrived of which seven were unsound. Presumably the Colonel purchased the horses without any veterinary opinion, and the unsoundness was only detected on their examination at the Barracks by the Veterinary Officer, in accordance with para. 28, *Regulations for the Performance of Veterinary Duties*.[1] This directed the examination of all remounts on joining and a report in writing to be made to the Officer Commanding before final approval of any not likely to " arrive at adequate strength for the Service, and every blemish or defect that may have escaped the notice of the officer who purchased the said horses." A report on

---

[1] This is the first mention of Veterinary Regulations I have met with. They certainly must have been published during Coleman's administration (see p. 95).

these remounts was made to the Commanding Officer, who nevertheless directed that the animals should be paid for. Johnston addressed the P.V.S. *direct* on this question and asked how he was to act in future. For this the Duke of Wellington, then Commander-in-Chief, ordered him to be severely reprimanded by the C.-in-C. Forces in Ireland. In this reprimand he was informed that he was not answerable for the soundness or unsoundness of horses when purchased, and that his duties were confined solely to veterinary practice. In the opinion of the C.-in-C. " great praise was due to the officer who selected these horses, and great credit to the dealer who furnished them"! It may here be added that independent veterinary examination confirmed Johnston's opinion of unsoundness; among the horses were even cases of blindness! Hearing that there was a vacancy in the 7th Hussars, Johnston applied for leave in order to obtain it; this was refused and he was accused of want of discipline. His Commanding Officer learning that he was not in possession of the full dress uniform of the regiment, ordered him to appear in it at Orderly Room in four days' time, a period within which it could not be made. Johnston resigned his commission in a fit of irritation, and later he recognized the consequences of his act; he had nineteen years' service, and had served in four parts of the globe, including India, where he had sunstroke. He appealed to the House of Commons, asking for an enquiry, and to be restored to his former rank. The Horse Guards having " summarily refused" to reinstate him, *The Times*, in its issue of 10th August 1847, took up his case. This paper appealed to the Duke of Wellington " to save from absolute ruin a man who appears to have long and faithfully served his country." *The Times* fully admits the danger of meddling with the discipline of the Army, but thinks that where it can be shown that unnecessary harshness has been exhibited, no evil can arise by bringing such cases to the notice of the country, in order that they may be sifted, and feels that in the present case it has a public duty to perform.

This case is a good example of one of the evils of the regimental system. Johnston was not the first officer driven out of the regiment under Colonel Jackson's command, nor were these remounts the only unsound animals Jackson had purchased; in seven months thirty-seven horses were cast, nearly a third of which had less than two years' service. The result of the appeal by *The Times* to the Commander-in-Chief was negative; the Duke of Wellington never changed an opinion once given.[1] Johnston's place in the regiment was taken by Cherry's son (A. H.); this does not look as if Johnston obtained any sympathy in that quarter.

During 1848 Cherry, who had for some time past adopted a remarkably hostile attitude towards the newly obtained Charter of the Royal College of Veterinary Surgeons, was openly charged with admitting men to the Service without a qualification. The charge was absurd; he admitted Dick's graduates, and some of the best men who entered our Service came from the Edinburgh School. His unpopularity among civil practitioners increased when he refused to furnish the names of the Veterinary Surgeons serving with the Cavalry, for entering in the Register of members of the College which was then, with infinite labour, being compiled. His son was the Secretary of the Registration Committee, and some regrettable scenes occurred in Council. Among other things the son attacked the system of shoeing in the Service, and insisted that the smallness of the part played by the Regimental Veterinary Surgeon was due to his ignorance of the subject. Friction between father and son was frequent for the next seven years. It is believed they were never reconciled. Finally the father was rejected at the poll for a seat on the Council. It is difficult to understand the dislike to the London School which Cherry continued to exhibit now that Coleman was dead. Perhaps he had learned of the attempt of Sewell to obtain the Principal Veterinary Surgeoncy of the Cavalry? Cherry appears to have been opposed to every measure of advancement in the civil profession, and whole-heartedly championed Dick in his skilful counterstrokes against the Royal College of Veterinary Surgeons.

In 1848 appeared the first communication from an Army Veterinary Officer on the subject of Sickness and Casualties among Horses at Sea.[2] The writer, J. Mellows, 1st Dragoon Guards, accompanied the regiment to Canada and returned with it. On the outward voyage the casualties were 11 per cent. and

---

[1] The unfairness of the Duke of Wellington was notorious. Stocqueler in his *History of the Horse Guards* 1750–1872 says that in matters of discipline recommendations to mercy made to the Duke rarely served the offender, unless weighty political or family influence was brought to bear. In one well-known case thirty-one years had to elapse before justice could be done to an officer; indeed the authorities had to wait until the Duke died. Nor was this arbitrariness confined to junior officers. General Sir de Lacy Evans, a distinguished officer, had incurred the Duke's displeasure and was passed over sixteen times for the Colonelcy of a regiment.

[2] *Veterinary Record*, vol. iv. 1848, p. 101.

on the homeward journey 5 per cent. This article contains the first account of "Ship Staggers," but the whole is worth reading as giving a good idea of transport in the days of sailing-ships. Suffocation was a common cause of death in bad weather owing to the hatches being closed.

In 1850 Mr. C. Cullimore, Veterinary Surgeon to the Bengal Horse Artillery, was presented at Court by Viscount Gough, under whom he had served in the Sikh Campaign, and there was a hope that the rule excluding veterinary officers from Court would now have been altered and an undeserved stigma removed from the profession. However, no such result followed for another thirty years. But Cullimore was not the first Veterinary Surgeon presented. Percivall in the April number of the *Veterinarian* for 1850, tells us that Professor Sewell had already been presented as Veterinary Surgeon of Volunteer Light Horse. This is the first and only reference to Sewell having served the State in a military capacity. He was appointed Veterinary Surgeon to the London and Westminster Light Horse in July 1805.

In 1853 Cherry took up the question of establishing a uniform pattern of shoe for the Cavalry, and in January a Committee was convened of which he and Siddall of the Blues were members. Seven Army Veterinary Surgeons gave evidence, among others W. Percivall and J. Wilkinson, but in addition to these, three civil practitioners, all first-rate men, were called upon. This gave rise to some adverse criticism, it being felt that only those with a knowledge of Service requirements should have been consulted. The Board had great difficulty in coming to a decision in consequence of the great diversity of opinion expressed. It finally decided to adopt: (1) A shoe "seated" on the foot and flat on the ground surface. (2) Counter-sunk nail holes without a fuller. (3) A calkin on the outside heel of the hind shoe and a thickened inside heel. (4) The shoe to weigh from 12 oz. to 15 oz. according to its size. (5) The number of nails to be six in front and seven behind. The Board further gave as its opinion that there was no lateral expansion in the foot, but that there was a movement from before backwards; the nails, therefore, could not interfere with expansion.

In the preparation of the foot for the shoe the Board decided that as little as possible should be pared out, but that exfoliating parts should be removed. Percivall in his evidence objected to the forcible removal of exfoliating sole, on the ground that it facilitated evaporation. He also considered that the shoe should be flat on the foot surface and concave towards the ground, holding that with this pattern five nails were sufficient. In the *Veterinarian* for December 1854 he freely expressed his opposition to the recommendations of the Committee, and it would appear as if he and Cherry had made a personal matter of their professional differences.

The shoe flat on the ground, seated on the foot surface stamped and without fuller, lasted as a Service pattern from 1853 to 1882.

During Cherry's period of office, *Regulations for the Performance of Veterinary Duties* were issued in March 1853. They are the earliest which have survived to us,[1] though as we know from the Johnston case, p. 122, they were not the first regulations issued. They were remarkably complete and many of the clauses remain at the present day. Cherry had a genius for organization. These regulations show his grip of Army requirements. Everything which experience could suggest was provided for. The preamble states that the Regulations apply to Cavalry regiments. They were not issued to the Artillery until July 1856, and were not made officially applicable to that regiment until 25th July 1857, by which time Cherry was dead. In the Appendices to these Regulations is a form of "Requisition for Medicines" identical with that still in use. There was as yet no monthly return, but a half-yearly return was furnished. The nomenclature of diseases was very logical and arranged in sixteen classes. The Veterinary Officer continued to furnish and maintain his pocket case of instruments.

In 1852 the Duke of Wellington died at the age of eighty-four. After Europe had settled down he had entered political life and forgotten the Army. His second period as C.-in-C. began in 1842; he watched the rusting of the whole machine, and took no interest in the progress of the science of war, nor of Artillery, which he regarded as inferior to infantry, and believed there was no weapon like the flint-lock musket. Though he was Master General of the Ordnance no reserve of guns was maintained, and there were less than fifty in the Arsenal at the time of his death! He was succeeded by Lord Hardinge, who thought it well to bring together in the open what was left of the British Army and see what it looked like. It was he who formed the camp at Chobham in 1853, an event of national importance, for the country became aware for the first time in forty years that an army existed, and the

---

[1] A copy exists in the Library R.C.V.S.; it belonged to the late J. B. W. Skoulding, Veterinary Surgeon (1st Class) Royal Artillery.

various branches of that army saw each other, in very many cases, for the first time. During the Wellington regime not once had the troops been brought together for instructional purposes; see Stocqueler's *Personal History of the Horse Guards 1750–1872*.[1] Almost all who had had practical experience of soldiering were now dead or passed out of the Service. The Cavalry were greatly concerned at the notion of putting their horses in the open during the autumn at Chobham! They had forgotten that any other than ceremonial duties were expected from them and little dreamed that not many months later they would be living in the open in a bitter winter on the Heights of Balaclava! Tented stables were accordingly erected and proved insufferably hot. It is well to note that tents were used for army horses as far back as 1853; indeed, they had been used on service several centuries earlier. The stables at Chobham were 30 yards long, 15 yards broad, and held 30 horses which stood in two ranks face to face with a four-foot passage between their heads.

We must now briefly turn to India, which we last saw in 1834, p. 102. Before the close of Mr. Cherry's administration matters in that country were becoming increasingly difficult, owing to the Veterinary Service being unrepresented either in military districts or at the head quarters of the Presidencies. In the early fifties there were rather more officers on the Indian than on the Home Establishment, yet they were without a head. Who can doubt that had an administrative veterinary service existed in India from the time the Department was formed, the mismanagement and ignorance of those in charge of the Studs could not have escaped as long as it did? We have seen that the attempt of a veterinary officer of the Stud to ventilate abuses led to his court martial and dismissal. A veterinary officer of the Imperial Service of very wide experience, Mr. R. G. Hurford, 16th Lancers, in 1849 drew attention to the worthlessness of the Stud horse, in a letter addressed to the Board of Management of Indian Studs; it was subsequently published in the *Veterinarian* in 1852. Had he been P.V.S. in India at this time, as he subsequently became, his letter might have done good. Curiously enough, when a P.V.S. was appointed to India, he had no jurisdiction over the Studs or the veterinary officers attached to them.

For other causes, unconnected with the Studs, the necessity

[1] Hardinge attempted to repair the Duke of Wellington's neglect of the Artillery, and armed the infantry with an improved weapon, but he was blamed for the disasters in the Crimea which obviously were due to the Duke.

of appointing a P.V.S. in India was urgent. In one of the Studs was a Captain Apperley (a son of the celebrated "Nimrod," a true friend to our profession), who had inherited the keen abilities of his father both for horse management and quackery. It is beyond belief that at a time when veterinary aid was available, this young officer was left in sole charge of a depot of young horses, numbering from 1,000 to 1,500, and responsible not only for their management but veterinary treatment! Some day the mortality statistics of this depot will be published; it suffices at present to say that Apperley acquired a certain amount of knowledge of treatment which did not lose in value by being made public. He became quite an authority, and so completely did the name of Apperley fascinate the lay mind, that we find his treatment for "Bursattee" forming the subject of a General Order dated 7th July 1851. All officers commanding mounted corps were directed to try this "valuable recipe," of which a copy existed in the adjutant's office for the guidance of the Veterinary Surgeon! The treatment consisted of calomel to the point of salivation and black wash to the ulcers. The order also notified the Veterinary Surgeon that not only did it cure Bursattee but Quittors! This occurred in Bengal. In the Bombay Presidency the Adjutant General of the Army issued a circular on 16th March 1854 on a new method of castration recommended and practised by Major Tapp of the Poona Irregular Horse.[1] The circular directed its employment in the Bombay Army, and appended full instructions. The operation was one well known in the castration of bulls in India; it was the terrible method of destroying the spermatic cord by forcible kneading with finger and thumb. An expert required half an hour to perform the operation!

The hideous cruelty of this method was protested against by Mr. J. H. B. Hallen, Veterinary Surgeon 1st Light Cavalry, who stated that, if it was still the C.-in-C.'s wish, he would of course perform the operation though it meant putting the animal to needless and excruciating torture. The A.G. of the Army in replying intimated that upon consideration of the objection raised, the Commander-in-Chief did not wish the system tried in the 1st Light Cavalry. His Excellency could not, however, allow the remarks on the cruelty of the operation to pass without comment. They were uncalled for, highly improper, and reflected indirectly on Major Tapp, whose well-known humanity was sufficient guarantee that the intense suffering *assumed* by Mr. Hallen did not exist!

[1] *Veterinarian*, vol. xxvii. 1854, p. 520, and vol. xxviii. 1855, p. 74.

Four months later a General Order was published forbidding the experiment, and stating that the Commander-in-Chief was satisfied that the operation was attended by the greatest suffering. Such an instance of ignorant cruelty could never have occurred had there been a P.V.S. at the C.-in-C.'s elbow.

In the *Veterinarian* for 1854, a senior officer of the Madras Veterinary Service urges the appointment of a P.V.S. He takes up the question from another aspect, that of departmental discipline, and emphasizes the necessity for professional supervision, in order to keep officers alert and efficient, especially in a country where habits of idleness are so rapidly contracted. This officer, Mr. J. Western, Madras Horse Artillery, points out that at the date of his letter a Veterinary Service had existed in India for twenty-seven years, and yet in that time not a single volume on the diseases of the country had been produced; he rightly cites this as evidence of want of professional interest. At p. 100 reference has been made to the channel of communication between the Veterinary Surgeon and the higher military authorities. Western gives us an excellent example of how the system worked. He was anxious to change the stable management of a unit of which he had temporary charge, so as to have the horses watered before instead of after feeding. This meant a change in Army Regulations, which the C.O. of the unit was only too anxious to obtain. Western being a regimental officer, could write no letter that did not first pass through his own C.O., who refused to send the recommendation on, as it reflected on a unit of which he was not in command. Western obtained the permission of the other commanding officer for the letter to the authorities to pass through Western's Commanding Officer, but the latter still refused to forward it. The officer commanding the station was next tried: he also refused. Western in despair addressed the Superintending Surgeon, who returned the correspondence with the remark that Government must be addressed through the proper channel! We see from this how completely the Veterinary Service was muzzled through lack of administrative officers.

The only person in this country who gave any thought to India was Percivall; the pages of the *Veterinarian* testify to the interest he took in getting the profession in that country placed on a sound basis. He drew attention in the *Veterinarian* in 1854 to the case of a veterinary officer reported upon as incompetent by his commanding officer. This alone, Percivall says, shows the need for an administrative staff in the Veterinary Service. It was many years before such appointments were made.

To return to Home affairs, war with Russia broke out in the early part of 1854, and an army which had wasted away under incompetent administration was about to be highly tried. Mr. Cherry was still alive, but at the age of seventy-five he was obviously unfitted for office in such a crisis. He died 11th July 1854, not quite four months from the outbreak of hostilities. During his fifteen years of administration he had neglected no opportunity of advancing his Service, and had done more solid work for his officers than Coleman had during the forty-three years he held the appointment. No obituary of Cherry appeared in the *Veterinarian*. No one knew him better than Percivall, but Percivall appears to have been rendered inarticulate by the fact that within a few *hours* of Cherry's death his successor had been chosen and he was not Percivall!

In July 1854 the senior officers on the Cavalry List were J. Siddall, Royal Horse Guards, whose commission was dated October 1812, and William Percivall, 1st Life Guards, whose date was November 1812. J. Siddall's services are recorded at p. 53. William Percivall was now sixty-two. He and Youatt had for many years been the most prominent men in the profession, and Percivall stood out as the representative of culture, sound professional judgement and experimental research. His text-books were not compilations, but the outcome of long personal experience and sound training; they will ever remain classics, and his profession, even at the present day, may read them with advantage; for lucidity, gift of expression and pure English they have never been equalled in veterinary literature.

It was a crushing blow to Percivall to find that he was not to succeed Cherry. J. Wilkinson, an officer fourteen years his junior in the Service, was selected. Percivall deals with the appointment in the August number of the *Veterinarian* for 1854, p. 479, in which, with restraint, he shows the bitterness of defeat. He speaks of the " injustice of two senior officers being passed over, both undeserving of the cruel military stigma which such rejection has fastened on them." He publishes the War Office reply to Lord Combermere's[1] recommendation of Percivall for the appointment, in which it is made to appear that Viscount Hardinge, the Commander-in-Chief, had personally selected Mr. Wilkinson. Hardinge was attacked in the House of Commons for

---

[1] Combermere was the Colonel of Percivall's regiment.

favouritism in appointments, and there was evidence to justify the charge, but it is well known that the appointment of Wilkinson was secured through the active interference of the Duke of Cambridge,[1] who was Colonel of Wilkinson's old regiment, the 17th Lancers. Percivall knew the cause; his last words on the subject are: "'Kings (*princes*) have long arms,' and so the matter ends."[2] Correspondence appeared in the following issue of the *Veterinarian* expressing something more than surprise that a man unknown outside his own regiment, who had made no discoveries, nor contributed to the common stock of knowledge, should have passed over the head of one to whom the whole profession was indebted.

Alma, Balaclava and Inkerman had been fought before Percivall wrote his last editorial in the December number of the *Veterinarian* for 1854. His thoughts were for the men and horses, and he asks what provision is being made for the veterinary care of the sick and wounded? He refers to the Peninsular and Waterloo campaigns, when little else was done than drag the sick, lame and wounded along at the tail of a regiment, and destroy them when they could proceed no farther. It is evident that he had in his mind the creation of veterinary hospitals. It was fitting that his last thoughts should have been directed to the Service he loved so well, in which he had passed his whole life and of which he was so distinguished an ornament.

He died, after a few days' illness, on 12th December 1854, at the age of sixty-two, almost on the anniversary of the death of his father, precisely five months after Cherry, and was buried in Fulham cemetery. His grave, unlike that of Coleman and Youatt, may still be seen. The cause of his death was Bright's disease, but there can be little doubt that the bitterness of spirit engendered by official neglect told against him.

William Percivall (1792–1854), the only child of John Percivall, was born before his father entered the Veterinary College. In 1809 William entered the College as a resident pupil of Professor Sewell, and obtained his diploma in 1811 at the early age of nineteen. The next

[1] See also Wilkinson's speech at the Annual Dinner, May 1855, *Veterinarian*, vol. xxxviii. p. 367. The Duke of Cambridge became C.-in-C. in 1856. Stocqueler, *op. cit.*, writing in 1873 says that his inclination to be just when making appointments was counterbalanced by the fear of giving offence to his old associates and friends, and that under intimidation and pressure, his judgement in certain Court Martial cases was defective, if not worse.

[2] The insertion by Percivall of " princes " into the quotation refers to the Duke, who at this time was better known as " Prince George."

year saw him in the Service commissioned to the Royal Artillery Drivers, and serving in the Peninsula War, where he was present at the battles of Orthez and Toulouse. In his writings there are remarkably few references to the Peninsula or to his active service experiences. It is presumed that on return from the Peninsula he worked under his father at Woolwich. When the Waterloo Campaign began he proceeded to Belgium; he was not at the battle, but references in his *Hippopathology* tell us he was in the vicinity, for he says, in dealing with tympany of the stomach, that he would probably never again see so many cases " as I witnessed on the march of the British Army from Waterloo to Paris in 1815," owing to a Brigade of Cavalry being allowed to feed in a field of growing wheat. On the reduction of the Army after Waterloo he was placed on half pay, July 1816. He took up the study of human medicine, entering St. Thomas's Hospital, where he dressed for Travers. He qualified in 1819 at the Royal College of Surgeons, and later became a Licentiate of the Apothecaries Company. His original intention was to take up the practice of human medicine, but changing his mind he worked under his father at Woolwich, where he devoted himself to study, anatomical, physiological and clinical. His first work, in which he was greatly assisted by his father, was *A Series of Elementary Lectures on the Veterinary Art*, 3 parts, 1823–26, which gave great offence to Coleman, who owing to jealousy, intensified by a criticism of his opinions,[1] appears to have endeavoured to prevent their publication. From this time is dated the coolness between Coleman and the Percivalls. A copy of this work was sent to the Emperor of Russia, and in return a gold snuff-box was received as a mark of Alexander I.'s appreciation.[2] This was the only recognition ever bestowed on his zeal and professional ability. In May 1827 he was offered the appointment of Veterinary Surgeon to 1st Life Guards, with which regiment he served until his death. In 1828 he began the *Veterinarian*, a further cause of annoyance to Coleman. The foundation of this periodical was the first step towards co-ordinating and educating the profession; he was soon joined by the able and indefatigable Youatt; on the death of the latter he carried on the work alone. It was in the *Veterinarian* that his *Anatomy of the Horse* first appeared, separately published in 1832; it was followed by his *Hippopathology*, brought out in the same manner and separately published in 4 vols. 1834–52, a second edition being issued at the time of his death. In 1850 appeared his *Lectures on the Form and Action of Horses*, and at the time of his death he was engaged on a *Manual for Veterinary Students* which never appeared. During the early part of his professional life he was a frequent visitor at the Veterinary Medical Association, but later on, as his works came out, he was the subject of such jealousy that he gradually withdrew

[1] "We have suffered our opinions to be taken into bondage by those to whom we are too apt to look up with oracular reverence."—Percivall, Part iii. 1826, p. 402.

[2] We do not know why a copy of this work was sent to the Emperor, but suggest that Percivall may have acted in a professional capacity to him at Paris.

from the society he had previously so much enjoyed. It is said that he was not a good public speaker; it is true he spoke seldom but always to the point; he once lectured for Youatt at the University of London in 1833, and this lecture bears no evidence of disability. The probability is that Percivall shunned the limelight.

It is remarkable how very little personal information is obtainable regarding the great men of the past. Youatt knew the value of such information, for on the death of Coleman he begged the readers of the *Veterinarian* to send him their personal impressions of the man, that these might receive permanent record in the periodical. Apparently there was no response. Of Youatt himself I am absolutely unable to obtain a tittle of information, although in touch with his descendants. Delabere Blaine is merely a name, the man is lost to us. And so with William Percivall; nowhere is there a published account which would enable us to visualize him. Writing in the *Veterinarian* for May 1830, W. Field Junr. describes him as " a cheerful and instructive companion, a truly honourable man and faithful friend." The celebrated "Nimrod" (Colonel Apperley) in July 1834 writes of him as " the man of science, the practitioner, the scholar and the gentleman," a delightful description. It was not known to the writer until too late that the youngest child but one of William Percivall was living up to the present year (1926).[1] The family of this gentleman, who was not in the profession, tell me how deeply their father revered the memory of his father, of whom he was always talking. Through this channel I have learned the correct date of William Percivall's birth and some slight but precious touches. He was a handsome man, extremely kind, of a quiet, deeply religious character. A great deal of his work was done at night; he would wake up and if a point of importance struck him, would sit up and write perhaps for hours. So well known was this habit that a notebook was always kept ready at his bedside. It is through the courtesy of Mr. Charles W. Percivall, M.A., the grandson, that I am enabled to present a portrait of William Percivall which forms the frontispiece to this book.

William Percivall was the greatest man the Army Veterinary Service has produced; we are proud to think that one so gifted belonged to our ranks. His name will be remembered so long as the veterinary profession lasts.

John Wilkinson (1804–1876) was Veterinary Surgeon 2nd Life Guards when selected in July 1854 to succeed Mr. Cherry as Principal Veterinary Surgeon to the Cavalry. At the time of his appointment he was in Turkey buying horses for the Crimean War, so that it is clear he had nothing to do with the jobbery which obtained his selection. He had qualified in January 1825 and entered the Service the same year. At the date of his appointment as P.V.S. he was fifty years of age, and had spent the greater part of his life in the 17th Lancers without having seen either active or foreign service. During his regimental service

---

[1] The profession is indebted to Mr. H. L. Roberts, F.R.C.V.S., of Ipswich, for notifying the fact.

he was well known as an exceptionally good judge of a horse; so great was the confidence in his judgement and integrity that for years he purchased all the remounts for the 17th Lancers.[1] This confidence in his ability no doubt inspired the idea of sending him to Turkey.

He was tall, slight, distinguished looking, well set up, very reserved in manner, austere, with a keen penetrating glance and somewhat severe expression. The writer met him within a few weeks of the completion of his career; he still carried himself stiffly and in spite of his seventy-two years was upright in his carriage but looked his age; his moustache and hair were then quite white. No one could recollect having seen him in uniform; he invariably wore a frock coat and tall hat. He was a strict disciplinarian of the old school. He lived for years in the quarters attached to the Royal Horse Infirmary, Woolwich, and held aloof from his officers, among whom he was decidedly unpopular. The author has none but respectful recollections of this cold reserved man, who treated him with every consideration on the two occasions on which they met. Mr. Wilkinson visited the Hospital stables regularly, though for some years a senior administrative officer, who was, of course, responsible, was attached to the Woolwich garrison. When he took over office his appointment was to the Cavalry only; the Artillery still possessed their Senior Veterinary Officer, J. Stockley. When Stockley retired in 1858 (at the age of 82!), the powerful Board of Ordnance was dead; no more Senior Veterinary Surgeons were appointed to the Artillery, and Wilkinson became Principal Veterinary Surgeon of the Army.

During the whole of his period of office Woolwich remained the Head Quarters of the Department. It was here that every young officer joined for duty and during his "probationary" period he was kept under the eye of the P.V.S. Probationary officers were originally known as "Acting Veterinary Surgeons"; the term was in use until July 1873, when they were entitled "Veterinary Surgeons on probation." The stores for the Department were held at Woolwich; they were jealously guarded, and received from the P.V.S. the closest personal attention. He employed towards the end of his life a senior officer as Storeholder, but still the eye of the P.V.S. scrutinized every indent and approved all material for issue. He never lived up to the amount allowed him in the estimates,[2] and was ruthless in cutting down indents. The Percivall-Stockley Museum was in existence to the end of his days, but the room was kept carefully locked.

He wrote very little; as a young man he published some observations on the value of the *Stomach Pump* in veterinary practice, *Veterinarian*, vol. iv., February 1831, and promised additional information on a new type of instrument, but no further article appears to have been published. Another communication was on the *Supply of*

---

[1] This was not the only regiment where this arrangement existed. Conspicuous examples were the 6th Dragoons (H. Hallen) and 6th Dragoon Guards (Hayward). *Veterinarian*, vol. xxii., August 1850.

[2] P.R.O. W.O. 32/60. Memorandum by Mr. Wilkinson dated 7th April 1859.

Horses for the Army, with Notes on the Remount System of the French Army. This was published in the *Journal of the Royal Agricultural Society* and *Veterinarian* for 1863, p. 229. In this paper he gives a few vital statistics of the British Army in 1862, and shows that the total wastage was 13 per cent. per annum, of which only 2 per cent. was due to deaths and destructions. He compares this with the French Army with its annual mortality of 8½ per cent., of which 5 per cent. was due to glanders. In this communication to the Royal Agricultural Society he is described as "Veterinary Surgeon General"!

He rarely spoke in public, only twice so far as I know. At the Annual Dinner of the Royal College in 1863 he stated that it was his duty to do all in his power to raise the status of the profession, and that the facilities now within his reach for securing the best candidates for the Army were far greater than when he joined. He urged that the profession should be better educated to enable it to occupy a higher social position. He spent the whole of his official career under the wing of the Duke of Cambridge, Commander-in-Chief. Between these two men a comradeship existed and to this friendship Wilkinson's long tenure of office was doubtless due. He was actually forced out of the Service in the end, as we shall see later, and died suddenly as the result, before his retirement could be gazetted, on 28th May 1876, aged 72.

The Veterinary arrangements for a campaign in the year 1854 were of a very primitive kind; we can best describe them by outlining the veterinary features of the Crimean War. The veterinary equipment for a regiment of Cavalry consisted of two Regimental or Head Quarter Chests and two Troop Chests. The former contained all the drugs and surgical appliances allowed, the latter were small and contained only an assortment of compounded medicines. The Head Quarter Chests were of thick wood bound with iron, the interior divided into compartments for bottles and canisters. In the scale of drugs, among other items, 10 lbs. Resin, 12 lbs. Aloes and 7 lbs. Potassium Nit. were allowed for 350 horses for six months. Diuretics and purgatives were prominent. Among the surgical supplies were 3 lbs. fine tow, 8 yards of linen for bandages, one dozen bladders for the purpose of enemata, and a perforated tin lantern which gave no light. Iron mortar, ladle, pots and kettle added to the weight. We need not describe this equipment further, which even in those days hardly seems up to date, especially as regards the treatment of wounds. The regimental system of medical care was the only one thought of for both men and animals. It did not occur to anyone at this time that a regiment has no use for either men or horses which are sick or wounded, nor has it facilities for looking after them. The veterinary officer had one trained assistant in the Field, the Farrier Major. The sick and lame marched with the baggage in the rear of the regiment and men had to be detached to look after them, a further drain on the strength of a troop. No provision existed for veterinary hospitals, though it was known that in the Peninsula so-called " sick-horse depots " or "Cavalry Depots " had had to be established, into which the human and equine debris of war were thrown to get along as best they could.

The number of veterinary officers in the Crimea in March 1855 was 18 out of a total strength of 44 officers at home and abroad. In June 1856 forty-three were serving in the Crimea, the total strength of the Army Veterinary Service then being 64. As in recent years a number of these appointments, eighteen out of forty-three, were temporary, though many were subsequently confirmed. The eighteen were made up as follows: Land Transport 12, Turkish Contingent 4, British Foreign Legion 1, Osmanli Horse Artillery 1. All the temporary officers were gazetted with the *local rank* of " Veterinary Surgeon in Turkey." It is obvious that this was no rank, but it is the earliest indication of rank being regarded as essential to the performance of military duty. A step further was taken in 1856, when the Veterinary Surgeon of the Osmanli Horse Artillery, J. K. Lord, was gazetted with the local rank of " Lieutenant in Turkey." All this was immensely superior to the organization of forty-four years later, which sent veterinary surgeons as civilians to an army in the Field in South Africa without authority or protection.

From a notice in the *Veterinarian* of March 1856 it is evident that the number of candidates for temporary employment in the War fell short of requirements. The article quoted laments the dearth of applicants, but adds that none need apply who fear the test of an examination. It also states that the Government is resolved to render the Army Veterinary Service more attractive, and that the P.V.S. is anxious to forward the interests of his officers. It is characteristic of our Government that during time of peace little or nothing can be obtained to encourage the Veterinary Service; see the remarks on p. 120 on Cherry's proposals for betterment. It is not until the country is involved in war that the sop of prospective improvement is held out; once the crisis is passed every effort is made by the civil branch of the War Office to evade its promises.

At first there was no Principal Veterinary Surgeon with the Army in the Crimea, no co-ordination of veterinary duties, no

PLATE F

To face p 136

systematized method of dealing with the sick. The losses during the winters of 1854-55 on the heights of Balaclava were a scandal, but the country was too deeply roused by the shocking sufferings of the men and the unorganized medical service, to pay much attention to the horses, which died like flies from starvation. In the Sebastopol orders of 21st January 1856, nearly two years after the war began, a Principal Veterinary Surgeon was appointed to the *Land Transport Corps*; no better selection could have been made than J. W. Gloag. He had long experience, was a most capable officer and had been present with his regiment throughout the war. On appointment he was directed to proceed to Constantinople to superintend the purchase of veterinary medicines and stores, and subsequently to the Dardanelles to examine the state of the animals at the depot there.[1] His visit to Constantinople to purchase medicines is interesting; the stores were lying on board the *Medway* in the Black Sea, where they remained for six months before they were discovered, a typical example of Crimean administration.

Mr. Gloag's appointment could only have been made as the result of dire necessity; no provision existed in the regulations for an administrative veterinary officer on the Staff of the Army, though, as we have seen, there were over forty officers in the Field under no professional control or organization. So far as can now be made out, the only officers directly under Mr. Gloag's control were the temporary officers in the various sick depots on the Black Sea. The regimental Veterinary Surgeons were locked up with their regiments in the Crimea, having practically nothing to do, as the regiments were skeletons; yet not one of these officers could be claimed for duty outside his regiment. The evils resulting from such a hopeless system are so obvious, that it is incomprehensible why nearly a quarter of a century had to elapse before they were rectified.

The earliest reference I can find to the evacuation of the sick from the Crimea for treatment in depots on the Black Sea is September 1854; it is in a notebook of the A.Q.M.G. Cavalry Division.[2] The animals had to be carried by boats to the ship in Balaclava Harbour, and then hauled aboard; no doubt similar methods had to be adopted at the receiving base. It must be remembered that these depots were unorganized, staffed by untrained temporary veterinary officers, each doing the best he

[1] *Veterinarian*, vol. xxix. 1856, p. 178.
[2] P.R.O. W.O. 28/159.

could in the absence of military knowledge, with the limited appliances at hand and the particularly villainous local labour engaged. It is noteworthy that with but two exceptions the only information we have of the diseases met with during the campaign was furnished by officers in these depots and by a temporary veterinary officer with the Turkish Contingent on the Bosphorus. The *Veterinarian* of 1856 reminds the Veterinary Surgeons of the Army that they have not sufficiently contributed to the march of progress. Among the most notable of the Black Sea contributors was a young officer, recently qualified, George Fleming. The best communication was made by another young officer, F. de F. Elkes, who unfortunately did not live to write a second; the most prophetic, by another temporary officer, T. W. Mayer, who gave a good account of Cattle Plague, and stated definitely his opinion that nothing would prevent the disease from reaching this country. This view was in direct opposition to that of Professor Simonds, who did so much to lull Britain into a false sense of security: in a very few years it was proved that the Army practitioner was right and the expert adviser to the Privy Council wrong.

The various contributions bearing on the Crimean War will be found in the *Veterinarian* as follows: vol. xxviii. 1855, 1 paper; vol. xxix. 1856, 5 papers; vol. xxx. 1857, 9 papers.

In April 1856 the Crimean War came to an end, and in the November number of the *Veterinarian* for that year, p. 625, opportunity is taken to record the zealous work done by the Army Veterinary Service during the campaign, and the approval of those services expressed by the Duke of Cambridge, in his public speech in May 1855.[1] Only two officers were specially decorated. Mr. J. W. Gloag received the Legion of Honour and the 5th Class Medjideh, and Mr. J. S. Stockley, son of the old Senior Veterinary Surgeon to the Ordnance, who was attached to the Head Quarter Staff in an executive capacity, obtained the 5th Class of the Legion of Honour. The Veterinary aspects of the campaign have never been described, though a fair amount of material exists.

The name of J. W. Gloag has occurred so frequently, that a brief account of this most excellent officer must be given. He joined the Service in 1832 and served at different times in the 10th and 11th Hussars. With the latter regiment he went to the Crimea, and was present at Alma, Balaclava, Inkerman, Tchernaye, Affair of the Bulganac, Siege and Fall of Sebastopol. He retired in 1870 and was appointed Veterinary Surgeon to the Royal Irish Constabulary, with

---

[1] *Veterinarian*, vol. xxviii., p. 359.

which he served up to the time of his death in 1886, at the age of 74. He was an extraordinarily popular man, and full military honours were paid him at his funeral, which was described in a professional periodical as one of the most imposing ever seen in Dublin. His genial disposition and goodness of heart, his upright gentlemanly bearing, endeared him to all. He was described at the time of his death as the most estimable, sympathetic and lovable of men. Throughout his life he had been a careful observer and was possessed of a large store of knowledge. His first contribution dealt with the introduction of the casting hobbles we still employ. Though they are generally known by the name of the manufacturer, it was Gloag who invented them. They are described and figured in the *Veterinarian*, vol. x. 1837. In 1848 he published in the *Veterinarian* a series of articles on the *Physiology of the Foot of the Horse*, subsequently published as a pamphlet, based on a sound, carefully controlled series of observations, supported by experiments, some of these being of a most ingenious nature. His most important contribution, from a Service point of view, was that dealing with the *Conduct, Duties, etc., of Veterinary Surgeons in the Army*, in the *Veterinarian*, vol. xii. of 1839, to which attention has already been directed at p. 108. In 1852 he published in the *Veterinarian* an article on *Broken Wind* which will repay re-reading.

T. W. Mayer, whom we have mentioned as writing prophetically on Cattle Plague reaching this country, graduated in 1835, so that he was not a young man when he volunteered for service in the Crimea. He did remarkable work in connection with the obtaining of our first Charter, which was the primary step towards the emancipation of the profession from the fetters with which Coleman had bound it. He helped to finance the movement, and the money he freely gave would have helped him in his declining years. After the Crimean War he obtained a commission in the Royal Engineers, which he held until 1870, when he was retired for age. Always keen on Veterinary Medical Societies, he founded the Army Society at Aldershot in 1861 and was present at its resuscitation in 1887, in which year he died at Aldershot aged 73. The veterinary profession has had none in its ranks who have had its advancement nearer to their hearts than T. W. Mayer.

In the Crimean Campaign errors abounded: this is not the place to deal with them, but it is impossible to avoid reference to the transport of animals by sea. So deep had been the sleep of the military service, that when the Expedition had to be sent to the Crimea, those in authority preferred the *sailing* vessel which took a month to reach the Black Sea, to the steamer which completed the journey in a fortnight! The losses at sea were consequently heavy, and advice tendered by the veterinary profession as to the best method of shipping horses, by carrying them on sand and shingle ballast in the hold and allowing them to lie down, was not taken by those responsible for transport operations.[1] One vessel employed in the work is of especial interest to our Service, from the terrible calamity which befell it. The *Europa* was lost by fire at sea with the Head Quarters of the Inniskilling Dragoons on board, and seventeen lives were lost including those of the Veterinary Officer and Farrier Major. There is a memorial to the regiment in Chelsea Hospital which reads as follows:

"Erected by Command of Her Majesty Queen Victoria in Memory of Lieut.-Colonel Willoughby Moore, Inniskilling Dragoons, and of the undermentioned non-commissioned officers and soldiers of the same regiment, who perished on board the *Europa* Transport when that vessel was burnt at sea on 31st May 1854, affording a noble example of courage and discipline in the discharge of duty.

"LIEUT.-COLONEL MOORE,
VETERINARY SURGEON KELLY."

Then follow the names of fifteen N.C.O.'s and men.

It will be observed that Mr. Kelly's name is not mentioned in the dedication, the defective wording of which suggests that he is included with the N.C.O.'s and men of the regiment. The unfortunate young Veterinary Surgeon, F. de F. Elkes (p. 138), was the victim of a tragedy of another kind. He was quartered in a camp at Baljik near Varna on the Black Sea. The place was infested with ruffians of every degree of criminality, and two officers had been murdered. Elkes occupied the same accommodation as G. Western, afterwards of the Madras Veterinary Service, and having occasion to go outside at night apparently forgot to wake Western, who hearing a noise on Elkes' return fired at what he believed to be an intruder, and killed Elkes. I have often heard it said that the accident cast a permanent cloud over Western's life. The following officers died in the Crimean Campaign, though the list may not be complete:

R. Kelly of the Inniskillings, J. Fisher 5th Dragoon Guards, Elkes of the Land Transport Corps, Scott-Gavin of the Turkish Contingent, Siddall of the 10th Hussars, and A. H. Cherry of the Royal Dragoons. The last-named officer was the youngest son of the late P.V.S., and like all the Cherry family was extremely able. He studied human medicine after taking his veterinary qualification, and joined the Service in 1846. There is a notice of his death and a short account of his useful life in the *Veterinarian* 1856, vol. xxix.

The Crimean War was a supreme test of physical endurance;

[1] *Veterinarian*, vol. xxviii. 1855, p. 295.

we know that at least nine veterinary officers served throughout the campaign and were present in every action; these were Stockley, Withers, Harpley and Cottrell of the Artillery, and Gloag, Constant, Gudgeon, Delany and Grey of the Cavalry. Their active service is worth recording: they were present at the affairs of the Bulganac and McKenzie's Farm, the Alma, Balaclava, Inkerman, Repulse of the Sortie on 26th October 1854, and the Siege and Fall of Sebastopol. Hicks-Withers was wounded at the Alma by a fragment of shell and the man holding his horse killed. He did not report his wound, but fifty years later received a pension for it ! He saw Nolan at Balaclava vainly endeavouring to direct the Light Brigade to their correct objective and witnessed his death. Among the young officers in the Crimea was a W. Partridge, whose conspicuous act of gallantry during a skirmish the 10th Hussars had with the Russian Cavalry at Kertch, led to his name appearing in an account of the fight published in the *Cornhill Magazine*, vol. vii. 1863. He subsequently went through the Mutiny, where he nearly succumbed to disease, to die at a comparatively early age in 1875.

There were two remarkably able men in our ranks at this time: John Keast Lord and William Barry Lord, brothers. They came from Tavistock, and John Keast returned there to practise after qualifying in 1844. A few years later he left his practice at Tavistock to roam in a whaler and became a trapper in the Hudson Bay Territory. When the Crimean War broke out both brothers joined the Army. We shall now deal with them individually.

J. K. Lord (1818–1872) was appointed Veterinary Surgeon to the Osmanli Horse Artillery in 1854 and was present at Balaclava. On 4th January 1856 he was re-gazetted with " the local rank of Lieutenant in Turkey while serving with the above Corps." He was therefore the first of our profession to be assigned military rank in a professional capacity. He left the Service after the War and henceforth devoted himself to travel and the study of Natural History. He was appointed naturalist to the Commission which was sent out to define the boundary between the United States and British Columbia, and here he had a great opportunity of studying the mule as a transport animal. His views are contained in the work *At Home in the Wilderness* and are of great professional interest. When in practice he had recorded in the *Veterinarian* of 1849 an observation which appears to us a commonplace, but which in those days was a distinct addition to knowledge. In writing on Tetanus following Castration he says, "almost every case I find recorded is traumatic in origin." At this time, and for long afterwards, the disease was generally believed to be capable of arising spontaneously. He published *The Naturalist in Vancouver Island*, 2 vols. 1866, *At Home in the Wilderness* 1867, 1876, *Handbook of Sea Fishing*, helped in producing an enlarged edition of Galton's *Art of Travel*, wrote many papers on Sea Fisheries and other topics in *Land and Water*, which for a short time he edited, and contributions to *The Field, Leisure Hour* and other Journals. Later he was engaged in archæological and scientific researches in Egypt, and in 1871 published a Catalogue of his Collection of lepidoptera and hymenoptera formed by him there. Finally he was invited to become the first manager of the Brighton Aquarium, where he died a few months after taking up his appointment. His valuable collection of birds, fishes, insects, etc., is now in the Natural History Museum, South Kensington. He described two new mammals. His memory is preserved to his country in the *Dictionary of National Biography*, on which notice we have freely drawn.[1] The great naturalist F. Buckland describes him as a big, unostentatious, large-hearted man, a delightful companion and a first-rate naturalist. He possessed the most remarkable dexterity in handling poisonous snakes.

William Barry Lord qualified in 1848. In 1854 he was gazetted Veterinary Surgeon Royal Artillery and proceeded to the Crimea; on the close of that War he was sent to India and served in the Mutiny. He retired upon half pay in 1864 and would appear to have then travelled widely; like his brother he became a student of Natural History. He published *Sea Fish* 1862, 1863, *Fishing Gossip* 1866, *The Silkworm Book* 1867, *Crab, Shrimp and Lobster Lore* 1867, *The Key to Fortune in New Lands* 1869, *Report on Mines in the County of Cork* 1870, *Diamonds and Gold* 1871, *Shifts and Expedients of Camp Life* 1871, 1876. It is curious to notice the parallel lines on which the genius of these brothers ran. W. B. Lord died in 1909.

There was a third Lord, W. C., in the Army but no connection of the above. He qualified in 1842 and wrote on " Gastritis mucosa " in 1865 and *Five Years' Practical Investigations of Homœopathy* 1869. He appears to have been one of the earliest converts in our profession to this system of medicine.

The Crimean War was barely over before the Indian Mutiny broke out and 70,000 troops, including eleven regiments of Cavalry, were despatched from this country. Many of the veterinary officers so engaged had served in the Crimea. The operations were long and severe; the veterinary arrangements for the campaign were of course regimental. All the Cavalry regiments from this country had to be remounted in India, and the supply of horses was drawn from that country, Australia and the Cape.

The Mutiny began at Meerut, 10th May 1857, and on the first day two veterinary officers, J. Philips and C. J. Dawson, were murdered. Dawson was ill in bed with fever; he and his wife were hacked to pieces and their house burned down. Philips

[1] Curiously enough the *Dictionary of National Biography* gives his Christian names as William Keast instead of John Keast.

was attacked on the road while driving home. A month later Veterinary Surgeon E. G. Chalwin, 1st Bgd. Bengal Artillery, was killed at Cawnpore while defending his wife and child from the mutineers, and shortly afterwards Veterinary Surgeon Vincent Nelson, 10th Light Cavalry, was beaten to death by the men of his regiment at Ferozopore. Veterinary Surgeon F. H. Hely, 7th Light Cavalry, was killed in the Defence of Lucknow. The death roll of the Veterinary Service was accordingly heavy.[1]

There was no time in this campaign, nor is there in any campaign fought under stress, to distinguish between combatant and non-combatant officers. In the campaign in Afghanistan of 1840 the 2nd Regiment of Bengal Native Cavalry behaved badly; their officers, including the Veterinary Officer, W. McDermott, were left to fight it out and suffered severe casualties. The Court of Directors in disbanding the regiment expressed their admiration of the gallantry and devotion of the officers. We see the same devotion of the Veterinary Service in the Mutiny. Veterinary Surgeon J. Siddall, together with Captains Hastings and Jackson, all of the Bengal Army, headed a small party of volunteers and against overwhelming numbers succeeded in relieving the Garrison of Arrah which was severely pressed. Only Siddall survived the exposure and hardships experienced during this operation. Among the Imperial Forces Veterinary Surgeon M. Harpley, Royal Horse Artillery, was twice mentioned in despatches for military service of which unfortunately I cannot trace the record, though undoubtedly for gallantry in the Field. This was the first " mention " obtained by a Veterinary Surgeon. Veterinary Surgeon Hicks-Withers, Royal Artillery, commanded two guns in the absence of officers through sickness, in the pursuit of the notorious Tantia Topee.

M. Harpley was in his day the best-known man in London in Household Cavalry circles. He served for many years with the " Blues " and was the father and counsellor of the Regiment. He bore a striking resemblance to the late Duke of Cambridge, and a member of the Royal Family, it is said, always referred to him as " Uncle George."

---

[1] The death of Veterinary Surgeon Charles Henderson, Bengal Army (son of Alexander Henderson, Veterinary Surgeon to the Queen Dowager), who died in December 1858 while on passage home, was probably attributable to the Mutiny. The son had inherited from his father an attractive personality which endeared him to his friends. Charles Henderson had been for some time in the Stud at Saharanpur. In the church of that place will be found a tablet erected to his memory by public subscription among those " who loved him in life and follow him in Death with affectionate Remembrance."

He was a man of great charm, and extraordinarily popular. When he retired for age the complimentary dinner given him by his regiment was attended by some of the best-known men in the land; when he died the Regimental Dinner for that year was abandoned as a mark of respect to his memory.

The Crimean losses aroused the nation to a sense of its duty in making financial provision for those who had suffered during the operations, and a new scale of pensions and allowances for those wounded or injured in action was promulgated by Royal Warrant in June 1857. It is typical of the War Office civilians that to judge from the correspondence which took place on this subject between the various branches of that institution, one would think they were ignorant of the fact that the nation had a big war on hand. The Veterinary Service came out very badly in this warrant. No matter what relative rank the officer held, £50 a year was all that was allowed, the same as was awarded to a Cornet, Ensign, Quarter Master, Apothecary and Hospital Assistant. This was no improvement on previous scales; he had been entitled to £50 a year for wounds since the Warrant of June 1812. Under the 1857 Warrant a Lieut. and Asst. Surgeon obtained £70 per annum, and a Captain, Chaplain and Surgeon £100 a year.

In the early days of 1858 an anonymous writer in the *Veterinarian*[1] closely examined the cost of making a veterinary surgeon and compared it with the pay and expenses in the Service. He decided that the Army was no place for his son. This communication is worth studying, as from it and the subsequent correspondence on the subject, a good idea may be formed of the cost of living in the Service nearly seventy years ago.

In December 1858 the *Veterinarian* examined the then recently issued medical warrant, and pointed out that it secured to medical officers all that was rightfully their due. " Rank and position are among the things for which most men have a predilection." The *Veterinarian* urges the Veterinary Officers of the Army to take immediate steps to improve their position both in rank and pay, and promises them every support. It suggests that a meeting be held, resolutions adopted, a standing committee formed, and a deputation chosen to wait on the Authorities. Mr. Wilkinson had already been moving in this direction. His first communication on the subject is dated 25th November 1858, addressed to the Military Secretary,[2] in which, in presenting a memorial from Army

[1] Vol. xxxi., pp. 12, 56, 80.   [2] P.R.O. W.O. 32/60.

Veterinary Officers, he gives an account of the education and training of the Veterinary Surgeon, and the method by which he enters the Service. This document, which is wholly holographic, is accompanied by a scheme for an improved warrant. It found its way in due course to the Finance Department of the War Office. One of the first comments made by that branch was that every candidate for the Army should possess the diploma of the only chartered body, and that it was open to the Scotch students to take that qualification! The writer adds: "The P.V.S., after mature consideration, authorizes me to say that he is prepared to concur." The significance of this sentence is only apparent to those who know the history of our Charter, and the bitter internecine war which followed its grant. Wilkinson was by no means in favour of excluding the Edinburgh graduates, but we find him concurring in this measure, owing to the attitude of a Finance man in the War Office who possessed an astonishing knowledge of the inner history of our profession. This he acquired, as the papers in the Public Record Office show, from a private letter addressed to General Peel, Secretary at War, by Mr. W. Robinson, M.R.C.V.S., of Tamworth, who urged that none but Members of the College should be admitted to the Army.[1] Another long memorandum from Wilkinson followed, deploring the schism between the Royal College and the Schools; he thinks it is not a controversy in which the Secretary of State or Commander-in-Chief could be implicated. Further he finds that if he restricts his selection of candidates to those holding the diploma of the Royal College, his field of selection, "none too large," would be reduced by half. He strengthens his new position by saying that he heard yesterday (6th April 1859) that the London School threatens to break away from the Royal College and issue a diploma of its own! He, therefore, thinks it would be better to leave him the full advantage of selecting from the whole number of properly educated Veterinary Surgeons. We are glad to record that he recovered from the weakness he first exhibited.

The Memorial, mentioned above, signed by 67 Veterinary Officers, is not in the file, but there is a Memorandum on the subject, which points out that no improvement of any importance

[1] Mr. W. Robinson was a remarkable man whose popularity has rarely been exceeded. He was three times Mayor of Tamworth, in which town he practised for fifty years. He and the Peel family were on terms of friendship (*Veterinarian*, vol. xxv., p. 350). Robinson was one of the foremost in obtaining the Charter. See *Veterinarian*, vol. xxvii. 1854, p. 582.

has been made in their position for half a century, excepting the addition of 2s. 6d. a day to the pay of those who have served upwards of 25 years; that many desirable men decline to join the Army as the remuneration is too small, averaging £135 p.a. for the first twenty years; and that several have left since the Crimean War for more promising occupation. Wilkinson suggests that the saving he has effected of between £500 and £600 a year on the £1,000 a year allowed him for the purchase of drugs would go far to meet the proposed increase in pay. Then follows a strange paragraph: " There appears to be a Warrant in existence relating to a portion of the Artillery, which if extended to the whole Army would more than meet the case of sixty out of the sixty-seven practitioners." The wording of this sentence suggests that at this time the Artillery was not in Wilkinson's administration, though the last Senior Veterinary Officer of the Ordnance had retired. This officer selected his own men, entirely from the London School, and it is evident was able to give them better terms than were obtained in the Cavalry, but what these were we are ignorant. Evidently Mr. Wilkinson did not become P.V.S. of the Army until 1859, some little time after Stockley's retirement.

The scale of pay put forward by Mr. Wilkinson in his proposed new warrant was rejected by the Civil Committee of the War Office on the ground that it was higher than the Medical Service for the particular work; they added that there was a desire on the part of the War Office " to make a distinction between the pay of the horse doctor and the doctor of human patients." The Committee made a strong point of keeping the proposed relative rank low " as these officers serve with regiments and corps where it is important to prevent any approach to the rank of the Commanding Officer." They even proposed that the Veterinary Surgeon should not be promoted after a successful examination *without the certificate of his Commanding Officer!* Wilkinson defeated this proposal by pointing out that in the conscientious discharge of his duties he might incur the displeasure of his commanding officer; evidently he had not forgotten the Johnston case. It is clear that the hand of this Civil Committee was against our Service and the definition of it given above is offensively expressed.

Mr. Wilkinson in his proposed warrant asked for the creation of administrative officers whom he describes as Staff Veterinary Surgeons; he desired they should rank as Majors; to this the Committee agreed, but said they were to be the junior officers of that rank, no matter how long their service. Wilkinson tried to get this amended so as to read " junior of all combatant officers of that rank," but failed. Our officers remained the permanent juniors of their rank in the Army for the next thirty-two years.

There had been a Medical Warrant in 1861 conferring the relative rank of Major on Surgeons; it also stipulated they were to be junior of that rank, but the clause was cancelled in 1863. In the interval, the question of who was the junior major in the Service, the Surgeon or the Staff Veterinary Surgeon, would have proved a puzzle had it ever been raised. Prior to this, Surgeons of Cavalry ranked as Captains but junior of that rank; Assistant Surgeons ranked as junior Lieutenants, but in the Guards and Infantry the Surgeons ranked with Captains according to the date of their commissions.[1]

When the warrant was issued the authorities evidently considered it desirable to deal with the question of relative rank, and defined it as carrying all precedence and advantages attached to the rank to which it corresponded,[2] except as regards Presidencies of Military Courts, Committees and Boards, when the Senior Combatant Officer was always President. It was made clear that relative rank conferred no military command whatever, nor the compliments paid by regimental and garrison guards, but it regulated choice of quarters (but not if the veterinary officer happened to be senior to the commanding officer), rates of lodging money, field allowance, forage, servant's allowance, prize money and compensation for wounds and injuries received in action. It also entitled the widow and family to the allowances granted by Royal Warrant to the widows and children of combatant officers. There was one important thing which relative rank failed to do. It gave no military protection to the officer himself.[3]

In due course the Wilkinson Warrant of 1st July 1859 appeared. It was the first to *grade* Veterinary Officers, by the introduction

[1] See *Roll of Commissioned Officers in the Medical Service of the British Army* 1727-1898, by Colonel W. Johnston, Army Medical Staff, and Lieut.-Colonel H. Howell, R.A.M.C., 1917.

[2] As our officers were junior of the rank this statement was misleading.

[3] In 1862 the Veterinary Surgeon of the 11th Hussars was tried by G.C.M. and dismissed the Service for striking a young officer under circumstances of gross provocation. His case is sympathetically referred to in an article on " Military Law " published in the *United Service Journal* 1862, Part ii., p. 404. If the Veterinary Officer in this case had held actual rank the trouble could never have arisen. Relative rank gave him no protection whatever against the grossest insults, and knowing this he very improperly took the law into his own hands.

of a principle of classification intended "to promote zeal and to encourage ability." The grades were Veterinary Surgeon, relative rank Lieutenant; Veterinary Surgeon 1st Class, as Captain; Staff Veterinary Surgeon, as Major; but in all cases junior of that rank, excepting for choice of quarters, throughout the Army. Mr. Wilkinson, who suggested the grading, may have borrowed the classification from the French Service, where it had been in force for a few years; on the other hand, in 1840 the distinction of first and second class existed among Staff Surgeons of the Army Medical Department, a branch quite distinct from the regimental medical officers, and did not disappear until 1858.

The basis of the Wilkinson Warrant was that promotion was to be given not necessarily by seniority, but by selection for professional ability and meritorious conduct, the selection to be made by the P.V.S. and followed by an examination. A V.S. was eligible for promotion to V.S. 1st Class at five years' service, a V.S. 1st Class to Staff V.S. at 15 years. In practice promotion was not given at these periods, as there was a fixed establishment for each grade and a vacancy had to occur before a promotion could be made. The establishment was as follows: Staff Veterinary Surgeons 3; Veterinary Surgeons 1st Class 25; Veterinary Surgeons 40. In order to maintain efficiency, all V.S.'s and V.S. 1st Class were to be placed on the retired list at the age of 55, and all Staff V.S.'s at the age of 65. The right to retire after 20 years' service, granted under a previous warrant, was withdrawn. Six months' notice had to be given if an officer wished to retire, and if he was under orders for foreign service notice could not be accepted until he had been a month at his new station!

The following were the rates of full and half pay granted by the Warrant of 1859. It is to be noted that in one or two of the articles the term "Veterinary Officer" appears for the first time in an official publication:

RATES OF PAY.

	After 25 Years' Service (p.d.).	After 20 Years.	After 15 Years.	After 10 Years.	After 5 Years.	On Appointment.
Staff Veterinary Surgeon	23s.	22s.	21s.	—	—	—
Veterinary Surgeon (1st Class)	20s.	17s.	15s. 6d.	14s. 6d.	12s. 6d.	—
Veterinary Surgeon ..	14s.	14s.	14s.	13s.	11s. 6d.	10s.
Veterinary Surgeon who entered prior to the date of this Warrant	17s. 6d.	15s.	14s.	13s.	11s. 6d.	10s.

All increases in pay for length of service to be governed by the duties having been discharged with zeal and ability.

HALF PAY.

	After 25 Years' Service (p.d.).	After 20 Years.	After 15 Years.	After 10 Years.	After 5 Years.	After 3 Years.
Staff Veterinary Surgeon	15s.	14s.	Half-pay of former rank.	—	—	—
Veterinary Surgeon (1st Class)	13s. 6d.	11s. 6d.	10s. 6d.	9s. 6d.	Half-pay of former rank.	
Veterinary Surgeon	—	—	9s. 6d.	8s. 6d.	7s.	4s.
Veterinary Surgeon who entered prior to the date of this Warrant	10s.	9s. 6d.	9s. 6d.	8s. 6d.	7s.	4s.

Sidney Herbert was responsible for this warrant. In the letter transmitting it to the Commander-in-Chief occurs the passage: "I am to express to you the confidence with which Mr. Sidney Herbert anticipates that every member of that Branch will respond to the boon thus conferred, by the most constant exertion and zeal in the duties confided to them." In spite of his wishes the warrant did not give satisfaction. The real value of the 1859 Warrant to our Service was first the creation of Administrative Officers and thereby the recognition of control, supervision and staff organization in the Veterinary Service, and secondly the promotion thrown open by retirement of men at a definite age. It was significant that the warrant laid down no maximum age for the P.V.S.

There was nothing in the Warrant of 1859 which affected the prospects of the Principal Veterinary Surgeon, and accordingly in October 1860, Mr. Wilkinson asked that as regards full pay he might be placed upon the same footing as a Deputy Inspector of Hospitals, so as to give him 30s. a day after 35 years' service.[1] He was then in his thirty-fifth year of service and in receipt of 25s. a day pay. In the correspondence which follows it is pointed out that he was not included in the Warrant of 1859, his position being considered rather as an office or appointment and not a rank, "though he holds the relative rank of Colonel" (this had been secured to him by the Duke of Cambridge). The question was submitted to the Treasury, Wilkinson being described as "a most meritorious officer who had done good service to the public," but though Sidney Herbert recommended he should be allowed the same rates of full pay, allowances, half and retired pay, as a Deputy Inspector of Hospitals, it was refused.

A peculiarity of some of Mr. Wilkinson's correspondence may here be noted. In one of his letters, two pages in length, there

[1] P.R.O. W.O. 32/60.

is not a single period; it is one long sentence necessitating the introduction of innumerable "and's," each of which was duly underlined in pencil in the War Office. It is not observed in his professional papers.

After the Mutiny the amalgamation of the Indian and Imperial Armies took place. Officers of the Company's Service were given the opportunity of transferring to the British Establishment or remaining on a local list. Seven Veterinary Officers passed over; twenty-four elected for the local list in India. They were the senior officers who had everything to lose by transfer, for they thereby automatically forfeited their subscriptions to Pension Funds, not only for themselves but for their widows and children.

Prior to the Mutiny very little improvement had been made in the financial conditions of service in India. The first Warrant of 1826 has been referred to at p. 103. In 1847 the Veterinary Surgeons of the Bengal Establishment petitioned the East India Company for the rate of pay and retiring allowance granted to the officers of the Imperial Service under the Royal Warrant of 1846, but this was not granted on the ground that the rates were higher than those paid to combatant officers of corresponding rank. The Court of Directors, however, stated that it was prepared to grant to Veterinary Surgeons the allowances drawn by combatant officers of the same relative rank. Under this arrangement the juniors suffered a loss, but the seniors benefited, although the highest relative rank at that time was only that of Captain. The Royal Warrant of 1859 was not acknowledged by the Government of India, which by now had passed from the "Company" to the Crown. In consequence no administrative officers were appointed and no promotions among officers of the local list were made. The decision was announced in the *Fort William Gazette* of April 1860, in which it is stated that "it was not considered expedient at present" to give effect to the Warrant ! Wilkinson saw to it that the officers of the British Service were promoted as vacancies occurred in the establishment, but the officers on the Indian List received neither promotion nor increase of pay. It was not until May 1865, *six years later*, that the warrant was honoured and made applicable to India. Articles dealing with this disgraceful breach of faith may be consulted in the *Veterinarian*.[1] It was not the last instance of such chicanery.

---

[1] Vol. xxxvi. 1863, pp. 341, 402, 608; vol. xxxvii. 1864, pp. 98, 398, 590, 830; vol. xxxix. 1866, pp. 893, 966; vol. xlii. 1869, p. 580.

When the Royal Warrant of 1859 was accepted by India the rates of pay of both Local and Imperial Forces were fixed as follows:

Staff Veterinary Surgeon of	25 years' service,	Rupees 976 monthly.
,, ,, ,,	20 ,, ,,	,, 964 ,,
,, ,, ,,	15 ,, ,,	,, 952 ,,
Veterinary Surgeon (1st Class) of	25 ,, ,,	,, 627 ,,
,, ,, ,, ,,	20 ,, ,,	,, 590 ,,
,, ,, ,, ,,	15 ,, ,,	,, 572 ,,
,, ,, ,, ,,	10 ,, ,,	,, 560 ,,
,, ,, ,, ,,	5 ,, ,,	,, 535 ,,
Veterinary Surgeon of	25 ,, ,,	,, 426 ,,
,, ,,	20 ,, ,,	,, 426 ,,
,, ,,	15 ,, ,,	,, 426 ,,
,, ,,	10 ,, ,,	,, 414 ,,
,, ,,	5 ,, ,,	,, 395 ,,
Veterinary Surgeon under	5 ,, ,,	,, 377 ,,

Retired Pay for officers of the Indian Service:

After 20 years' service ..	..	£200 per annum.
,, 25 ,, ,,	..	£250 ,,
,, 30 ,, ,,	..	£300 ,,

The chief cause of complaint in the sixties was, as we have seen, the non-application of the 1859 Warrant to India, and that consequently no Staff Veterinary Surgeons were created and no Principal Veterinary Surgeon. To escape their responsibility the Government of India actually asked the opinion of Officers Commanding Brigades of Artillery and Regiments of Cavalry, as to whether *they* thought such administrative appointments necessary! The majority were in favour of the measure. In spite of this the appointment, for Inspecting duties, of combatant officers selected from the *Stud Department* was contemplated, and in one year was actually carried out! But in 1862 the Bombay Government took upon itself to act on the 1859 Warrant, and promoted an officer to the rank of Staff Veterinary Surgeon and subsequently, as an " experimental measure," to Principal Veterinary Surgeon of that Presidency,[1] but nothing was done in Bengal until July 1866, when two *Inspecting* Veterinary Surgeons were appointed, one of the Royal, the other of the Local List.[2] The senior of the two was created Principal Veterinary Surgeon in India.

[1] The officer so promoted was Mr. Hallen of the Bombay Service.
[2] Officers on the local list were examined as to their fitness for promotion by Mr. Wilkinson, the examination questions being sent to India.

The first P.V.S. to hold office in India was Mr. R. J. G. Hurford, an officer of vast Indian experience. He had taken part in every campaign in that country since 1839 and his war service deserves permanent record. With the 16th Lancers he served in the Afghan Campaign of 1839 under Lord Keane, including the Siege and Capture of Ghuznee (medal). He was in the Gwalior Campaign of 1843 and present at the Battle of Maharajpore (medal). He served with the 9th Lancers in the Sikh War, and was at the Battle of Sobraon 1846 (medal). He was in the Punjab Campaign of 1848–49, including the passage of the Chenab at Ramnugger, and Battles of Chillianwallah and Goojerat (medal and clasps). He also served throughout the Mutiny of 1857, and was present at the Siege and Capture of Delhi, actions at Boolundshur and Alighur, Battle of Agra, and the Reliefs of both Cawnpore and Lucknow.

No better selection could have been made for the appointment. Mr. Hurford knew his own mind; he was a man of great presence and firmness, tall and dignified, while his knowledge of the care and management of the troop horse in India was unrivalled. He held office until 1871, when he was retired for age. The second officer selected was Mr. J. Siddall of the Indian Service, the hero of Arrah; he only held office for a few months, dying, strange to say, close to the scene of his great exploit.

At the time of the Bengal appointments, Inspecting Veterinary Surgeons for each of the Presidencies of Bombay and Madras were created. The designation "Inspecting" was adopted in India, whereas in the Warrant the appointment is called "Staff."

In October 1866 instructions were issued respecting the duties of the Principal and Inspecting Veterinary Surgeons; these included an annual inspection not only of the Imperial but Local Forces, but the Stud Department, and the Veterinary Surgeons employed there, who nearly all belonged to the local service, were exempted from veterinary supervision, perhaps for the reason that the abolition of that sink of iniquity had been decided, or perhaps because the officers of the local service were not under the Principal Veterinary Surgeon in India! The same order laid down the sanitary and other duties of executive Veterinary Surgeons, and enjoined a daily inspection of forage, grooming and shoeing of all units under their care, for "Improper diet, bad grooming and careless shoeing are the most frequent causes of all diseases to which the horse is liable." Then follow instructions

PLATE G

1864

To face p 152

for the training of the farriers in hospital duties, to which great importance was attached.[1]

During the six years the Government of India withheld the 1859 Warrant, great hardships were inflicted on both Imperial and Local officers in the matter of pay, and on Local officers in promotion. Officers on the Imperial List were promoted by the War Office as their turn arrived, but no promotions were given to the Local officers; the result was they lost seniority. One of them writing to the *Veterinarian*[2] says, in an able and temperate article: "Officers of the Home Service have passed over our heads, who were children at school when some of us were assisting in the struggles on the frontiers of India." Their grievance in the matter of promotion was primarily due to the attitude of the Government of India and not to the War Office, but there were ways in which the War Office could have rendered the lot of the Local officers more endurable had it cared to do so. But beyond examining them as to their fitness for promotion the War Office left them severely alone, and allowed them gradually to die out, disgusted with their treatment; a few obtained administrative appointments, but as these had to be shared with the Imperial Service they were few and far between. The Local officers were compelled to live in India, even when there was no duty for them to perform, until the time arrived for their retirement. The old army of India had no friends at the War Office; collectively and individually they were unknown. Those combatant officers who transferred from the Indian to the Royal Artillery were placed in a separate list, were generally known as "Hindoo Gunners," and at the Head Quarters of the Royal Regiment were practically ostracized.

From 1860–66 a War in New Zealand dragged on and caused great anxiety owing to many mishaps. Among the officers of the Veterinary Service present was Mr. John Anderson; he was the second Veterinary Surgeon to be mentioned in despatches for rendering outstanding military service. He volunteered to carry despatches through a country occupied by an extraordinarily astute enemy who spared neither prisoners nor wounded, and succeeded. He served in the Taranaki and Waikato Campaigns. At the storming of the Gate Pah, where we suffered heavy loss and were repulsed, he commanded two guns, there being no other officer available owing to casualties.[3] We shall meet with him again.

[1] The full order is published in the *Veterinarian*, vol. xl. 1867, p. 18.
[2] Vol. xlii. 1869, p. 580; vol. xliii. 1870, p. 43.
[3] There is no official record of this. The information was given me many years ago by officers who served in the campaign.

The Warrant of 1859 had done nothing to improve the status of the Veterinary Service, and as we have already indicated it gave no satisfaction. In March 1866 an appeal was submitted to the Principal Veterinary Surgeon, signed by 42 officers headed by Mr. Gloag, asking for an improvement in their position.[1] They point out that the 1859 Warrant fails to confer advantages commensurate with the advances made by other Departments. They indicate the existence of a feeling of growing dissatisfaction. A favourable consideration of their proposals would arrest this and ensure a continuance of zealous service, and the influx into the Army of the best men, who are always the cheapest to employ. The memorialists ask that the Principal Veterinary Surgeon should be a Veterinary Director General, that Staff Veterinary Surgeons should be known as Principal Veterinary Surgeons with the relative rank of Lieut.-Colonel, a small increase in full and retired pay, financial recognition for the Head of the Department in the Field, the relative rank of Major at 20 years' service, good service pensions, retirement for all ranks at 55 years of age in the interests of efficiency, and finally on retirement the conversion of relative into honorary rank. This memorial is of very great interest; it shows that in spite of the deadening influence of Regimental Organization our officers sixty years ago recognized the extraordinary weakness of their position and the disadvantages under which they laboured. The memorial, greatly to his credit, was approved by Mr. Wilkinson, who regarded the appeal as fair and reasonable; the financial cost he pointed out would be only £4 17s. 6d. per diem. The opposition came from the military authorities, who stated that no strong case had been made out, that there was no dearth of candidates and they were unable to see the disadvantages under which the Veterinary Surgeons "imagined" themselves to be labouring.[2]

The earliest attempt to draw up an organization for our Service in war was made in 1866. Mr. Wilkinson was by now firmly seated in office and the lessons of the Crimean War not entirely forgotten. The *Regulations for the Supply of Military Stores to an Army in the Field* 1866, set forth the Veterinary Organization for an "army" consisting of 15,000 fighting men of all arms; for the movement of this Force 10,000 *hired* transport animals were required. To look after them the Wilkinson scheme engaged 40 Acting or Temporary Veterinary Surgeons, holding no commission, but the relative rank of Lieutenant to regulate allow-

[1] P.R.O. W.O. 32/60.   [2] P.R.O. W.O. 32/60.

ances. It is distinctly stated that these 40 civilian gentlemen are *to have the control and management of the Transport duties!* There was to be one Veterinary Surgeon to every 400 transport horses and in addition a reserve was to be formed, termed a "Staff Corps," from which Veterinary Surgeons could be drawn to meet casualties in regiments. There was a Chief Staff Veterinary Surgeon on the Head Quarter Staff, and 4 Staff Veterinary Surgeons, one with each Division, one with the Cavalry Brigade, and one with the "Field Arsenal." An officer as "Purveyor" of medicines was also provided. The subordinate staff consisted of 200 civilian farriers and 200 civilian shoeing-smiths—*i.e.* one of each to every 50 transport animals plus a reserve. Altogether, *exclusive* of the Veterinary Surgeons with the various regiments, Wilkinson's scheme had to furnish for the care of 10,000 transport animals 51 Veterinary Surgeons military and civil; 436 Clerks, Farriers and Shoeing Smiths; 117 camp followers; 51 forge waggons; 102 chests of farrier's tools; a pair of chests for each veterinary officer, weighing 160 lbs.; and six months' supply of drugs in the custody of the "Military Store Dept.," but administered by a Veterinary Officer, the Purveyor.

It is significant of the period that no provision is made for the care of the sick, either of the fighting forces or transport, although in the former case the regimental system accounts for this. The burden of the veterinary regulations for the field is mainly confined to the shoeing of the 10,000 transport animals, for which, as has been seen, elaborate provision was made. Yet with all its deficiencies the scheme was infinitely superior to the arrangements of thirty-two years later, which sent a large army overseas without any organization of its veterinary service.

The Campaign in Abyssinia took place in 1867; it was small but arduous, and everything depended on transport animals. This campaign is of especial interest to us, as it was the first in which the Commander-in-Chief of the Forces in the Field drew attention to the services of the Veterinary Department. He was well served, as his Director of Veterinary Services, though not so styled, was Staff Veterinary Surgeon Hallen, "an able and valuable officer," whose name was known throughout India; his right-hand men were Veterinary Surgeon (1st Class) W. Lamb and Veterinary Surgeon J. Anderson, the latter fresh from New Zealand. There was considerable discontent in the profession that though mentioned in Despatches no honours came their way. As the *Veterinarian* of November 1868 expressed it, "There was no precedent for the recognition of the services of Veterinary Surgeons in the Army, though for sixty years they had shared in the toils, dangers, hardships and victories of the British Arms."

At length some recognition came, not, however, to Staff Veterinary Surgeon Hallen, who being a Veterinary Surgeon was not eligible for a C.B. ! Mr. Lamb was promoted Staff Veterinary Surgeon in consideration of his valuable services during the War. The extraordinary circumstance of the senior officer going unrewarded, while his junior was recognized, shows the strength of the opposition against granting to our Service the honours given to other branches. Veterinary Surgeon John Anderson, though employed three times on Special Service and mentioned in despatches, went unrewarded.

The Abyssinian Campaign is of great historical interest to us, because for the first time an effort was made to deal with casualties among animals by the immediate formation of hospitals, or as they were called, "Sick Depots," on the Lines of Communication. They were necessarily crude, being improvised in the Field instead of being an integral part of the Expedition. The subordinate personnel was untrained, the veterinary officers doing their own dispensing and dressings. But it was a step forward, and the results were so superior to anything previously obtained, that the Commander-in-Chief made a special point of introducing the subject into his Despatch. Many years later, among the last letters written by Lord Napier, was one to Dr. Fleming in which he referred to the value of the Veterinary Service in Abyssinia.[1]

The official position of the Principal Veterinary Surgeon in the Army List has already been referred to (p. 83). On the advent of Cherry we find him shown at Chatham in the "Garrison Infantry and Invalid Depot." Evidently the authorities were in difficulties as to his posting, but in order to show that he was not at Chatham the word "Clapham" is inserted after his name. For the first year of his term of office he officially remained at Chatham, but for all other years he is shown under the heading "Cavalry Depot, Maidstone." He was not on the Staff of the Depot, but like the "Superintendent of Sword Exercise," evidently for convenience, is shown under Cavalry Depot, the word Clapham appearing after his name. Proximity to the Cavalry Depot no doubt suggested Cavalry Depot Staff uniform as the most appropriate for the P.V.S. and later on for his administrative officers.

[1] *Veterinary Journal*, vol. xxx. 1890.

When Wilkinson came into office in 1854 he also was shown under the heading "Cavalry Depot, Maidstone," but in 1859 under the head of "Staff, Great Britain." Up to this time there was no page in the Army List showing collectively the officers of the Veterinary Service, but in 1859 a page appeared headed "Veterinary Medical Department"; in May of that year it showed two Acting Veterinary Surgeons, but by December Wilkinson was shown as head of the Department, and the names of his staff of Administrative Veterinary Officers, and those of the Acting Veterinary Surgeons followed. In January 1861 the word "Medical" was dropped and the designation became "Veterinary Department." No regimental officers appeared on this page until October 1869; they were then inserted, and after their names the regiments to which they belonged were shown. This arrangement lasted until 1878, when the veterinary officers of the Artillery, Engineers and Army Service Corps having become departmental their regiments were omitted; finally in 1881 the Cavalry being departmentalized all regiments were omitted. In both cases the officers automatically disappeared from the regimental lists.

At no time were Coleman, Cherry or Wilkinson members of the War Office Staff. The Medical Department of the Army was not included in the War Office until April 1856, and the Veterinary Department was not admitted until July 1876.

The state of Europe had never been considered more peaceful than in the year 1870. Statesmen in this country with the best opportunities for knowing, declared the political horizon to be perfectly clear. Precisely the same ignorant official optimism existed when the Indian Mutiny broke out; and the year 1914 was no exception. In the summer of 1870 France and Germany were locked in the throes of a desperate struggle, in which France was shattered for nearly fifty years. The suddenness of the conflict, and the extraordinarily perfect organization of Germany, led to introspection in this country. One of the first reforms was the abolition of the purchase of commissions and of regimental commands. This occurred in 1871; from that time onwards it was possible for a poor man to rise steadily in his regiment and by ability finally to command it. It may be thought that this has no bearing on the Veterinary Service, but it was by no means without effect, as we shall show later. Among general effects it led to the study of war as a profession, and the improvement in the fighting branches necessitated corresponding improvement in the ancillary services. In the case of our own department improvement came very slowly and extended over very many years, nevertheless the Franco-German War may be taken as opening the eyes of the nation to the helplessness of an unorganized army in a struggle with an organized and powerful neighbour.

In 1872 new Regulations for the Veterinary Service were introduced; none had been published since Mr. Cherry's period of office in 1853, so that they were long overdue. I cannot say that I have not seen a copy of the 1872 regulations, inasmuch as they were in use when I joined, but I have only a general recollection of their contents and so far as I know no copy exists. Autumn manœuvres in 1875, the first since the camp at Chobham just before the Crimean War, showed that the military authorities were taking the Continental lesson to heart. The publication in 1876 of *The Organization and Composition of an Army Corps* must have come as a surprise to many. It was the first time that any effort had been made to organize the Army for War. The Army Corps consisted of three Divisions, and the total number of animals was 11,863. The Veterinary Service consisted of a Chief Staff Veterinary Surgeon on the Head Quarter Staff, and a Staff Veterinary Surgeon as administrative officer to each Division. The number of executive officers for an Army Corps was 35, or one to every 340 animals. It is not clear where and how the P.V.S. proposed to obtain his executive officers and replace wastage, for his total number of officers at home and abroad was only 122, and he had no reserve. No provision of any kind existed for the care of the sick, other than being dragged along by their units; precisely as the men had been up to the end of the eighteenth century, when if they were unable to keep up they were left on the side of the road, to be robbed or murdered by camp followers or peasants, or with any good fortune to fall into the hands of the enemy. It must be remembered that this veterinary organization was initiated or accepted by an old man, who had never been on service, foreign or active. Yet if John Wilkinson were with us to-day he would undoubtedly defend the regimental treatment of the sick, though a little study of the Crimean Campaign must have shown him the worthlessness of such a system. The only reference made in the professional literature of the day to this organization was in the *Veterinary Journal*[1] by Fleming, whose criticism is directed against the titles of the administrative

[1] Vol. ii. 1876.

officers. He considered them most confusing, and urged the title of Inspecting Veterinary Surgeon. He does not comment on the lack of provision for the care of the sick, yet he had active service experience in the Black Sea depots during the war with Russia, and subsequently in the war with China.

Among other indications of the desire for change growing out of the gradual reorganization of the Army, was the effort made to give practical expression to a feeling, which had long existed in the Veterinary Department, that Principal Veterinary Surgeon John Wilkinson had outlived his usefulness, and that his retention of office year after year was a block to promotion and progress. He was now seventy-two years old, had served continuously for fifty-one years, and for twenty-two years had been head of his department. There is no doubt that he regarded his office as a life-appointment, such as his predecessors had enjoyed. This idea was rather rudely upset on 13th March 1876, when a question was asked in the House of Commons as to the duration of the appointment. The reply was that no warrant fixing the period existed, but that it was a question for consideration whether it would not be prudent to make a change in this respect, and place the appointment on the same footing as that of the Director General of the Medical Service. On 28th April a further question was put asking what decision had been arrived at; the reply was that Mr. Wilkinson's retirement was in progress and that application had been made to the Treasury for his pension. It was further decided that there was to be a time limit to the appointment. This decision was Mr. Wilkinson's death warrant; before his retirement could be carried out he died suddenly on 28th May 1876, his widow following him a few weeks later.

It is impossible to pass over without further comment the administration of an officer who for nearly a quarter of a century directed the destinies of our Service. Unlike Coleman he had no other irons in the fire; he concentrated on his duties, and safeguarded the Army against disease by inculcating sound sanitation and rational horse management. He exercised rigid care in his selection of candidates for the Veterinary Service. During his long tenure things stagnated, for old men with new ideas are rare and he doubtless regarded the regimental system of the Veterinary Service as perfect. His care of stores and parsimony regarding them has already been mentioned. Improved equipment had been introduced during his period of office, the chests being in pairs, but the date of the change is unknown. It is quite certain that in the matter of stores we were not only far behind the times, but the reserves for the Field were most inadequate. We have seen (p. 134) that he would not spend more than half the money allowed him, and it was very many years after his death before the stores and reserves were satisfactory. We may feel sure that he considered that in pattern they were all that could be desired, and this conservative attitude was in accordance with the military spirit of the age. At the time of his death we had a citizen army of 200,000 men armed with a muzzle-loading rifle, though after the Franco-German War every other nation possessing these had consigned them to the scrap-heap. Our Artillery were armed with a muzzle-loading gun hopelessly inefficient, though it was known throughout the world that the breech-loading field gun had won the war for Germany. Stagnation must always occur where only old brains are employed and retained in office. Young receptive minds can look ahead, but the old can only look back.

CHAPTER V

THE EVOLUTION OF THE ARMY VETERINARY SERVICE, 1876-1919

ON the death of Mr. Wilkinson the Authorities showed considerable judgement in choosing his successor. We do not know to whom Mr. James Collins owed his selection, for he was promoted over the head of a very senior officer, a difficult matter under the then Commander-in-Chief.

James Collins (Plate 1), 1830-95, was of Irish birth. He graduated from the Edinburgh Veterinary College in 1852 and joined the Service in 1854, being appointed to the Inniskilling Dragoons, then in the Crimea. He was present at Balaclava, Inkerman and Sebastopol, and left the Crimea in 1856. In 1858 he proceeded to India, where he served for twelve years, being promoted to 1st Class after eight years' service, and to administrative rank as I.V.S. Bombay Command at the phenomenal service of twelve years! On returning from India in 1870 he served in Ireland until 1876, and on 28th June of that year at 46 years of age and 22 years' service, he was selected as Principal Veterinary Surgeon of the Army. This is an astonishing record of early promotion; his advancement to 1st Class and to administrative rank was clearly due to Mr. Wilkinson, who exercised the wide powers of selection placed in his hands by the Warrant of 1859.

Mr. Collins was a tall, soldier-like man, direct in speech, sharp and decisive in manner, with a firm face which he occasionally permitted to relax, a strict disciplinarian, kindly to the deserving, straightforward and impartial. He was short-sighted and wore an eyeglass. His appointment was for seven years. We intend to show that he deserves to be remembered as the strongest administrator and most thorough reformer who has ever occupied office. When he took up office a new era opened for our Service, and from his day to the present time the Department has steadily gone forward. He assumed duties at the period already indicated as critical when the British Army was in the melting pot. He had perfectly clear-cut views as to what was necessary for the regeneration of the Veterinary Service. He had seen the evils of the regimental method of dealing with sick animals in war and the impotence of any veterinary organization based on a regimental system. His wise administration will ever be remembered for the abolition of regimental Veterinary Officers and the unification of the

Department. In addition he secured for his service a long catalogue of concessions, none of which, it is safe to say, were granted on request.

He was only 53 when retired on completion of appointment, and lived twelve years longer.

The establishment of the Veterinary Service when Mr. Collins took over office was 1 P.V.S., 8 Staff Veterinary Surgeons (five at home and three in India), 67 Veterinary Surgeons of Artillery, 31 of Cavalry, 6 of Army Service Corps, 2 of Royal Engineers, 2 with Remount Depots, 12 General Service and 8 Probationers; total 137; the strength was 122.

One of the first changes made was to get his office recognized as part of the War Office; it was accordingly moved from the Royal Horse Infirmary, Woolwich, to Pall Mall. In Mr. Wilkinson's time the office of the P.V.S. had no connection with the War Office (p. 157); it was a room in his own quarters, and he received a monetary allowance and provided his own clerk. Later he was given a soldier clerk, who at the time of Mr. Wilkinson's death was a Bombardier in the Coast Brigade of Artillery. On the transfer of the P.V.S.'s office to London, he became a War Office clerk, and remained at the War Office until his death many years later, having served no less than seven heads of the department. Mr. Bathurst's name was known to two generations of veterinary officers.

Before he had been six months in office, Mr. Collins began his fight for an improved Veterinary Service.[1] On 18th December 1876 he drew the Adjutant General's attention to the fact that he could not fill the vacancies on his establishment, as the emoluments in private life were higher than in the Army, and the prospect of long Indian service acted as a deterrent. He then put forward a scheme for placing all veterinary officers in one department and stationing them for duty in the various military districts. At the same time he expressed his doubts as to the wisdom of the step so far as the Cavalry was concerned, as not only was that branch more popular but there were important remount duties to perform which would suffer by frequent changes of officers.[2] He was prepared to include them in the scheme if they were permitted to be attached to a regiment for five years. When this proposal reached the Financial Authorities it was negatived on the score of expense. The P.V.S. soon returned to the attack and submitted another scheme. In this he proposed that all new

---

[1] P.R.O. W.O. 32/60.
[2] In those days each cavalry regiment remounted itself.

entrants should join on a ten years' engagement at £250 per annum, half of them to be retained at the end of that period, and the other half to be discharged with a bonus of £800. He was here following the Medical Service, which was recruited on the short service basis. The struggle with the Finance branch lasted throughout the whole of 1877 and part of 1878, so that before looking at the new warrant we must see what events of interest to our Service were happening outside the War Office.

India had been a source of great trouble; the course of events up to 1866 has been described at pp. 127, 150, 153. The Government of India had then after years of delay appointed a P.V.S. and other administrative officers, but subsequent vacancies due to death or retirement (the P.V.S. retired for age in 1871) were not filled up. For reasons unknown the Government had determined not to make any permanent appointments, and filled vacancies by employing " officiating " officers; this state of affairs continued for six years, with the result that dissatisfaction was general. Finally in 1876 Mr. F. F. Collins (brother of James) was appointed P.V.S. in India. It was also decided that the P.V.S. at home could communicate on professional questions with the P.V.S. India, so that matters were in a fair way of settlement. The difficulty was to know what to do with the surviving group of local officers. They had no status in the Imperial Army, and few of them could have understood anything of its organization. Among this small group was Mr. Hallen, one of the ablest men who have ever entered our profession. We shall see little or nothing of him, for his work lay in India and outside our Service. His appointment as Superintendent of Horse Breeding Operations, and his duties in connection with Cattle Plague and the abolition of the old Indian Studs, kept him employed for several years. It fell to Mr. Hallen, as the working member of a Commission, to break up the effete and hopelessly incompetent Stud administration, and to start, under competent management, something less expensive and better suited to the requirements of the country. There is, however, a sequel to this story which will appear later.

Mr. J. Collins had served several years in India and was well aware how hardly Indian service pressed upon some officers, especially those of the Artillery. Artillery Veterinary Surgeons accompanied their Brigades to India, and Veterinary Surgeons of Cavalry accompanied their regiments, in every case with the prospect of twelve years' foreign service. So-called Heavy Cavalry were not sent to India, so that veterinary service in these regiments was greatly sought after. The P.V.S. therefore, in order to equalize Indian Service, which was being largely borne by junior officers of Artillery, determined to establish a roster for Foreign Service even while our organization was purely regimental. In 1876 there were 62 Veterinary Officers in India and 58 on the Home Establishment; of these 58, thirty held commissions in Cavalry and therefore did not come into the general roster for service abroad. This left 28 officers to relieve 68 in India. Consequently, while many officers had been from eight to twenty-two years continuously on the home establishment, officers who had already served from six to ten years in India found themselves after four years at home again under orders for Foreign Service. Further, in 1876 out of 42 officers of the 1st Class only 10 were in India, so that among the class next for promotion to administrative rank, few had the necessary training in service abroad. Orders were issued that no officer would be promoted Staff Veterinary Surgeon who had not completed a tour of foreign service; further, if an officer declined to leave his regiment in order to go abroad he would automatically forfeit claim to promotion. This order created consternation and the strongest personal ill-feeling against the P.V.S. Yet it is obvious the legislation was just and reasonable; to send an officer to India in an administrative capacity who had never previously served in that country was a farce; his ignorance led to trouble. Nevertheless, such an appointment actually occurred. It is obvious also that the disproportionate share of foreign service which fell to the Veterinary Officers of Artillery was a serious hardship.

In 1876 died a well-known officer of our Service whose name must be mentioned. James Thacker had served with the 12th Lancers in the Kaffir War of 1851-53, subsequently in the 15th, and later in the 10th Hussars. He was not only highly skilled professionally, but in his day was one of the best known amateur riders in the country. He had had many falls steeplechasing, and was popularly believed to have broken at one time or another every bone in his body. He rode with a short cane, which in one of his numerous accidents actually destroyed the sight of one eye. As a judge of a horse he had no superior, and when he retired in 1875 the Government of India appointed him Remount Agent for Bengal, a well-deserved recognition of his remarkable ability. He died in the following year at Melbourne, where he had gone to purchase horses.

During 1877 the first Veterinary Statistical Report on the Horses of the British Army was published; it covered the financial year 1876–77. Such a publication had long been needed. An anonymous writer in Colburn's *United Service Magazine* in 1872 had urged that this information should be tabulated and given to the public, but nothing was done until Collins entered office. A summary of the Report may be seen in the *Veterinary Journal*, vol. v. 1877, p. 426.

During the years 1877–1878 there was great dissatisfaction in the Veterinary Service and the P.V.S. was blamed for not getting his Warrant through. Having been behind the scenes, as the correspondence in P.R.O. W.O. 30/60 takes us, we know now how hard he was working at the subject and how his efforts were being frustrated. On the 22nd April 1878 the long looked for Warrant appeared. It abolished the regimental system in all but Cavalry. It introduced limited service for all new entrants, the period being ten years; at the end of that time not more than four officers annually were to be selected for retention. The new entrant received £250 a year exclusive of allowances, as against £182 10s. for the officer of corresponding rank under the old warrant, who received no allowances. It fixed the period of promotion to first class at 12 years' service instead of approximately 10 years as under the previous warrant. It increased the pay and retiring allowances of the Administrative Veterinary Officers, but as the maximum retired pay was not obtainable until 30 years' service, instead of 25 years as in the previous warrant, it created a block in promotion. All officers had a right to retire at 20 years' service and retirement was compulsory at 55 years for all ranks. Nothing was done for the P.V.S. excepting to fix his retired pay at £500 a year; his pay remained at £750 consolidated, and the title of Veterinary Surgeon General which had been asked for was refused. The relative rank of the P.V.S. remained as Colonel, but the Administrative Officer, now known under this Warrant as Inspecting Veterinary Surgeon, remained a Major and junior of that rank, excepting the P.V.O. in India, who ranked as a Lieut. Colonel. The Warrant did not authorize the conferment of Good Service Pensions, of Honours for Active Service, or give the right of Presentation at Court. It had been hoped that these grievances would have been removed.

The Warrant accordingly gave no satisfaction, excepting at the extreme ends of the scale; the new men were better paid, and the Inspecting Officers were both better paid and received a better retiring allowance. No one could have been more dissatisfied than the P.V.S., who had had to surrender much in order to departmentalize two-thirds of his officers. He knew well the hardship of the twelve years' rule as regards promotion to first class, and before he left office he got the period brought back to ten years. Nevertheless the Warrant of 1878 was the first big step towards efficiency. It is evident, however, that no organization for war was possible until *every* officer of the Service was at the disposal of the P.V.S. and no longer subject, so far as his professional duties were concerned, to the orders of the regiment to which he belonged. The regimental system was a peace system with great drawbacks. True it furnished amenities which were lost on its abolition, but it was a strangle-hold on development and efficiency. There are still some fourteen regimental officers alive to-day.

The year 1878 saw a further attempt at the organization of the Army for War. On 1st June there was published *Regulations for the Organization of the Lines of Communication of an Army in the Field*. It was there laid down that the charge of an executive veterinary officer was 250 animals, while there was to be an administrative officer for every 3,000. The P.V.S. must have known that on service the effective charge would be much more than 250, but no doubt he found it either difficult or impossible to extract a reserve from the authorities, so fixed the charge per officer as low as possible in order to admit of the numbers being increased. Actually this scale required more officers than the establishment could provide. It will be observed that the charge is expressed in terms of " animals " and it is made clear that this includes horses, mules and other animals employed in transport, also slaughter cattle. The Regulations clearly state that veterinary officers will be posted to the Army in the Field by the P.V.S. Curiously enough there is a scale of Farriers laid down, one Farrier Q.M.S. for every 500 animals, and one Farrier Sergt. and one Shoeing Smith for every 50 horses or mules.[1] These men were intended for veterinary purposes, namely the care of the sick in the Field, but where were they to come from? They simply did not exist, excepting in regiments, and a regiment, whether going on service or not, required its Farriery Staff. We do not know what really were Mr. Collins' proposals to the authorities, as there are no papers bearing on the question, but it is clear that he was endeavouring to obtain a subordinate staff. Short of enlisting and training men for the purpose, the only

[1] There is much about this organization which recalls the Wilkinson scheme of 1866 (see p. 154).

alternative was to attempt to borrow men from regiments, a system followed for the next quarter of a century.

In these regulations of 1878 will be found a scale of drugs and instruments for 5,000 animals in the Field. Some of the items are interesting: ox bladders for administering enemata, pewter syringes for wound dressings (the piston of which always bent), iron mortar, ladle, pot and kettle, perforated tin lantern which gave no light, a case of dissecting instruments providing the only knives furnished. All this equipment was a relic of the Wilkinson administration. Simplicity and inefficiency were the characteristics of the stores issued; everything was out of date and belonged indeed to the pre-Crimean period. For this Mr. Collins was not responsible; existing supplies had to be used up and new equipment could only be obtained after a prolonged fight and years of delay in manufacture. At this time the officer's personal technical equipment, apart from the instrument case over his shoulder, which was his own property, consisted of a pair of Wilkinson Veterinary Field Chests Nos. 1 and 2, each weighing complete 77 lbs. and when empty 29 lbs. To supplement the instruments mentioned above, the chests contained a phleme and blood stick, seton needles, bullet forceps, also bull's eye lantern. There were no surgical knives, artery or other forceps. The number of bandages provided was *three* and there were no absorbent dressings. One chest was the complement of the other, so that when one was lost the usefulness of the other was greatly impaired. In 1881 *Regulations for the Supply of Stores in the Field* were issued and provided for a veterinary depot of stores, sufficient for six months, to be held by the Ordnance Store Department. It was located anywhere on the L. of C. between the base and front, and a specially appointed officer of the Veterinary Service, technically known as a Purveyor, was attached to the Ordnance Store Department to supervise and issue stores. This arrangement is almost identical with the Regulations of 1866, p. 155. Two points will not escape observation: the Veterinary Service was still being dry-nursed, another department holding its stores, and the stores were not located in the best position.

The hopelessness of the veterinary equipment for the Field may be judged from what we have said; the Campaigns in South Africa and Egypt, during the administration of Mr. Collins, brought many defects to light, and gave an impetus to a reorganization of equipment which began in the next administration. The arrangements for Veterinary Hospitals in the Field are for the first time laid down in the above-quoted *Regulations for the Organization of the Lines of Communication for an Army in the Field* 1878. They are not referred to as hospitals but as Remount Depots, one at the Base and one Advanced. They were entirely under combatant control and received the healthy horses for issue to the troops as well as the war-worn and diseased from the front. Presumably Mr. Collins accepted this disgraceful organization, but there are no papers on the subject in the old veterinary file in the P.R.O. The personnel of these depots consisted of men of the A.S.C., convalescents and hired local labour.

In 1878 occurred the first Afghan War, which was fought on a purely regimental basis. It was soon followed by the second Afghan Campaign, and administrative officers were now appointed to the two Field Forces employed, and Base Hospitals established. Their organization was haphazard, having no definite basis; the veterinary department was under-staffed, and the loss of animals from want of professional supervision and general neglect, gave rise a year or two later to prolonged discussion in the House of Commons, which was all to our advantage.

When the new Warrant of 1878 was published the Government of India refused, as usual, to recognize it, and for over a year officers who joined on the promise of £250 a year received in India the old rate of pay, which was much less. It was not until August 1879 that India agreed to recognize the Warrant, but nevertheless did not restore the back pay !

In 1878 occurred the Wars in the Cape, finally terminating in the Transvaal Campaign. A P.V.S. was appointed to South Africa during hostilities, a decided advance in organization. We learned much from the South African Campaigns both as regards diseases and equipment and organization. We also learned a good deal from both the first and second Afghan Wars, but in this case the lessons, though stated officially to have been taken to heart, led to no increase in the efficiency of the Veterinary Service.

There was much feeling when the war honours for India and South Africa came out and nothing fell to the Veterinary Department. It was not until the following year that the P.V.S. at the Cape was granted a Good Service Reward of £50 a year. Two executive officers received the thanks of H.R.H. the Commander-in-Chief for their services in that campaign, or rather series of campaigns, while one of them, V.S. (1st Class) F. Duck, was specially mentioned in Colonel Buller's Despatch, published

PLATE H

To face p 168

in the *London Gazette* 5th July 1879, for his skill and unremitting attention and for his gallantry in action. Nothing was done for the officers in India, who were not even referred to in the C.-in-C.'s Despatches. The *Army and Navy Gazette*, ever a staunch friend to the Department, over and over again referred to the good work done by our Service and urged some recognition.

In July 1880 a Royal Warrant was published providing for the special promotion to the rank of 1st Class of Veterinary Surgeons who had rendered distinguished service in the Field. It will be observed that this warrant only applied to one rank of officer; only the junior branch was provided for. The V.S. of the 1st Class, or the P.V.S. were not mentioned. The Department and its friends had long been pressing for recognition for war service. This was the outcome, the promotion of junior officers " without reference to seniority " to the rank of 1st Class. Perhaps no previous legislation ever inflicted so cruel a blow on a small service. This Warrant of July 1880 subsequently damned the career of more than half the senior officers in the Department. Officers found themselves passed over for no cause within their control, and their accession to administrative rank owing to the age limit was rendered in some cases impossible. This order was followed by the gravest discontent, which increased within the next few years as junior after junior passed over the heads of seniors (one officer passed over thirty-seven heads) and by the mere accident of age blocked promotion for years. This was the Authorities' idea of recognizing valuable service in the Field. It was the cheapest and worst conceived scheme ever devised; it ruined the future of all officers passed over, and created a feeling of discontent and disgust which did not die out until all these officers had left the Service for age. If Mr. Collins agreed to this Warrant it was the greatest mistake of his administration. It is more than likely that he was never consulted, and that the scheme was devised by the Military Secretary and the Financial Branch, who had not considered its ultimate effect on the Department.

Let this matter be fairly stated. No one in the Department objected to juniors being rewarded for active service. For years recognition had been asked, but it was expected to take the form of brevet promotion, which would have given the officer the financial advantages of the higher rank without altering his position on the list of seniority. Further, it was not thought possible that awards would be limited to the junior rank alone, but would apply equally throughout. In no case, excepting in the selection of administrative officers, was it ever supposed that one man would be put over the heads of others, no matter how distinguished his service. The chaos such a system would have provoked in a regiment was recognized, and such promotions were never made; why a Department of the Army was selected for such an experiment is beyond comprehension.

We have previously noted (p. 166) that the number of Veterinary Surgeons to be employed in War exceeded the numbers available. In November 1880 a reserve of veterinary officers was approved, consisting of officers on half pay and Yeomanry veterinary officers; in this way a reserve of 43 was obtained (on paper). In April 1881 £150 a year, inclusive of all allowances, was approved for these officers if called up, and they were permitted to be employed up to the age of 65. How Mr. Collins expected to secure the services of the Yeomanry officers is not quite clear; they were all regimental and under their Commanding Officers, and so remained for the next thirty years.

A project strongly advocated by Mr. Collins was the creation of an Army Veterinary School. He started his agitation in 1878. His scheme embraced the instruction of combatant officers in the care and management of animals, the veterinary treatment of simple cases when no veterinary officer was available, and the selection and purchase of remounts. Probationary veterinary officers were to be trained in their military duties and regimental farriers and shoeing smiths taught their duties as hospital assistants. In addition, he proposed that the school should be a centre of research; his proposals on this subject may be reproduced, for they have never previously been made public.[1] He begins by saying that the Instructor of the School must not be classed with Instructors of Musketry and Garrison Classes: "I desire that the Veterinary Instructor should be something more than these. He will require close application, constant observation, study and original research. He will require to travel in order to ascertain what is doing in Continental Veterinary Schools, and gather information from every source to impart to his class of Veterinary Surgeons. All this will entail demands on his income." It is evident that this far-seeing reformer realized the value of research work, but it is also evident that he could not carry out this ambitious programme single handed, and it was another eight years before any research work was produced. Behind the

[1] P.R.O. W.O. 32/60 $\left[\text{See File } \frac{7017}{920}\right]$.

P.V.S. in the formation of this School was the General Officer Commanding the Cavalry Brigade at Aldershot, Major General Sir Fredk. Fitzwygram, himself a member of the profession. He entered into the scheme heart and soul, not only in the interests of the rising generation of veterinary officers, but also of the combatant officers, whom he was anxious to see assume a position as horse-masters, to which at that time few of them could lay claim.

Lieut. General Sir Frederick Fitzwygram, Bart., qualified at Edinburgh in 1854 when a Captain in the 6th Dragoons. His professional experience was necessarily limited as he never practised excepting on the occasions when the veterinary officer of the regiment he later commanded (15th Hussars) went on leave, when he was always good enough to act for him. His *Notes on Shoeing Horses* (1861-63) were based on the information he received from Mr. H. Hallen, Veterinary Surgeon 6th Dragoons. One may easily miss the author's acknowledgement in this respect, as it appears only in the last paragraph of the book. *Horses and Stables*, published in 1862, 69, and 86, is believed to be from the same pen; the second and third editions were revised by officers of the Army Veterinary Service. Both works were full of sound common sense, and unquestionably played an important part in the education of the combatant officer in the care and management of horses and the prevention of disease.

Sir Frederick Fitzwygram was a good friend to the profession and especially interested in educational questions. He was a member of Council of the Royal College of Veterinary Surgeons for twenty years and a President for four years. In 1875 when President he founded the Fitzwygram Prizes and thus gave practical evidence of his interest in the profession with which he had for so long been identified.

To understand the position of combatant officers of Cavalry regiments at this time, we must remember that the Cavalry was being regenerated, it was about to get rid of the shackles which had fettered it for the better part of two centuries. The abolition of purchase in the year 1871 had given new life to the Army, for officers could now look forward to merit and zeal, rather than a large banking account, helping in their advancement.[1] With this emancipation came the necessity for study, for they were now really responsible for the unit of which they had command, instead of nominally responsible as in the old purchase days, when

---

[1] The price of a Lieut. Colonelcy in the Cavalry of the Line was a little over £6,000. This was the regulation price. Sums four or even five times larger were paid in special regiments. It cannot be wondered at that under these conditions regiments were regarded as personal property, and their owners converted into autocrats.

a Cavalry regiment was run by the Adjutant and Regimental Sergt. Major, while officers commanding troops—as they were called before the introduction of the squadron as a unit—had no more control over the drill and training of their men and horses than the man in the street. Under the old system in the usual course of events the officer hung on until he got his "troop," which gave him a captaincy, and he then retired, unless he was comfortable in his regiment and it was not going abroad. The process of emancipation, as well as the growth of capability to assume the powers now gradually being placed in the hands of unit commanders, was extremely slow; a new generation had to arise. A man who for years had never had a voice in the feeding or management of his horses, whose men were paid by a regimental Paymaster, drilled by an Adjutant or Regimental Sergt. Major, and who had not the power to take a horse of his own troop out of the stable without permission from his commanding officer, was not likely to embrace with zeal a newly found freedom which he was not trained to use.

This digression enables the reader to understand why General Fitzwygram and others attached such importance at its inception to the Army Veterinary School. It was to be a training ground in horse management. Many years had to elapse before some regiments threw off their conservative prejudices, and at last perceiving the benefits of a system which potentially made every officer of a regiment a soldier instead of an ornament, entered whole-heartedly into the work of the School. Necessarily it was in the so-called "poor regiments" that the change came quickest. For many years every commanding officer that succeeded to his regiment had been brought up under the old vicious system, and very grudgingly gave power to his unit commanders; and in some regiments none was given. A new race of cavalry officers had to grow up, and in this the Army Veterinary School played its part. In the Artillery the situation was entirely different; commissions had always been unpurchasable in that regiment; the officers were frequently poor men, devoted to their profession, and ever since the year 1822, when the abolition of the Corps of Artillery Drivers gave them control of horse management, battery commanders had had a free hand in their unit, and in return gave considerable latitude to the subaltern officers under them. The regimental system in the Artillery was then, as now, to foster independence, to teach officers while young to accept responsibility, and to think and act for themselves in an emergency.

The result is to turn out such officers and other ranks as are unequalled in any army in Europe.

A rate of pay of £150 a year was given to the Instructor, but the Financial Authorities were determined to spend no money on the scheme, and consequently the P.V.S. had actually to surrender one of his few staff appointments in order to secure a stipend for the Instructor. The loss of this appointment meant in the course of years that several men who would have been promoted and subsequently retired on the pay of an administrative officer, were not promoted and retired on a lower rate of pay.

The School was opened on 1st June 1880, the P.V.S. attending the opening. V.S. 1st Class J. Lambert had been appointed Instructor. Mr. Collins remained sufficiently long in the Service to see the School permanently established. He caused an Artillery School he had formed at Woolwich in 1878 to be merged into that at Aldershot.

The first Annual Dinner of the Department was held on 11th June 1880, and of the thirty-six officers present, five are still alive at the date on which this is written (16. 11. 26).

Veterinary History Sheets were introduced in 1880.

In this year, under the Presidency of Major General Sir Fredk. Fitzwygram, a War Office Committee sat to enquire into the organization of the Veterinary Department. It is significant that the P.V.S. was not a member of the Committee; our interests were represented by a civilian, Professor G. T. Brown, a very able man but absolutely ignorant of military requirements. For the information of the Committee the P.V.S. stated his views on the foreign service question; he drew attention to the facts that in time of war India did not increase her establishment of veterinary officers to meet the extra work, and that an increase in pay for the officers serving in that country was long overdue. He also took occasion to represent the deep sense of injury and unfair treatment then general in the Department owing to their non-participation in honours and rewards for active service, adding that not one officer's name had been brought forward for the recent campaign in Afghanistan.

This Committee recommended the complete departmentalization of the Veterinary Service, thus bringing in the Cavalry and abolishing all Cavalry appointments in future. It urged that India should act with greater liberality in the matter of the number of officers employed, especially on service, and that an increase in pay should be given. It expressed no opinion on the unfair treatment of veterinary officers in the distribution of mentions and rewards for active service.

On 1st April 1881 the regimental veterinary system in Cavalry was accordingly abolished and henceforward the Veterinary Service was known as the Army Veterinary Department, all officers, excepting those of Household Cavalry, being transferred to one list and wearing one uniform.

A Royal Warrant was published in April 1881 granting "charge pay" to the Senior Veterinary Officer in a command abroad (the Warrant did not apply to India) when the total number of animals exceeded 1,500, and to the Senior Veterinary Officer in the Field when the number of animals exceeded 5,000.

In July 1881 the profession was made acquainted with the remarkable discovery made in India by Dr. Evans, Army Veterinary Department, of the presence, in the blood of horses and camels affected with "Surra," of large flagellated organisms, since named Trypanosoma. No importance was at first attached by the medical authorities in India to this momentous discovery. Why the military authorities referred Dr. Evans' report to the Sanitary Commissioner to the Government of India was never known, but his views were condemned by this authority in very unmeasured, in fact insulting language, and Dr. Evans was informed that he had mistaken effect for cause. Considerable feeling was created in the Veterinary Service by the attitude of the Sanitary Commissioner, and the *Veterinary Journal* in its July issue for 1881 hit back very hard. The *Army and Navy Gazette* also took up the case, and said that the Military Department of the Government of India had aggravated their offence by publishing a further criticism on Dr. Evans' discovery, this time from the pen of the Editor of the *Indian Agriculturist*, a gentleman who admitted that he knew nothing of the subject, but forwarded a preparation which would cure animals in any stage of the disorder!

Dr. Griffith Evans (Plate 6) was born in Wales in 1835 and entered the Army Veterinary Service in 1860. He proceeded to Canada in 1861, where he served several years with the Royal Artillery, taking part in the Field Operations against the Fenians in 1866 and 1870, for which he received the Canadian General Service Medal with two bars. While at Montreal he graduated in medicine at the McGill University. At Toronto he met a young medical student who subsequently became Sir William Osler, Regius Professor of Medicine at Oxford. Osler refers to Evans' scientific enthusiasm.[1] In 1879 Evans was in India, and in 1880 made his important discovery of *Surra*

[1] *Life of Sir William Osler*, by Professor H. Cushing, 1925.

PLATE VI

GRIFFITH EVANS, M.D., D.Sc., Ch.M.
Inspecting Veterinary Surgeon, Army Veterinary Department.

To face p. 174.

being due to flagellated protozoa in the circulating blood. This, as we have seen above, was not appreciated for many years, not indeed until long after Dr. Evans had left the Service for age. We now know that it was the initial step in the discovery of the causes of nine or ten plagues due to members of the genus Trypanosoma affecting both animals and man, and of such terrible malignity as to be capable of depopulating a country. The University of Wales conferred on him the Doctorate of Science, and that of Liverpool awarded him the Kingsley Medal in 1917, for distinguished work in Tropical Medicine. In 1918 our own College conferred on him the Steel Medal. These were the only and belated distinctions he received for his outstanding discovery. When the writer was at the War Office an effort was made to obtain an Honour for Dr. Evans, but his name and services had long been forgotten! He was of medium height, and on medical grounds for some years wore a beard, one of the few officers in the Service so permitted. In manner he was somewhat brusque, and rapid in conversation. He is happily still alive at the date of this notice, and the father of the profession.

The year 1882 saw an Expedition sent to Egypt at very short notice to deal with the rebellion organized by Arabi. With this Force was sent for the first time a duly accredited P.V.S. on the Head Quarter Staff; the officer selected was Inspecting Veterinary Surgeon J. J. Meyrick, under whose management the Department earned golden opinions for its devotion to duty. The *Army and Navy Gazette* published some of the letters it had received from combatant officers on the efficient and zealous services rendered. Our officers now found their names mentioned in Despatches, and for the first time a Companionship of the Bath in the Military Division was conferred upon a Veterinary Officer. In addition the P.V.S. received the order of the Osmanieh. The departmental report on this campaign is a damning indictment of a Hospital Service comprised of the men shed by the Cavalry on being dismounted, unorganized, untrained, and as usual, when no longer under regimental control, wanting in discipline. The picture Mr. Meyrick presents of the so-called Sick Depot on the bank of the Canal is one which should be read by those anxious to learn something of our early difficulties.

Inspecting Veterinary Surgeon J. J. Meyrick joined the Service in January 1860 and was gazetted to the Royal Artillery. He served in Canada from 1861-68 and in India from 1868-81. In 1882 he was sent as P.V.S. with the Expeditionary Force to Egypt, and in 1889 was retired under the age clause. During his long period of service in India he took an important part in Horse Breeding Operations under the Hallen scheme. He was an extremely quiet, closely observant man and a student of his profession. He published a work on *Stable Management and the Prevention of Disease among Horses in India*, which was translated into Urdu. His general reading was wide, and he was an authority on the lives of Mahomet and Napoleon, though he published nothing on either. He was also an authority on rifles, sporting guns and ammunition, and was a first-class shot. During his Indian service he had been a very keen sportsman. As a student of Art he has left behind an album of beautiful botanical paintings executed while in Egypt. He was of medium height, most unobtrusive, earnest and thorough in everything he took up; few knew that this quiet retiring man had a great fund of general information. His memory even at the advanced age of ninety was phenomenal. He furnished many notes which have been incorporated in this history. He died in 1925.

During 1882 *Regulations for the Army Veterinary Department* was issued, a great improvement on its predecessor. In it there was an Appendix on *Hints for the Selection of Remounts*, which was written by General Fitzwygram. In the same year a new form of Confidential Report on Veterinary Officers was issued. In regimental days the form used for all other officers had been employed, but on a department being created a special and very comprehensive inquisition was held each year. The Commanding Officer, among other questions, was called upon to report on the officer's strict sobriety! This was the only Confidential Report in the Service in which this question appeared, and it remained for ten years, until it was unofficially brought to the notice of the Adjutant General of the Army at that date (Sir Evelyn Wood), when the question was expunged.

In 1883 occurred the first promotions for war service made under the Royal Warrant of 7th July 1880 (see p. 169), three Veterinary Surgeons being promoted over the heads of their seniors for service in Egypt. This was the beginning of a dissatisfaction which almost rent the Department in twain. What other result could have been expected?

Just before Mr. Collins retired he succeeded in obtaining for all Inspecting Veterinary Officers the relative rank of Lieut. Colonel, and he saw rescinded the iniquitous paragraph in the Royal Warrant of 1878, fixing promotion to first class at 12 years' service: promotion was now to be given at 10 years' provided three years had been spent abroad. It was also approved that a V.S. 1st Class with ten years' service in the rank, should be promoted to the relative rank of Major. Finally, he brought his period of administration to a close by obtaining the removal of the restrictions against Presentation at Court.

PLATE VII

GEORGE FLEMING, C.B., LL.D., 1833-1901
Principal Veterinary Surgeon, Army Veterinary Department.

This great administrator retired in June 1883, and the *Army and Navy Gazette* gave a long and well-merited notice of his services. He left without receiving any honour from the State, but a Good Service Reward of £50 per annum was conferred on him shortly afterwards. He died in 1895. Mr. Collins was succeeded in office by Dr. George Fleming.

Dr. George Fleming (1833-1901; Plate 7) was born in Glasgow, and, like Mr. J. Collins, he qualified at the Edinburgh College of Professor Dick. He entered the Service at 22 years of age. The following month he proceeded to the Crimea, where he served with the Land Transport Corps in one of the Black Sea Depots. He was just too late for the medal for the campaign. Two years later he served in China with the Military Train and was present at the Bombardment of the Taku Forts and the Capture of Pekin. He remained in that country after the close of the campaign and travelled through Manchu Tartary, on which he published a book. He left China in 1862, joined the 3rd Hussars in 1864, was then transferred to the Royal Engineers, was for a short time in Syria purchasing animals for the Abyssinian War, and in 1877 was appointed to the 2nd Life Guards. Two years later he was promoted Inspecting Veterinary Surgeon, and in 1883 at 50 years of age succeeded Mr. Collins. He suffered under the disadvantage of not having served in India.

He was about the middle height, slight in build, with good features and a bright attractive manner. He was a dispenser of unbounded hospitality, a great talker, and an admirable public speaker. He wrote well and clearly, but his writings are frequently marred by an intolerance of opposition which showed itself in much he undertook. He was the victim of hero-worship by the civil profession in this country, to which he had rendered outstanding services; this did much to spoil a character that needed restraint rather than undue encouragement. His weaknesses were an incurable optimism, extraordinary impetuosity, a love of popularity and insatiable ambition.

There was nothing of the old school about him; he was modern in every sense of the term, and adopted views on glanders and tuberculosis which were greatly in advance of the veterinary thought of his day. He was anxious to see the Army Veterinary School at Aldershot a seat of scientific research, and during his period of office gave it every support. His ambition to be first in everything led him towards the end of his professional life to exhibit a jealousy which certainly was not evident during the middle period; it also tempted him to the production of works urgently required by the profession, but which by training and experience he was unable to supply from his own knowledge.

The account of his services to the profession as a whole has yet to be written. They were of outstanding value, and he has left behind a name which is permanently fixed in the history of the veterinary profession in this country. It is not generally known that he financed from his own pocket the Veterinary Surgeons Act of 1881, the obtaining of which has by many been regarded as his greatest service to the profession.

During his first year of office as Principal Veterinary Surgeon the University of his native city conferred upon him its LL.D. in recognition of his services to his country and to literature, and on the occasion of the Jubilee of Queen Victoria in 1887 he received the Companionship of the Bath (Civil Division). His period of office was in some respects less arduous than that of his predecessor as the Department had already undergone a thorough overhauling, but there were questions which yet required to be settled; among others, veterinary equipment for peace and war, and the reorganization of the Army system of shoeing, and to these he applied himself with characteristic energy. Over the latter years of his official career hung a cloud. The reason of this will appear later in the text.

After his retirement in June 1890 he continued to conduct the *Veterinary Journal*, which he had started in 1875, and to take an interest in Army questions. In 1892 he lectured on the *Shoeing of Army Horses*, and the paper on the subject, published in the *Veterinary Journal*, vol. xxxv., may always be read with advantage. In the same year he urged the trial of mallein in this country on the strength of Nocard's report. The Army had been free from glanders for two years before he retired, but with 2,000 cases occurring annually in London, or in the vicinity, the risk of infection was ever present. At the end of the year 1894 he resigned the editorial chair of the *Veterinary Journal*, a periodical he had conducted for twenty years with conspicuous zeal and ability. Only those who have held similar positions are capable of realizing what twenty years of this class of work means; it is incessant drudgery. The creation and conduct of this Journal was not the least of the great services he rendered to his profession. It is interesting to note that the two monthly periodicals of the profession were both of them initiated and conducted by Army officers, and that from 1828 to 1894 the profession was largely indebted to the military service for its monthly literature. We are unable here to give an account of Dr. Fleming's literary activities other than those affecting the Army. From the first article he wrote in the Crimea in February 1857 down to the above-mentioned lecture in 1892 his pen was never idle. It is gratifying to record that he received a Good Service Pension in 1896. Dr. Fleming died in 1901 at the age of 68.

It is difficult at the present day to understand the State having a contract with its servants for the supply of equipment or stores; such, however, had been the case from the first creation of a standing army, when Colonels of Regiments clothed their men and fed their horses on a contract system, and the Surgeon of the regiment provided his own medicines. Nor were contracts confined to officers; as we have already seen, p. 14, Farriers held a contract for shoeing, themselves providing iron, nails, tools and coal, the State providing labour, a forge and shoe-turning appliances, and further back still in the eighteenth century they had held a contract for the supply of medicines. If the eighteenth century Farrier had returned to life, his bitterness at the loss of the medicine contract could not have been greater than that of his successor of the nineteenth century, when he found his special shoeing perquisites seriously threatened. The contract system for shoeing worked well in peace, but failed in war. The men could not make the shoes even had coal, forges and iron always been available. This had been recognized as far back as the Peninsula, when boxes of hand-made shoes were sent out for the use of Farriers. At first a penny a day per horse had been allowed for shoeing; in due course this was reduced to three farthings per horse per diem, still the farrier made it pay; the last reduction was to a halfpenny per diem, but even then the contract was welcome. The Crimea was no test for shoeing as the troops did no marching, nor was the Mutiny, for the shoeing was mainly done by natives. The Abyssinian Campaign was worked by India, so the same explanation holds good. It was not until South Africa in 1879 and Egypt in 1882 demonstrated the rottenness of the contract system, that any attention was attracted to the matter. Dr. Fleming wrote on many subjects of which he was not master, but when it came to questions of shoeing there was nothing any army or other farrier could teach him. He knew the impossibility of dragging heavy forge carts with an army over unmade roads, the impossibility of forging shoes in the Field in sufficient numbers to meet wear and tear, and the many other objections to the established method. In 1884 he succeeded in attracting the attention of the authorities to a system which made use of machine-made shoes, the shoes being put on cold if there was no appliance for heating them, and machine-made nails being employed instead of hand-made.

It is not intended to recount the difficulties of revolutionizing the shoeing; the advocates of the new system were sometimes too optimistic, and like Dr. Fleming saw no difficulties; the opponents, who were legion, Commanding Officers and Farriers, had to be fairly beaten in spite of their capacity for obstruction. In 1885 the new method was first tried on Service at Suakim, and was of course successful; it could not be otherwise; it crept into the Service through the Cavalry in March 1888, and finally that powerful fortress the Artillery succumbed under pressure from above. All this took years to accomplish, for another generation of Farriers and Commanding Officers had to grow up. It is impossible to carry out such radical changes excepting over a long term of years, and Dr. Fleming had been some time out of the Service before the Army fully adopted machine-made shoes, so great was the prejudice in favour of the hand-made article. He was, however, in office when the State relieved the Farrier of his contract, and purchased the stock he had on hand, not at very liberal prices. This treatment reduced these valuable men into growling, sulky laggards, whose work was done with disgust, and with bitterness and hatred in their hearts. The fact is the Farriers were badly treated; they should have been given either five years' notice or five years' purchase. What their profit actually amounted to was a secret never discussed; we were always given to understand that it was something extremely small, but when the farrier lost his contract, it was evident that something substantial had been struck off his income. During the years of transition the Veterinary Service had a very difficult and painful task; they knew the soundness of the new system, and also the hard manner in which the Farriers had been treated. Dr. Fleming claimed for the change that he had introduced a better pattern of shoe. He converted the shoe from a "seated" shoe, flat on the ground surface, with counter-sunk holes, to a shoe flat on the foot surface, concave, and fullered on the ground surface. Such changes of pattern, however, are of no moment if the principles of shoeing are observed. The seated shoe went back to the time of Coleman and was officially adopted in 1854. It was in use for 30 years, and its successor has lasted 30 years. To preserve soundness of the feet of Army horses there is nothing to choose between the two patterns.

In 1884 a Dr. Cameron in the House of Commons determined to bring the authorities to book over the Commissariat and Transport Services in the Afghan and Egyptian Campaigns, especially in the former, in which 60,000 camels and 30,000 baggage animals died. The Government of India admitted the losses and defective system, and promised reform. The Minister representing India in the House stated that the report from that Government was "the most melancholy piece of reading ever published." Unfortunately Dr. Cameron withdrew his motion for a Select Committee to enquire into the working of the Commissariat and Transport Services of India, on the assurance of that Government that full steps were being taken to reorganize those services. But a Select Committee inquired into the British

Commissariat and Transport Service in Egypt; as a result the present efficient Army Service Corps was created. What India did after escaping the inquisition of a Select Committee, was to increase the number and efficiency of the native veterinary practitioners and threaten a wholesale reduction in the British Veterinary Service. This, however, did not take place; on the other hand, the Department was strengthened by thirteen officers. It was very gratifying in the discussion in the House to hear on all sides of the "thoroughly efficient" Veterinary Service in the Egyptian War, and the "admirable manner" in which the officers had performed their duty. Mr. Collins must in his retirement have felt that his seven years of hard work had borne fruit.

In May there occurred two more of those unjust promotions under the Royal Warrant of July 1880: two officers of the first class ranking as Captains were promoted to first class ranking as Majors,[1] and so passed over the heads of their seniors. This intensified the indignation previously felt throughout the Department (pp. 169, 176).

In this year (1884) died Veterinary Surgeon 1st Class F. W. Going, who for years had served with the Royal Horse Artillery. He was a typical Irishman, extremely popular, and there was nothing he could not or would not ride. At a pig-sticking meeting at Kampti he had the misfortune to break his girths; placing his saddle on a bush he rode after the pig bare-backed, was charged, and both he and the horse came down. The pig stood over him ripping the clothes off his back, and then tried to turn him over to get at his belly. Going told me that he held on to a tuft of grass as long as possible, and finding he could no longer keep face downwards, he "laid hold of the pig's ears and nipped on to his back"! The story created a great sensation, and was duly embellished to the extent that Going rode the pig to a standstill. Actually the animal was so astonished that he never moved, and a member of the party coming up put his spear through him. The only wound Going sustained was on the inside of the knee from his friend's spear. Pluck and presence of mind had saved him from an ugly situation. The incident was duly recorded in the official account of the meeting.

The year 1885 saw fighting on the Nile and in the Sudan, and also in South Africa, necessitating an increase of 12 officers to the establishment. All these forces were accompanied by properly appointed administrative officers. The Nile, Suakim and Bechuanaland Expeditions led to further promotions of

[1] In the original warrant there was no provision for promotion in the grade of first class for service in the Field.

V.S. 1st Class ranking as Captains to V.S. 1st Class ranking as Majors, so that the prospects of the senior officers passed over were finally destroyed.

In this year the conditions which had to be satisfied by candidates for admission to the A.V.D. were for the first time set out in a printed paper, also instructions for the examination of officers for promotion. Hitherto a discretion in these matters had been left to the P.V.S.; they were now to be governed by Regulations.

In April (1885) the Government of India issued an order fixing the rates of pay from the P.V.S. downwards, and giving a substantial increase to all ranks. In 1886 further rumours of the reduction of the Veterinary Establishment in India led to questions being asked in the House of Commons, where it was stated that these reductions had been decided upon, and that the formation of a Civil Department was under consideration. Dr. Fleming attacked the scheme in the *Veterinary Journal*, and subsequently the establishment was reduced but not to the level contemplated.

The early history of the Army Veterinary School at Aldershot has already been told (see p. 170). Under Dr. Fleming's administration it assumed the position of a centre of research so earnestly desired for it by its founder Mr. James Collins. Dr. Fleming appointed to the School two officers, Mr. C. Rutherford and the writer, and the designation of the staff was changed from Instructor to Professor and Assistant Professor. At this time there were no facilities for study, no laboratory, no appliances and no subordinate staff. These had all to be created, a slow process in the absence of public funds. The only building available as a laboratory was an unoccupied hut possessing a kitchen, and the kitchen in due course became the centre of considerable activity, where questions of army animal hygiene and the physiology of the horse were for some years studied. In course of time the old hut camp at Aldershot disappeared and with it the Army Veterinary School and laboratory, which were transferred to permanent brick buildings on a new and more convenient site. It is interesting to look back and compare the present excellent institution with its weather-beaten, tumble-down wooden predecessor, which represented the acme of discomfort.[1]

The losses among horses and mules during our various cam-

---

[1] A detailed History of the Army Veterinary School appeared in the *Veterinary Journal* for January 1927, by its late Commandant, Colonel A. G. Todd, C.B.E., D.S.O.

paigns in South Africa owing to " Horse-sickness " led to an officer of the Department being sent out to that country in 1886 to investigate. Mr. J. A. Nunn had previously been trained in technical methods of bacteriological enquiry in London, Cambridge and Paris. His results, published eighteen months later, threw no light on the disease. At that time no one realized the special difficulties connected with the investigation of " Horse-sickness."

Colonel J. A. Nunn (1853-1908) joined the Army Veterinary Service in 1877 and shortly after was gazetted to the Royal Artillery. He saw active service in Afghanistan 1878, and with the Chin-Lushai Expedition 1889-90 (D.S.O.). In India he carried out much professional work in a civil capacity for the Punjab Government, and some years later was appointed Principal of the Punjab Veterinary College 1890-96. On his vacating this position his services were recognized by the conferment of the C.I.E. After his return to England he qualified as a barrister. On the outbreak of war in South Africa he was appointed Deputy Director General Army Veterinary Service, which office he held until 1904. He was then appointed Principal Veterinary Officer in South Africa and shortly afterwards transferred in a similar capacity to India, where his health broke down. He died soon after his return home. He translated a work from the French on the *Diseases of the Mammary Gland*, was the author of a *Manual of Veterinary Toxicology*, and a frequent contributor to periodical literature.

An Army Veterinary Association had been formed at Aldershot as far back as 1861 through the energy of Veterinary Surgeon T. Walton Mayer, Royal Engineers, an enthusiast (see p. 139). The Society had, however, become moribund owing to the frequent changes of officers, and the retirement from the Service of its energetic secretary Mayer. In January 1887 it was resuscitated, a luncheon being held to celebrate the event, at which Dr. Fleming and Mr. Mayer, now long retired, were present. It held several meetings during 1887, when many professional subjects of the greatest military importance were discussed, the earliest being the *Working of the Army Veterinary Department in the Field* by V.S. 1st Class F. Duck. It is not too much to say that this paper initiated a serious study of the subject. It was published in the *Veterinary Journal*, vol. xxiv., and may be read with advantage as a historical contribution to the most important question in Army Veterinary organization. It is gratifying to know that in spite of the frequent changes of officers which military service entails, the Association is still not only in existence but extremely active, and has held its meetings regularly for the past thirty years, but for unavoidable gaps caused by wars.

Fifty have been held since the Great War at the time this note is written.

In 1888 the name of a young officer of the Department was frequently found in the public press. Veterinary Surgeon J. R. D. Beech had joined the Service less than seven years previously, and had almost immediately been sent to Egypt, where he took part in the 1882 Campaign, the 1884 Campaign in the Soudan, and the Campaign of 1884 on the Nile. In these, especially in 1884 and 85, he had shown great military abilities which brought him notice, and in 1887, when a Mission was sent to King John of Abyssinia, he accompanied Mr. Gerald Portal in the capacity of second Secretary of H.M. Diplomatic Service. This expedition was extremely hazardous, a fact well known beforehand, and the selection of Beech was doubtless made on account of his known determination and cool courage. The *Standard* of the 9th January 1888, in giving an account of the success of the Mission, says that Beech on more than one occasion saved it from destruction. It was currently stated that but for Beech the Mission would never have reached King John; even on the return journey the members had a narrow escape from being murdered. Beech was rewarded with a C.M.G., a decoration never previously given to anyone under the rank of a field officer and never at all to an officer of the Veterinary Department. The *World* of 8th February pointed out that this was the first occasion on which a Veterinary Surgeon had been employed on a Diplomatic Mission, and that he must be a man of exceptional capacity and one of whom his Department had reason to be proud. It also quoted the evidence of Mr. Knox, Chief Accountant at the War Office, who expressed the opinion before Lord Randolph Churchill's Committee that there was no body of officers more able and zealous in their duties than those of the Army Veterinary Staff.

We shall complete the history of Mr. Beech. In September 1888 he surrendered his veterinary for a combatant commission as 2nd Lieut. in the 21st Hussars, there being only one previous instance of such an exchange on record in our Service, that of Veterinary Surgeon S. Newman, 29th Light Dragoons (see p. 54). In 1889 he was in command of the Egyptian Cavalry at the Battle of Toski. In 1890 he was promoted to a Lieutenancy in the 4th Hussars, and in the same gazette to a Captaincy in the 20th Hussars, a record in promotion for fifteen months' service. In 1891 he commanded the Egyptian Cavalry at Tokar, and secured victory by a charge in which he was slightly wounded in endeavouring to rescue a wounded Egyptian officer. Shortly after this his brilliant and meteoric military career ended, but he returned from retirement to take part in the war in South Africa, where he commanded a regiment of Scottish Horse. He also took part in the Great War, and was killed in 1915.

Another officer of the Department, Colonel G. R. Griffiths, D.S.O., if not so well known to the public was equally well known in Egypt, where he had served since 1882. In due course he became Principal Veterinary

PLATE I

To face p 184

Surgeon of the Egyptian Army and the late Lord Kitchener's right hand man in everything connected with animal management and supply. He was of a remarkably attractive personality, bright, cheerful under all difficulties, and was universally known in the Egyptian Army as the "Friendly." He was in every campaign in Egypt and Soudan from 1882-1889, and required about a foot of ribbon to accommodate his bars. The Sirdar's confidence in his professional judgement was a pleasing feature in one who trusted so few. "This is all the money I can spare you, Griffiths; go and buy me as many Camels as you can." No account was asked for on his return. Griffiths' rigid integrity was well known. He died while still a comparatively young man in 1920, and left behind a host of friends.

In 1888 it was decided that a tour of foreign service was to be six years instead of five and that appointments to Remount Depots at Home were to be for five years, the officer meanwhile being struck off the Foreign Service Roster.

A change in the pattern of the infantry rifle having been decided upon (the bore being reduced), the question of whether these lighter bullets would have a stopping effect on horses arose; to answer this the services of the Department were called in. Horses were employed for the experiments, which were made by the Small Arms Committee and extended over two or three years. The animals were fired at immediately after destruction. The Lee-Metford rifle was the outcome of this work, the veterinary features of which are fully recorded elsewhere.[1]

Somewhat later, experiments were made by another committee to test a new type of Cavalry sword, and again horses were used for the trials. They were slung in the riding school and ridden at. The swordsman employed was a Farrier Qr. Master Sergt., a very fine man-at-arms, and in his hands the new sword inflicted the most remarkable injuries, including a fracture of the tibia from a cut! The specimens resulting from both of the above experiments were placed in the museum of the Army Veterinary School, Aldershot.

In 1888 occurred an important expansion of the Army Veterinary Service, the early history of which is as follows. In 1887 V.S. 1st Class F. Duck and V.S. F. Smith paid a private visit to some of the Veterinary Schools and Military Establishments of France, Germany and Belgium. In consequence of what they saw a conjoint report was furnished to the War Office, dealing first with professional matters and secondly with military questions. Both parts of the report were subsequently published in

[1] *Journal of the Royal United Service Institution*, vol. xxxviii. 1894.

the *Veterinary Journal* 1887, vol. xxvi., pp. 35, 183. In the professional report an account was given of the State Vaccine Establishment in the Veterinary School of Brussels, which supplied calf lymph for the whole of Belgium. It was suggested that the Army Veterinary School at Aldershot should undertake Vaccine production and supply the Army. It so happened that in 1888 smallpox was rife in the country, and the Local Government Board had such numerous calls on its resources that it was unable to supply the Army with the amount of lymph required. This was especially felt at large military centres such as Aldershot, and a proposal was made to the P.M.O. to provide him with calf lymph if he would obtain the authority of the Medical Department at the War Office. The question was taken up energetically by the Medical Service, and in due course the operations were sanctioned and an *Army Vaccine Institute* created as an annex to the Army Veterinary School. Buildings were obtained and the writer went through a course of instruction in calf vaccination at the Local Government Board Institute; in May 1888 work was commenced. In 1897 it was decided to include the Navy as well as the Army. The Institute remained in operation for 22 years, when the Local Government Board, owing to the great decline in public vaccination in this country, was able once more to take over the work. During these years this Institute issued lymph for over 2,000,000 people.

In 1888 occurred the first retirements of officers under the limited 10 years' service regulation. This short service system had been tried in the Medical Service and had failed, as it deserved to do. It was abolished in the Medical Department, but still retained by us, and in due course two officers were retired. Within a few months both were restored to the establishment and promoted. The inner history of the transaction was never properly known. The farce of Short Service was a little later practically ended by the issue of a warrant, dated 20th October 1888, which permitted of " a number " of Veterinary Surgeons being retained at the end of their ten years' service, instead of four originally intended; the warrant did not cancel the short service clause, but stated that the officers' service *may* on completion of engagement be dispensed with, and stipulated that the retention of the officer lay with the Commander-in-Chief on the recommendation of the P.V.S. In order to bolster up the old warrant it was notified that an officer had the right of voluntary retirement with gratuity after 10 years' service. I never heard of one availing himself of the privilege ! The Finance Branch saw to it that the advantage the 10 years officers had had in pay was to be returned to the State, 6d. per diem being deducted from their pay as 1st Class when they were selected for retention.

The first step towards extending the departmental system to Volunteer formations was taken in the same year, by defining the uniform of the newly added Veterinary Officers of batteries of position as being that of the A.V.D., but with silver in place of gold lace. Veterinary Officers of Yeomanry nevertheless remained regimental.

Towards the end of the year there died in India one of the fast diminishing band of "Company" officers. Inspecting Veterinary Surgeon W. Lamb was an officer universally beloved and conspicuous among sportsmen. The whole of his service had been in the Bombay Presidency, and he was intimately concerned with the Army Veterinary School at Poona and with Horse Breeding operations. His record of active service comprised Persia in 1857 and Abyssinia 1868, where he was second senior. In the Persian War he distinguished himself by capturing the colours of the enemy in a charge made by his regiment, the 3rd Bombay Light Cavalry. Professionally he held a very high position; socially no man was better known on his side of India.

Still in the year 1888, the Royal Warrant of 1878 was amended by Army Order 473. Among other questions it dealt with rank. It begins by saying that "Officers of a Department of our Army not having honorary rank, shall rank as follows for purposes of precedence and other advantages attaching to corresponding military rank." It then gives the various veterinary *grades*, with their corresponding military rank, which did not differ from the last orders on the same subject. Under the section on "retired pay" some small advantages were conceded, which were neutralized by the statement that no officer could claim on voluntary retirement the pension of his rank, unless he had served three years in the rank, or ten years abroad in all ranks, or five years with an army in the Field. So that the voluntary retirement clause at 20 years' service was killed. This amending order further stated that no V.S. 1st Class could be appointed I.V.S. until he had completed 15 years' service. This was doubtless introduced owing to the phenomenal promotion of junior officers to which we have already alluded. This order made it clear that all promotions were to be for ability and merit, there is not a word on seniority.

The year 1889 was chiefly remarkable for a disaster arising out of the operations for "roaring" undertaken by Dr. Fleming.

The preliminary work connected with this operation was carried out at Aldershot in 1888, and a note of it will be found in the *Veterinary Journal*, vol. xxvii., p. 1. As a result of the first operations it was found that when a portion of a cartilage of the larynx had been excised, a growth in due course occurred which assumed serious proportions, while simultaneously portions of the other cartilages became ossified. This could not have been anticipated. Dr. Fleming was informed of this serious set-back and saw the cases. The operating work was now removed from Aldershot to Woolwich, as Woolwich was more accessible from London. There a large number of horses were operated upon, with a secrecy unusual in surgery.

We need not follow the further history of this lamentable affair. It will be found in the columns of the periodical literature for 1889-1890. The failure could have been avoided had less impetuosity been exhibited, and above all, had the lessons of the preliminary failures been seriously taken to heart.

A paper on the *Physical Condition of Horses for Military Purposes* was read before the Aldershot Military Society in this year by Dr. Fleming. It was subsequently published in the *Veterinary Journal*, vol. xxix., p. 42. In the discussion which followed the paper an officer of the department pointed out to regimental officers where they failed in an important branch of horse management. It was doubtless the first time that the regimental officer had had his defects publicly criticized by the Veterinary Service, and an acrimonious discussion followed which was carefully edited in the published proceedings. The substance of it may be read at p. 115 of the above-quoted volume of the *Veterinary Journal*.

The question of the Employment of Dogs for Military Purposes in our Army was first introduced by an officer of the Department, Veterinary Surgeon (now Lt. Col.) E. E. Bennett, in March 1889. He lectured on the subject at the *Royal United Service Institution*, and his paper will be found in that Journal for 1889. He dealt with the employment of dogs on outpost duty, reconnaissances, patrols, as despatch and ammunition carriers, as searchers for the wounded, etc., and their training for these duties. He also suggested the employment of dogs for Naval purposes. The Chairman of the meeting dwelt on the novelty and importance of the subject, and the Army's indebtedness to the Veterinary Service. In all that has subsequently been published on this question, and on the practical value of dogs in the late War,

I have never seen it stated that the subject was first introduced and demonstrated by an officer of the Army Veterinary Department.

Dr. Fleming's period of office terminated on 28th June 1890. He left with a damaged reputation, after an undoubtedly brilliant and useful career. His services to the profession form no part of this history, and have yet to be written. As P.V.S. his outstanding service was the introduction of machine-made shoes to the Army and the abolition of the contract system with Farriers. He also devoted considerable attention to improving veterinary equipment for the Field. Indeed he radically reorganized equipment; instruments were modernized, ample surgical dressings provided, and Field panniers introduced, though later on these had to be abandoned owing to their great weight. He also introduced the Veterinary Wallet carried on the Field by Farriers; this wallet was suggested and devised by I.V.S. J. J. Meyrick.

On Dr. Fleming's retirement an official scandal occurred. It so happened that the next senior officer on the list, Mr. (afterwards Veterinary Colonel) J. D. Lambert, was due to retire under the age clause twenty-four hours before the Principal Veterinary Surgeoncy would become vacant.[1] To the surprise of the Service a Royal Warrant was published in June, dated 16th May 1890, which opened with the very ancient information that the appointment of the P.V.S. shall be for seven years, and the retirement of all other officers A.V.D. shall be compulsory at the age of 55, " except that if it should in any particular case be considered that the interests of the public service would be materially advanced by the further retention of an I.V.S. on the active list, the age of retirement of such I.V.S. shall be extended to sixty." The effect of this warrant, which was made for one man only, was to block the departmental flow of promotion for seven years, and ruin the prospects of more than one officer. It was undoubtedly a piece of official jobbery, and was understood to be effected by the powerful influence of two old officers of the 17th Lancers, a regiment in which V. Colonel Lambert had long served. This was the second occasion on which influence gained in this regiment was employed to the detriment of our Service.

[1] There is no desire in the subsequent remarks on this case to withhold the sympathy which all feel when an officer by sheer force of circumstances loses heavily by an inability to complete the needful qualifying service. Many officers have left the Service on a lower rate of retiring allowance than they would have received had they been permitted to serve twenty-four hours longer.

James Drummond Lambert (1835-1902; Plate 8) entered the Service in October 1857 and was gazetted to the Royal Artillery in July 1858; in 1862 he proceeded to India, where he served until 1865. In January 1863 he joined the 17th Lancers, with which he served until April 1880. He was with this regiment in the Zulu War of 1879, being slightly wounded at the Battle of Ulundi. In 1880 he took up the Instructorship at the Army Veterinary School, Aldershot, which he held for a few months, being promoted to Inspecting rank in February 1881. He was then sent to the Cape and took part in the Transvaal Campaign of that year. He returned home in 1882, and on 28th June 1890 was appointed Principal Veterinary Surgeon. In 1891 the designation of his office was changed to Director General and the compound rank of Veterinary Colonel was conferred; in the same year he was appointed a Companion of the Bath. He retired in June 1897 and died in 1902.

He was rather below the medium height, thick set, had a florid complexion, and pleasant expression. In his long service with the Cavalry he had imbibed all their venerable prejudices, good and bad. In discussing with the writer the weight carried by the Cavalry horse, he was opposed to any reduction and stated that the greater the weight placed on the saddle the more care the soldier took of his horse's back !

By nature he was extremely cautious. Long years of regimental training had taught him to lean on the Authorities; what they thought he thought, what they desired he carried out. He was equally cautious professionally; every case of skin disease was mange, while ozœna and glanders were almost brothers ! He looked with suspicion on recent advances in knowledge in case they should prove unsound; the employment of mallein met with a chilling reception; it might possibly produce glanders.

His administrative principles were simple; for example, when Commanding Officer and Veterinary Officer failed to agree, he told the writer that he always knew beforehand that the Veterinary Officer was at fault. Had he not blocked promotion for seven years, it would be permissible to regard his term of office as of benefit to the Service, in the sense that during this long period of rest it recovered its lost position, but there is no reason why this should not have occurred under another Chief.

Veterinary Colonel Lambert entered upon office at a critical period in our history; the Authorities were greatly exercised at the turn events had taken in connection with the operation for "roaring," events which the Remount Department were not slow in utilizing to our disadvantage. Peace and freedom from all disturbing activities were desired by the War Office, and it was well known that the new Principal Veterinary Surgeon could in this respect be relied upon. To live in peace with all branches and all persons in authority was with him a cardinal principle. Recent events had intensified his natural caution.

PLATE VIII

VETERINARY-COLONEL JAMES DRUMMOND LAMBERT, C.B.,
1835–1902
Director-General, Army Veterinary Department.

The subject which during his administration occupied his attention more than any other was "frost-shoeing." He listened to everybody's opinion, but it was the advice of his brother, an able practitioner of Dublin, which made the deepest impression upon him. His brother rightly favoured the employment of frost nails and many types were placed on trial. V. Colonel Lambert's administration was favoured with one long and very severe winter, which enabled all the various frost-shoeing contrivances to be very thoroughly tested, including a test in draught work on the frozen canal at Aldershot. Such an opportunity rarely occurs. Many years later, when at the War Office, the writer desired to refresh his memory from the valuable information accumulated by all branches of the Service in Aldershot at this particular time, but the papers had been destroyed without reference to the department concerned, and the whole of this work was lost!

Although Mr. Meyrick had been made a Companion of the Bath (military) for the 1882 Campaign, it was discovered in 1890 that no authority existed in the regulations governing the Order for this creation. Accordingly a new statute was added, which embraced the Veterinary Service in the Military Division of the Bath. Under this Colonel Lambert was made a C.B. in June 1891.

There died in India in 1890 a young officer of the A.V.D.—J. H. Steel, son of Mr. C. Steel, Veterinary Surgeon 12th Lancers—who had already during his short life made a name for himself by his literary and professional activities. A brilliant student, he qualified in London in 1875, entered the Service, leaving it almost immediately for a teaching appointment at the London School. He remained a few years at the College, publishing in 1876 an *Equine Anatomy* and in 1881 a work on *Bovine Pathology*. He also took the first B.Sc. (Honours) at the London University and intended taking his D.Sc. Being disappointed by a breach of faith in the matter of promotion, he resigned the College and rejoined the Service. Going to India he entered with enthusiasm into the immense field of work afforded by that country. He investigated Surra in Burma, describing it as *Relapsing Fever of Equines*, due to the organism found by Dr. Evans. He established a *Quarterly Journal of Veterinary Science in India*, became Principal of the Bombay Veterinary College, and among numerous other activities wrote a work on the *Diseases of the Elephant* 1885 and another on the *Diseases of the Dog* 1887. Invalided home with abscess of the liver, contracted when doing field work on Cattle Plague,[1] he wrote during his illness

[1] He lost his way, and night coming on was compelled to remain where he was. He was in thin white clothing and spent the night in a tree, which was safer than remaining on the ground. He was chilled to the bone by the heavy dew and cold night, and liver trouble followed.

works on the *Diseases of the Camel* 1890, and *Diseases of the Sheep* 1890. On his return to India against all medical advice his trouble soon recurred and he died. With his death the Service lost its ablest young officer, a scientist and worker whose enthusiasm was infectious. The *Quarterly Journal* founded by Steel, with whom the author was co-editor, was not only the first veterinary periodical in India, but the first and up to the present only publication devoted to the diseases and management of Army animals. It lasted from 1882-1890 and died with its founder.

The Army Medical Service had long been dissatisfied with their military position, and in 1890 urged they should be granted substantive rank. The British Medical Association gave the movement its whole-hearted support. A derogatory remark made by this body concerning the Army Veterinary Service was taken up by the *Veterinary Journal*, vol. xxxi., and some plain writing resulted. No worse spirit could have been exhibited than that in which the question of rank was treated by the military authorities from the Duke of Cambridge downwards. Their opinions and views are on record in the proceedings of the Camperdown Committee; an analysis of the evidence was published by the British Medical Association in July 1890. In June 1891 a question was asked in the House of Commons whether substantive rank would be granted the Veterinary Service, and the reply was that it would naturally follow the grant of titles to medical officers. In October 1891 a Royal Warrant was published by which compound rank was conferred on serving officers of the A.V.D. The Principal Veterinary Surgeon became Director General A.V.D. with the substantive rank of Veterinary Colonel, and so throughout the various "grades." Our officers were now no longer the permanent juniors of their rank in the Service (see p. 147). A few months later it was granted to Veterinary Surgeons of Yeomanry, Hon. Artillery Company, and Volunteers. This Warrant further directed that in future the designation of Veterinary Surgeon should be amended to that of Veterinary Officer. Opinion was divided as to the utility of compound rank, the consensus of opinion being that it was a label of inferiority, so long as compound rank did not apply to all branches of the Service. The question was, therefore, bound to arise again.

In the same year (1891) it was announced that the Secretary of State for India had (at last) approved of a Civil Veterinary Department for that country, for the purposes of educating natives in veterinary work, of controlling cattle disease, and to facilitate and extend Horse Breeding operations. Early in 1892 the Department was created, 17 officers of the A.V.D. being permanently transferred, while Mr. Hallen, as he then was, was made Inspector General Civil Veterinary Department, the title of General Superintendent of Horse Breeding Operations being abolished. The pay granted to the transferred officers was their Departmental pay, plus civil allowances varying from Rs. 150 to Rs. 400 a month.

We have seen earlier (p. 170) the attempt made under Mr. Collins to secure a reserve of Veterinary Officers, but the results do not appear to have been satisfactory. Under V-Colonel Lambert an appeal was made for 66 Veterinary Surgeons to register their names for Home Defence only. No definite rates of pay were laid down, but it was stated they would not be less than those given to officers A.V.D. The scheme evidently failed, nothing more being heard of it.

Towards the end of 1892 the Secretary of State for India permitted the assumption of compound military rank by the three remaining officers of the Indian Army, Lieut. Colonels Hallen, Kettlewell and Shaw. The titles of P.V.S. and I.V.S. in India were amended to P.V.O. and I.V.O.

At home the designation Inspecting Veterinary Officer was altered to District Veterinary Officer in November 1891; this absurd term lasted until October 1902, when it was replaced by Principal Veterinary Officer. The Principal Veterinary Officer of a Command in 1902 was allowed a Staff Officer; the arrangement continued in force until February 1905, when it was abolished. The designation Principal Veterinary Officer lasted until 1912, when it was replaced by Assistant Director of Veterinary Services.

In 1894 new *Regulations for Army Veterinary Services* were published. They embodied several features introduced since the issue of the 1882 regulations, and gave much more information on the Organization of the Veterinary Service for War.

Colonel W. B. Walters, the second senior officer of the Department now living in 1926, retired in 1894. He joined the Service as far back as November 1861, and the following year was gazetted to the Royal Artillery, with which he served in Canada for some years, taking part in 1866 in the operations against the Fenians—medal with clasp. In 1871 he was gazetted to the Inniskilling Dragoons and in 1877 to the Royal Engineers. In 1879 he took part in the Zulu War—medal. Shortly afterwards he was appointed to succeed Mr. Lambert as Instructor at the Army Veterinary School, Aldershot, and in 1883 was promoted to administrative rank. He proceeded to Egypt in 1885 and took part in the Operations around Suakim, being mentioned in Despatches—Egyptian Medal and Star. At the end of the Campaign he was posted to Ireland, later to Aldershot, and subsequently to London. Some few years before retirement he received the C.B. He was re-employed both during the South African War and the Great War. The assistance he has given the writer in drawing upon his memory for facts in connection with the history of our Service is acknowledged elsewhere.

Lieut. Colonel J.H.B. Hallen (1829-1901; Plate 9), Inspector General of the Indian Civil Veterinary Department, was retired for age in 1894. He was the son of Mr. H. Hallen, for many years Veterinary Surgeon Inniskilling Dragoons. The father seldom appeared in print, but in his day was recognized as one of the best men in our profession, in or out of the Service. It is generally understood that he took an active part in the production of General Sir Frederick Fitzwygram's publications *Notes on Horse Shoeing* and *Horses and Stables*, and was responsible for the so-called Fitzwygram shoe. He also greatly improved the horse slings then in use. The son, the subject of this notice, qualified in human and veterinary medicine, and passing out from Professor Dick's School in 1848 he entered the service of the East India Company in 1850, joining the Bombay Veterinary Service. He served with 1st Bombay Lancers 1850-55, was Remount purchasing until 1858, then served with the Bombay Horse Artillery until 1862. In that year, at twelve years' service, he was made Inspecting Veterinary Surgeon of the Bombay Army; he organized the Veterinary Service of that Force and established an Army Veterinary School at Poona. In 1863 he was made Superintendent of the Stud Department of Bombay. In 1867-68 he was head of the Veterinary Service in the Abyssinian War, and in consideration of his great services Lord Napier put forward his name for the special consideration of the Government. Nothing was done. A C.B. could not be conferred upon him because he was a Veterinary Surgeon! In 1869 his services were asked for by the Government of India in connection with Cattle Plague; he became President of the Commission which sat until 1872 and furnished the official publication on the disease. For this he received the thanks of the Government of India. From 1872-76 he was one of the Commissioners charged with the breaking up of the old Indian Studs. The creation of the Indian Civil Veterinary Department with its schools was due to his initiative; he also organized the Horse Breeding Operations of India, of which he was Superintendent, and finally in 1892 became Inspector General of the Civil Veterinary Department of India and was created a C.I.E. He was a remarkably able man who would have shone in any calling in life. After his retirement his Horse Breeding scheme was reported a failure, and in 1903 control was handed over to the Indian Remount Department. Colonel Hallen died in 1901, so had not the mortification of seeing his life's work destroyed.

No mention of the Veterinary Schools of India can be made without a reference to the devoted work of Colonel H. T. Pease, formerly A.V.D., whose energy and ability have raised the Lahore School from very

PLATE IX

VETERINARY LIEUT.-COLONEL J. H. B. HALLEN, C.I.E., 1829-1901
Inspector-General, Civil Veterinary Department, India.

humble beginnings to its present position of importance.[1] He translated textbooks into Urdu for the use of the students and lectured in that language; he conceived the Imperial Bacteriological Laboratory at Muktesar, originated and edited with others the *Journal of Tropical Veterinary Science*, was one of the earliest, if not the first, to diagnose the existence of Dourine in India, and did a great deal of work on Surra. The Cattle Survey of India claimed much of his attention, the earlier series of books on the subject being from his pen. He has been a great and untiring worker and has inspired others.

For years there had been growing dissatisfaction over the paltry sum of nine shillings a day retiring allowance for officers of the A.V.D. after 20 years' service, as the Warrant of 1878 only permitted half the rate of full pay on voluntary retirement, while a medical officer received one pound; even in 1807, the pension at twenty years' service was 7s. a day! The A.V.D. did not expect the same pension at 20 years as the A.M.D., but they thought that a pound a day at 25 years' service, instead of 15s. as provided by the Warrant of 1878, was reasonable. In 1893 the Director General of the Department was made acquainted with the growing agitation for reform in retired pay. Considerable Parliamentary influence had been secured, principally by Major J. A. Woods. A statement had been drawn up showing what the Veterinary Service had accomplished since its creation in 1796, and modest demands for improvement were formulated. The leading spirits in this movement were V-Majors J. W. Evans (now dead), J. A. Woods, and the writer. To the last of these was allotted the work of informing the profession how matters stood and asking for their co-operation. This was done through the columns of the *Veterinary Record* 1892 and took the form of a narrative entitled *Veterinary Life in the Army*, under the *nom de plume* of "Kudyard Ripling." The story served its purpose. Then precisely when the prospect looked brightest the Government unexpectedly went out of office; with it disappeared the powerful interest enlisted, and our hopes of reform were temporarily destroyed. It may be well to record the chief points of the scheme because of future developments: (1) The Director General to be given the rank of Major General; (2) the Seven Administrative Officers to hold the rank of full Colonel; (3) Veterinary Majors

---

[1] The first school began, I believe, in a mud hut under Mr. Batt of the Indian Veterinary Department; he was followed by Kettlewell, a man of great ability, and later by Nunn. The Indian Government has been served by many officers of great ability, but has generally left the impression that it has not fully appreciated them.

of five years' service to rank as Lieut. Colonel; (4) Officers promoted for service in the Field to receive Brevet promotion, thereby not affecting Departmental seniority; and (5) no increase in pay was asked, but only increased pensions, that of the Director General to be raised from £500 to £650 p.a., and, for other ranks, £300 a year at 20 years' service and £365 at 25 years' service. It was strongly represented that something should be done to repair the disaster which had overtaken so many senior officers by the special promotion of junior officers over their heads for war service, and it was believed that the proposed rates of retired pay at 20 and 25 years' service would help to meet their case. The appeal concluded by saying " we are only seeking for a retiring allowance sufficient to enable an officer worn out in the service to live in moderate comfort."

Three years after the effort above related a Royal Warrant was published in August 1896, the preamble of which runs, that it having been represented " that the rates of retired pay hitherto granted to officers of our Army Veterinary Dept. are insufficient " etc. From this it may fairly be assumed that the representations in 1893 bore fruit. In this warrant the D.G.'s retired pay was raised from £500 to £600, the Administrative Officers also benefited, while the V-Major or V-Captain of 20 and 25 years' service, though not receiving what had been desired, obtained an increase of £69 at 20 years and £86 at 25 years' service. Further the three different rates of pension for age, and infirmity under the 1878 warrant—which in the memorial we had asked to be abolished—were abolished, and one scale only for age or sickness laid down. Other representations made in 1893 seem to have attracted attention, for example the hardship of having to serve three years in a rank before obtaining the pension, especially hard on Lieut. Colonels promoted late through no fault of their own; it was gratifying to find that this order did not appear in the new warrant.

A remarkable article appeared in vol. xiii. of the *United Service Magazine* for 1896 written by a senior officer of the Army Medical Service, in which he advocated the abolition of the Army Veterinary Department and the assumption of its duties by the Army Medical Service ! The suggested change, it was pointed out, would enable more officers of the Medical Service to be retained in time of peace, whose services would be immediately available for their own Department in time of war ! The logical result would have been that on the outbreak of war the Veterinary Service would have ceased to exist. The writer replied to this

PLATE X

VETERINARY-COLONEL SIR FRANCIS DUCK, K.C.B.
Director-General Army Veterinary Department.

communication in vol. xiv., September 1896, but it is doubtful whether under the circumstances any reply was necessary, had it not been that the suggestion was put forward in all seriousness. It may be added that this officer made the notable statement that as the phenomena of disease are identical throughout the animal kingdom, the only preliminary training the medical officer required, in order to assume veterinary duties, was a few months spent in acquiring the technique of handling horses.

The positions accepted by some Veterinary Surgeons in Yeomanry regiments had for several years caused dissatisfaction and scandal in the profession. No one objected to a member of the College serving as a trooper or as a combatant N.C.O., but it was known that in several regiments, not entitled by their establishment to a Veterinary Officer, members of the College were serving as Farriers and Shoeing Smiths! This caused considerable feeling, and in 1897 the attention of the profession was drawn to the practice by the *Veterinary Journal.* In 1898 the Council of the R.C.V.S. passed a resolution against Veterinary Surgeons holding Farriers and Shoeing Smiths' appointments, and said that in future acceptance of such appointments would be regarded as unprofessional conduct. In 1899 the Council of the College represented the matter to the War Office, and desired that each regiment, notwithstanding its establishment, should have a Veterinary Officer. This was at once agreed to. In 1901 V-Lieuts. of the Auxiliary Forces were made eligible for promotion to Captain at ten years' service instead of fifteen as formerly. Notwithstanding there were members of the profession who continued to serve as Farriers and Shoeing Smiths, and to these in October 1902 the Council sent a copy of its resolution of 1898. This appears to have had the desired effect, as nothing more was heard of the matter. It is somewhat remarkable that men should have been found willing to occupy positions inferior to those for which they had been rendered eligible.

By the year 1896 no case of glanders had occurred in the Army for over eight years!

V-Colonel Lambert retired on completion of his seven years in office in June 1897 and was succeeded by V-Colonel F. Duck.

Veterinary Colonel Sir Francis Duck (Plate 10) entered the Service at 22 years of age in July 1867 and was at once gazetted to the Royal Artillery, with which branch he served until the introduction of the Departmental System in 1878. In 1867-68 he was engaged on transport duty in connection with the Abyssinian Campaign, and for these services he was thanked by the Secretary of State for War. He then proceeded to India, where he served six years. In 1878 he was in the Cape, where he remained until 1885. During this time he served in the Gaika and Galika Wars, the Zulu War, the Boer War and Bechuanaland Expedition. He was thanked by H.R.H. the Commander-in-Chief for his services in connection with the Zulu War and was mentioned in Despatches.

Colonel Buller's Despatch of his operations in 1879, published in the *London Gazette* of August 1879, says: "Veterinary Surgeon F. Duck, Royal Artillery, has been attached to the Frontier Light Horse for twelve months and has had charge of the horses of all mounted corps. We have to thank his skill and unremitting attention for their efficiency. Mr. Duck has also accompanied the troops on all large patrols, and has frequently rendered me great assistance in action."

On a previous occasion he was reported by Colonel Buller for his gallantry in action, particularly during the retreat from the disastrous defeat at the Zlobane Mountain on 28th March 1879, when "taking a dead man's rifle he volunteered his services with the rear guard and rendered excellent service at a most critical moment."[1] Further, on this occasion he was recommended for the Victoria Cross, but his name was struck out by the supreme commander on the ground that he had no right to be there! I had this fact from the Commander's own lips, so that it may be accepted. About this time Duck was not a *persona grata* with the Officer Commanding the Column, in consequence of a circumstance which is worth recording. A horse had obtained access to a sack of Commissariat tea and having partaken largely he was seized with serious symptoms from which he shortly died. Tea poisoning is sufficiently rare in horses to warrant a post-mortem examination even in the presence of the enemy.[2] So absorbed was he in the examination that he did not notice the Column had moved off; after a time he was missed and the Force had to return in order to find him! The Commander was furious and Buller advised the absent-minded officer to keep well out of his way. A short time afterwards the Zlobane incident occurred. The impression left on my mind is that he was never forgiven for the serious upset he caused to the Commander's plans.

In 1885 he received a step in relative rank for Meritorious Service, and in June 1890 was promoted Inspecting Veterinary Surgeon. In 1894 he proceeded to India as P.V.O., and in 1897 returned to England to take up the appointment of Director General.

Colonel Duck was a man of few words, deliberate in speech, extremely quiet in manner and most unselfish. He held the scales with a fairness and firmness long unknown; such a thing as a "job" was in his time unthinkable.[3] He was full of wisdom but a slow thinker, and his

---

[1] *Veterinary Journal*, vol. ix. 1879, p. 439.

[2] The case is recorded in the *Veterinary Journal*, vol. ix. 1879, p. 154.

[3] I cannot resist the temptation of recording an example of his chivalrous fairness. When the Zulus were broken at Ulundi the mounted troops were released from the square and went in pursuit. Duck stopped a Zulu with a bullet in the hip; he could easily have killed him with his

monosyllabic utterances failed to reveal his personality excepting to the few privileged to know him. He was in favour of drastic changes, but he wished them to come slowly; he had confidence in his younger officers but doubted whether the seniors could adapt themselves to changes when long years of repression had eliminated initiative and stunted growth. It was on the shoulders of the seniors that the increased responsibility would fall, and he foresaw failure unless changes were gradually introduced.

When he retired in 1902 his services were marked by the special distinction of a Knighthood of the Bath, the first ever conferred upon a Veterinary Officer.

During his period of office the two subjects, apart from a big campaign, which occupied his mind were Veterinary Field Equipment and the Transport of Horses by Sea. He was opposed to the old heavy pair of Field chests described at p. 167, one of which was useless without the other, and in their place introduced a single chest complete in itself, and weighing less than the original pair. It took a long time to effect this change, but the chest was a great success during the 1899-1902 Campaign in South Africa; its disadvantage was that it contained so many articles, that it required almost a special training to be able to get everything back into place. These chests continued in use until the art of compressing drugs, bandages, etc., led to a simpler and lighter chest being adopted. He had great experience in the transport of animals by sea, and his strong point was the use of pens instead of individual stalls. Nevertheless, he failed to convince the authorities, and during the long war in South Africa, when hundreds of voyages were made by horse-ships, the old system of stalls was employed throughout. He succeeded, however, in getting the use of slings abolished as a regular routine, and also the worthless nitre and vinegar treatment, reminiscent of Coleman's days.

The year 1898 saw the death of a young and most promising officer, V-Captain Haslam. He joined the Service in 1885, after a brilliant career as a student, and served in Egypt and India. From these countries he wrote papers on the Camel and Horse which attracted attention. Returning from India in 1893 he took his M.D. and Ch.M. at Edinburgh University. In 1895 he wrote on the Pathology of "Roaring," attributing it to a flattening or jamming of the left recurrent nerve as it passes around the aorta. The theory was not

---

revolver, but did not regard it as fair to a wounded man, so he fought the Zulu on foot with his own national weapon, the assegai, and killed him. One would like to think that the Zulu appreciated the situation.

new, but his observations were precise and based on dissections. He went to East Africa in 1897 in the service of the Colonial Office. Dr. Koch, when at Zanzibar, was so struck by Haslam's ability that he urged the Governor to send him into the interior to investigate an outbreak of Cattle Plague then raging. From this expedition he never returned, being murdered on 17th July 1898 by natives. His papers were lost, but his work is highly spoken of by E. Austen in *A Monograph on the Tsetse Flies*. Haslam's most important observation was the possibility that flies other than *Glossina* might convey the infection of *Nagana*. This officer, so well equipped educationally, was a great loss to our Service.

The compound rank which had been conceded to officers of the R.A.M.C. and subsequently extended to the A.V.D. in 1891, had, under pressure from the civilian medical profession, been abolished for the R.A.M.C. and non-compound rank substituted in June 1898. It had been hoped that in due course this would have been made applicable to the A.V.D., but by 1899 nothing in this direction had been done. We were the only Department of the Army so earmarked, and it was realized that it was not the intention of the authorities to make any alteration. The Council of the Royal College of Veterinary Surgeons took the question up in April 1899, the champion of the A.V.D. being Mr. J. F. Simpson, whose name in this connection must never be forgotten. Year after year, as we shall presently see, he brought forward motions at the Council meetings, urging that representations be made to the War Office, and the Council ultimately gave him whole-hearted support. His first effort in April 1899 to obtain a deputation to wait on the Secretary for War and press for the removal of the compound title, was opposed by General Sir F. Fitzwygram, a member of Council, while V-Colonel Lambert pleaded for "a little further delay." At the next Council Meeting in July it was decided to send a deputation, or, if that was not acceptable to the War Office, to submit a statement of the case. The fight by the Council of the Royal College of Veterinary Surgeons on behalf of the Army Veterinary Department lasted from 1899 to 1902. It would disturb the chronological order of events to tell its history as a whole; it is best dealt with incidentally.

October 1899 saw this country involved in war in South Africa, and by December the military situation was serious. The position of the Department and its readiness for war must now be examined.

We have seen (p. 154) that the first attempt made to organize the Veterinary Service for War was in 1866 under Mr. Wilkinson. In 1878 Mr. Collins had drawn up revised regulations. We have adversely criticized both schemes, which showed a strong family likeness. Under the scheme of 1878, the Campaigns in South Africa 1878-1881, and in Egypt and the Soudan 1882-85, had been conducted. These demonstrated our weakness in technical equipment, subordinate personnel and veterinary hospitals, but no action was taken to remedy defects. Nine years after their publication the 1878 regulations were discussed at a meeting of the Aldershot Army Veterinary Association, on a paper read by Mr. (afterwards V-Colonel, Sir) Francis Duck. It is safe to say that until this paper appeared the full extent of our liabilities had not been properly appreciated by the Department. This paper proved of momentous importance, inasmuch as it caused the Department to reflect on the blots on their organization, especially the grave risks incurred by combining a veterinary hospital with a remount depot.[1]

Defective equipment can always be remedied, given time and money. To obtain suddenly a trained subordinate staff was quite another matter. Over 150 men a year belonging to all branches were being trained at the Aldershot School; but when trained they were locked up in their regiments and unavailable. Regiments very naturally regarded the training of these men as intended for regimental purposes only.

A year before the War of 1899-1902, the War Office initiated a proposal for the formation of a Station Veterinary Hospital in this country as an experimental measure. Since 1886 they had existed in India, and in the Medical Service they had long been recognized as the only solution of dealing with the sick. The Station selected was Salisbury. The Cavalry opposed the suggestion, and for very different reasons Colonel Duck was not a supporter. He had no hospital staff belonging to his own Service and to keep the hospital going would have had to depend upon the loan of men from other branches with consequent constant changes. The Adjutant General, Sir Evelyn Wood, the Qr. Master General, Sir George White, and the Commander-in-Chief, Lord Wolseley, were all in favour of the proposal. Lord Wolseley brought matters to a focus in a minute he wrote on 5th February 1899, of which the following is the substance:—

"The proposal is a step in the right direction because the new system for peace would be a preparation for war. In war we could not

[1] The paper was published in the *Veterinary Journal*, vol. xxiv.

allow Cavalry Regiments to take seriously sick horses about with them. Officers Commanding Cavalry will object to the scheme, that branch is more conservative in its instincts and prejudices than the officers of other arms. All Commanding Officers protested loudly when the sick soldiers of many corps were collected into one Station Hospital, but firmness based on military knowledge carried the day, and now it is only a stray fossil here and there who would go back to the old expensive system of Regimental Hospitals."

This minute by Lord Wolseley should never be forgotten. It constitutes the first real step towards the efficient organization of the Army Veterinary Service.

In consequence of the decision given above, the Director General (F. Duck) urged the formation of a subordinate Veterinary Staff for hospitals, and the withdrawal of Farrier Quarter-Master Sergeants from Cavalry Regiments. Such a sweeping change takes months to discuss, and before any decision was arrived at the storm of 1899 broke over our heads. The precise position of the Army in respect of arrangements for the care of sick animals in the Field in the month of October 1899, must now be clearly grasped, and for this purpose it is necessary to look back.

Ten years before the War, the Field Army Establishments of 1888 provided *one* "Sick Horse Hospital" for a Force consisting of an Army Corps, a Cavalry Division and L. of C. Troops. It was located at an "advanced depot," immediately in the rear of the army. It was not only a hospital, but was to receive and issue remounts. For this purpose it was divided into two troops, one for the sick and one for the healthy horses, the total capacity being sufficient for 300 animals. There was an Inspecting Veterinary Surgeon with this Hospital who was subordinate to the Major in Command! At the Base was a "Remount Depot" which received both remounts from overseas and sick animals from the Hospital at the advanced depot!

To put the case briefly, Veterinary Hospitals were utilized to hold healthy remounts, while Remount Depots contained both healthy and sick animals. Had it been desired to ensure the general infection of the army with contagious diseases, no better arrangement could have been devised!

In 1891 the above regulations were revised, though no attention was paid to their potential capacity to infect the army in the Field, against which the Department had previously protested (see p. 201).

In 1892 these regulations were again issued with minor amendments, such as the employment of the designation "squadron" for "troop," and of "Veterinary Lieut. Colonel" for "Inspecting Veterinary Surgeon." One other change made in the 1892 Establishments was the substitution of the term "Sick Horse Depot" for "Sick Horse Hospital."

In 1898, the year before the War in South Africa, another edition of War Establishments was published. In this it was astounding to find that *no provision of any kind existed for the care of sick animals in the Field.* The "Sick Horse Depot" was swept away, but the Remount Depot had been very greatly enlarged. The only indication of the existence of a Veterinary Service, is a Base Depot of Veterinary Stores, and an Advance Depot of Stores under a Farrier Sergeant! Further, *every V-Lieut. Colonel had been abolished from the Army in the Field;* the Principal Veterinary Officer alone remained, with no administrative staff to carry out his orders!

We shall probably never know who was responsible for destroying the Veterinary Department as an active service unit. That all veterinary arrangements for a campaign were intentionally cut out in 1898 admits of no doubt, but the instigators of this crime against efficiency must be left to conjecture. It is significant that the Remount Department was not paralysed by the War Establishments of 1898; on the other hand it was considerably strengthened.

Thus the outbreak of War in 1899 found the Veterinary Service without the shadow of an organization, nothing more indeed (save for the P.V.O.) than the British Army took with it to Flanders in 1799 and subsequently into the Peninsula and Crimea. It fell to the authorities at the Base of Operations in South Africa to organize a system to meet the deficiency, and their methods were not only archaic but opposed to all common sense and experience.

The Director of Transport and Supply at Cape Town was constituted the head of the Remount and Veterinary Services, and the organization adopted was that laid down in 1888-92, which was doomed to infect the army with contagious diseases. Care also was taken to place the Veterinary Service under the Remount Department. Thus was initiated a system which resulted in the army being riddled by contagious diseases and deprived of all means of dealing with them. Never in the history of any British War has there been such a deliberate sacrifice of animal life and of public money. For this no one was ever called to account. The Royal Commission on the War was muzzled by the rigid limitation of enquiries, and not a single member of the Veterinary Service who had been in the Field was called upon to appear before it.[1]

When the War Establishments of 1898, to which we have referred, were being drawn up, by one of those remarkable vagaries of irony the Staff of the War Office included a man the greater part of whose professional life had been devoted to the study of the organization of the Veterinary Service for War. Veterinary Colonel F. Duck, Director General of the Army Veterinary Department, was not even consulted when his Department was emasculated. Nevertheless, he took the initiative on the outbreak of War in 1899 of recommending the Authorities to send Field Veterinary Hospitals from India to South Africa, and throughout the first year of the Campaign these were the only semblances of organization we possessed.

When every Remount Depot in South Africa was full of horses suffering from glanders and mange, the Veterinary Service was called upon to eradicate these, and other contagious diseases, which by now were spread over a sub-continent. Only forty or fifty regular officers and about a hundred civilian Veterinary Surgeons were available for the whole army. The Civilian Service had their military work to learn in the rough school of war, often without a guide or teacher. They were also handicapped from the first by not holding even temporary commissions.[2] A civilian with an army is a mere camp follower without power or authority. Hospitals, however, were now taken in hand, and every effort made to stem the flood of disaster, but the subordinate personnel had to be trained and a system evolved. Organization for War cannot be undertaken during hostilities; this is the duty of peace time.

We have no intention of following the course of the War, or tracing the evils resulting from placing the work of the Veterinary Service in the hands of the Remount Department. The two and a half years of the Campaign will be found fully considered in my *Veterinary History of the War in South Africa* 1899-02.

The year 1900 was devoted by the Council of the Royal College of Veterinary Surgeons, headed by Mr. J. F. Simpson, to an

[1] It is interesting to note how history repeats itself. During the Crimean War a Commission sat to enquire into the scandals attached to that campaign, but though the losses in horses occupied considerable attention, not a member of the Veterinary Service was called to give evidence. It is through the evidence of an Engineer Officer we learn that Mr. Wilkinson's quest for horses in Bulgaria (see p. 133) was a failure.

[2] Yet, curiously enough, when they died they were given a Lieutenant's funeral.

endeavour to obtain a redress of grievances of the A.V.D. and secure its effective reorganization. The Deputation to the Secretary for War proposed in July 1899 was declined by the War Office. The statement of the case was then submitted, but no reply was given for nearly a year, when the Council was informed that they must await the conclusion of the War before any further consideration could be given to their case ! This did not further matters; and a letter was sent back hoping that a favourable reply would be received at an early date. Meanwhile the professional press was busy, the *Veterinary Journal* firmly supporting the action of the Council. An article in the *Nineteenth Century* for June 1900 brought to the notice of the public " *The Cruel Case of the Wounded War Horse.*" This article strongly urged that Veterinary Hospitals should be commanded by Veterinary Officers with power to deal with subordinates, and that full rank was a necessity for the officers instead of the compound titles which they alone in the Army bore. Letters also came from the seat of War, sent by accredited correspondents to the leading papers, giving graphic accounts of what they saw, and recording the appalling losses of horses due to want of properly organized Veterinary Hospitals, and pressing for reconstruction of the Department on modern lines. The professional periodicals, especially the *Veterinary Journal*, for 1900 will furnish the facts to which attention is here briefly drawn.

Throughout 1901 the Council of the Royal College, including our Department's doughty champion, J. F. Simpson, continued their representations to the War Office; there had been a change in War Ministers, and it was hoped that the new minister might prove more helpful. The *Church Society for Promotion of Kindness to Animals* also addressed the Secretary for War in 1901, on the much needed reform in the A.V.D., but this, like all representations by the Council of the College up to this time, appeared to fall on deaf ears.

The administrative work of the Veterinary Service at the War Office could not be carried on by one man, especially during War; in November 1901 the appointment of a Deputy Director General was authorized, which office lasted until 1904, when it lapsed.

Anticipating matters, an Assistant Director General was appointed in 1907 and has continued up to date.

We have already drawn attention to the disastrous results of promoting officers for Field Service at the expense of their brother officers. In 1901 a great change was made, an officer being promoted for service in China by brevet, instead of passing over the heads of his seniors.

In 1902 the Civil Veterinary Department in India received a serious set-back relative to the Horse Breeding establishments. The very words " Horse breeding in India " stink in the nostrils of those who know the story. Its history requires a volume to itself, which the Author hopes one day to furnish. In 1873 the old Indian Studs had been swept away after 80 years of organization, reorganization and disorganization, and a scheme devised by Lt. Colonel Hallen of the Indian Veterinary Service was instituted. During the many years he supervised this work there were no complaints so far as I am aware, but after his retirement for age in 1894, which has already been noticed at p. 194, opportunity was taken to condemn his system as having " completely failed to answer the expectations it was intended to fulfil " and reorganization was demanded. A Commission sat in 1900-01; they attributed the shrinkage in remount supply to the officers of the Civil Veterinary Department, who, it was stated, had proved unsuitable for the work. " Their training does not specially fit them for it; no practical knowledge of breeding is gained by them during their Veterinary training, and few of them have more than a limited knowledge of Native languages."[1] The reorganization recommended by the Commission was a partial reversion to the old Stud system, which had so lamentably failed, *viz.*, the removal of horse breeding from civil veterinary to military remount control, the Civil Veterinary Department being left to concentrate on education and the study of the diseases of stock. Behind this desire for reorganization was the feeling expressed in the statement, freely repeated by the Commission, that " friction has always existed between the Remount and Civil Veterinary Departments," and therein doubtless lay the reason for the outcry for reform. It is not our intention to go further into this question, excepting to note that the essential feature of the new system was the appointment of a Veterinary Staff Officer on whom the Director of the new Department was to lean, for in enumerating the qualifications required of the Director it is distinctly stated that if he has some knowledge of breeding so much the better. In other words, the Veterinary Service was to continue to do the work while the Remount Service received the credit.

[1] This is an old complaint against our officers. Even in the "Company's" Service so few took the trouble to learn the language of the country, that they were penalized by deprivation of certain allowances.

As the result of the repeated representations of the Council of the Royal College to the War Office events took a somewhat unexpected turn in April 1902, when a new Veterinary Warrant was issued. The first intimation the Council of the Royal College had of its existence was through the daily press, an unfortunate piece of official neglect, but not of course unintentional.

This Royal Warrant, dated 20th March, was intended to accelerate promotion. It fixed the tenure of office of the D.G. at three years with a maximum of five; the promotion of V-Lieutenants at $7\frac{1}{2}$ years' service, of V-Captains at 15 years' service, and of V-Lieut. Colonels by *selection* from V-Majors who had served three years in India. The extension of service of a selected officer over 55 years of age was annulled, and there were improvements in pay and retired pay. This warrant abolished the ten years' short service scheme, though not in express terms. It, however, permitted the retirement of an officer at ten years' service, where such retirement might be deemed expedient.

In this warrant no mention was made of the main point to which the Council of the College had for so long been inviting the attention of the Authorities. The compound rank remained, and Mr. J. F. Simpson, in his criticism of the warrant at a meeting of Council on 11th April 1902, stated that in an interview which the deputation of the Council had with the Secretary for War in June 1901, that official held out no great hope that the prefix would be removed, and had suggested that there was not much in the question so long as the officers received other considerations which *in his* opinion were more valuable!

The Council agreed to represent to the War Office that the improvements in pay, promotion and pensions granted by the new warrant were regarded as utterly inadequate, and would not help to fill the depleted ranks of the Department, in which there were then thirty vacancies, and no candidates. This letter, dated 7th June 1902, directs attention to (1) the persistent refusal to grant non-compound military rank to Veterinary Officers; (2) the lack of authority in their own hospitals and over their own subordinates; (3) the appointment of a combatant officer as Inspector of Veterinary Hospitals in South Africa; (4) that veterinary officers were ineligible to purchase remounts, and (5) were ineligible for appointment as A.D.C. to a General Officer, even when their services had been specially asked for. The Council described these disabilities as degrading, and as lowering professional status. This firm letter contained recommendations on Promotions and Pensions, Indian Pay, Charge Pay, Specialist Pay, and Study Leave. It further asked the rank of Colonel for Administrative officers, of Major General for the Director General, with the rate of pay and pension " now drawn by the D.D.G. of the Medical Service." The acknowledgement of the War Office was that a further communication would be sent thereafter. In *The Times* of 5th September following, it was announced that a Committee would assemble to consider what alterations were necessary " in the terms under which officers now serve in the A.V.D." This epoch-making Committee was presided over by the Earl of Hardwicke. Its members were Major General Wynn, D.A.A.G., Colonel Marling 18th Hussars, Mr. Higgins, Accounts Department, V-Colonel Thomson D.G.A.V.D., Professor W. O. Williams, President R.C.V.S., Mr. J. F. Simpson, F.R.C.V.S., and Mr. C. Watherston, Secretary.

On the 15th October 1902 V-Colonel Duck, after serving five years in the appointment (the term having been reduced from seven to five), was succeeded as Director General A.V.D. by V-Colonel H. Thomson.

Major General Henry Thomson (Plate 11) joined the Service in 1871 at 20 years of age. He was gazetted to the "Veterinary Department," and so remained until July 1878, when he was gazetted to the Royal Artillery. This is a curious gazette, as there was no Veterinary Department proper in those days. It is assumed that he had to wait for a regimental vacancy to occur, and was included among the twelve "General Service" officers mentioned as being on the establishment in June 1876 (see p. 102). He served in India from 1873-79. In 1881 he was attached to 19th Hussars, and with this regiment served in the Egyptian Campaign of 1882, being present at Kassassin and Tel El Kebir. For his services in this campaign he was mentioned in Despatches and promoted 1st Class. In 1883-84 he was serving in the Soudan Campaign with 19th Hussars, and was present at El Teb and Tamai. He was again mentioned in Despatches, and was promoted for service in the Field to the relative rank of Major. In 1890 he was promoted Inspecting Veterinary Surgeon, serving in this capacity at Home and in India; in 1898 he was made Principal Veterinary Surgeon in India, where he remained until 1902, and in that year was promoted Director General. In 1900 he was created a Companion of the Bath.

Veterinary Colonel Thomson, as he then was, entered on office at an extremely important period in the history of our Service. He held very advanced views on the question of Army rank, and insisted that the status and rank to which our officers were

PLATE XI

MAJOR-GENERAL H. THOMSON, C.B.
Director-General, Army Veterinary Service.

entitled, in spite of the attempt to extinguish it by a prefix, should be as fully recognized as that of combatant officers. His appointment as a member of the Hardwicke Committee was a source of great strength, as neither of the two civilian members had the technical knowledge of service conditions necessary to meet and combat the military objections which were sure to be raised, or to avoid the pitfalls certain to be created.

The Hardwicke Committee held its first meeting on 28th November 1902. While it was sitting the attention of Parliament was drawn by Captain Norton, M.P., to the waste of animal life in South Africa, owing to an insufficiency of Veterinary Officers, and the same member asked the question why officers of the Veterinary Service were not employed as purchasing officers for remounts. The reply given by Mr. Brodrick to the last question is worth recording; he said it was not considered advisable to institute the proposed system, and then defined the respective responsibilities of the Veterinary and purchasing officers. The Veterinary Officer was responsible for soundness and age, the purchasing officer for fitness, quality, appearance, strength and action.

During the deliberations of the Hardwicke Committee a portion of the Veterinary press continued its campaign against the War Office. The *Veterinary Journal* protested against this policy while negotiations were pending, and later on gravely read the profession a lesson in good taste and manners! This zeal in defence of the War Office was quite misplaced; for several years it had treated the Council of the Royal College with something less than scant courtesy, and as we shall presently show it was not without hope of defeating that body even while conceding its demands.

The Warrant which *made* our Service was signed by King Edward VII. on 5th October 1903 and was published in Army Order 180, November 1903. It began by conferring non-compound rank on all serving officers of the Department; it gave an increase in pay and retiring allowances for most ranks; it accelerated promotion, Captains being created at five and Majors at fifteen years' service. The Director General remained a Colonel but was "to rank as Major General"! His appointment was for three years with power of extension for two years. The rank of Colonel was now opened to senior officers; the age of retirement for Colonels was fixed at 57, and for all other ranks at 55. Brevet rank for meritorious service was also instituted.

The last clause in the Warrant provided for the creation of an

Army Veterinary Corps from among the N.C.O.'s and men already employed on Army Veterinary Services, but the Warrant says nothing as to how this Corps was to be trained or officered. It was not, in fact, for another two and a half years that the officers of the Army Veterinary Department and the N.C.O.'s and men of the Army Veterinary Corps were amalgamated into one unit, the Army Veterinary Corps. This took place in March 1906 and was published in A.O. 48 of that year. The omission to amalgamate and to define the duties of the officers relative to the Corps can only be attributed to the unwillingness with which all vital principles were conceded. The Council of the Royal College of Veterinary Surgeons wrote to the Authorities thanking His Majesty for the Warrant.

The man by whose courage and persistence the Warrant was obtained which rendered our Service effective was the late Mr. J. F. Simpson, F.R.C.V.S., of Maidenhead. It is not too late for the Royal Army Veterinary Corps to place on the walls of the Council Chamber a memorial plate to one who rendered it such outstanding service.

On the creation of a new branch of the Army an immense amount of work has to be done in laying down foundations. There were Standing Orders to be compiled, calculated to meet any point in management and command likely to arise. There was training, technical and military, to provide for. Familiarity with the system of accounts, messing, clothing and equipment had to be acquired. The spade work done at this time reflects the greatest credit on those concerned,[1] but it was necessarily slow: for example, it was not until eleven years later that a *Field Service Manual* was produced. For the first time in its history the Veterinary Service had been given charge of its affairs and had become wholly responsible for its own efficiency. It took these duties very seriously.

On the formation of the Corps the subordinate service was largely composed of Farriers and Shoeing Smiths, who were transferred from other branches of the Service, but it was soon evident that this was an undesirable course in which to continue. In due time the farriery element was reduced, so that the highest attainable rank in that branch became Farrier Corporal, though it was open to Farrier Corporals to qualify for promotion to the

---

[1] Major-General Thomson had as his Asst. Director General, Major (now Major-General) E. R. C. Butler, on whose shoulders this work fell.

higher rank of Sergeant, Staff Sergeant, Serg. Major or Warrant Officer, all of which had been instituted in the Corps by the year 1907.

Meanwhile hospitals were being created, at first two, Woolwich and Aldershot, then two more, Bulford and the Curragh. It is significant of the difficulties attending the birth and development of our Corps that hospitals could only be obtained from the Treasury by sacrificing fifteen officers. The establishment was reduced by that number, and to meet the shortage it was decided (1905) that in future officers would be allotted to stations and not to units. The Army itself was not favourable to the introduction of Hospitals. One writer, speaking for the Cavalry, said they aimed a direct and deliberate blow at horsemastership among combatant officers and farriers.[1] He advised squadron commanders to treat all minor cases, and said that an allowance should be made them for drugs and dressings ! A Cavalry Commander protested against the presence of a hospital in his barracks as it was not under his control; far deeper reasons lay behind his official objection.

Even the War Office did no more than was absolutely necessary to help the development of this young Service. Under-currents began to make themselves felt almost immediately after the vital warrant was issued; to one some reference must be made.

A few months after the publication of the Warrant of October 1903, the Director of Transport and Remounts put forward a scheme of his own for veterinary reorganization, on whose prompting we do not know. The essential point was the reduction in the number of veterinary officers from 180 to 102, together with the following provisions:—

All young officers of mounted units were to receive six months' training at a "Military Veterinary College," of which there were to be two, three, or if necessary, four. Other officers besides subalterns were to be encouraged to go through an advanced course of instruction at the Royal Veterinary College, to qualify for appointments in veterinary hospitals and pass into the Veterinary Staff ![2] The age of entry was to be raised, the rank of Lieut. abolished, and that of Captain given on entrance. We need not follow this wild scheme any further; the intention was very clear, and the attitude of the Whitehall

[1] *Cavalry Journal*, vol. ii. 1907.
[2] I do not profess to understand with precision what this means, I merely quote the language employed in the scheme.

mind at that particular period is made evident. While this attempt to strangle the infant A.V.C. was being made, the Editor of the *Veterinary Journal* was lecturing the profession about its attitude towards the War Office !

By 1906 Revised Regulations for the Army Veterinary Services had been issued, a heavy task considering the complete reorganization which had occurred. In the meaning of the term " Service " or " Services " there have been more than one change. In 1906 an officer above the rank of Lieut. Colonel belonged to the Army Veterinary Staff. In 1909 the same rank of officer belonged to the Army Veterinary Service. In the Royal Warrant of that year it is laid down that an officer of the A.V. Service includes the Director General, a Colonel removed from the Corps, an officer of the Corps, and a Veterinary Officer of Household Cavalry. It is not clear why " Staff " was converted into " Service."

In 1906 the rank of the Director General was more clearly defined. He remained a Colonel in the Army, but was granted the Honorary rank of Major General. The question of Honorary rank gave rise to difficulties and attempts were made to weaken it. More or less lame methods were adopted in successive Royal Warrants to make the position clear. Finally, twelve years later, the Authorities abolished Honorary rank and made the appointment that of a Major General.

About this time a retired officer of the Department came prominently before the public as a painter and sculptor. Captain Adrian Jones joined the Army in 1867, and in the following year saw active service in Abyssinia with the 3rd Dragoon Guards. He was in the Boer War of 1881 with the 1st Dragoon Guards, and served on the Nile in 1884 with the Royal Artillery. He retired in 1891, while serving with the 2nd Life Guards, and took up with enthusiasm his new profession. It is impossible in the space at our command to enumerate the many public monuments which are his work. Whether painting or modelling he is equally successful. That wonderful group the Quadriga of " Peace," given, as it deserves, the finest site in London, has never been approached in craftsmanship by any previous worker in this country at least, or possibly in any other. The equestrian statue of the Duke of Cambridge in Whitehall is Meissonier-like in its accuracy of detail and faithful likeness; he has captured the precise gesture and attitude of the Duke. The Cavalry Memorial in Hyde Park is doubtless the most dignified statue of St. George in existence, the figure has all the attributes of a Saint and a Knight. Captain Jones' genius is entirely of his own development; his military career precluded him from passing through the usual schools, with the result that his superb gifts are unrecognized by the Royal Academy.

In 1907 a special building erected at Woolwich for mobilization and other veterinary stores was handed over for occupation.

A Depot for the Corps at Aldershot and another at Woolwich had originally been contemplated; finally one depot was decided upon, and it was located at Woolwich.

In October 1907 Major-General Thomson's period as Director General expired. To him had fallen the spade work consequent on the inception of the Corps, and it is fortunate that he had as his Assistant Director General, Major (now Major-General) E. R. C. Butler, who in spite of his other heavy duties found time to write an official text-book on *Animal Management*.

No mention has hitherto been made in these pages of Burma as a military station, for the reason that its occupation by mounted troops was found too costly in horses, in consequence of epizootic paraplegia and other diseases. Nevertheless that country has not been neglected by the Army in Veterinary development; much good work was done in the early days by the late Veterinary Surgeon 1st Class Frost, Royal Artillery, and later by the present Colonel G. H. Evans, whose name has been associated with Burma for nearly forty years. No man is better known in that country and doubtless no one knows the country as well as he. His remarkable personality has enabled him to visit parts that no white man could enter and make certain of returning alive. A keen naturalist, he has contributed greatly to the knowledge of the fauna of Burma, especially the Reptilia, and his work has received scientific recognition in this country. His knowledge of Elephants, their management and diseases, constitutes him the highest authority we have ever had on the subject. His fame as a sportsman has among other reasons rendered him the best known and most popular man in Burma. Shortly after the period we have now reached in this History, he retired for age and settled down in a country from which most people are glad to escape.

Major-General F. Smith became Director General in October 1907.

Born 1857 he entered the Service in 1876 and was the last officer but two to join under the old regimental system. He was gazetted to the Royal Artillery in 1877 and to the 12th Royal Lancers in 1880. In 1886 he joined the staff of the Army Veterinary School, Aldershot, as Assistant Instructor and was made Professor in 1887. On the expiration of his period of office in 1892 he was appointed to the Remount Department. He served with the Nile Expedition in 1898 and in the South African War 1899-1902, becoming P.V.O. South Africa in 1903. He retired in 1910 at 53 years of age, was re-employed on Home Service during the Great War, and relegated to unemployment in 1919.

His assumption of office in 1907 was coincident with the introduction of one of the greatest military changes ever made in our system. Mr. (afterwards Lord) Haldane had introduced his scheme for a Territorial Army. He was the first Minister of War to recognize the potential value of the thousands of men who as Artillery, Yeomanry and Infantry gave voluntary service to the State. His decision to give them an organization on the lines of regular formations met with destructive military criticism, but fortunately for the country he was in a position to carry his scheme through.

When the organization was published by the military experts it was found that the Territorial Veterinary Service was *regimental* instead of departmental. This of course was intentional; never during the construction of the Territorial scheme had the Veterinary Branch of the War Office been consulted. The scheme as published was simple. It comprised 220 officers and 14 other ranks as clerks; there was absolutely nothing else, no provision for the care of the sick and consequently no authority for stores or equipment. One would have thought that the newly created Army Veterinary Corps had been hatched outside the War Office and that the experts responsible for the Territorial Army Organization had never heard of it. But no such ignorance obtained among them; to return to the antiquated and worthless regimental system for the New Army was their deliberate policy and as such it had to be contested. To say that the New Army was regarded by the Service with disfavour is to state the case very mildly; a leading military adviser of the Crown confidently asserted that it could never be made an efficient military force, and if it were ever employed he hoped it would be but for a very short time. It should be explained that at this period it was never contemplated to employ this force for any other purpose than Home Defence. Such an attitude did not inspire confidence in the New Army nor encourage those who were at work on its construction, but no doubt it did encourage the tactics of delay, obstruction and indifference which marked the attitude towards its Veterinary development.

It was at once represented to the authorities that whereas 220 officers were required, there were only 32 in the old forces and there was nothing to show that these 32 would transfer to the New Army. Permission was asked, and granted by the War Minister, for the Council of the Royal College of Veterinary Surgeons to be approached and their co-operation invoked in securing officers. This was the first time in our history that a War Minister had empowered the Parliament of the profession to be consulted. The same step had been taken in regard to the Medical Service.

In January 1908, therefore, before a meeting of Council, the Director General gave an outline of the Territorial Scheme and proposed that the Veterinary Service of that Force should be based on that of the regular Army Veterinary Service. This necessitated the existing regimental officers of Yeomanry and Artillery surrendering their regimental commissions and being formed into one body; experience of war had shown such an organization to be absolutely essential to success. About one in every eleven of the practitioners then on the Register would be required in order to obtain the number desired. As far as possible the Veterinary Service for each of the fourteen Divisions and fourteen Mounted Brigades would be raised in the military districts in which these were being formed. The officers of the entire force would come on to one general list for promotion by length of service and those now holding commissions would have their seniority in the new force.

The creation of a subordinate Veterinary Service of non-commissioned officers and men for duty in hospitals was next dealt with, and here it was explained that this part of the scheme had no official sanction at present, but was put forward to render the account as complete as possible. All experience had shown that the only effective method of dealing with sick animals on service was by means of properly equipped self-contained hospitals. A service not self-contained was unworkable and led to chaos. Then followed an account of the fourteen Divisional Hospitals which it was hoped to create, together with the subordinate personnel required, the rates of pay of each rank, and the proposed method of training of all ranks.

A scheme for the creation of a Reserve of Officers was also brought forward at this meeting. It will be considered later; it suffices to say that the Council greatly appreciated the confidence placed in them by the Minister of War and promised this somewhat technical communication full consideration, subsequent deliberations being greatly assisted by the fact that two retired heads of the Department were then serving on the Council.

Two months later, in March 1908, the Council R.C.V.S. invited the War Minister to reconsider the status of the Director General, and urged that he should be placed under the Q.M.G. and not under the Director of Remounts. To this communication the War Office replied a year later, stating it was undesirable to make a change in arrangements which had worked satisfactorily for five years. It was notorious, on the contrary, that the arrangement had never worked satisfactorily.[1] As a consequence of this letter the President of the R.C.V.S. (Sir John M'Fadyean) interviewed Mr. Haldane in June 1909, and a letter was afterwards received agreeing to give the Director General direct access to the Q.M.G. on all matters regarding the administration of the personnel of the Army Veterinary Service. The President, in acknowledging this communication, accepted this solution as going " a long way towards removing what many of us have felt to be a grievance," and added that when the Territorial and Special Reserve Schemes were before the Council " no effort will be spared to make them a success." The Committee of the Council which had dealt with the question, in passing a resolution approving the President's reply, regretted that the dual control of our Service had not been completely swept away, and hoped that time would prove direct communication on some matters between the D.G. and the Q.M.G. to be of such practical advantage as to lead to its complete adoption. Further resolutions were then passed, recommending to the professsion the schemes for Territorial Officers and for a Reserve of Officers.

It will be observed that eighteen months had elapsed between the date when the Council was addressed by the Director General in January 1908 and the time when they were able to declare

[1] It is desirable to explain that prior to the Esher Committee, which sat a few years earlier than the period we are speaking of, the position of the Director General Army Veterinary Department was under the Adjutant General. The Esher Committee made many sweeping changes in the constitution of the War Office, all of which failed to stand the test of experience and had been dropped. Almost the sole relic of this scheme was the position of the D.G.A.V.S., who was placed under the Director of Remounts in the Quarter Master General's Department. The objections to this were that the Remount Directorate had always been hostile, that it was also an alien branch, being concerned with recruiting (the Medical Service was quite distinct from the Recruiting branch of the Army); everything had to pass through the Remount Directorate to reach the Q.M.G. Many of the questions were technical, so that the entertaining spectacle was afforded of a man knowing nothing of a subject endeavouring to explain it to someone as wise as himself. Further, the co-operation of the Remount Branch could not be expected on matters to which by tradition it was opposed, so that it was possible for a scheme, while filtering through that department, to be blocked before reaching the Q.M.G. The latter officer would not depart a hair's-breadth from the prescribed channel of procedure; in this matter he was punctiliously insistent.

their intention of helping the scheme. This delay was due not to the Council but to the War Office. The War Office, however, had itself taken steps early in January 1909 to discuss the question of the formation of a Veterinary Service for the T.F., and the Director of Remounts, who was responsible for organizing the conference, had actually to ask permission for the D.G. of the Veterinary Service to attend! This shows the atmosphere of the conference, at which the D.G. of the Territorial Force, the Civil Member of Council (the virtual C.-in-C. of the Territorial Force), the Q.M.G. and others were present. The attitude adopted by the Q.M.G. was that the conference had met to discuss the means of providing a general list of Veterinary Officers for duty during the next Training Season, and not the formation of a Corps for War. He said that he did not consider it necessary to go to the R.C.V.S. for the officers, and proposed to obtain them through County Associations! The Civil Member in supporting him stated that the Secretary of State refused to recognize the Veterinary Service of the War Office as a separate Directorate; finally the Q.M.G. declared, evidently as his considered opinion, that the Territorial Force required no Veterinary Service for War! A minute on this conference was subsequently written by the Director of Remounts urging that something should be done to save the horses and to mitigate the hardships and sufferings of animals in war. During the following six months, January to June, the Civil Member and Q.M.G. vainly endeavoured to obtain Veterinary Officers through the County Associations. One gentleman was found, over 60 years of age, who had never done any soldiering, and so determined were the Q.M.G. and Civil Member to have their own way that, presumably on the strength of this gentleman's age, his name was actually put forward as the Administrative Veterinary Officer of a London Division! As we have seen above, Lord Haldane agreed in June 1909 to the D.G. having access to the Q.M.G. on all questions of personnel, and the formation and Organization of the Veterinary Service of the T.F. was then begun with the co-operation of the R.C.V.S.

An organization for the officers having been secured, the next point which had to be taken up was sanction for the establishment of the subordinate personnel of the Corps and of Hospitals; hospitals were of no use without personnel nor the latter without hospitals. To both of these measures the Civil Member and Q.M.G. were opposed; we have seen that they had decided no veterinary organization was necessary for war and consequently no personnel or hospitals were required. Neither question was settled for many weary months; interviews and minutes were alike equally unavailing. Attempts were made to get authority by whittling down the numbers; even then the Civil Member would not agree to the men being clothed !

Since no approval for hospitals could be obtained, no Ordnance Equipment could be earmarked for these units. So extraordinary was the opposition to the creation of an effective Veterinary Service, and so lukewarm the attachment of those not actively hostile to the scheme, that it was thought well to place the case more fully before the authorities. It was evident they did not realize the situation which would arise on calling into existence an Army with 130,000 animals, consigned to the care of officers and men who knew little or nothing about their care and management, for they had no experience of these in peace time, as the horses were hired and remained under the care of the contractor.

Accordingly in March 1909, at a time when matters were in a bad way, a memorandum was addressed to the Director General Territorial Force pointing out that the position of the mounted branches of the T.F. might be likened to that of a man, the embarrassed recipient of a strange animal, to the habits, peculiarities and care of which he is totally ignorant; that the knowledge of the care and management of horses among civilians was year by year growing less and becoming confined to the relatively small and diminishing class of grooms. This difficulty had not been felt during training, as the horses were generally accompanied by their attendants, but this would not be so in war. It was stated that had the Secretary of State on the inception of the T.F. asked for an opinion on this question he would have been advised that training in horse management was the first essential, guns being of no use unless they can be got into position and dismounted cavalry never being other than a disorganized mass. To commit such a delicate mechanism as a horse to unskilled hands was like giving a child a chronometer to play with. The Director General T.F. was reminded that the last time a civil army went to war in this country was in the days of Cromwell, when technical experts had to be appointed for Artillery, Engineers, Forage and Transport services, but none were appointed for the care of horses, as in those days everybody rode who could afford it and trained servants were to be found in abundance. It was urged that all this was changed and that Commanding Officers would require a " Horse Master " through whom they could pull the needful strings. This duty would naturally fall to the Veterinary Service of Units; this Service in the T.F. should be charged not only with the prevention and treatment of disease but with the care and management of horses. Nothing came of this appeal to common sense. (It was not many years after, that " Horse Masters " had to be appointed during the Great War to carry out what neither officers nor men could learn without years of experience.)

By January 1910 the struggle to obtain Hospitals and hospital personnel for the T.F. had resolved itself into a war of position where neither side would yield. Amongst other arguments it was said that the creation of hospitals would encourage animals being kept near the fighting line; it was pointed out in reply that the proposed hospitals would be well back from the front. This was countered by the statement that in this case civilian practitioners could be employed under County Associations, and the care of sick and wounded men in Civil General Hospitals was referred to as evidence of the practicability of such a scheme; it was also added that these hospitals were not demanding either equipment or buildings; the reply was that the General Hospitals were already staffed and equipped for dealing with the civil population and were in fact working institutions; to expand them to meet the exigencies of war would not be difficult, and it was also pointed out that the comparison made between hospital organization for men and for animals could not be a true one, until public sentiment and the private purse provided some means of relief for animals against the hardships of war. It was urged that it was the duty of the State to make this provision; that the organization necessary for the accommodation and treatment of 10,000 war-worn and war-injured animals could not be evolved out of the imagination of any County Association, but that this knowledge had been acquired by the Veterinary Department and was embodied in the proposals submitted. To this it was replied (and this objection was considered final) that since the proposed hospitals were not to be located near the fighting line, there was no use in having hospitals far back as the sick could not be evacuated from the front ! This argument was met by pointing out that the troops had to be fed and that every supply train returning empty could be made a hospital train for animals. So good, indeed, were these facilities for evacuation during war that an important part of veterinary administration was the careful inspection of those being sent back to avoid including any soon likely to be fit for duty. We must now leave the matter of subordinate personnel and Veterinary Hospitals, saying only that they were sanctioned in the term of office of the next D.G. It must be remembered that much of this correspondence was carried out by a civilian with no knowledge of war and by a military officer of very limited active service experience. Whenever, as in the case narrated, they found themselves defeated, refuge was taken in months of silence and inactivity; they appeared literally to have gone to earth, for although the room of the Q.M.G. in the War Office and that of the D.G. A.V.D. were not twenty-five yards apart, on one occasion six months passed without their setting eyes on each other.

Technical equipment for Territorial Officers was another big difficulty, and until the issue of this was approved no money could be spent. When sanction was at last given, no approval could be obtained for its storage. So senseless was this opposition that the Civil Member was asked whether he expected the officers concerned to keep the equipment under their beds. To ensure the War Equipment of the T.F. remaining intact it had, in consequence of the decision to provide no storage, to remain at Woolwich until War was declared.

The Territorial Force was not the sole subject of legislation; there was a good deal requiring attention in the Regular Forces. No Reserve of Officers existed for the Army, and a Special Reserve for all Branches was projected. The Army Veterinary Service fixed their Reserve at 150 officers and had taken up the question of their supply with the Council of the R.C.V.S., as mentioned above, in January 1908. Like the other scheme it was held up for eighteen months, to the astonishment of candidates, who of course could know nothing of the cause of delay. Eventually it appeared two years later than had been hoped and a corresponding period of training had necessarily been lost. What the Service generally owed to its Special Reserve in the Great War will never be properly known.[1] As a matter of fact, at the time the Special Reserve was asked for we were 33 officers short of War Establishment even if every officer on the Home list had been available to take the Field.

On the termination of the War in South Africa the technical

[1] A Financial Official of the War Office, who was opposed to the creation of a Special Reserve of Officers, informed the Director General that when war broke out he could go into the streets and obtain any number of veterinary surgeons. The fact that they were untrained did not concern him.

equipment then in store, together with the best of it returned by the troops on demobilization, was sent home. In 1907 this represented all we possessed for the Field Army; it consisted of the chests introduced by Colonel Duck, referred to at p. 199, which had done yeoman service but were now out of date. Great improvements in manufacture had occurred in consequence of the war; for instance, drugs had been compressed, also dressings and bandages. Instruments had been improved and some rendered obsolete. It was evident that the whole equipment would have to undergo a radical change. All necessary steps had been taken to devise a chest of more up-to-date pattern, when the military authorities decided that in the future the maximum weight of veterinary stores per unit must not exceed 25 lbs. This required a total revision of the scheme, and it was decided to introduce a unit chest of drugs and dressings of the simplest kind which would be within the prescribed weight and expendible. These chests were calculated to last a fortnight, when a new one would be issued. As the chest was expendible it was made of the lightest, strongest, and cheapest material—*i.e.*, three-ply wood bound with tin, with webbing strap and buckle. A special Veterinary Chest for each officer, complete with drugs, dressings and instruments, was also devised, which remained with him as part of his personal equipment. Chests for Hospitals were the next consideration, and a set was devised to meet all requirements. This took many many months to arrange, the whole of the work being carried out by Major (now Major-General) E. R. C. Butler, and the resulting patterns were highly approved. It had been decided during the administration of Major-General Thomson that the Veterinary Service could no longer live from hand to mouth in the matter of stores; the War in South Africa had proved what a haphazard and expensive system this was. The special building erected at Woolwich (see p. 213) was opened shortly after the new D.G. came into office. Everything was now ready for the process of manufacture; the numbers required and the cost were ascertained; nothing remained but to obtain the needful money. To the utter consternation of the department it was now learnt that the Q.M.G. had decided not to ask for the money! Behind him in this matter were the Financial Authorities, opposed to the expenditure of any money in peace but prepared to " pour it out like water in time of war." The argument of this branch was that everything could be bought when the necessity arose. It was pointed out that one could not buy what did not exist, and that war would not wait for manufacture. The whole experience of South Africa had been lost; it was well known that it took a year to manufacture the pattern chest then in use. The light unit 25 lb. chest, above mentioned, we could buy by the thousand as it was a trade article, but empty chests were of no value; these thousands had each to be packed complete for issue. All this was duly represented, but no attention paid to the matter. Our position, with no equipment for units, out-of-date and insufficient equipment for officers and equally out-of-date equipment for hospitals, was ludicrous, while the Territorial Army, which was rapidly taking shape, had nothing of any kind!

Relief came in a wholly unexpected way. In a conference held at the War Office all heads of departments were asked the short question, "Is your branch ready for War?" The D.G.A.V.S. replied, to the astonishment of all present, that the A.V.D. was not. When desired to explain the position, he said he had no stores, that he had asked for the money and that the Q.M.G. had refused to put forward the estimate for sanction! Within a week or two the money was found and orders were given to proceed with manufacture, the total expenditure to extend over three years, the period which it was estimated would be required for production. That is how the stores were obtained which afterwards saved our department from reproach in the Great War. We were in due course able to put every war unit in possession of its equipment, also every officer, every mobile section and every hospital. Stores for a three months' issue to the Field Army were lying packed at Woolwich, also the whole of the Stores for the Territorial Force, and in addition a three months' reserve was in hand. During the whole of the War the question of the sufficiency of Stores never caused any anxiety.

It was now desired to render the probationary period on joining, which was fixed at six months, a real test; six months was too short a time in which to impart instruction, military and technical, to the young officer. Percivall thought that he ought to be on probation for a few years; in 1908 one year was asked for as a minimum, to serve the double purpose of adding to the officer's knowledge and revealing his weaknesses. Further it was recommended that he be examined at the end of his probationary period and his final position on the list decided by this test.

During the next twelve or fifteen years the gradual growth of an officer's experience takes place; at the end of that time he is about 40 years of age and either of exceptional ability, of which there are few, of so-called average ability, of which there are many, or else has passed through the most critical period of his life without materially adding to his knowledge. During the critical period examinations are held to test what progress is being made; failure to pass these within the prescribed period should be dealt with by relegation to retirement with a gratuity.

The examination for promotion to Major was the most important test, being both professional and military. At the time these questions were taken up an officer could evade this examination by taking his Fellowship, so that though he might fail in his Service test his promotion was assured him by his Fellowship; such actually occurred. The Fellowship test for promotion was therefore withdrawn. It was also proposed that all examination papers should be adjudicated by a Board of Examiners, the mean of whose marking should be taken, and in cases of doubt an assessor called in. In the past the papers had been marked by the Head of the Department, which was regarded as undesirable.

The importance of weeding was urged, as it would leave selected Majors who on an average became Lt.-Colonels ten years later. The final step of Lieut.-Colonel to Colonel occurred about 55 years of age if a vacancy existed. Experience had shown that there were few men of 55 years of age, who had spent half a lifetime on foreign service, who yet retained sufficient mental and bodily energy to be worth retaining for another two years. The final step to Colonel ought not to be made solely because a vacancy existed, but for the reason that the best interests of the Service were met by retaining the officer. The opinion formed by long years of observation was therefore expressed that automatic promotion was ruinous to efficiency.[1] Up to the year 1908, of the last 36 officers who had retired between 45 and 55 years of age, no less than 30 were unfit for further advancement; and of the last 13 officers of a mean age of 55 years only 3 were mentally and bodily active. Hardly any of these recommendations were accepted. Even the evil of automatic promotion remained unrecognized, until something occurred as the result of it which forcibly drew attention to the question.

During this administration every effort was made to encourage

[1] These recommendations to facilitate the flow of promotion, and the careful weighing in the balance of the officers of 55 years of age, were also given in evidence to a War Office Committee on "Promotion of Regimental Officers," which sat in 1907.

officers to employ modern instruments of precision—for example, electrical illumination of the various body passages, of the eye, of sinuses and deep wounds—and to adopt improved methods of examining the heart and lungs and such-like. Winter essays for officers of all ranks were tried as an experimental measure, but appeared unpopular, yet as necessitating reading up a subject and expressing one's views on it in a clear and systematic manner, they were a useful training to those who looked forward to one day occupying the higher ranks.

If greater efficiency were expected from officers, greater opportunities for acquiring information should be given; this was impressed on the Authorities. Increased facilities for post-graduate courses, which were limited to the meagre number of eight annually; the encouragement of officers to proceed abroad and study in Paris, Berlin and Vienna, not only purely professional but also military questions connected with their profession; the formation in Commands of circulating libraries of text-books and periodicals; the supply to every officer of a case of instruments and microscope as a free issue on joining, and the putting into actual operation of the authority, which existed, but had never been acted upon, for rewarding merit by brevet promotion, were the bases of the recommendations made. The Authorities were reminded that the higher education of the Veterinary Officer was as imperative as that of the combatant officer. There was no Veterinary Staff College, but the concessions above asked were calculated to overcome this lack.

It was further recommended that the flow of promotion in the higher ranks should be encouraged by limiting the tenure of the appointments of Lt.-Colonels and Colonels; in the past these had been held for an average of eight years, in the future they would be held for twelve or thirteen years and so further increase the block in promotion.

Few of the suggestions above mentioned were adopted, not always because they received no military support, but for the reason that the Finance Branch vetoed them on the ground of expense.

The Establishment of the Veterinary Service in time of peace was fixed on a minimum basis; it was pointed out that this allowed no provision to be made for sickness, for leave of absence, for study leave, for the shortage which occurred every year during the relief season, and further that there were stations abroad (Gibraltar, Malta and China) where Veterinary Officers should be located and local civil assistance no longer employed. Owing to the fact that foreign stations insisted on the arrival of the new officer before parting with the old, this country had to bear a minimum of four months' loss of service each year for every officer relieved; the officer proceeding abroad required a month's leave, his journey occupied a month, while the relieved officer required a month for his journey and a further month's leave on arrival in this country. Year after year this had happened, and in years of heavy reliefs the home service had suffered, officers desiring leave having to pay civil practitioners to perform their duty. In consequence of this representation five extra officers of the ten asked for were added to the Establishment, and it was arranged that foreign stations were to send home half their officers due for relief without waiting for the arrival of the relieving officers. This was one of the few instances where the Q.M.G. supported the recommendations put forward; but when the final decision was given by the Chief of the General Staff, the Director General was not invited to be present at the conference, his duties being performed by the Director of Remounts!

In consequence of the formation of a Corps the work of the Department at the War Office had greatly increased, while the staff remained the same, viz., the Director General and a Deputy Assistant Director General. There was no officer in charge of Records, the routine work of which had to be done at the War Office. It was the only branch of the Service whose Record Office was in that building. An Asst. Director General of the rank of Lt.-Colonel and a D.A.D.G. of the rank of Major or Captain were asked for at suitable rates of staff pay. The authorities offered a Staff Captain at £14 per annum remuneration, though an Infantry Staff Captain received £235 per annum, one of Royal Engineers £107, and one of A.S.C. £144 per annum for his services. The question was not settled until the next D.G. came into office.

Now that an Army Veterinary Corps had been formed a feeling got abroad that it was part of its policy to take Farriers away from units and embody them in its Service. There was never any such intention, but we were anxious to see this class more economically employed, and knew that this could best be effected by the formation of a Corps of Farriers on the lines of the Corps of Armourers, the administration falling to the Ordnance Service. There was only an insignificant reserve of Farriers and Shoeing Smiths, and the wasteful regimental system of employing them in the dual capacity of soldier and tradesman necessitated the engagement of large numbers over and above those actually requisite for shoeing. We continued to pursue the old system of training, requiring years to be spent in the forge, indifferent to the fact that the system of Army Shoeing had undergone a complete revolution. Now that the horses were shod with machine-made shoes it did not appear to be necessary that more than a small percentage of men should be capable of making a shoe; and if we gave attention to training in fitting the ready-made article and nailing it on, we had accomplished all that was essential for the vast majority of men. In this way many more men could be trained in the same time and a reserve accumulated. A proposal on the above lines was put forward in 1908. The scheme met with the stoutest opposition from the Artillery and Cavalry. The only person who gave it support was the Director of Organization, who invited the Director of Recruiting to say whether the suggestion of passing trained Shoeing Smiths to the Reserve at seven years or earlier would be a disadvantage to the Army as urged by the Artillery. The reply of the Director of Recruiting, whose aid to defeat the scheme had been previously secured, was that we would not get many men to undergo the prescribed training with the penalty in front of them that they were not to extend or re-engage " owing to their acquired efficiency "! He appeared to forget that passing to the Reserve was the penalty inflicted on the man who had learned his trade as a soldier. The authorities were pressed to give consideration to a proposal which promised simplification in training, a reserve, and a smaller number of men per unit. An official definition of the duties of a farrier was also asked for. Nothing came of this effort to obtain the economical employment of Farriers and Shoeing Smiths nor the building up of a reserve. The sequel to the story occurred during the War, when Schools of Farriery had to be established for the purpose of training Shoeing Smiths to meet the enormous demands in the Field.

The Cavalry School at Netheravon was established after the War in South Africa, and among its functions was the training of officers in horse management. Hitherto this subject had been taught at the Army Veterinary School at Aldershot; its transfer to Netheravon was portion of a secret scheme for imparting to officers what was termed veterinary knowledge which they were not taught at Aldershot. The ultimate aim was to qualify combatant officers to treat the sick horses of the State. With this object in view the syllabus of instruction at Netheravon was carefully drafted by the Cavalry Officers concerned, but between the time of its War Office approval and printing the designation of the subject "Horse Management" was changed without authority into "Veterinary Subjects."

All Schools of Horsemanship in the past had annexed veterinary matters as a sort of prescriptive right. In the seventeenth and part of the eighteenth century this was justified by tradition, but the parting of the ways had long since occurred, and in this country at least, no serious effort had ever been made to oust the regular veterinary schools since their establishment. Our Cavalry Officers had recently been to the celebrated Cavalry School at Saumur and had imbibed the ritual which was carried out there with an almost religious solemnity. They had seen what a handful of supermen could do with horses trained to unnatural movements, such as a circus proprietor might have envied, and they had seen the officers and other ranks put through a course of veterinary instruction and shoeing. On their return their ambition to create a Saumur in England was evident, and they pressed for veterinary instruction for their school. The syllabus produced was elaborate, drawn up by enthusiasts anxious to emulate Saumur, and forgetting that that Institution was not the growth of yesterday. It aimed at too much; for example, "The Art of Farriery in all its Branches" was among a dozen other subjects to be acquired in a few months. The officers who drew up this scheme were ignorant of the fact that the Art of Farriery in all its Branches could only be acquired by a five years' apprenticeship in a busy forge and did not ask themselves whether this knowledge would make a better squadron leader. It was contended that the officer could learn at the Aldershot School and with his regiment all that really mattered of shoeing, saddlery, forage or "first aid," but that all this could not be learned in ten months, as was projected at Netheravon. There was no short cut to horse management; the principle could be taught in the class-room, but the practice only by object lessons in the stable.

With regard to the veterinary side of the case it was actually urged by the then Director of Military Training (under the pressure of his Cavalry advisers) that as a shortage of veterinary officers would occur in war, the training of the Cavalry in these duties was a distinct advantage. This argument was met by the logical reply, that as a shortage of Veterinary Officers was anticipated the proper course was to increase their Establishment to meet the deficit rather than to assume that the Cavalry officer was a fit and proper person to treat a sick troop horse. Secondly, a shortage of Combatant Officers would certainly occur in war; was it therefore proposed to train veterinary officers to take their place? Further, if the Cavalry in the future carried out the functions for which they alone existed, they would have no time to devote to the treatment of animals in war. The whole of the veterinary experience in the Army indicated that what was required of Cavalry officers was a knowledge of horse management and the conditioning of healthy animals. The Director of Military Training argued that it was proposed that only " common " cases should be treated by Squadron Officers; he was reminded that the term " common " was indefinite and frequently misleading. A " common cold " might be the precursor of serious trouble. As an instance of the danger of giving combatant officers the authority desired, he was reminded that during the War in South Africa an officer of Artillery, travelling in charge of horses at sea, on the S.S. *Cervona* in 1901, insisted against civil veterinary advice in destroying no less than 251 horses for glanders when they were only suffering from a common cold! But nothing could discourage these people. The *Cavalry Journal* contained indignant articles on the manner in which instruction was being withheld, and one writer suggested an allowance for medicines should be drawn by Squadron Officers! It is a remarkable fact that the amateur when he has anything wrong with his own horses always goes to the professional man for advice, but is extremely anxious to treat animals the property of others.

Closely allied to this question of Cavalry Officers treating their sick animals was the opposition offered by the Cavalry Commander at a large military station to the surrender of the regimental horse infirmaries for conversion into a central veterinary hospital for the Cavalry. The policy of instituting these hospitals was already fixed; the question so far as this station was concerned was where it should be located. On the question of suitable sites for veterinary hospitals some curious notions prevail. When a veterinary hospital was to be built at Pretoria it was sited on the edge of the sewage farm, well away from the Cavalry Lines. A mere accident brought this site to notice before building operations began. The explanation was that a veterinary hospital was something insanitary; the real fact was that, as it was not to be under Cavalry control, the regimental authorities pressed for it to be kept as far away from them as possible. The hospital above alluded to was proposed to be erected on a site well away from all other units, in disregard of the fact that the sick have to march to hospital. As at Pretoria, the choice of site was no accident but a set design, intended to provide an excuse for not sending animals to hospital.

The Cavalry Commander was informed that his late regimental infirmaries would be converted into a station Cavalry hospital, and in reply said this would be detrimental to the training of officers and farriers; further, he was opposed to the system of station hospitals and especially to one over which he had no authority being instituted in his barracks, adding: " No longer could the Commanding Officer superintend the condition of his horses as *well as their care and treatment in sickness ;*[1] no longer was it possible to train the Regimental Staff for their veterinary duties in time of war, and no longer *could the men of a regiment be given practical illustrations of treatment and cure.*"[2] In all my service I never saw the Commanding Officer superintend the treatment of his sick, nor the men of a regiment being given veterinary training in hospital, nor can I conceive what useful purpose such training was proposed to serve ! The reply to this criticism was that on service the combatants had other duties to perform than treating sick animals, that a separate branch existed for that purpose, and it was this branch which must be trained. The Cavalry Commander above alluded to, when asked what he would do with the sick under regimental arrangements, replied that if unfit to move with their unit he would leave them behind in charge of a Farrier. When reminded that the Farrier was intended to shoe horses and his absence would necessarily be felt, he said that the shoeing could be done by the cold shoers ! It was represented to the authorities that if a Farrier can be detached from his unit and left behind in the open with a collection of sick for which he can do nothing, he is not performing his duty as a shoer of horses, and if the shoeing can equally well be carried out in his absence, it is obvious the Farrier is a supernumerary ! No more was heard of these objections, and the hospital in due course appeared in the place where it was required.

In 1909 the Commander-in-Chief in India drew attention to the loss of animal life in that country in consequence of epizootic diseases, and attributed it to little or nothing having been done for the preservation of animals and to the lack of veterinary knowledge. It is unfortunate that it was not made clear that

---

[1] The italics are mine.—F. S.   [2] *Idem.*

these remarks applied only to Transport animals, not under the charge of the Army Veterinary Service, for which officers of that Service are only called in when outbreaks of disease have occurred. In consequence they see nothing of oxen or camels in health. It was brought to the notice of the Authorities that before officers proceed on a tour of service in India, increased facilities for instruction in Tropical Diseases should be given them, and this training supplemented by continuous practical experience in India; that the whole of the Transport should come under Veterinary control and that the methods of dealing with the prevention of disease should be centralized. If these recommendations were adopted and the needful staff given, the suppression of disease among transport animals was as certain as anything could be. In no instance had veterinary preventive medicine failed when properly organized.

India in effect desired that the study of Tropical Diseases should be taken up. Compared with ourselves, Germany had but a trifling interest in the question, yet she had a school dealing with the Tropical Diseases of Animals, while this country was without one. It was therefore proposed to establish such a school at Aldershot, employing a civilian pathologist at £1,000 a year, India contributing its share towards his salary, the school to be not only for the purpose of instruction but also of research, and every veterinary officer to be trained there before proceeding abroad. Unfortunately nothing came of the proposal.

It was felt that the Annual Veterinary Statistical Report of the Army, the origin of which is dealt with at p. 164, should serve a double purpose, not only as a record of animal wastage, but also furnishing an analysis of its causes and means of prevention. It was thought that the dry study of figures could be rendered more interesting by making the Report educative, dealing with researches undertaken during the year, improved methods of treatment, and such like. After much difficulty the authorities agreed to issue the Annual Report for 1909 as a Command Paper, so that it was presented to both Houses of Parliament, and obtained the same circulation as is accorded the Army Medical Report. In the next administration, however, the Report was reduced to bare figures and tables.

What most impressed one at the War Office was the utter neglect of the authorities to consult the Veterinary Department before taking measures which directly affected it. This was due to the subordinate position which it occupied under Remounts and the policy of some branches of deliberately ignoring its existence. Thus questions of Training, Mobilization, Regulations for Field Service and other matters of supreme importance, in which it was concerned, were not referred for opinion. A good example of this is given earlier in this History, when the Veterinary Service was destroyed as a War unit without any reference being made as to its views (p. 203). Similarly Regulations for Field Service were drawn up at this time, embodying the lessons of the War in South Africa, and without reference to the Department, the Director of Veterinary Services was allotted a useless position on the L. of C. instead of being with G.H.Q. Representations were made, but no notice was taken. We now know that as soon as we took the Field in 1914 the position allotted was found to be unworkable in all theatres of war.

It was evident that our senior officers, as those of other branches, required training in Staff Duties. The day when an Administrative Officer's duties were mainly confined to dealing with official correspondence and returns had passed. He had to be identified with the work of the Staff, study the conditions under which modern armies fight, and learn how far these affected the arrangements he would have to make for his Service in War. A knowledge of these problems could only be effectively acquired in Staff Rides, which had the double advantage of not only training our officers but of bringing the Staff itself face to face with veterinary problems. Though the War in South Africa had effectively closed the door against the haphazard methods of the past in dealing with sick animals on a campaign, many Staff Officers had still to be taught its lessons, and had yet to learn to listen to advice and reasoned opinions. A minority was hostile to the Veterinary Service being associated with Staff Training, but this conservative attitude has long passed.

The reason why the veterinary case was fought with such persistence during these years was that our newly established Service might not be found wanting in the next war. There was to be no more hand-to-mouth system of supplies; no more employment of civilian practitioners without military status and authority; no more conversion of remount depots and regiments into a collection of sick and war-worn animals; no more begging from regiments the loan of subordinate personnel, and no more hopeless confusion. Our aim was the creation of properly equipped hospitals, organized and staffed by ourselves, of the success of which we were assured, the whole of the veterinary arrangements being placed in the hands of a well-trained administrative staff.

The marking of army animals by clipping the number on the coat was doubtless the earliest system employed; it is referred to at p. 17. Subsequently hoof branding was adopted, and when army numbers, as opposed to regimental numbers, were introduced, all four feet were branded. On service the system of hoof branding is impracticable, and skin branding has been used in its place, a cruel and mutilating process. During wars in South Africa horse-stealing has always been prevalent; the last war in that country was no exception. To provide a complete identification, the writer, after losing a horse, thenceforth tattooed his name inside the mouth above the incisor teeth; it was a natural step to suggest army numbers being so placed. Few outside the Corps realized the advantages which had thus been secured, and for years afterwards the antiquated hoof brands were employed. It is gratifying to learn that all army animals now bear their number tattooed in the mouth.

Only one other matter remains to be drawn attention to. During this administration it was arranged with the Director of Supplies and the Director General Army Medical Department that in all stations where the military authorities had their own abattoirs an officer of the Veterinary Service should inspect the stock for slaughter during life and examine the animals after death. In addition, arrangements were made with the same departments for the inspection, by a Veterinary Officer, of dairies and dairy stock supplying milk to military hospitals.

Before introducing the next Director General we shall consider the length of time for which the appointment could be held. In the days of Messrs. Coleman, Cherry and Wilkinson the appointment as head of the Department was for life; in 1876 it was made seven years; in 1897 five years; in 1902 a three years' appointment with a possible extension of two years; in 1913 a four years' appointment unless extended under special circumstances. Under the regulation of 1902 the occupant of the post was asked at the end of the third and fourth years whether he desired an extension. When that question was asked the writer he declined any extension unless his Department was placed on a sound footing by being wholly brought under the Q.M.G. without any form of Remount control. This being refused, he left at the end of his three years, the shortest period of office on record.

PLATE J

Major General R. Pringle took over the appointment of Director General on 15th October 1910.

Major General Sir Robert Pringle joined the Service in 1878 at the age of 23, and was among the first candidates under the new Departmental scheme. He became 1st Class ten years later and a Major at 20 years' service. His promotion to Administrative rank occurred at 23 years' service; he was P.V.O. 3rd Army Corps in 1902, Inspecting Veterinary Officer in India 1903-07 and P.V.O. Aldershot Command 1908-10. He was over 55 years of age when he succeeded as Director General; had his predecessor occupied office for the full period of five years General Pringle would have been retired for age before the appointment became vacant.

He served in the Afghan War 1880, the Wuzeere Expedition of 1881 (Despatches), the Zhob Valley Expedition of 1884 and during the last phase of the War in South Africa 1899-1902 (Despatches and D.S.O.). In 1909 he received the C.B. and for his services in the Great War the K.C.M.G., being the first officer of our Service to receive this reward. He died in 1926.

General Pringle was a Scotsman, level-headed, shrewd and cautious. He had been amongst horses all his life, and there was little of practical importance connected with them he did not understand; on the other hand he took little interest in science or the development of modern methods of enquiry. In his prime his judgement was ripe and his opinion highly valued. In his early days he made three contributions to veterinary literature, but nothing after 1884.

In 1911 the long-hoped-for Reserve of Stores was supplied by the contractors, and our position in this respect was one of less anxiety; by the following year all the medical and surgical equipment required for units, hospitals, etc., for a Field Force consisting of seven Divisions and a Cavalry Division had been delivered and the position was one of security.

In 1912 a Record Office in connection with the Corps was opened at Woolwich and the work removed from the War Office, an officer in charge of Records being appointed. This year also saw a change in the official designation of administrative officers of Commands, the title of Asst. Director of Veterinary Services being substituted for that of P.V.O. This brought the designations of our officers in peace into line with those already decided upon for Veterinary Staff Officers of Divisions in the Field.

In 1911 it had been laid down that no candidate for the A.V.C. could compete more than twice; in 1913 it was added that the maximum age for candidates should be 25 instead of 27 years of age.

In this latter year a most important Veterinary Field Unit was instituted to serve as a connecting link between the Troops in the Field and Veterinary Hospitals. Experience during the War in South Africa had shown that some means of collecting and taking over the sick and injured animals shed by a Force during its advance was absolutely necessary. Local efforts made in South Africa were more than encouraging where large numbers of animals " left on the veldt " had been swept up by mounted men following in the wake of a Force, and subsequently transferred to the nearest hospital. Under the administration of the previous Q.M.G. the organization of such a unit as part of a modern Division was out of the question. After his departure from office in 1913 and the accession of a new Q.M.G. no difficulties were raised, and sanction was given for the creation of Mobile Veterinary Sections, one to each Cavalry Brigade and Infantry Division.

Another result of the appointment of a new Q.M.G. was that a Veterinary Directorate was granted independent of the Remount Department. This change had been urged on the Authorities for the previous six years; it was now instituted by A.O. 402 of 1913 and the Veterinary Service was free to function, responsible only to the Quarter Master General of the Army.

Similarly approval of a subordinate personnel for the Army Veterinary Corps T.F. was also granted. It is almost unbelievable that this question, debated since 1908, was only settled early in 1914. Personnel was approved for seven Veterinary Hospitals T.F. About the same time equipment for fourteen such hospitals —the result of the old struggle—came to hand; the position was thus assured. It was these seven reserve sets of hospital equipment which saved the Veterinary position after the loss of matériel in the Retreat from Mons.

The unsuitable designations of Professor and Asst. Professor at the Army Veterinary School, Aldershot, were altered to Commandant and Instructor in 1913, an undoubted improvement.

In 1914 the Field Manual, Veterinary, was published; it had long been expected, but there are so many branches to consult and oppositions to be contested for works of this kind that their production is a matter of years. Fortunately it appeared before war broke out, so that every officer of our Service knew what his duties were in the Field.

As a result of the years of fighting narrated in the previous pages, the outbreak of War in 1914 found our Service prepared. We were, however, without that supplemental aid which the

Red Cross Society affords to the Medical Service, but this was not for long. The Royal Society for the Prevention of Cruelty to Animals patriotically came forward and offered financial assistance for sick and wounded animals of the Army. The magnificent work accomplished through the aid furnished by this wealthy body can never be forgotten: without it the high degree of excellence attained by Veterinary Hospitals could not have been reached. The Society was represented by its Secretary, Captain E. G. Fairholme, on whom an Hon. Commission in the A.V.C. was conferred. His enthusiasm was unbounded; he went overseas soon after war began, so was on the spot to meet all demands, which were never made in vain. Large sums of money were expended in rendering hospitals complete with modern requirements; as a consequence results were attained hitherto beyond our most sanguine expectations.

One of the many important questions which had to be dealt with was the Transport of Animals by Sea. The system laid down did not give good results and something better was demanded. The whole question is thoroughly dealt with in the Veterinary History of the Great War, but it is impossible to avoid reference to the order, smoothness and reduced mortality which resulted when the Veterinary Service was given a free hand to organize its own system based on experience. The transport of animals in pens, advocated thirty years before by Colonel Sir Francis Duck (see p. 199), was adopted with the happiest results. In all matters dealing with the reorganization of the system of Sea Transport, Mr. A. E. Boyer, M.B.E., a civilian veterinary practitioner, stands out pre-eminent as supreme organizer, tactful disciplinarian and first-class horsemaster.

Less than six months after the War began the old question of shortage of farriers arose. Not only were these required in regular formations, but also to meet the demands of the large forces being raised. In June 1915 a School of Farriery was established, a second, third and fourth school followed within a few months, and through these for the remainder of the war some thousands of men were converted into horse-shoers by a system of intensive training. A full account of this remarkable chapter in the history of the war is given in the official publication. An Hon. Commission in the Corps was conferred on Captain Budd, M.B.E., to whose capacity and technical skill one of the schools owed its success.

Some set-backs were experienced by our Service during the War, of which the most serious was due to the uncontrolled mortality among the remounts in Canada and the United States. The loss from disease among these was heavy; the depots were congested, and the Veterinary Service imperfectly organized. In 1917 it was decided to send Colonel Olver as D.D.V.S. to the British Remount Commission in Canada. It is very difficult to get rid of a bad system which has been in force for any length of time; the Official History tells us of the conditions existing in this vast concern, containing several thousand horses, of which large numbers were affected with epizootic diseases; it was a truly Augean stable he was called upon to cleanse. It is unfortunate that this officer, with his capacity for organization, firmness and knowledge of modern methods of controlling epizootic diseases, was not sent out in the first instance.

In 1917 Colonel J. J. Aitken was despatched to the United States to assist the Military Authorities in the formation of an American Veterinary Corps, which it had been decided should be based on that of our Army. The exercise of great tact, moderation and diplomacy was required, and the results obtained fully justified this officer's selection.

In October 1915 Major General Pringle's period of office expired under the terms of the Royal Warrant of 1902 under which he was appointed. It came as a great surprise to his Service to find that his appointment was extended under conditions justified neither by the military position nor by his state of health. He was now just over 60 years of age. It will be remembered (p. 223) that under the previous administration the attention of the authorities had been drawn to the inadvisability of retaining officers over 55 years of age; these recommendations were rejected, and the then Q.M.G. remained long enough in office to regret bitterly an appointment he insisted on making in opposition to the opinion of his adviser. The same mistake was here repeated by his successor, in the case of a much older officer whose state of health, the result of advancing age, was such that vitality, judgement and interest were being gradually sapped by arterial sclerosis, and whose growing disability ultimately rendered him unable to concentrate on the serious work in hand or to undertake the necessary inspections. In this way he lost touch with the actual workers in Hospitals and in the Field, and accordingly was not in sympathy with their difficulties or requirements. For reasons unknown he did not employ his Staff Officers on Inspection duties as was done by other Branches.

Two years from the time of his extension, owing to continuous ill-health, he was compelled to relinquish his appointment on 11th October 1917, in his 63rd year.

The Q.M.G. of this period has been shown to be a man of much broader views than his predecessor, but his previous training—like that of most Staff Officers—had not been in a mounted branch of the Army, and it is doubtful whether he took that interest in the Veterinary Service which his position demanded. Nevertheless, we sincerely thank him for the legislative advances made during his period of office.

In consequence of the Great War there were many deaths among officers during Sir Robert Pringle's administration, which it is impossible to deal with individually. An exception, however, must be made in the case of Lt. Colonel F. U. Carr, whose brilliant career during his relatively short period of service had attracted attention both within the Department and throughout the Service generally. Commissioned in 1895, he served on the North-West Frontier of India in the Mohmand and Tirah Expeditions of 1897-8, receiving the medal with two clasps. His next service was in the War in South Africa 1899-1902, where he came to the front not only as a first-class professional officer but as a leader of men. During the guerilla war he organized a body of native scouts, and was frequently out all night gaining intelligence. He was offered and refused command of French's Scouts, and was also offered a commission in the 10th Hussars, which he also declined. Towards the end of the War he was severely wounded and unable to take part in further active operations. He was subsequently attached to the Staff of the Remount Commission under Lord Downe, and with it toured South Africa, Australia and New Zealand. Lord Downe applied for his services as A.D.C.; the request was refused (see p. 207). For his services in South Africa he received the Queen's Medal with six clasps and the King's Medal with two clasps. Among other operations he was present at Sannah's Post.

From 1903-1906 he was employed in the operations with the West Africa Force in Northern Nigeria, receiving the medal and clasp. In 1908 he joined the Egyptian Army and was present in the Operations in Southern Kordofan in 1910, receiving the medal and clasp. On the outbreak of the Great War he proceeded to France with the 2nd Division, taking part in the retreat from Mons and the Battles of the Marne and Aisne. He was recalled to the Sudan in October, 1914, and was in the Operations in Darfur in 1916. In addition to being mentioned in Despatches he received the 4th Class Osmanieh and the 3rd Class Order of the Nile.

In 1907 he was made Director of the Veterinary Department of the Sudan Government, and set to work with characteristic energy to build up an export trade in live stock with Egypt. He had to establish a quarantine station, where the animals were held before the approval of the Egyptian Government could be obtained to their entry, and this with practically no financial aid. Still he was positive of the soundness of his scheme and the benefit it would confer on the Sudan; the proof that he was right is afforded by one of the most remarkable facts in the economic history of that country; in seven years the value of cattle exports rose from £40,000 to £380,000. These results were obtained solely as the result of Carr's thoroughness, energy, knowledge, and the capacity he had of inspiring his subordinates with affection and loyalty. At the time of his death he was organizing cotton production in the Sudan, and had he lived, would have been created Director of Agriculture. He died at the end of 1917 at the early age of 45 years.

Carr was a quiet, modest, unassuming man, of great strength and determination; he was devoted to his work, and possessed a charm of character which secured for him the affection of all who knew him. His death was an irreparable loss both to the Sudan and his own Service, and his life is an object lesson to future generations of veterinary officers.

Major General Sir Robert Pringle was succeeded by Major General L. J. Blenkinsop, who took over the appointment of Director General on arrival from India in December 1917 while the War was still in progress.

Major General Sir Layton Blenkinsop, K.C.B., D.S.O., entered the Service in 1883; he was promoted 1st Class in 1893, Major in 1900, and to Administrative rank in 1903, at 20 years' service, becoming full Colonel in 1908. He held many Administrative positions, being successively P.V.O. 3rd Army Corps, Irish Command, South Africa, Northern Command, Southern Command, Aldershot Command, and Director of Veterinary Services in India, where he was granted the temporary rank of Brigadier General while so employed.

He was Senior Veterinary Officer, British Troops, in the Nile Expedition of 1898, present at the Battle of Khartoum, being mentioned in Despatches and receiving the Egyptian Medal and Clasp, Queen's Medal and D.S.O. In the South African War of 1899-1902, he was Senior Veterinary Officer Cavalry Division, and received the Queen's Medal with six clasps, King's Medal with two clasps, was mentioned in Despatches and promoted V.-Major. He was mentioned in Despatches for his services in the Great War, received the War and Victory Medals and the Companionship of the Bath.

In 1921 he was created a K.C.B. in the Military Division and shortly before his retirement was appointed Colonel Commandant Royal Army Veterinary Corps; he was placed on Retired Pay in December 1921.

During the years 1890-93 he was in the employment of the Punjab Government as Veterinary Adviser and held a Professorship at the Lahore Veterinary College. He made several contributions to Veterinary literature and is Co-Editor of the Official Veterinary History of the War. At a time when scientific studies were looked at askance, he instituted a laboratory in his hospital at Woolwich, where advanced clinical enquiries were carried out. He has been prominent in urging a higher professional education and the employment of modern methods of scientific research, and jealous that his department and profession should occupy a high position.

Though Sir Layton Blenkinsop filled the appointment of Director General for four years, only a portion of his term of office can here be noticed, owing to the limitations of this work, which ends with the War. Unquestionably the outstanding feature of this period was the demobilization of the Veterinary Service, including animals. The Official History of the War does not appear to me to give sufficient prominence to this question, the difficulties and attendant risks of which are not generally realized. He had before him as an object lesson the demobilization of animals in South Africa, carried out by agents of the Remount Department, who with a few strokes of the pen disposed of all surplus stock at the nearest civilian centre. The Veterinary Service drew attention to the grave risk of the wholesale spreading of disease by this system, but it was held that the expense of their keep prohibited the necessary period of isolation and the delay in malleining many thousands of animals was not justified. Consequently large numbers were disposed of without the Veterinary Service being informed as to their sale. Animals were even sent home against veterinary advice, and brought with them Epizootic Lymphangitis, which they spread widely in the kingdom. It may be noticed in passing that the authorities had been warned by the then Senior Veterinary Officer, Remounts (Major L. J. Blenkinsop), what would follow as the result of taking these animals to England, but all to no purpose.

With this experience before him we may be certain that when the demobilization of animals was being planned in 1919 the arrangements were made with especial care. The Directors of Veterinary Services in the various theatres of war submitted their proposals based on a knowledge of local conditions, and from these a well-considered scheme was drawn up, whereby, step by step, animals were tested with mallein and examined for lymphangitis and then sold, a corresponding proportion of men of the R.A.V.C. being simultaneously liberated. Of the thousands upon thousands of animals disposed of, in no case was it subsequently shown that a single one affected with glanders had been sold. We cleared up as we went along. No disease was left behind in the various countries, and no disease introduced into this country, a vast contrast to the state of affairs after the War in South Africa.

It must not be supposed that these results were obtained solely by the methods having been well thought out; the scheme had to be upheld against the many attacks made, some by well-meaning, others by irresponsible persons, anxious at any risk to get the matter over. A stout resistance had to be offered to these, and even to official pressure which sought to relax the stringency of the regulations in favour of certain animals, but the Director General's attitude was that of uncompromising firmness, and it saved the name of this country from reproach.

Nothing gave more trouble than the dogs. Popular sentiment demanded that they be permitted to return with the troops from countries abroad, quite forgetting that rabies is enzootic there. It is quite certain that dogs would have been permitted to return with their owners without quarantine but for the attitude of the Director General; the question was a national one and had to be firmly faced, and the arguments against uncontrolled entry eventually won the day. A costly scheme was introduced, the expense of which was mainly defrayed by the Royal Society for the Prevention of Cruelty to Animals. Very early proof was afforded of the wisdom of the opposition offered; among the first batch of military dogs from overseas a case of rabies occurred in quarantine three weeks after landing ! We are glad of the opportunity afforded us of emphasizing the admirable Staff work done at this time. The general community of this country have no idea of the horrors arising from hydrophobia and rabies, nor of the heavy financial loss of stock from contagious diseases, from both of which they were saved by the excellence of the veterinary arrangements dealing with demobilization.

The number of officers serving with the Royal Army Veterinary Corps during the Great War was 1,668, of whom 381 were Decorated, while the total number of Mentions in Despatches was 857. The number of Warrant Officers, Non-Commissioned Officers and men who served with the Corps was 41,755, of whom 443 were Decorated and 499 Mentioned in Despatches.

The losses from all causes among officers was 63, and other ranks 420.

The sacrifices made by the Corps have been commemorated by a mural tablet and Corps Banner in St. George's Garrison Church, Woolwich. The Memorial is of mosaic with marble panels bearing the pre- and post-War Corps Badges (Plate 12).

PLATE XII

WAR MEMORIAL, ROYAL ARMY VETERINARY CORPS, AT ST. GEORGE'S GARRISON CHURCH, WOOLWICH

PLATE XIII

WAR MEMORIAL, ROYAL COLLEGE OF VETERINARY SURGEONS

To face p. 241.

It commemorates those who were members of the Regular and Territorial Royal Army Veterinary Corps, including the men transferred from the Corps to combatant units. The Memorial was unveiled on 22nd June 1923 by Major General Sir Layton Blenkinsop, Colonel Commandant Royal Army Veterinary Corps.

A War Memorial Tablet was also erected by the Profession in the Royal College of Veterinary Surgeons (Plate 13), which was unveiled by the President (Dr. O. C. Bradley) on 7th April 1921. The Council of the College has also established a War Memorial Library.

With the termination of the War, the limit we set ourselves in this History has been reached. The R.A.V.C., purely civilian in its inception,[1] has become purely military. It has not, however, ceased to play a part in the affairs of the Profession. The services of our officers to Veterinary Literature we have alluded to, but by no means fully treated, in the text. Since 1856 the Department has furnished eight Presidents, nineteen Vice-Presidents, twenty-four Members of Council, seventeen Examiners for the diploma of Membership and six for the Fellowship diploma. As already pointed out at p. 177, the most active member in securing the Veterinary Surgeons Act of 1881 was a distinguished officer of the Department, Dr. George Fleming.

The evolution of our Service began in 1876, reached its maturity in 1914, and the fruits of 38 years' work were gathered during the Great War. Our Sovereign was the first to graciously acknowledge the results of our work by conferring on the Corps the much-coveted title of "Royal." This was promulgated to the Army on 27th November 1918.

The Quarter Master General to the Forces, in congratulating the Director General and all ranks of the Army Veterinary Service on this proud distinction, expressed himself as follows:

"On the occasion of His Majesty the King being graciously pleased to raise the Army Veterinary Corps to the status of a 'Royal' Corps, the Quartermaster-General to the Forces wishes to convey to all ranks his congratulations and appreciation of the good work which they have performed during the present War.

"The Corps by its initiative and scientific methods has placed Military Veterinary Organization on a higher plane. The high standard which it has maintained at Home and throughout all theatres has resulted in a reduction of animal wastage, an increased mobility of Mounted Units and a mitigation of animal suffering, unapproached in any previous Military Operations."

---

[1] All army ancillary services were at one time designated "Civil Departments." In the case of the Veterinary Service this was accentuated by having a civilian at its head for forty-three years.

APPENDICES

APPENDIX I

The Uniform of the Army Veterinary Service, 1796–1911

It is extremely difficult to give precise information of the early uniforms worn by the Army, as all patterns and official information were lost in two disastrous fires—the last in 1841. The descriptions which have survived through the medium of letters or orders are very incomplete.

The general tendency in dress was in the direction of extravagance; especially was this the case during the Regency, when the future George IV. took a keen personal interest in uniform, and was responsible for tight-fitting, elaborate dress. Colonels of regiments were also given a very free hand, and this did not tend towards economy or uniformity. Many references are made by writers of the period to the great extravagance in dress in the Peninsula War, especially in the Cavalry. Lord Combermere was so elaborately dressed as a General of Hussars that he was said to have been worth £500 to anyone who had captured him. Lord Wellington, on the other hand, though by no means indifferent to his personal appearance, set an example by the plainness of his dress, yet he made no attempt to stem regimental extravagance, nor did he insist on uniformity of pattern.

From 1796 to 1822, a period of special interest to us, precise details are wanting, but in the latter year Dress Regulations were published. I have accordingly submitted my remarks for the earlier period to an authority on uniform, Mr. Percival Reynolds, who has been good enough to advise me in the matter and supplement my deficiencies.

Though in the following account I specifically refer to the Veterinary Officer, yet in the Regulations he is rarely referred to individually. This is due to the fact that he formed one of a small group in each regiment known as the " regimental staff," and the regimental staff with minor differences were dressed alike. This staff consisted of the two surgeons, the paymaster, quarter-master and veterinary surgeon. There was no riding master until 1855. In the Dress Regulations the designation " Regimental Staff " is employed; I have made the question more individualistic by referring only to the Veterinary Surgeon as if the regulations were drawn up specially for him.

1796.—The uniform worn by the Veterinary Service in 1796 was identical in pattern in each branch of the Cavalry, but differed in colour, it being either scarlet or blue, depending on the colour worn by the regiment. The coat was extremely plain, not even the facings of the regiment being borne on the collar and cuffs. In shape it was single-breasted, cut away in front to the hips and had a pair of long tails (Plate A, p. 40). The buttons were of regimental pattern. The sword belt was worn under the coat and no sash worn around the waist, the sash being a combatant distinction. The breeches were white, and high boots or gaiters were worn. When not on parade the coat could be worn open, displaying a white waistcoat. The head-dress was a cocked hat worn transversely; it was without lace or plume, but had a plain black silk loop and rosette with regimental button. The queue or club was worn according to regimental custom. The sword and sword belt were probably of regimental pattern. The coat shewn in Plate A is based on a knowledge of the period, and is approved by Mr. Reynolds.

Between 1796 and 1799 the cut of the coat was altered throughout the Army; it was no longer open, but made to button up as low as the waist.

1804.—As far as can be determined the above uniform, with the modification last mentioned, was worn until 1804, when an addition was made to it, the collar and cuffs being now of the same colour as the regimental facings.

Clubs were abolished from the Army between 1798–1800 and queues followed in 1808.

In 1812 the uniform of the Cavalry generally had undergone great changes: a helmet had been substituted for a hat in heavy cavalry, a shako for the helmet of Light Dragoons, and extensive changes in pattern made in the coat, but these did not affect the Veterinary Service; the coat and head-dress still remained as in 1804. Epaulettes or wings had been sanctioned for the Regimental Staff in 1804, but withdrawn in 1810; again sanctioned in 1813, but withdrawn in 1817. The Cavalry in 1812 lost their breeches and boots, and overalls of a grey colour ornamented with a stripe took their place, so that overalls of regimental colour were now worn by veterinary officers. The hat remained cocked for the Veterinary Service, but was worn fore and aft and no longer transversely. It still remained perfectly plain with the black silk loop, rosette and button. It was high, though every effort had been made by Wellington and his staff in the Peninsula to introduce a low cocked hat.

1817.—In 1817 the collar and cuffs were now embroidered according to regimental pattern, being laced or plain, depending on the branch of the Cavalry Service to which the officer belonged. In other respects the coat remained as before, the sword belt still being worn under it.

1822.—The earliest known copy of the Dress Regulations was published in 1822. In this year the first break away from a distinctive uniform for veterinary officers was made n the Household Cavalry and Waggon Train. In both these services the coat of the regiment was worn, but without epaulettes or aiguillettes, and there was of course no sash. The head-dress remained as before.

In all other branches of the Cavalry, excepting Hussars, the coat worn by the veterinary officer had the collar, sleeves and sometimes the tail of regimental pattern, but it was single-breasted as before with ten buttons down the front. The chief distinction now introduced was ten narrow double stripes of silk braid across the chest corresponding to the buttons on the coat. This narrow braid gave the appearance of an elongated sewn-up button-hole and the arrangement was technically referred to as a "notched hole" or "twist hole." In scarlet regiments the braid was crimson, in blue regiments black in colour. The collar was enormous, three inches in height; a black silk cravat encircled the neck. This is well seen in Percivall's picture, though it is of a later period. This Prussian collar lasted until 1855. The tails of the coat were short in Light Dragoons and Lancers and ornamented with three long "twist-holes" and three buttons; they were longer in Dragoon Guards and Dragoons and of regimental pattern. The edge or "turn-back" of the tails was of the same colour as the regimental facings. No shoulder straps or aiguillettes were worn by Veterinary Officers of Dragoons or Dragoon Guards, but epaulettes were worn by those of Lancer and Light Dragoon regiments, and aiguillettes in Lancer regiments. No sash or girdle was worn in any branch.

In Hussars there was no attempt to adopt the regimental dress, which at this time consisted of an elaborate jacket and pelisse (flying jacket) richly embroidered with lace and covered with small buttons. In its place the Veterinary Officer of Hussars wore a blue long-tailed coat cut away in front, with cuffs and collar of regimental pattern; both these and the "turn-back" of the tails were of the same colour as the regimental facings. The tails of the coat were ornamented with the regimental badge. On the breast of the coat were ten rows of narrow double black silk braid as described above.[1]

This dress is shewn in Plate B, p. 72, 8th Hussars. The star in the hat is not regulation but was worn in this regiment. The wide Cossack overalls were characteristic of the period.

In all branches of the Cavalry the sword, belts and overalls were of regimental pattern. The colour of the overalls in the Cavalry was blue-grey for ordinary occasions; for levée dress, and in some Light Cavalry regiments for reviews, various coloured overalls were worn by officers. The Hussars in certain orders of dress had embroidered waistcoat and pants with Hessian boots. The lace was either gold or silver.

The head-dress for regimental staff officers remained the cocked hat in all regiments wearing helmets. In regiments wearing chakos or lance-caps these head-dresses, but without the gold or silver ornaments, were worn by the regimental staff, the date of the change being uncertain.

1828.—In April 1828 the distinctive coat of the Veterinary Officer described above was abolished throughout the Cavalry and replaced by the coatee or jacket of the regiment, with the exception that the epaulettes were of infantry pattern. In Dragoons and Dragoon Guards the coat now possessed a long skirt, the front as usual being cut away.

[1] Mr. P. Reynolds drew my attention to the fact that a coat of this period exists in the Museum of the Royal United Service Institution, being originally worn by Surgeon Smet of the 8th Hussars.

In Light Dragoons and Lancers it was also cut away, the skirt being represented by two diminutive tails shorter in Light Dragoons than in Lancers.

In Hussars the elaborate full-dress jacket of blue cloth was now worn by the Veterinary Officer, with a blue cloth pelisse. Both were heavily laced and covered with small buttons and the pelisse possessed an edging of fur.

The head-dress was still the cocked hat in all but Light Dragoons, for in 1826 the lance-cap was replaced by the cocked hat and not restored until 1834. In Light Dragoons a plain black bell-topped beaver chako with peak was substituted for the cocked hat, but without gold ornaments (Plate C, p. 88). This chako was ornamented with a white plume of drooping cock's feathers, gilt scales chin strap, together with gold lines and gold bullion tassels. In those regiments wearing the cocked hat gold and crimson bullion tassels were added to the corners of the hat, and a black ribbon to both front faces, but no plume was worn.

The Dress Regulations of 1828 for the first time give information on the horse furniture for the Veterinary Officer. It consisted of a black sheepskin and shabraque instead of the dress " housing " worn by combatant officers of the regiment.

It is interesting to observe the evolution of the Veterinary Officer's coat as just recorded. At first plainer than that of a private soldier of the period, it was not until eight years after our creation that approval was given to wear the facings of the regiment on the collar and cuffs. Then came orders and counter-orders respecting epaulettes, features which one might regard as insignificant, until it is pointed out that epaulettes were a mark of rank. Their sanction and withdrawal extended over a period of thirteen years, and indicate the doubt felt by the authorities as to the advisability of recognizing the rank of the Regimental Staff. In 1817, or thirteen years after the introduction of facings, the collar and cuffs of the coat were embroidered with the distinctive lace of the regiment. Five years after this the Veterinary Officers of Household Cavalry and Royal Waggon Train were put into regimental uniform; in the Line the coat was rendered distinctive by rows of braid across the chest, while the tail assumed a semi-regimental or regimental character. Six years later practically all distinctions in coat were swept away, and the whole of the Regimental Staff wore the uniform of the regiment to which they belonged. In the case of the Veterinary Officer, the period of evolution occupied thirty-two years.

1834.—In 1834 the Veterinary Officers of Household Cavalry were permitted to wear epaulettes and aiguillettes, but no sash. The horse furniture laid down for these regiments, and for Dragoons and Dragoon Guards, was a black sheepskin and shabraque: the regimental dress housing of blue cloth (shabraque) was not worn. On the other hand, in Light Dragoons and Hussars the regimental horse furniture was worn.

In Lancer regiments the lance-cap for the Veterinary Officer was again taken into use in 1834.

1846.—In 1846 the Veterinary Officers of Hussar regiments wore the busby (Plate D, p. 104), the 15th Hussars alone wearing a scarlet chako; the busby lines were of gold, excepting in the 8th and 11th Hussars, where they were black. The lance-cap was still worn in Lancer regiments, without gold ornaments, though gold cap lines were worn (Plate E, p. 120).

The pattern of lance-cap shewn in Plate E is not accepted by experts whose advice I have sought. It has been suggested that it should be all black, but the regulations give us no such instruction, they merely stipulate that for the Regimental Staff the cap is to be without gold ornaments. It does not appear to me that this excludes the scarlet top or the front plate, and I accept the responsibility for Captain Haswell-Miller's figure.

The dress of the Veterinary Officer of the Cavalry Depot was laid down in 1846; it consisted of a blue coat with scarlet collar and cuffs faced with gold. The overalls were blue with gold lace stripes; the head-dress was the cocked hat without a plume.

1855.—In the year 1855 the cocked hat was now ornamented with a plume of drooping black cock's-tail feathers three inches long (see Plate F, p. 136, 1856); the same was worn by the medical officer.

In this year the elaborate jacket and pelisse of Hussars was abolished from the Army and its place taken by a single-breasted jacket with six loops of gold chain gimp across the chest, with caps and drops fastening to gold olivettes.

Hitherto no mention has been made of the uniform worn by Veterinary Officers of Artillery for the reason that from 1796–1855 no information has survived. In 1855 we learn that, in what is now known as Field Artillery, the uniform was identical with that worn by other officers of corresponding rank, excepting that the pouch belt was of white patent leather with a black instrument pouch.[1] The pouch was decorated with the Crown and Royal Cypher. The Regulations make no mention of the fact that on the front of the white patent leather belt was an eight-pointed star, within which was the Garter and Royal Cypher. The whole was surmounted by a crown. This distinctive star was worn by both medical and veterinary officers. Its survival may be seen on the pouch belt worn by the Corps of Commissionaires. The cocked hat was worn in Field Artillery, but the Regulations make no mention of a plume.

It is evident that the year 1855 saw the distinctive pouch belt of our Service introduced; a similar belt was already worn in the Medical Service of the Cavalry, consisting of a black morocco belt and pouch, but the pouch belt of the Veterinary Officer of Cavalry still remained regimental, though, as we have seen, not in the Artillery.

1857.—In 1857 the busby for Veterinary Officers of Hussars, the lance-cap in Lancer regiments and the chako in Light Dragoons were replaced by a cocked hat with black cock's-tail feathers. With the

---

[1] Captain Macdonald in his *History of the Dress of the Royal Regiment of Artillery* 1625-1897, says that in 1859 both the Veterinary Officer and Medical Officer of Artillery wore a *black* morocco shoulder belt.

substitution of the cocked hat, busby, chako and cap lines disappeared in these branches. In Lancer regiments an addition was made to the uniform, the gold girdle being worn.

Throughout the Army the overalls for mounted duties were in 1857 "booted"—that is, strapped with leather on the inside from the thigh to the boot, the leather being carried completely around the outside for several inches above the boot (see Plate G, p. 152). This lasted until replaced by the jack-boot. Another change made in this year was that badges of rank for all officers were introduced and worn on the collar.[1]

1861.—In 1861 the black feather in the cocked hat of all veterinary officers was replaced by a red feather, excepting in the Household Cavalry, where no feather was yet worn.

The newly created Veterinary Staff, consisting of the Principal Veterinary Surgeon and the Staff Veterinary Surgeons, was in 1861 provided with a distinctive uniform. It was laid down that these officers were to wear the uniform of the Cavalry Depot, consisting of a blue Light Dragoon coatee with five gold cords running across the breast with caps and drops and fastening with five gold olivettes. On each side of the breast the top loop was eight inches long and the bottom one four inches. On the shoulder was a double cord with button. The skirt of the coatee was nine inches long, the collar two inches high and edged with gold cord. The collar and cuffs were scarlet, the cuffs pointed. The sleeve for a Colonel had gold lace one and a half inches, and tracing of narrow gold braid eleven inches deep; the other distinguishing feature of rank was a silver crown and star on the collar. The overalls were blue with a double gold stripe; in undress a scarlet stripe. The usual cocked hat was worn, with gold bullion tassels at its corners, one row of gold gimp chain up the side and button; the feather was red. The white patent leather pouch belt with black pouch was worn, the belt of the P.V.S. being distinguished by two rows of gold embroidery. This was the first uniform ever laid down for the Veterinary Staff; it can hardly be called distinctive, being that of the Cavalry Depot, as mentioned above.

1864.—In 1864 there was a change, Light Dragoons having ceased to exist, but the uniform of the Veterinary Staff was still that of the Cavalry Depot, which was now Hussar. The tunic was blue, single-breasted, with six loops of gold chain gimp with caps and drops, fastening to six gold olivettes; in fact it was the Hussar tunic of to-day. The pouch belt was of white patent leather; the overalls had a single gold lace stripe. The cocked hat now had four rows of gold chain gimp up the sides, and button besides the bullion tassels (Plate G, p. 152).

In 1864 the uniform of the Veterinary Officer of Royal Horse Artillery is described for the first time. The busby was worn with a red plume and black busby lines. The jacket, overalls and sword belt were identical with those of other officers, but the pouch belt was white enamel leather and the pouch black morocco with the Royal Cypher

---

[1] They were as follows: Colonel and Captain, a crown and star; Lieut.-Colonel and Lieutenant, a crown; Major and Cornet, a star.

(Plate H, p. 168). The horse furniture was the same as that worn by other officers, including the shabraque in Review Order.

The uniforms of a Veterinary Officer of Royal Engineers and of the Military Train were also laid down in 1864; in both cases they were purely regimental, excepting that a cocked hat with red feather and a white patent leather pouch belt were worn.

In 1864 the Veterinary Officers of the Household Cavalry now wore a red feather in the cocked hat.

1874.—A third change in uniform for the " Veterinary Staff " was introduced in 1874. It had been Light Dragoon in 1861, Hussar in 1864; it was now made Dragoon (Blue), but for the first time rendered distinctive by the introduction of maroon-coloured facings. The Dragoon tunic is the one still in use; it possessed a maroon velvet collar and cuffs, gold staff lace and universal buttons. The stable jacket was also of Dragoon pattern, with staff lace and maroon velvet collar and cuffs. The forage cap was of the staff pattern, a cap with almost vertical sides, gold band, embroidered peak and a button and tracing on the top. The belts were white and the cocked hat of the pattern previously described. The horse furniture was as for the officers of the Staff of the Army.

No provision was made for the uniform of probationary veterinary officers, who actually wore undress Artillery uniform with maroon velvet collar and cuffs! In the Household Cavalry the white patent leather pouch belt replaced the belt of regimental pattern previously worn. Gold tassels were added to the cocked hat in this branch, but the black silk loop and rosette remained. Pants and jack-boots for mounted duties replaced booted overalls throughout the Army in 1872, and appeared in the Dress Regulations of 1874. Mess waistcoats were also authorized in 1872.

1883.—By 1883 all regimental uniform had been abolished, excepting in Household Cavalry, and the Army Veterinary Department had been formed (Plate I, p. 184).

The tunic laid down in these regulations was as in 1874, the rank being indicated by the number of twists given to the Austrian knot on the sleeve—single for Lieutenants and Captains, double for Field Officers and triple for Principal Veterinary Surgeon. The badges of rank were now worn on the shoulder cords and were as at present. A full-dress pouch belt was introduced of departmental pattern gold lace with a maroon stripe, but it was only to be worn at levées, balls and State occasions and by no officer under the rank of a Captain. The full-dress pouch was of maroon velvet embroidered. Full-dress sword belt was worn by all ranks in review order. Full-dress overalls with a maroon stripe through the gold were introduced for review and mess order; in all other orders of dress, overalls or pants with a single scarlet stripe were worn. A patrol jacket with upright collar, the sleeves and breast trimmed with black mohair braid, was worn by all under administrative rank; for these officers a frock coat of Dragoon pattern was laid down.[1] The cocked hat remained as before, but the length of the feather was regulated by rank, the P.V.S. wearing an eight-inch feather, I.V.S. six inch, other ranks four inch. The forage cap for administrative officers was of staff pattern with upright sides and peak, the band being of departmental gold lace with a maroon stripe. For all other ranks the ordinary forage cap without peak was used, set at an angle on the head; it had a band of departmental gold lace and maroon stripe, on the top of the cap a gold button but no tracing. A black sabretasche bearing the Crown and Royal Cypher was worn on mounted duties. The belts were of white patent leather, the shoulder belt possessing the usual buckle, tip and slide; but the star and crown on the front of the belt was now obsolete. Probationary officers wore the undress uniform of the Department.

1891.—In 1891 the upright collar of the frock coat for the P.V.S. was altered to a roll collar so that a white linen collar and black bow tie were worn with it.

For all officers of the relative ranks of Lieutenant and Captain the Infantry pattern helmet was now worn instead of the cocked hat. On the helmet plate was the monogram A.V.D. in silver on a black ground. Gold tracing on the top of the forage cap was sanctioned.

1894.—In 1894 the full-dress pouch belt for the Director General was directed to be worn on all occasions, but the full-dress pouch at levées, balls and State occasions only. All executive officers were now permitted to wear full-dress pouch and sword belts, but only at the above functions. A departmental button was approved, an eight-pointed star surmounted by a crown, on a circle Army Veterinary Department and within the circle the Royal Cypher. Up to this date the buttons had been of universal pattern.

1900.—In 1900 the buttons remained of the same pattern but were indented, those of 1894 having been raised. A plain blue patrol jacket known as a frock was introduced for the Director General, with shoulder straps of maroon cloth with a blue cloth centre, upright collar, cuffs pointed and departmental buttons.

1904.—At no period within living memory did the uniform of the Army undergo so many radical changes as in 1904. Many of these were the outcome of experience gained during the war in South Africa, others were introduced ostensibly to reduce expense, and still others were the result of that desire for change which is periodically evident in everything.

The most valuable of all the changes was the introduction of a definite drab service dress. Khaki in one form or another had been worn on service since 1880, but it was not official. The last time the British Army went to war in red and blue tunics was as recently as 1879. In India khaki drill had been worn for years before that date, but had not been adopted by the home army. Nevertheless when war broke out in South Africa in 1899 the force sent to that country wore

---

[1] The frock coat and staff cap of the period may be seen in Plate 6.

drab clothing, though it was not embodied in the Dress Regulations until 1904.

Another sweeping change in this year was the introduction of a peaked forage cap of so-called staff pattern which replaced the absurd forage cap of pork-pie shape placed on the head at a sharp angle. Also the patrol jacket for all branches of the Army was replaced by a frock coat.

A fourth great change was the entire remodelling of the mess dress.

The changes in dress in our own Service in 1904 were numerous. Maroon cloth was substituted for velvet on the collar and cuffs of the tunic. The tracing on the sleeves of the tunic was a triple Austrian knot for the Director General, but a single knot for all other ranks. The D.G. also wore on the tunic the plaited shoulder cords of a General Officer; other ranks wore the twisted cord of infantry pattern. On the collar of the tunic a departmental badge was worn consisting of a gilt laurel wreath surmounted by a crown and enclosing in silver the monogram A.V.D. The scarlet stripe on the overalls and pants was replaced by a double stripe of maroon cloth for all ranks excepting the Director General, who, being a General Officer, wore a wide scarlet stripe.

The white pouch belt, sword belt and slings disappeared, as the tunic was only worn at levées, balls and State occasions, when gold lace shoulder and waist belts were worn by all ranks.

The cocked hat was limited to the Director General and full Colonels; all other ranks wore the black infantry helmet with ball. The D.G. wore a red swan feather plume ten inches in length, the Colonel one of eight inches. The sword and scabbard of the D.G. were of the pattern of a General Officer's; for all other ranks the Cavalry pattern was used.

The undress was a double-breasted blue frock coat with two rows of buttons; the coat reached nearly to the knees. The collar was stiff and upright, bearing in metal the departmental badge.[1] The frock coat of the D.G. was that of a General Officer, with blue velvet collar and cuffs and full-dress shoulder cords. Both the D.G. and his officers continued to wear the sword belt over the tunic and frock coat, no sash being approved until a year or two later, when the D.G. wore the sash of a General Officer, other ranks wearing the waist belt.

The forage cap was of blue cloth with a maroon band and departmental badge in front; for the Director General the band was scarlet; the badge in gold embroidery was that of a General Officer, also the embroidery on the peak of the cap.

The service jacket was of drab cloth, single-breasted with a turned-down collar bearing the departmental badge in bronze metal; the buttons were bronzed; there were four pockets, shoulder straps, and the badges of rank were worn on the sleeve. With this jacket a khaki collar and tie were worn. The breeches were of Bedford cord laced on the leg, with gaiters of brown leather. The belts were of plain leather, Sam Browne pattern. The cap was peaked, with stiff sides and expanded top, and bore on the front the departmental badge in bronze metal.

The mess jacket was of blue cloth with a roll collar faced with

[1] The frock coat was abolished during the Great War.

maroon cloth, as were also the cuffs of the sleeves. On the collar was worn a gilt departmental badge. The shoulder straps were of blue cloth, edged with gold lace for the Director General and Colonels, but plain for all other ranks. On the straps were the badges of rank, in silver embroidery for the D.G. and Colonels, in gilt metal for other ranks. The waistcoat was of blue cloth with departmental buttons. A collar and black tie were worn.

1911.—The Dress Regulations of this year are entitled Army Veterinary Service and distinguish between the administrative rank, as representing the Service and the Army Veterinary Corps.

The buttons of the administrative officer bore the words Army Veterinary Service; the collar badge was of the departmental pattern, but with A.V.S. in silver, and the cap badge of Colonels was the same but of a larger pattern. A blue serge jacket had been introduced for the Staff of the Army and was worn by the Director General and Colonels; it resembled the service jacket in pattern, with gorget patches of scarlet with line of gold chain gimp for the Director General only. The sword slings now laid down for the D.G. were those for a Field Marshal, consisting of one-inch Russia leather and gold oak-leaf lace. The horse furniture for the D.G. was that for a General Officer, but with brown leather brow band and rosettes instead of blue.

The Colonel had now a double Austrian knot on the sleeve of the tunic, and instead of a waist belt for the tunic and frock coat, a sash of gold and crimson silk net was worn, while the sword slings were of crimson Russia leather with gold lace and lion's head buckles. Horse furniture for a Colonel was Staff pattern with brown leather brow band and rosettes.

For all ranks below Colonel, buttons of the pattern described bore the words Army Veterinary Corps. The head-dress was the black infantry helmet with plate of eight-pointed star, within the Garter in silver was A.V.C. in monogram on green enamel. The shoulder belt and pouch, waist belt and sword slings were all of gold lace, departmental pattern as in 1904; in fact, but for the above trifling changes, the full dress of the two periods was identical (Plate J, p. 232).

The horse furniture was of universal pattern with brown leather brow band and rosettes.

Uniform of the Indian Army

The early uniform worn by the Veterinary Officers of the Indian Army is unknown; it was probably regimental from the first, it certainly was so later on. I have met with no distinct account earlier than the Dress Regulations of the Madras Army 1851, in which it is stated that the uniform for veterinary officers is the same as that worn by Horse Artillery and Cavalry, excepting that the girdle or sash is not worn. A slight description of these two uniforms may be given, and in this connection it must be borne in mind that they, with a head-dress which offered no protection against the sun, were worn in a tropical climate. *Horse Artillery* wore a single-breasted blue jacket with scarlet cuffs and collar three inches deep, the collar and cuffs ornamented with gold lace. The breast of the jacket was trimmed with straight lines of gold braid in double rows running the full width of the chest, but narrowing to six inches at the bottom. A small space was left between each row. Three rows of ball buttons ran from the top to the bottom of the jacket attached at the centre (where the jacket was hooked) and to the extremities of each row of lace. The helmet was very imposing, being Roman with a black glazed skull and peak, and a red horse-hair mane behind, gilt chin scales, and a front plate bearing the regimental device and distinctions. The trousers were dark blue with a single stripe of wide gold lace. The shoulder and sword belts were white leather, the shoulder belt bearing on a gilt plate regimental distinctions and having chains and pickers.

The *Cavalry* wore a black beaver chako with gold cap lines and swan feather plume. The tunic was blue and had five rows of buttons; it was laced across the chest in silver. The collar was high and it and the cuffs were ornamented with silver lace. The overalls were sky blue. The pouch belt, sword belt and sabretasche slings were all of silver lace.

APPENDIX II

NAMES OF VETERINARY OFFICERS IN THE PENINSULA 1808–14, TOGETHER WITH THE BATTLES AT WHICH THEY WERE PRESENT[1]

(Compiled from the Returns in the Public Record Office.)

1808

18th Light Dragoons.	J. Nesbitt.	Rolica, Vimiera, Corunna. Regiment returned to England in 1809.
20th Light Dragoons.	J. S. Darley.	Rolica, Vimiera.
Royal Artillery Drivers.	H. Coward.	Corunna. Returned to England in 1809.
Royal Waggon Train.	F. C. Cherry.	Corunna. Cherry returned to England in 1809; went back to the Peninsula in 1812; present at Salamanca, Vittoria, South of France.
3rd Hussars K.G.L.	F. Erdmann.	Corunna. Regiment returned to England in 1809 and did not subsequently take part in the Peninsula War.
7th Light Dragoons.	No Veterinary Surgeon.	Regiment returned to England in 1809 after Corunna.
10th Light Dragoons.	J. Denny.	Corunna. Regiment returned to England in 1809.

[1] I have taken the Army List honours, but as a matter of fact this is incomplete, and regiments were present at engagements for which no official recognition is accorded; this is especially true for the *Pyrenees, Nivelle, Nive, Orthez,* and *Toulouse*.

15th Light Dragoons.	J. Castley.	Corunna. Regiment returned to England in 1809. Castley returned to the Peninsula with 12th Light Dragoons in 1811.

1809

3rd Dragoon Guards.	T. Rose.	Albuera, Vittoria.
4th Dragoons.	T. Bird.	Talavera, Albuera, Salamanca, Vittoria, Toulouse.
14th Light Dragoons.	R. Thompson.	Douro, Talavera, Fuentes d'Onor.
16th Light Dragoons.	J. Peers.	Talavera, Busaco.
23rd Light Dragoons.	J. Shipp.	Talavera. Regiment returned to England in 1809.
Royal Artillery Drivers.	C. O'Connor.	
1st Royal Dragoons.	W. Ryding.	Fuentes d'Onor.
1st Hussars K.G.L.	F. Precht.	Talavera. Died December 1810.
	T. Power.	Salamanca, Vittoria, South of France.

1810

13th Light Dragoons.	S. Chard.	Busaco, Albuera. Died October, 1812.
	J. Constant.	Joined 1814.

1811

4th Dragoon Guards.	A. Kirwan.	
5th Dragoon Guards.	J. D. Stanley.	Succeeded by J. Jons, who was present at Vittoria.
3rd Dragoons.[1]	J. Barrington.	Salamanca, Vittoria. Succeeded by J. Lowes in 1814, who was present at Toulouse.
9th Light Dragoons.	J. Gain.	Regiment left the Peninsula in 1813.
11th Light Dragoons.	R. Gouldthorpe.	Died 1813. Regiment left the Peninsula in 1813.
12th Light Dragoons.	J. Castley.	For previous service see above, 15th Light Dragoons 1808.
Royal Artillery Drivers.	J. Lythe.	Ciudad Rodrigo, Badajoz, Salamanca, Vittoria, Orthez, Toulouse.
2nd Hussars K.G.L.	F. Eicke.	Salamanca. Regiment left the Peninsula 1813.

[1] The Veterinary Surgeon of 3rd Dragoons was J. Blanchard; he did not accompany the regiment to the Peninsula. Barrington was posted locally, also his successor Lowes. The name of Lowes does not appear in the Army List of the period, but it is in the Peninsula returns. See footnote, p. 77.

1812

Royal Waggon Train.	F. C. Cherry.	See the year 1808.
Royal Artillery Drivers.	G. Price.	Died a few months later.
1st Life Guards.	F. Dalton.	
2nd Life Guards.	Jeremiah Field.	
Royal Horse Guards.	J. Siddall.	
1st Dragoons K.G.L.	L. Heuer.	Salamanca, Vittoria, South of France.
2nd Dragoons K.G.L.	H. Hogrefe.	Badajoz, Salamanca, Vittoria, South of France.

1813

7th Hussars.	R. Darvill.	Orthez.
10th Hussars.	H. Sannermann.	
15th Hussars.	C. Dalwig.	
18th Hussars.	D. Pilcher.	
Royal Artillery Drivers.	J. Percivall.	Orthez, Toulouse.

APPENDIX III

NAMES OF THE VETERINARY OFFICERS PRESENT IN THE WATERLOO CAMPAIGN

1st Life Guards.	Francis Dalton.
2nd Life Guards.	Jeremiah Field.
Royal Horse Guards.	John Siddall.
1st Dragoon Guards.	Officer absent. Sick ?
1st Dragoons.	William Ryding.
2nd Dragoons.	John Trigg.
6th Dragoons.	Richard Vincent.
7th Hussars.	Richard Darvill.
10th Hussars.	H. Sannermann.
11th Light Dragoons.	Officer absent. Sick ?
12th Light Dragoons.	James Castley.
13th Light Dragoons.	John Constant.
15th Hussars.	Conrad Dalwig.
16th Light Dragoons.	J. W. Jons.
18th Hussars.	Daniel Pilcher.
23rd Light Dragoons.	John Shipp.
Royal Waggon Train.	F. C. Cherry.
Royal Artillery Drivers.	H. Coward. J. Burt. C. O'Connor. J. Lythe. W. Percivall. H. Smith.
	A seventh officer, name unknown, joined the Army in July; perhaps T. Peall.

APPENDIX IV

Veterinary Officers of the King's German Legion

(All these officers held the Diploma of the London School.)

Artillery.	J. F. Hilmer.	August 1805.
1st Dragoons.	W. Clarkson.	December 1803; transferred to King's Dragoon Guards, March 1805.
	L. Heuer.	May 1805.
2nd Dragoons.	H. Hogref.	July 1806. Appointed 15th Hussars August 1817 and changed his name to Hogreve.
1st Hussars.	F. Precht.	October 1804. Died in Portugal December 1810.
	T. Power.	July 1811.
2nd Hussars.	F. Neynaber.	January 1806. Died at Canterbury October 1806.
	F. Eicke.	January 1807.
3rd Hussars.	F. Erdmann.	July 1806.

Served in Copenhagen 1807. Hilmer, Eicke, Erdmann, Precht.
Served in Walcheren 1809. Eicke.
Served in the Peninsula 1808–14. Heuer, Hogref, Precht, Eicke, Power, Erdmann.
Served in North Germany 1813–14. Hilmer, Erdmann.
Served in Waterloo Campaign 1815. Hilmer, Heuer, Hogref, Power, Eicke, Erdmann.

APPENDIX V

Names of Veterinary Officers Present in Various Campaigns from 1799–1908

For Campaign in Holland 1799, *see page* 74; Campaign in Egypt 1801, p. 74; Mahratta War 1803, p. 54; Copenhagen 1807, p. 74; Campaign in South America 1807, p. 74; Corunna Campaign 1808, p. 75 and Appendix II.; Walcheren Campaign 1809, p. 75; Peninsula War 1808-14, Appendix II.; Waterloo Campaign 1815, Appendix III.

Siege of Bhurtpoore 1826.—*British Cavalry:* C. Percivall, G. Spencer.

Anglo-Spanish Legion 1835-37.—F. B. de Vine, T. S. Beech, R. Bailey (all temporary officers).

Afghan War 1839.—R. J. G. Hurford, W. McDermott.

Afghan War 1841-42.—W. McDermott, A. C. Hulse, W. P. Barrett, W. Edlin.

Gwalior Campaign 1843.—R. J. G. Hurford, G. Johnston, H. C. Hulse, W. P. Barrett.

SIKH WAR 1845-46.—W. Edlin, R. J. G. Hurford, W. McDermott.

KAFFIR WAR 1846-47.—B. C. R. Gardiner.

SIKH WAR 1848-49.—R. J. G. Hurford, A. W. Caldwell, H. C. Hulse, W. McDermott, J. Siddall, A. Turnbull, J. Harris, W. Johnson.

KAFFIR WAR 1851-53.—W. Thacker.

CRIMEAN WAR 1855-57.—*Royal Artillery*: J. S. Stockley, H. Withers, M. Harpley, F. Cochrane, F. Cottrell, W. B. Lord, J. Brennan, J. Mason, W. Huke, C. Saunderson, J. Cleaveland. *Cavalry*: J. Barker, J. Byrne, J. Collins, S. P. Constant, F. Delaney, E. S. Grey, R. Kelly, T. Gudgin, A. J. Owles, H. Sewell, T. J. Towers, J. W. Gloag, T. Hurford, A. H. Cherry, G. Fisher, T. Siddall, W. Partridge. *Land Transport Corps*: W. Death, W. Varley, J. Channon, T. Paton, H. Hussey, J. Burr, W. J. Fenner, W. Darrowfield, G. Fleming, J. Ball, J. Moir, G. Western, F. de F. Elkes, G. Poyser. *Turkish Forces*: J. K. Lord, T. W. Mayer, R. Wilkinson, J. Dollar, J. Quallett, H. W. Cannell, Scott-Gavin.

INDIAN MUTINY 1857.—*Royal Artillery*: J. S. Stockley, H. Withers, M. Harpley, W. B. Lord, G. I. Rollings, C. Saunderson, J. B. Skoulding. E. Kelly, J. B. Hall. *Cavalry*: A. J. Owles, R. J. G. Hurford, T. Hurford, F. Baily, H. J. Parker, E. S. Grey, T. Gudgin, W. Partridge, H. Dawson. *Military Train*: W. Death. *Indian Service*: R. B. Parry, J. Harris, I. Bicknell, H. C. Hulse, J. Philips, R. Willis, W. Barrett, W. McDermott, J. R. Hoey, A. C. Williams, J. Siddall, W. Johnson, A. Turnbull, C. J. Dawson, S. M. Jeffery, E. G. Chalwin, T. T. Page, F. A. Hely, J. S. Woods, V. Nelson, C. Henderson, J. W. Garrad, T. Hickman, G. Kettlewell, M. J. Marshall, C. Corker, R. W. Murray.

PERSIAN WAR 1857.—H. Dawson, W. Lamb (*Indian Service*).

CHINA WAR 1860.—G. Longman, G. Fleming, J. B. Skoulding.

NEW ZEALAND WAR 1860-65.—G. Blake, J. Anderson, W. Appleton.

CANADA, FENIAN RAIDS 1866—G. Evans, J. J. Meyrick, W. B. Walters; 1870 G. Evans.

ABYSSINIAN WAR 1868.—J. H. B. Hallen, W. Lamb, J. Anderson, J. Kettle, J. C. Berne, C. G. Reilly, A. A. Jones, G. I. Rollings.

KAFFIR WAR 1877-78.—F. Duck, B. L. Glover.

AFGHAN WAR 1878-80.—C. Steel, J. B. Skoulding, G. Oliphant, W. Appleton, G. A. Oliver, R. Poyser, W. Walker, F. Plomley, A. E. Queripel, F. Garrett, J. A. Woods, T. J. Symonds, W. F. Blanchard, C. Clayton, C. W. Gillard, J. K. Grainger, J. J. Philips, J. Burton, J. P. Adams, M. C. Mitchell, W. B. Spooner, S. D. Gillespie, A. C. Webb, A. Bostock, T. Flintoff, J. D. Edwards, J. A. Nunn, J. W. A. Morgan, W. R. Hagger, R. Pringle, R. Moore, K. Lees, F. W. Forsdyke, A. W. Mason, S. Slattery.

ZULU WAR 1879.—T. Gudgin, J. Lambert, W. B. Walters, W. Burt, F. Duck, C. Phillips, B. L. Glover, S. Longhurst, J. W. A. Morgan, W. R. Hagger, G. Fenton, T. A. Killick, R. Moore, F. Raymond.

Transvaal War 1881.—T. Gudgin, J. Lambert, C. G. Reilly, F. Duck, G. Durrant, A. A. Jones, B. L. Glover, C. W. Gillard, D. C. Pallin, C. Rutherford, T. Caldecott.

Egyptian Campaign 1882.—J. J. Meyrick, J. Anderson, W. Burt, F. Walker, J. A. Rostron, F. C. Boulter, M. F. Case, S. Sartin, S. L. Pallin, J. W. Evans, D. Whitfield, H. Thomson, I. Matthews, G. J. R. Rayment, M. C. Mitchell, W. B. Spooner, M. Anderson, W. A. Crow, W. R. Hagger, J. B. Savage, H. T. Mann, G. R. Griffiths, E. E. Bennett, J. R. Beech, R. W. Burke, S. M. Smith.

Nile Campaign 1884-85.—W. Burt, A. E. Queripel, C. Phillips. A. A. Jones, C. Clayton, W. B. Spooner, G. R. Griffiths, E. E. Bennett, J. R. Beech, S. M. Smith.

Bechuanaland Expedition 1884-85.—F. Duck, J. C. Berne, J. H. Cox, J. A. Woods, C. Rutherford.

Suakim Campaigns 1885-96.—W. B. Walters, J. Baldock, D. I. Hinge, M. F. Case, G. Aitkin, C. W. Gillard, H. Thomson, C. J. R. Rayment, W. Gladstone, W. B. Spooner, W. R. Hagger, G. Fenton, H. T. Mann, G. R. Griffiths, J. R. Beech, T. A. Mitchell, C. H. Betser, P. W. Dundon, F. W. Sharpe, E. Taylor, H. T. Mann, J. Moore.

Burma Campaigns 1885-96.—B. A. Powell, W. Gladstone, E. R. C. Butler, G. Fenton, G. C. O. Fowler, E. Taylor, E. J. Lawson, F. Eassie.

Hazara Campaign 1888.—E. Ewing.

Hazara Campaign 1891.—W. R. Hagger.

Chin-Lushai Campaign 1889.—J. A. Nunn, G. H. Evans.

Manipur Campaign 1891.—F. Eassie, F. C. Stratton.

Miranzi Campaign 1891.—W. A. Crow.

Waziristan Campaign 1895.—G. J. R. Rayment, E. Taylor, C. Rose.

Chitral Campaign 1895.—R. Poyser, F. Raymond, G. M. Williams, A. C. Newsom, H. T. Sawyer, E. Taylor, H. B. Knight, F. Eassie, F. W. Forsdyke, G. J. R. Rayment, T. G. Peacocke, W. N. Wright, C. B. Freeman.

Matabeleland Campaign 1896.—A. England.

Dongola Campaign 1896.—G. R. Griffiths, T. E. Lewis, W. D. Smith, A. H. Lane.

Tochi Campaign 1897-98.—G. J. R. Rayment, C. B. M. Harris, F. W. Hunt, R. L. Cranford, H. B. Knight, W. A. McDougall.

Mohmand, Malakand, Bunner Campaigns 1897-98.—F. W. Forsdyke, H. T. Mann, W. R. Walker, G. M. Williams, T. W. Rudd.

Tirah Campaign 1897-98.—B. L. Glover, F. W. Forsdyke, W. J. Tatam, W. F. Shore, C. Rose, F. W. Wilson, F. U. Carr, W. N. Wright, W. S. Anthony, A. E. Richardson, R. H. Holmes, E. P. Barry.

Nile Campaign 1897.—G. R. Griffiths, T. E. Lewis, W. E. Russell.

Nile Campaign 1898.—L. J. Blenkinsop, G. R. Griffiths, F. B. Drage, T. E. Lewis, W. D. Smith, E. J. Lawson, W. E. Russell, F. Smith.

SOUTH AFRICAN WAR 1899-1902.—*Regular Officers* : E. B. Bartlett, L. J. Blenkinsop, E. Brown, A. Bostock, F. F. Crawford, W. A. Crow, J. Cooper, F. U. Carr, G. T. Coley, R. C. Cochrane, G. Conder, F. B. Drage, H. M. Durrant, F. Eassie, A. England, W. B. Edwards, F. W. Forsdyke, T. Flintoff, J. J. Griffith, W. Gladstone, S. D. Gillespie, F. W. Hunt, C. B. M. Harris, R. F. Houston, A. H. Lane, E. J. Lawson, E. W. Larnder, I. Matthews, H. T. W. Mann, J. Moore, E. E. Martin, W. M. Millar, A. C. Newsom, A. Olver, J. J. Philips, D. C. Pallin, R. Pringle, G. J. R. Rayment, R. W. Raymond, A. E. Richardson, C. Rutherford, W. E. Russell, C. Rose, H. T. Sawyer, F. J. Short, F. W. Sharp, H. A. Sullivan, T. H. Shore, J. B. Southey, W. D. Smith, F. Smith, E. Taylor, W. J. Tatam, A. G. Todd, G. M. Williams, F. W. Wilson, A. J. Williams.

Civil Veterinary Surgeons, subsequently commissioned.—J. J. Aitken, H. Allen, E. P. Argyle, P. V. Beatty, L. Barnard, A. F. Deacon, A. J. Dalgleish, O. S. Fisher, F. Fail, H. Gamble, E. S. Gillette, M. St. C. Glasse, H. Greenfield, H. E. Gibbs, A. S. Head, C. H. Hylton-Jolliffe, G. T. Jackson, W. A. Jelbart, G. P. Knott, B. L. Lake, W. G. Lowe, W. Ludgate, A. Leaning, A. S. Laurie, H. S. Mosley, F. A. S. Moore, R. C. Matthews, W. H. Nicol, J. Nicholas, W. W. R. Neale, E. C. Orton, E. S. Oliver, A. Porteous, F. S. Probyn, R. A. Plunkett, S. F. G. Pallin, D. J. Quinlan, J. A. Russell, N. de E. Roberts, J. W. Rainey, A. N. Swanston, C. E. Steel, W. E. Schofield, J. R. Steevenson, J. J. B. Tapley.

Natal Volunteer Veterinary Corps.—H. Watkins Pitchford, F. A. Verney, S. B. Woollatt, A. X. Byrne, W. M. Power, S. T. Amos, ? Hutchinson, S. Webb.

Yeomanry Veterinary Officers.—Names unknown, being regimental officers; they are believed to have been about thirty in number.

Colonial Forces, South African and Overseas Veterinary Officers.—Names unknown, being regimental officers; they are believed to have been about sixty in number.

Civil Veterinary Surgeons.—R. Anderson, R. A. Anderson, E. Ashworth, D. A. Aitcheson, R. Armstrong, H. L. Anthony, C. Aggio, R. Brownrigg, J. W. Brownless, J. P. Bell, J. Buck, G. H. Butcher, G. W. Balfour, T. Bowhill, J. Brand, J. B. Brown, G. H. Barber, R. E. Beilby, K. Barber, J. H. Bell, R. S. Beattie, ? Byrne, P. Conacher, W. L. Cockburn, J. H. Christy, J. Crawford, C. Campbell, J. B. Cowx, J. R. Crone, S. G. Chellew, R. J. Collings, F. Crossley, J. E. Cockroft, J. Carpenter, J. A. Cunningham, J. Chalmers, F. Carless, A. Conisbee, G. T. Cameron, C. C. Clark, C. H. Cordy, J. Douglas, C. Dyson, J. Donaldson, J. P. Dunphy, E. M. Dyson, J. A. Duff, H. E. Davies, T. H. Dale, F. J. Dunning, J. S. Drabble, E. T. Ensor, P. M. Evershed, E. R. Edwards, J. S. Edgar, W. G. Evans, G. Ellis, F. W. Firth, J. R. Farrar, H. W. Fernandez, J. Forrest, F. C. Fountain, A. L. Farrant, A. B. Fowler, J. Fairclough, J. L. Frood, E. Fern, F. C. Gavin, A. G. Grist, F. G. Golden, C. Goundry, W. G.

Green, A. Goulé, G. Gardner, W. S. Gridley, F. B. Gresham, A. Hodder, T. R. Hoggan, A. Hawes, A. B. Holland, A. J. Hines, R. Henderson, W. Hill, J. H. Hulseberg, G. J. Harvey, W. Hepburn, J. C. Hingston, C. G. Hearn, J. R. Hamilton, A. Hart, H. A. Hazell, T. Hogg, W. H. Hirst, A. F. Jackson, W. Jowett, J. F. Joyce, E. M. Jarvis, E. Kellett, L. P. Knight, H. B. Kenny, W. Kidd, P. J. Kelland, W. A. Kendall, T. T. Kilpatrick, A. J. Lane, J. M. Lund, A. D. Lalor, H. Layshon, F. Lindsay, W. M. Malone, J. M. Magill, R. Miller, G. Montgomery, J. W. Masheter, H. F. MacVean, A. Main, H. E. Mason, A. Mitchell, R. MacDonald, A. MacNae, G. May, J. J. McGrath, W. McKie, J. Neill, H. H. Newcombe, C. R. Neale, ? Norgate, H. O. Oliver, H. S. O'Neill, O. A. O'Neill, J. O'Brien, J. Pollard, H. W. Phelan, J. Peddie, J. H. Plunkett, W. G. Pakeman, J. K. Pilkington, W. M. Pye, T. Parker, J. M. Parker, C. E. Parker, F. W. Pawlett, J. N. Pringle, G. H. Pickwell, T. Rennie, D. Rees, W. N. Rowston, J. M. Robinson, B. Runciman, R. S. Reece, S. Stockman, C. E. Smith, J. I. Smith, S. L. Stevens, T. J. Symes, W. Scott, C. D. Stewart, H. Sturge, J. P. Small, F. M. Skues, C. M. Sharpe, D. Stranaghan, A. C. Smart, A. J. Sellars, H. Scarlett, J. P. Stableford, M. H. Sowerby, H. L. Somers, A. Sykes, R. Stokoe, E. S. Soutar, W. S. Stevens, G. F. Stevenson, W. S. Taylor, J. M. Tait, H. K. Tasker, C. R. Twist, F. W. Trydell, J. Thompson, D. S. Tamblyn, R. P. Thomas, S. R. Tufts, T. Tranter, E. Vans-Agnew, H. M. Webb, W. Wadsworth, C. E. Wells, J. R. Wardrop, G. Waugh, F. F. White, W. T. White, R. F. Watson, E. A. Wilshaw, J. Walker, F. A. Wall, R. F. Wall, P. A. Wilks, E. A. Wilson, J. C. Young.

[The above list does not include those employed on Sea Transport Service.]

CHINA CAMPAIGN 1900-01.—E. A. Hazelton, H. J. Axe, W. A. Pallin, W. N. Wright.

SOMALILAND CAMPAIGN 1903.—A. T. Appleton, W. G. Russell, G. M. Williams, H. M. Lenox-Conyngham, W. A. Wood, C. B. M. Harris, J. A. McGowan, M. St. G. Glasse, A. Leaning.

THIBET CAMPAIGN 1903-4.—J. J. Aitken, R. C. Moore, W. A. Jelbart. A. J. Williams, H. Gamble.

BAZAR VALLEY CAMPAIGN 1908.—A. England, A. J. Thompson.

EAST AFRICA (SOMALILAND) CAMPAIGN 1908-10.—F. W. Hunt.

THE GREAT WAR 1914-18 (see p. 240).—It has not been found possible to print the long list of names of officers serving in the Great War. Through the courtesy of Major-General H. T. Sawyer, Director General Army Veterinary Service, Lieut.-Colonel J. W. Rainey has prepared a complete list of names, which has been deposited in the Royal College of Veterinary Surgeons as a memorial and permanent record of this struggle.

INDEX TO NAMES

The pages marked with an asterisk contain a biographical notice.

Aitken, Colonel J. J., 236
Anderson, J., 52, 153, 155, 156
Apperley, Captain, 128
Apperley, Colonel, 128, 133
Austen, E., 200

Barrett, C. R. B., 104
Barrington, J., 76, 77
Bathurst, J., 162
Batt, 195
Beech, Lieut.-Colonel J. R. D., *184
Beech, J. S., 106
Bennett, Lieut.-Colonel E. E., 188
Bird, Thomas, 75, 76, 77, 78, 119
Blagrave, Captain, 69, 70, 71, 72, 73
Blaine, Delabere, 33, 133
Blanchard, J., 75, 77
Blenkinsop, Major-General Sir L. J., *238-241
Blinman, C., 55
Bloomfield, Lord, 69, 70
Bloxham, S., 52
Blundeville, 105
Boardman, T., 51, 52
Bolton, Brigadier-General, 65
Bourgelat, 8
Boyer, A. E., 235
Brett, 105
Brodrick, 209
Brown, G. T. (Professor), 173
Browne, Ensign, 55
Budd, Captain, 235
Buller, General Sir Redvers, 168, 198
Burrowes, T., 54, 55.
Butler, Major-General E. R. C., 210, 213, 221

Cambridge, Duke of, 131, 135, 138, 143, 149, 192
Cameron, Dr., 180
Carr, Lieut.-Colonel F. U., 207, *237
Castley, James, 11, 51, 75, 76, 91, *92
Causer, E., 51
Chalwin, E. G., 143
Chard, S., 76
Cherry, A. H., 115, 124, 140
Cherry, F. C., 3, 30, 51, 75, 76, 77, 86, 87, 88, 89, 91, 107, *115-130, 136, 156, 157, 158
Cherry, W. A., 116, 124
Clarence, Duke of, 88
Clark, Bracy, 64, 86, 87, 88, 116
Clark, James, 8, 21, 28, 104
Clarke, A. E., ix
Cleveland, Colonel, 6
Cline, Professor H., 27, 28, 65

Coleman, Professor E., 2, 3, 14, 21, 23, *27-111, 112, 113, 114, 115, 116, 120, 124, 131, 132, 157, 159, 199
Collins, F. F., 52, 163
Collins, James, 2, 4, 52, 58, *161-178, 181, 182, 193, 201
Combermere, Lord, 130, 243
Constant, J., 77, 78, 141
Cooper, Sir Astley, 27, 28, 29, 31, 65, 68, 96, 100, 101, 115
Cottrell, F., 141
Coward, H., 57, 75, 102
Coxon, S., 74
Cullimore, C., 125
Cumming, R. S., 53, 73, 74

Dalton, F., 76
Dalwig, C., 77
Darley, J., 74
Darvill, R., 42, 51, 77, 78
Davies, Richard, 54
Dawson, C. J., 142
Delaney, F., 141
Denny, J., 51, 53, 75
Dick, Professor William, 3, 51, 52, 87, 91, 107, 114, 115, 124
Downe, Lord, 237
Duck, Colonel Sir Francis, 168, 183, 185, *197-208, 221, 235
Duncan, Colonel F., vii, 32

Eicke, F., 74, 75, 76, 77
Elkes, F. de F., 138, 140
Erdmann, F., 74, 75
Erratt, Joseph, 54
Evans, General Sir de Lacy, 124
Evans, Dr. Griffith, ix, *174, 191
Evans, Lieut.-Colonel G. H., *213
Evans, Major J. W., 195

Fairholme, Captain E. G., 235
Farrington, J., 46
Feron, J., 51, 55, 75
Field, John, 47, 76, *96, 100
Field, W., 133
Fisher, J., 140
Fitzwygram, General Sir Frederick, *171, 173, 176, 194, 200
Fleming, Dr. George, 1, 52, 138, 156, 158, *177-189
Fortescue, Hon. Sir John, viii, 6, 36, 37, 46

Gain, J., 75, 76, 77
Gamgee, Professor John, 29
Gauly, T. I., 51
George IV., 69, 70, 72, 73, 116

Gibb, Dr., 97, 98
Gibbs, Major H. E., ix, 58
Gloag, J. W., 10, 51, 56, 61, 108, 109, 110, 120, 137, *138, 141, 154
Going, F. W., *181
Goodwin, Joseph, 51, 59, *68
Gouldthorpe, R., 76, 77
Grellier, James, 51, 54
Grey, E. S., 141
Griffiths, Lieut.-Colonel G. R., *184
Grose, F., 6
Gudgeon, J. P., 141

Haldane, Lord, 214, 216, 217
Hallen, H., 107, 134, 171, 194
Hallen, Lieut.-Colonel J. H. B., 52, 128, 151, 155, 156, 163, 193, *194, 206
Harcourt, W., 40
Hardinge, Lord, 126, 127, 130
Hardwicke, Earl of, 208
Harpley, M., 141, *143
Harrison, James, 52
Haslam, Vet.-Captain, *199
Hastings, Captain, 143
Haswell-Miller, Captain, x, 247
Hayward, J., 134
Heathfield, Lord, 36, 37, 38, 40
Hely, F. H., 143
Henderson, Alex, 143
Henderson, Charles, 143
Herbert, Sidney, 117, 118, 119, 149
Heuer, L., 76, 77
Hexam, H., 5
Hill, Lord, 113, 114, 115
Hilmer, J. F., 74
Hinde, Captain, 7, 8
Hodgson, J. H., 51, 75, 98, 99, 100, *102
Hogrefe, H., 76, 77, 78
Howell, Lieut.-Colonel H., 147
Howick, Lord, 113, 114, 115
Hunter, John, 27, 45
Hurford, R. J. G., 24, 127, 172

Jackson, Captain, 143
Jackson, Colonel, 122
Johnston, G., 122, 123, 124, 146
Johnston, Colonel, W., 147
Jones, Captain Adrian, *212
Jons, J. W., 77

Karkeek, 104, 105
Keane, Lord, 152
Kelly, R., 140
Kettlewell, Lieut.-Colonel, 193, 195
Kirwan, A., 76, 77
Knight, Francis, 62
Koch, Dr., 200

La Fosse, 28
Lake, Lord, 54
Lamb, W., 52, 155, 156, *187
Lambert, Colonel J. D., 52, 173, 189, *190-197, 200
Lander, G., 74
Lane, John, 23, 49
Lawson, S., 67
Liverpool, Lord, 78
Lord, J. K., 136, *141
Lord, W. B., *142

Lord, W. C., 142
Lowes, J., 77, 78
Lythe, J., 76, 77, 78

Manners, W. E., 16
Markham, F., 5
Markham, G., 5
Marling, Colonel, 208
Marsh, Frederick, 73, 74
Mayer, J. (Senr.), 29
Mayer, T. W., 138, *139, 183
McDermott, W., 143
McFadyean, Professor Sir John, 216
Mellows, J., 124
Meyrick, Lieut.-Colonel J. J., ix, *175, 189, 191
Moorcroft, William, 27, 28, 36, 37, 47, 96, 97, 98
Moore, General Sir John, 74, 75, 115
Morton, Professor, 92

Napier, Lord, 156
Nelson, V., 143
Nesbitt, J., 74, 75
Newman, Samuel, 54, 55, 184
Norton, Captain, 209
Nunn, Lieut.-Colonel J. A., *183, 195

O'Connor, C., 57, 74, 75, 76
Olver, Colonel A., 236
O'Reilly, R., x
Osler, Professor Sir William, 174
Osmer, W., 28
Owles, J., 52

Parker, J., 75
Partridge, W., 141
Peall, Thomas, 50, 51, *59, 85, 94
Pease, Colonel H. T., *194
Peel, General, 145
Peers, J., 75, 76
Pembroke, 10th Earl, 8, 21, 117
Pembroke, 11th Earl, 38, 40, 117
Percivall, Charles W., 133
Percivall, John, 2, 28, 34, 41, 47, 49, 50, 52, 57, 58, 61, 72, 73, 79, 82, 87, *93, 94
Percivall, William, 1, 28, 29, 51, 58, 64, 77, 78, 84, 85, 86, 87, 90, 91, 94, 99, 100, 108, 117, 125, 129, 130, *131
Philips, J., 142
Pilcher, D., 77
Pitt, General W. A., 40
Power, T., 77
Precht, F., 74, 75, 76
Price, George, 69, 70, 72, 73, 74, 76
Pringle, Major-General Sir Robert, *233-238
Prior, L. M., 119
Purvis, J., 51, 106

Rainey, Lieut.-Colonel, J. W., ix
Rayment, Lieut.-Colonel, 106
Reynolds, P., ix, x, 243
Roberts, H. L., 133
Robertson, James, 108
Robinson, W., 145
Rollo, Dr., 33, 34, 79
Rose, T., 75, 76, 77
Rutherford, Colonel C., 182

Ryding, W., 51, 76
Rymer, 26

Sainbel, 27, 30, 34, 37, 40, 43, 86, 91, 97
Sannermann, H., 77
Sawyer, Major-General H. T., ix
Scott-Gavin, 140
Sewell, Professor William, 42, 100, 107, 113, 115, 124, 125, 131
Shaw, Lieut.-Colonel F. G., 193
Shipp, John, 51, 52, 73, 74, 75
Siddall, James, 52, 53, 55
Siddall, John, 53, 76, 125, 130
Siddall, John (Bengal), 53, 143, 152
Siddall, Thomas (10th Hussars), 140
Sievier, 29
Simonds, Professor J. B., 29, 86, 138
Simpson, J. F., 200, 204, 205, 207, 208, 210
Skeavington, J., 103
Skoulding, J. B. W., 126
Smith, Major-General Sir Frederick, 182, 185, 195, *213-232
Smith, Opie, 55
Smith, Thomas, 51, 54
Smythe, Sir John, 5
Somerset, Lord Fitzroy, 113, 114
Stanley, J., 76
Steel, J. H., *191
Stocqueler, 124, 127, 131
Stockley, J. S., 138, 141
Stockley, William, *37, 52, 57, 58, 134
Sumner, Rev. P., x

Tapp, Major, 128
Thacker, James, *164
Thompson, R., 75, 76
Thomson, Major-General Henry, *208, 213, 221
Todd, Colonel A. G., ix, 182
Trigge, John, 73, 74
Turner, James, 29, 50, 51
Turner, Sir James, 6

Walters, Colonel W. B., ix, *193
Walton, Colonel, 7
Watherston, C., 208
Wellington, Duke of, 31, 54, 78, 110, 113, 124, 126, 127, 243
Western, G., 140
Western, J., 129
White, Field-Marshal Sir George, 201
White, James, 50, 51, 52, 85, *86
Wilkinson, John, 3, 58, 125, 130, 131, *133-160, 167, 201, 204
Williams, Professor W. O., 208
Withers, Hicks, 141, 143
Wolseley, Field-Marshal Lord, 201
Wood, Field-Marshal Sir Evelyn, 176, 201
Woods, Major J. A., 195

York, Duke of, 36, 37, 38, 40, 53, 86
Youatt, William, 1, 29, 86, 87, 90, 91, 96, 106, 107, 115, 130, 131, 133

INDEX OF SUBJECTS

AGE limit. *See* Veterinary Service
American Veterinary Corps, 236
Annual Dinner, 173
Army in 1852, 110, 126
    in 1870, 157, 160
    Territorial. *See* Veterinary Service
    Vaccine Institute, 185
    Veterinary Association, 139, 183, 201
    Veterinary Corps. *See* Veterinary Service
    Veterinary Department. *See* Veterinary Service
    Veterinary School, 170, 173, 177, 182, 186, 201, 226, 230, 234
    Veterinary Stores, 213
Artillery:
    appointments in, 34
    commissions in, 44, 57
    constitution of, 31, 172
    farriers in, 12, 13, 17, 22, 24

Blood-letting, 17, 48, 49, 109
Board of General Officers, 9, 14, 38, 39
Burma, 213

Campaigns, 253 *et seq.*
    Abyssinia, 155, 184
    Afghan, 168, 180
    Copenhagen, 74
    Crimea, 130, 135-142
        articles on, 138
    Egypt, 74, 175, 181
    Great War, 4, 234
    Holland, 74
    Mutiny, 142-143
    New Zealand, 153
    Peninsula, 74, 75-78
    Second Mahratta, 74
    South Africa, 168, 181, 200, 203
    South America, 74
    Walcheren, 75
    Waterloo, 78
Cavalry, 7, 9, 10, 13, 38, 44
    appointments in, 36-37. *See* Officers, schemes to obtain
    care of horses, 8, 114, 170, 188, 211, 228, 229
    officers, training of, 170-171, 211, 226, 227
    Regimental Veterinary Service (abolition), 157, 162, 173-174. *See* Hospitals and Veterinary Service
    reorganization, 171
Coleman:
    administration, 27 *et seq.*
    appointments, 32-34, 35, 79, 112
    attacks on, 69, 87 *et seq.*

Coleman:
    attitude to profession, 29
    characteristics of, 28-30, 90
    commission, 35, 45, 80
    contracts. *See* Contracts
    contribution to science, 28
    curriculum, 30, 40, 41, 43
    designation in Ordnance, 34
        in Cavalry, 45, 83, 84
    duties with Ordnance, 35
    enemy of the profession, 30, 90
    evidence before C.M.E., 63
    hereditary diseases, 92
    "Instructions to Farriers." *See* Farriers
    jealousy of, 28, 30, 31, 50, 51, 90
    lectures, 30, 33-35, 50, 81, 82
    lowers social standard, 30, 41, 89, 90
    medical men and, 30, 41-43, 45, 89. *See* Medical men
    opposes progress, 90
    Ordnance. *See* Coleman appointments
    pay. *See* P.V.S.
    Percivall, J., and, 79, 82, 87, 94
    published works, 28, 30
    rank, views on, 90
    reforms, 30, 49, 80, 90
    relations with officers, 51, 55, 56, 89, 92, 110, 111
    successor, 112
    tool of Sir Astley Cooper, 29
    Veterinary Surgeon General, 83, 84, 107, 113
Commissioners of Military Enquiry, 63, 89
Commissions, 41, 43-45, 52, 57, 59, 197
Contracts, 46, 103, 116
    Coleman's, 14, 34, 43, 45-47, 63-64, 88, 89, 95, 96, 112, 116
    Farriers. *See* Farriers

Demobilization, 239-240
Dick College graduates, 51, 107, 145
Director General, 192, 196, 232, 234, 236
    assistance for, 205, 225
    rank, 190, 195, 208, 209, 212
    status, 215, 216, 217
Diseases, 35, 92, 152, 168, 174, 191, 195, 203, 204, 229
    nomenclature, 95, 126
    treatment of, 8, 23, 47-50, 170, 211, 228
    tropical, 229-230. *See* Glanders, Horse-Sickness, Roaring, Surra, Trypanosomiasis
Dogs in war, 188
    quarantine, 240

Equipment, 47, 63-64, 109, 112, 135, 155, 159, 167, 168, 189, 199, 214, 220, 221, 222, 234. *See* Stores and medicines
Esher Committee, 216
Examinations:
    entrance, 65, 114, 115, 136, 233
    promotion, 146, 148, 153, 164, 182, 223

Farrier Corporal, 11, 12, 210
    Major, 9-12, 16, 17, 19, 24, 25
    Q. M. Corporal, 11
    Q. M. Sergeant, 11
    Sergeant, 7, 10, 12, 13, 15, 24, 114, 203
    Sergt.-Major, 11
    See Shoeing Smiths
Farriery Schools, 226, 235
Farriers, 2, 5, 7, 25-26, 109, 155, 166, 210, 211, 225, 229, 235
    as veterinarians, 5, 7, 8, 17, 39, 40, 42, 54
    contract, 7, 13-15, 46-47, 64, 178-180
    corps of, 225
    "Directions for," 49
    dress, 15, 16, 20
    duties of, 5, 16, 109, 226
    education, 2, 8, 9, 23, 84
    enlistment, 26, 226
    "Instructions for," 23, 48, 83, pupilage, 26
    rank, 12
    regulations, 7, 8, 17-22
    reserve of, 226
    Veterinary Surgeons, acting as, 197
    warrants, 11
Field Service Manual, 210, 234
Flogging, 8, 16, 17, 41
Foreigners in Veterinary Service, 55
Foreign Service, 93, 148, 162, 163, 173, 185, 224-225
French Veterinary Service, 96

Glanders, 32, 33, 35, 54, 59, 85, 86, 109, 135, 177, 178, 190, 197, 204, 228
    Coleman on, 28, 48, 50, 83-85

Hardwicke Committee, 208, 209
Headquarters of Veterinary Service, 58, 134, 156-157, 162
History Sheets, Veterinary, 173
Honours for Service, 78, 138, 143, 155-156, 165, 168, 173, 175, 191, 199. *See* Promotions
Horses, 9, 17, 31, 49, 50, 91, 109, 127, 188
    demobilization of, 239
    "horse masters," 218
    losses of, 36, 137, 168, 180, 203, 205, 209, 236
    numbering of, 17, 22, 232
Horse-Sickness, 183
Hospitals, 109, 131, 134, 167, 168, 201, 204, 205, 211, 214, 215, 217, 219, 228, 229, 235
    evacuation to, 137, 219
    Mobile Veterinary Sections, 234

Hospitals, regimental system, 91, 94, 135, 142, 154, 161, 202
    remount depots as, 168, 202, 236
    sick horse depots, 137, 155, 156, 158, 159, 175, 203

Indian Veterinary Service, 1, 26, 46, 52, 54, 96, 98, 99, 101, 103, 107, 127-129, 150, 163, 180, 181, 182, 193, 229
    administration of, 100, 127-130, 151-153, 163
    Civil Veterinary Dept., 192
    local officers, 152, 153, 163
    pay, 103, 151, 153, 168, 173
    promotion, 150, 153
    P.V.S. (duties of), 152
    schools, 187, 194, 238
    stagnation in, 1, 129
    studs, 97, 99-102, 127, 128, 151, 152, 163, 175, 193, 206
    uniform, 252-253

Johnston Case, 122 *et seq.*, 146

Marshal, the, 7
Medical men in Veterinary Service, 41-43, 52, 53, 55-61
    Service, 33, 46, 62, 112-113, 115, 146, 192
    attitude of, to Veterinary Service, 29, 41, 61-62, 65, 90, 100, 101, 192, 196
Medicines, 47, 63-64, 103, 109, 112, 114, 135, 137, 155, 167, 221. *See* Contracts, Equipment, and Stores
Muster-Masters, 5

Netheravon. *See* Cavalry officers, training of

Officers. *See* Artillery, Cavalry, Campaigns, Commissions, India
    administrative, 3, 91, 100, 129, 130, 137, 146, 148, 149, 155, 158, 164, 165, 168, 169, 187, 193, 205, 231, 233
    age limit. *See* Veterinary Service
    casualties, Great War, 240
    civilians employed as, 136, 154, 204
    classified, 66, 73
    Coleman's choice of, 41-44, 88, 90
    critical period of life, 223
    early difficulties of, 41, 51, 55, 73, 90, 92
    entrance. *See* Examinations and Veterinary Service, patronage
    examinations. *See* Examinations
    graded, 148, 187, 192
    leave, 224, 225
    pay. *See* Pay
    pension. *See* Pensions and Pay, retired
    presentation at Court, 125, 165, 176

Officers, present day, ix, 3
    Principal V. Surgeon. *See* P.V.S.
    probationary, 134, 170, 222
    promotion of. *See* Examinations and Promotion
    rank of. *See* Rank
    repression, effects of, 199, 223
    reserve of. *See* Reserve
    retirement of. *See* Retirement
    schemes to obtain, 39-41, 43, 47, 52, 55, 165, 214, 217. *See* Veterinary Service, short service
    status. *See* Status
    temporary, 136, 154
    Territorial. *See* Veterinary Service
    training of, 222, 224, 230, 231
    Veterinary Surgeon General, 83, 84, 107, 113, 135, 165
    volunteer, 187, 192
    weeding of, 223
    Yeomanry, 170, 187, 192, 197, 214, 215
Ordnance Board, 31, 35, 134
    Medical Service, 57
Organization for War, 154, 158, 166, 193, 201-204, 231
    Col. Duck on, 183, 201
Ozœna, 48, 83, 190

Pay (rates of), 38, 39, 40, 43, 56, 60, 64, 103, 108, 117, 118, 120, 121, 144, 145, 148, 150, 162, 165, 170, 174, 187, 207, 225
    half-, 44, 56, 60, 93, 108, 118, 120, 149
    retired, 56, 60, 93, 108, 117, 118, 119, 165, 187, 195, 196
Pensions, 56, 60, 66, 119, 120, 121, 144, 187, 196, 207
Presentation at Court, 125, 165, 176
Private practice (by officers), 47
Probationary officers. *See* Officers
Promotion, 164, 165, 176, 187, 207, 223
    blocking, 169, 189, 196, 224
    brevet, 169, 196, 206, 209
    to combatant rank, 54, 184
    for service, 169, 176, 181, 182
P.V.S., 173, 189
    appointment, 45, 107, 115, 134, 154, 159, 190
    early designation, 34, 45, 83, 84, 134
    pay, 34, 45, 57, 64, 80, 81, 112, 113, 115, 149, 165
    position in Army List, 47, 156
    rank, 149, 154, 165

Rank, 208
    compound, 11, 192, 200, 205, 207
    relative, 56, 60, 62, 66, 73, 92, 108, 120, 121, 136, 144, 146-147, 176, 187
    substantive, 192, 205, 209
    veterinary officer, junior of rank, 147, 192
Record Office, 225, 233
Register (Sick and Lame Horses), 2, 82, 95, 122

Regulations, Cavalry, 17
    Farriers. *See* Farriers
    Field Service, 154, 166, 231
    Veterinary, 95, 122, 126, 155, 158, 167, 176, 182, 193, 201, 202, 212
Remount Department, 203, 204, 206, 211, 216, 217, 225, 231, 232, 234
    Depot. *See* Hospitals
    Purchase, 122, 134, 162, 176, 207, 209
Reports, 9
    confidential, 66, 110 *n.*, 176
Research, 50, 224
    See Army Veterinary School
Reserve, 155, 158, 166, 170, 193, 215, 216, 220
Retirement, 60, 93, 148, 165, 186, 187, 209
    pay. *See* Pay
Returns, 51, 67, 82, 106, 126
Roaring, 187
Royal College of Veterinary Surgeons, 197, 200, 204, 207, 210, 214, 216, 241
Royal Horse Infirmary, 33, 35, 58, 94, 134, 162
Royal Society for Prevention of Cruelty to Animals, 235, 240

Schools. *See* Army and Farriery
Sea transport. *See* Transport
Shoeing, 8, 15, 21, 22, 69-73, 124, 125, 155, 178, 179, 226
    Coleman on, 21, 47, 68-73
    frost, 22, 191
    smiths, 12, 13, 14, 17, 22, 25, 109, 155, 170, 210
Smallpox, 186
Stables, 32, 49, 109, 112, 127
Standing Orders, Regimental. *See* Farriers, regulations
Statistics (Annual Reports), 106, 135, 164, 230
Status (farrier), 6
    (veterinary officer), 30, 41-42, 44, 49, 50, 89, 90, 93, 117-120, 135
Stores, 134, 137, 155, 167, 203, 213, 214, 220-222. *See* Equipment and Medicines
    reserve of, 160, 222, 233, 234
Surra, 174, 191, 195

Training, post-graduate, 224
    probationary, 222
    staff duties, 231
    See Army Veterinary School
Transport by sea, 67, 124, 139, 199, 228, 235
Travelling allowance, 34, 56, 61, 121
Trypanosomiasis, 174

Uniform, 54, 156, 187, 243-253

Vaccine Institute, 185
Ventilation, 49, 67, 84, 104
Veterinary Colleges, 9, 30, 51, 88, 112, 145. *See* Dick College graduates
    Service, abolition suggested, 196, 217
    administrative officers. *See* Officers

Veterinary Service age limit, 55, 148, 149, 165, 169, 170, 189, 207, 223, 224, 232, 236
  and Medical Department, 57, 60, 61, 62, 65, 66, 157
  appreciations, 65, 118, 121, 156, 169, 175, 181, 184, 241
  Army Veterinary Corps:
    formed, 210
    attempt to destroy, 211
    Depot, 213
    Department, 58, 162, 165, 173, 174, 210
    destroyed, 203
    School. *See* Army
  creation of, Artillery, 33; Cavalry, 35, 38-47
  of situation prior to, 17, 23, 50
  departmentalization of, 173
  depots, 213
  Director General. *See* Director General
  duties, 94, 109, 123, 209. *See* Regulations, Veterinary
  entrance. *See* Officers and Examination
  equipment. *See* Equipment
  establishment, 136, 148, 155, 158, 162, 164, 166, 211, 220, 224, 227
  headquarters. *See* Headquarters and Royal Horse Infirmary
  in 1838, 108
  in 1858, 144
  in 1870, 157, 159, 160
  1876–1919, 3
  in 1903, 209
  introduction of, 34, 36-37
  meat and dairy inspection, 232
  medical men in. *See* Medical men and Medical Service

Veterinary Service, need for, 39, 65
  officers. *See* Officers
  organization aimed at, 231
  patronage, 51, 88, 94, 107, 114, 115
  presentation at Court, 125, 165, 176
  promotion. *See* Examination and Promotion
  rank. *See* Rank
  regimental system, 91, 94, 108, 110, 123, 137, 159, 161, 165, 173, 174, 214
  reserves. *See* Reserve
  retirements. *See* Retirement
  Royal Horse Infirmary. *See* R.H.I.
  short service, 163, 165, 186, 207
  stores. *See* Stores
  subordinate personnel, 25, 156, 166, 168, 170, 175, 201, 202, 210, 211, 215, 217
  Territorial, 214, 216, 217, 218-220, 234
  Veterinary Medical Dept., 66
  Volunteer, 187, 192
  warrants. *See* Warrants
  Yeomanry, 192, 197, 214, 215
Surgeon General. *See* Officers

War Memorials, 241
  organization. *See* Organization
Warrants, Farriers, 11
  Indian (1826), 103; (1865), 150; (1879), 168; (1885), 182
  Royal (1796), 43; (1798), 56; (1805), 60; (1807), 60; (1812), 66; (1815), 65; (1830), 93; (1837), 65; (1846), 119, 121; (1859), 148; (1878), 165; (1881), 174; (1883), 176; (1888), 169, 187; (1891), 192; (1896), 196; (1903), 209
Wounds, battle, 49, 105, 106, 185

www.ingramcontent.com/pod-product-compliance
Lightning Source LLC
Chambersburg PA
CBHW061124010526
44114CB00029B/2996